GLOBAL WEST, AMERICAN FRONTIER

A volume in the Calvin P. Horn Lectures
in Western History and Culture

GLOBAL WEST, AMERICAN FRONTIER

Travel, Empire, and Exceptionalism
from Manifest Destiny
to the Great Depression

DAVID M. WROBEL

University of New Mexico Press
Albuquerque

My thanks to *The Historian, Montana The Magazine of Western History*,
and the *Pacific Historical Review* for permission to draw
on my work previously published therein:
"Exceptionalism and Globalism: Travel Writers and the Nineteenth-Century
American West," *The Historian* 68 (Fall 2006): 430–60.
"The West in the World, the World in the West: Gerstäcker, Burton,
and Bird on the Nineteenth-Century Frontier," *Montana The Magazine
of Western History* 58 (Spring 2008): 24–34.
"Global West, American Frontier," *Pacific Historical Review* 78
(February 2009): 1–26.

Library of Congress Cataloging-in-Publication Data

Wrobel, David M.
Global West, American frontier : travel, empire, and exceptionalism from manifest
destiny to the Great Depression / David M. Wrobel.
pages cm. — (Calvin P. Horn lectures in western history and culture)
Includes bibliographical references and index.
ISBN 978-0-8263-5370-2 (hardback) — ISBN 978-0-8263-5371-9 (electronic)
1. West (U.S.)—Description and travel—History. 2. Travel writing—Historiography.
3. West (U.S.)—Historiography. 4. West (U.S.)—Public opinion. I. Title.
F595.3.W76 2013
978'.02—dc23
2013017317

BOOK DESIGN: Catherine Leonardo
Composed in 10.25/13.5 Minion Pro Regular
Display type is Matchwood Bold WF

For my brother Marek (1955–2012), in loving memory.

CONTENTS

ILLUSTRATIONS

ACKNOWLEDGMENTS

In November 2003 I delivered the Calvin Horn Lecture (formerly "lectures") in Western American History and Culture at the University of New Mexico (UNM). While grateful to have received that invitation, I was at the time more than a little relieved to learn that the format had changed sometime around the turn of the last century from four lectures to just a single one; I flippantly threatened to deliver a single four-hour lecture. *Global West, American Frontier* is a departure from the traditional four-essay structure of the Calvin Horn Book Series. I had the opportunity to deliver ten additional talks over the course of a decade, between 2002 and 2012, on western American travel writing, and part 1 of this book draws on those as well as the original Horn lecture. I am indebted to the Western Literature Association (Tucson, 2002), Phi Alpha Theta, the National History Honor Society (New Orleans, 2004, and Philadelphia, 2006), Yale University's Howard Lamar Center for the Study of Frontiers and Borders, Beinecke Rare Book and Manuscript Library, and Sterling Memorial Library (New Haven, 2005–2006), the Colorado Historical Society (Denver, 2006), the Pacific Coast Branch of the American Historical Association (PCB-AHA) (Pasadena, 2008), Ohio University (Athens, 2009), and the Huntington Library–USC Institute for California and the West (San Marino, 2012), as well as UNM (Albuquerque, 2003), for providing those forums for presentation. My thanks go to Dick Etulain and Virginia Scharff for including me in the Horn series, to David Holtby (former director of the University of New Mexico Press), and to all the history faculty and graduate students at UNM for being such kind and gracious hosts. I am also grateful to Clark Whitehorn of the University of New Mexico Press for his support and good advice over the past couple of years as I moved the study toward completion, and to the entire staff of the Press.

The majority of the research for *Global West, American Frontier* was done in two very special places. The Huntington Library in San Marino, California, has been a regular second home to me in the summers for two decades now. An Andrew Mellon Fellowship in the summer of 2003 provided the time to begin my scholarly acquaintance with western travel writing and the broader travel writing genre, one I had always been interested in as a causal reader. The Huntington, as so many western American historians know, is home to a wonderful intellectual community whose members are simply too many to mention but whose friendship and support have been invaluable. One member of that community who cannot escape mention, though, is Peter Blodgett, Russell Foundation Curator of Western Historical Manuscripts and executive director of the PCB-AHA. Peter has listened patiently and provided kind encouragement over the years. As so many scholars in the field know, he is a brilliant guide and facilitator of our efforts to navigate the Huntington's remarkable collections.

I was especially fortunate to spend academic year 2005–2006 as the senior research fellow in western American history and culture at the Beinecke Library and the Howard Lamar Center for the Study of Frontiers and Borders at Yale University and am deeply appreciative of the efforts made by the University of Nevada, Las Vegas (UNLV) College of Liberal Arts and Department of History to facilitate that annual leave. My thanks to Johnny Faragher, Jay Gitlin, Edith Ropotkoff, and, of course, Howard Lamar for making me so welcome at the Lamar Center, and to George Miles, the late Frank Turner, and all of the excellent staff of the Beinecke Library who helped make my time there both pleasant and productive. I am indebted also to the excellent community of Yale graduate students for welcoming me into their circle of New Haven westerners.

Students are often among the first audiences subjected to our ideas, and I am grateful to the UNLV history graduate students for their patience, forbearance, enthusiasm, and great insight in discussing the travel narrative genre as a window onto the western past and present. My faculty colleagues at UNLV helped to make my former intellectual home a wonderful one for more than a decade. Deepest thanks also go to my new colleagues in history at the University of Oklahoma for their warm and supportive welcome, especially to department chair Rob Griswold for granting me the time in fall 2011 to write, and to Dustin Mack and Jonathan Filler for their excellent research assistance. David Chappell, Sue Hodson, Barry Menikoff, Martin Padget, and Janet Ward all provided particularly insightful feedback on the study, and Dick Etulain's and Ronald Primeau's close readings and helpful suggestions made the work stronger.

During all the travels and travails of this project, my most important intellectual home has been quite literally at home, with my wife Janet Ward and our wonderful children Davey, Ethan, and Miranda; their company is my greatest reward.

I dedicate this book to my late brother Marek Wrobel (1955–2012), whose journey had to end too soon.

INTRODUCTION

Roads Traveled

From this hour I ordain myself loos'd of limits and imaginary lines,
Going where I list, my own master total and absolute,
Listening to others, considering well what they say,
Pausing, searching, receiving, contemplating,
Gently, but with undeniable will, divesting myself of the holds that
    would hold me.

      —Walt Whitman, "Song of the Open Road," in *Leaves of Grass,*
                              Second Edition (1856)

[He] kept his scalp in a little box, showed it to visitors with pride, and
rather enjoyed being probably the only person in the world who could
entertain his visitors with a description of the feelings produced by
suddenly recognising the top of your head on the ground at your feet.

      —John White, *Sketches from America* (1870)

Beyond the Mythic West

John White, a Fellow of Queen's College Oxford, toured the United States and Canada in the late 1860s and, like so many nineteenth-century European visitors, wrote up his experiences and impressions; they were published in 1870 under the title *Sketches from America*. A remarkably cynical and irreverent account, White's *Sketches* would have provided readers with a sobering corrective to the ubiquitous and purple prose of western land and town promoters in the post–Civil War years.

1

Speaking to the lack of interesting infrastructure in new western towns, he wrote: "The lions of a town like Omaha are wonderfully quickly gone through; and after a walk round the place, the irresistible politeness with which the townspeople forced one to get into a vehicle and be driven round it again, was but a cruel kindness."[1]

But while White's assessment of Omaha's place promoters would have deflated their efforts to expand their town's reputation to mythic proportions, he was, like a good number of travelers of the period, drawn to the more fantastic stories of western frontier distinctiveness—to the West of the imagination that mythmakers were creating. His real Nebraska coup de grace was the story of "the scalped man of Omaha." "Have you seen our scalped man yet?" White's Omaha guide inquired. White had heard about the recent Indian attack on a train but had no knowledge of the scalped man, so he asked whether the victim's body was still on show. "Body?" the guide replied. "No. Man's lively enough I guess . . . take him some 'baccy or something, and get him to show you his scalp." The guide proceeded to explain that the Indians had attacked the train, thrown it off the tracks, and immediately scalped all the men on board (fortunately it was a goods train with few passengers), except for one who had run back along the line toward an advancing passenger train; but then that lone escapee, too, was tomahawked and scalped, although his assailants acted in haste to ensure their escape, and the wounds they inflicted proved not to be fatal.

An Englishman by birth, like his chronicler White, the now renowned "scalped man of Omaha" had managed to survive the attack, and after the Indians departed he realized that he was alive, albeit conspicuously and painfully scalpless. But as luck would have it he found the missing scalp as he wandered along the tracks, and figuring that he "had a better right to it than anyone else" put "the recovered top of his head" into his pocket. He made a "happy recovery," although his crown "was a little ghastly to look upon." White explained that the man "kept his scalp in a little box, showed it to visitors with pride, and rather enjoyed being probably the only person in the world who could entertain his visitors with a description of the feelings produced by suddenly recognising the top of your head on the ground at your feet."[2]

If ever readers needed confirmation that the West was wild and weird, accounts such as White's provided it. The late Ray Allen Billington examined a mountain of travelers' reports on nineteenth-century western America in his *Land of Savagery, Land of Promise: The European Image of the American*

Frontier (1981) and emphasized those works that highlighted the unparalleled uniqueness of the place. The western frontier, in Billington's reckoning, was a mythmaker's dream: a land of ferocious, untamed Indians, rugged frontiersmen (and later cowboys), strange animals, and spectacular landscapes; a place already so incredible that even a mildly imaginative mind could render it truly astonishing. There was certainly no shortage of nineteenth-century travel writers who played up the unusual and fantastic aspects of the West and thereby contributed to the growth of western American mythology, which rested on a foundation of presumed western American exceptionalism. To the image makers, as Billington called them, the "Great West" was like no place on Earth. Whether they viewed it as a land of savagery to be derided or as a land of promise that inspired democratic movements in other parts of the world, these European visitors were imagining the West as a world of its own, a world apart, an absolutely unparalleled place.[3]

Nineteenth-century painters (such as Albert Bierstadt, Thomas Moran, and Frederic Remington), writers (including James Fenimore Cooper), and performers (most notably Buffalo Bill Cody) contributed greatly to this sense of the American West as a dramatic and adventurous landscape, a place like no other. The twentieth century also witnessed no shortage of western mythmakers in the aforementioned genres as well as in film, television, and the advertising industry. But despite the great weight of representations of a mythic, exceptional, and quintessentially American frontier West in the nineteenth and twentieth centuries, and the equally encumbering weight of scholarship on the mythic West, or the West of the imagination, that has piled up since 1900, it is important to remember that the trans-Mississippi West was also very often viewed in the nineteenth century as a global West, as one developing frontier, one colonial enterprise, among many around the globe.

Twentieth- and twenty-first-century scholars have exhibited a tendency to throw around the term "mythic West" with such enormous enthusiasm and abandon that we are left to wonder in astonishment at the intellectual limitations of nineteenth-century Americans, and their global observers, who presumably subscribed so readily, so unthinkingly, to that colorful vision of their West as a place like nowhere else. Even the late Robert Athearn, a truly accomplished and thoughtful western historian, demonstrated a tendency, when it came to the mythic West, to let his rhetorical proclivities overwhelm his usual good judgment. Writing in 1953 about nineteenth-century British travelers to the West, he proclaimed:

Without exception, these travelers were prepared for the worst. . . . Steeped in the traditions of Cooper and filled with the literary atrocities of Beadle, they came West expecting to see the landscape awhirl with beautiful maidens pursued by shrieking savages, who were in turn pressed by buckskin-garbed frontiersmen brandishing a formidable collection of hardware.[4]

Athearn offered this observation in the early Cold War years, a period that saw a revival of the notion of American exceptionalism rooted in the nation's frontier heritage.[5] In this cultural climate of the mid- to late 1940s and 1950s, it was common to assume not just the primacy but even the absolute hegemony of exceptionalist visions of America and its West in the previous century. This notion of the United States' pronounced difference from other nations was an essential aspect of the consensus-centered vision of the country's past that developed in those years. The divisions among regions, social classes, and racial, ethnic, and religious groups were deemphasized, while those factors that purportedly distinguished the United States from other nations in positive ways (its democratic traditions and technological prowess, for example) were highlighted. The idea of a benign westward movement of democratic and Christian people across the American continent, bringing progress and prosperity to a barren wilderness, amounted to a wonderfully positive reenvisioning of the nation's nineteenth-century past, a mental rerendering of John Gast's famous 1872 painting *American Progress*.

Generations of western history writing, dating all the way back to Helen Hunt Jackson's scathing critique of U.S. federal Indian policy in *A Century of Dishonor* (1881) and Josiah Royce's 1886 account of the deleterious impact of the conquest of California on the American character, and up to the New Western History of the 1980s, 1990s, and beyond, have provided us with a counternarrative to the nation's romantic entanglement with its western past.[6] *Global West, American Frontier* offers a new ear to some old voices that deserve another hearing: the writers of travel books about the West. From these travelers' accounts, written by Europeans and Americans, it becomes clear that a more complex understanding of the West was not just present in the nineteenth century but pervasive.

In addition to the steady diet of exceptionalist rhetoric and imagery surrounding the American frontier that has provided so much grist for the mythmakers' mills and so much food for academic thought, there was another cultural diet, often equally voluminous, of globally contextualized discussions and representations of the American West provided in travel books. Moreover, it is safe to assume that the concurrent intake and digestion of the exceptional and the global, of these visions of a remarkably distinctive American frontier and of a deexceptionalized global West (provided by the more perceptive travelers who explored the region), did not leave nineteenth-century American readers, or other readers around the globe for that matter, in a perpetual state of self-conflict. Rather, these varied visions gave nineteenth-century Americans more to ponder about their West and its relationship to their nation than scholars have generally assumed. It might be best to think of the American frontier and the global West of the nineteenth century as a current and a countercurrent that probably coexisted not all too uncomfortably in the consciousness of people who thought about such things, in much the same way that advancing and receding tides mark the same shoreline, leaving it looking different, literally from moment to moment.[7]

In *Global West, American Frontier* I use travel writing as a lens onto this broad countercurrent of thinking about the global West during the nineteenth century, and the considerably more frontier-centric and nation-centric envisioning of the West in the twentieth century. Travel writing constituted a genre that, prior to the professionalization of American academic disciplines in the latter years of the nineteenth century, offered people a lively and perceptive discourse about the world around them. Travel writers offered up their expertise as historians, geographers, demographers, anthropologists, and authorities on the natural and built environments, and displayed their talents as prose writers, all to a highly receptive and sizable reading public. Travel writing was voluminous, ubiquitous, profitable, and widely discussed. In the nineteenth century, publishers earned much of their income, and, more importantly, the reading public gained much of its knowledge about the world, from travel books.[8]

The travel writing form, as we will see, did not disappear as the nation entered the twentieth century and the world's most remote places became increasingly more accessible. With the growing specialization of knowledge—even while anthropologists, geographers, and others produced impressive storehouses of information about distant peoples and places—the reading public continued to turn to travel books to learn about the faraway, as well as for the pleasure that accompanies the reading of good writing. The travel book remained a key genre throughout the twentieth century, and still is today. In the early twenty-first century, when it is possible to fly to nearly anywhere in the world within a day and to travel virtually to anywhere via the Internet, a quaint, old-fashioned printed companion remains surprisingly popular. A distinctive hybrid of the fiction and nonfiction forms, of reflection and reportage, of anthropology, history, and literature, still serves as an essential accompaniment for actual travel or provides core background reading for a journey.[9] Such is the case with American-authored or America-situated classics of the genre such as Mark Twain's irreverent *Roughing It* (1872), D. H. Lawrence's stirring *Mornings in Mexico* (1927), Jack Kerouac's frenetically paced *On the Road* (1957), John Steinbeck's more leisurely *Travels with Charley in Search of America* (1962), or William Least Heat-Moon's engaging *Blue Highways: A Journey into America* (1982). Still, one suspects, most travel narratives are read in the comfort of the home, not in the course of "roughing it," no matter how liberally defined. The travel narrative is a vehicle for vicarious travel, enabling the reader to see the varied peoples and places of the world through the eyes of the writer but without the discomforts and inconveniences of the actual journey. Such has been the case for centuries, and the travel book has consistently found a large audience.

Moreover, travel writers are still playing a significant role in sustaining notions of the American West as a canvas for the curious and the fantastic in the early twenty-first century, as evidenced in the recent travelogue of French intellectual Bernard-Henri Lévy, *American Vertigo: Traveling America in the Footsteps of Tocqueville* (2006).[10] In 1831, Alexis de Tocqueville and his friend Gustave de Beaumont arrived in the young United States to begin their nine-month-long exploration of American society through the lens of its practices of incarceration and rehabilitation. The resulting book, *Democracy in America* (two volumes, 1835 and 1840), one of the most celebrated and widely read books about the United States since its "rediscovery" in the mid-twentieth century, explained much more than the American prison system; it dissected and illuminated the democratic pulse of a nation to the world and to Americans as well.[11] The achievements of the new country a half-century after forging its Constitution were in Tocqueville's account cause for national pride and an object lesson for other nations seeking paths to democracy. *Democracy in America*, which appeared in six editions between 1945 and 1959 as the United States engaged in a monumental process of Cold War–inspired self-definition, has become a core text in the annals of American exceptionalism.

One and three-quarter centuries after Tocqueville and Beaumont arrived in the United States, Lévy journeyed around the country (with his driver) for nine months and wrote *American Vertigo*. Tocqueville and Beaumont surely came to the United States with their own predilections and assumptions, but they clearly came also to learn. By way of contrast, Lévy it seems came only to confirm his rather well-established beliefs about America. Tocqueville's careful observations enabled him to write a book that served as a window onto the very political heart and cultural soul of America, a book that remains prescient in the twenty-first century. Lévy's book serves more as a mirror of his own preferences and biases than a window through which to view the nation. Furthermore, Lévy, like White nearly a century and a half earlier, demonstrates a penchant for finding and fixating on the extraordinary for the sake of shock value.

Traveling through southern Nevada, Lévy visits the Spearmint Rhino, one of Las Vegas's famous strip bars, the even more renowned Chicken Ranch brothel in Pahrump, in adjacent Nye County, and the Southern Nevada Women's Correctional Center in North Las Vegas. In the aforementioned establishments he interviews, respectively, a lap dancer, a prostitute, and a senior citizen on death row, thereby, one presumes, imagining that he is taking the pulse of the region. Indicative of his approach throughout the book, Lévy seeks to illuminate a place by emphasizing its margins, its outliers. With a remarkably diverse population of approximately two million residents, southern Nevada's female lap dancers, prostitutes, and condemned inmates are no more representative of that region in the early twenty-first century than the "scalped man of Omaha" was of the central plains in the post–Civil War years. Yet Lévy's lineup of social outcasts plays to a chord in the stigmatized contemporary popular consciousness of Las Vegas and its surrounding environs as America's Sodom and Gomorrah, much as White's scalped man of Omaha story played to public interest in the fantastically wild West.[12] All the characters are real—Lévy's three female exemplars of American culture at the margins, and White's scalped survivor of the exploding violence between whites and Indians on the plains. Their respective travel accounts do not use untruths to propagate the notion of a West that is and was like no place on earth; rather, they do so through their choices of which encounters to include and which to leave out of their accounts.[13]

Lévy, quite recently, and White, in the distant past, found what they came for. Their accounts are likely to be cited periodically in the coming centuries by scholars seeking some pithy accompaniments for their analyses of the West during the Indian Wars, or of the United States' purportedly most decadent and depraved metropolis in perhaps its most libertarian state in the new millennium. It is doubtful, however, that either book will find lasting significance; Lévy and White are unlikely to follow in Tocqueville's footsteps in that regard. Tocqueville's assessment of America has proven so enduring because he was so observant of the nation's norms as well as its exceptions, its commonalities as well as its peculiarities.

In *Global West, American Frontier*, I have been drawn primarily to travelers' accounts of potentially enduring value, ones that do follow in Tocqueville's footsteps. Most of my coverage emphasizes works that warrant resurrection, or at least a closer look, not as markers of western American wildness and weirdness but rather as a counterpoint to the mythic West. These works, such as George Catlin's *Adventures of the Ojibbeway and Ioway Indians in England, France, and Belgium* (1852), Richard Francis Burton's *The City of the Saints* (1861), and Mark Twain's *Following the Equator* (1897), are reminders of the messy and contradictory world of observations and interpretations that people have had to navigate in the past, much as they do in the present. They constitute, I hope, a testament to the ways in which the best travel writers have represented the West in challenging, probing, insightful fashion and how the conceptual roads they have traveled amount to a detour from the sorts of well-traveled paths that the existing scholarship on western travel writing has generally taken. Once this introduction is in the reader's rearview mirror, she or he will encounter no more scalped men of Omaha, no more women sex workers or death row inmates, or UFOs for that matter.[14] Yet I am hoping that the cast of characters and chronicles presented here will prove significant nonetheless as markers of an evolving West that existed and continues to exist in the popular consciousness, often in the shadow of western mythology yet always as an important accompaniment.

Roads Traveled and Not Traveled

Global West, American Frontier's five chapters emphasize the importance of the travel writing genre for understanding how the American and world publics have viewed the American West in the nineteenth and twentieth centuries, and more particularly in the century from the mid-1840s through the early 1940s. The two chapters in "Part One: The Global West of the Nineteenth Century" suggest that travel writers in that period, as often as not, presented the West in decidedly nonmythic fashion, emphasizing that place's connections to other frontier regions that lay at the edges of other expanding empires. The three essays in "Part Two: The American Frontier of the Twentieth Century" focus on the period that has generally been characterized by historians as the postfrontier era. I suggest, though, that the American frontier was very much alive as a concept and even a reality for many travel writers throughout the first four decades of the new century, as they (and perhaps their readers, too) searched for a quintessentially *American West* within the nation's borders or even for its American frontier equivalent, or extension, beyond them.

While the study covers a good deal of ground chronologically, geographically, and biographically, it is in no way intended to constitute a comprehensive examination of travel writing about the American West. I have been selective regarding choices of travelers and with respect to chronology. The study does not begin with the earliest published accounts by travelers on the eighteenth-century American frontier, or with the first American travel book (published after the Revolution), John Ledyard's *Journal of Captain Cook's Last Voyage to the Pacific Ocean and in Quest of a North-West Passage* (1783),[15] or even with the most famous of all European travelogues,[16] the naturalist and explorer Alexander von Humboldt's *Personal Narrative of Travels to the Equinoctial Regions of America, During the Years 1799–1804.*[17] Indeed, even the best known of all American journeys of exploration, that undertaken by Meriwether Lewis and William Clark from Saint Louis to the Pacific coast and back in the wake of the Louisiana Purchase of 1803, does not serve as my beginning.[18]

Instead, after some initial explorations in the opening chapter of the travel writing genre in relation to the history and historiography of the United States and the West, this study finds its chronological start at a pivotal moment in the nation's history: the middle of the nineteenth century. This is when the country acquired its Far West in the wake of the annexation of Texas, the war against Mexico, and treaty negotiations with Great Britain over the northern border. It is clear that the United States' attempted invasion of Canada during the War of 1812, the new nation's aggressive stance toward Spain as well as its own Indian peoples during the period 1810–1819 that culminated in the acquisition of Florida, and the broader policy of removal of Indian peoples from the southeast during the administration of Andrew Jackson, collectively amounted to a developing set of "habits of Empire," to use historian Walter Nugent's apt phrase.[19] Nonetheless, the mid-1840s witnessed a new scale of U.S. imperialism and an administration's willingness (in spite of the presence of significant opposition) to go to war for the purpose of expanding the nation's territorial footprint and securing its ostensible manifest destiny. For historian Elliott West, 1845 marks the beginning of the "Greater Reconstruction," a period marked by remarkable national growth and division that lasted until the formal end of Reconstruction in the South and the end of the last major war against Indian peoples (the Nez Perce War) in 1877.[20] It was certainly clear from the public debates of the time, in the mid-1840s, that the nation was in the midst of an imperial moment of a new scale and significance.

We start at that moment, not in the actual theater of the war against Mexico, but in Berlin, where the war became a topic of conversation for Alexander von Humboldt and the American travel writer John Lloyd Stephens. We begin also with the journeys of another American, the painter George Catlin, and the subjects of his art and performance, North American Indians—Iowas and Ojibways—in the European center of empire and colonialism, London. Our points of departure also include another European, the German travel writer and prolific author of western adventure stories, Friedrich Gerstäcker, who traveled in North America and across the globe comparing the impact of gold rushes in particular and colonialism more generally on indigenous populations. The coverage in the second chapter includes the British travelers Francis Galton, Richard Francis Burton, Isabella Bird, Robert Louis Stevenson, and Mary Kingsley, along with Mark Twain. Part 2 of the study comprises three chapters, the first of which is devoted in part to the global travels of John Muir and Jack London in the early years of the new century but more fully to the African and Brazilian expeditions of Theodore Roosevelt. The fourth chapter examines the transcontinental automotive travelogues of the early twentieth century and includes the antimodernist observations of Emily Post and a host of lesser-known figures, in addition to the well-known Mary Austin and D. H. Lawrence. The final chapter begins with the observations of a famous American writer and an equally famous British one, Ernie Pyle and J. B. Priestley, respectively, although the chapter is devoted largely to a tour through the West via the pages of the Federal Writers' Project (FWP) state guides, produced from the late 1930s to the early 1940s. The conclusion begins with the pronouncements made in the late 1930s and 1940s concerning the death of the travel book, and then examines the persistence and vitality of the genre since then and the place of the West as a still-favored subject and destination.

Global West, American Frontier focuses largely on travelers whose accounts were produced independent of government directives or those of other sponsoring agencies that might have limited the writer's vision or directed it in certain clearly prescribed ways (although, as I will explain shortly, the FWP state guides of chapter 5 are an important exception to this general rule).[21] For this reason, I have not included promotional writings about the West in this study, even though such accounts were ubiquitous from the mid-nineteenth to the early twentieth century and certainly often utilized the form of the travelogue. The West's boosters frequently adopted the word "travels" for the titles of their publications, almost certainly with the purpose of broadening their appeal to the readers of travel books and perhaps masking their motivations as sellers of place rather than detached observers, describers, and evaluators.[22] For similar reasons, I have chosen not to provide coverage of another voluminous body of western writing that described western places: the reminiscences of old pioneers. These works of memoir also mimicked the popular travelogue form as their authors recounted the trials and tribulations of western journeying and settlement experienced earlier in life. Like the grandiose claims of western promoters, these retrospective travel narratives were the product of ulterior motives—generally the desire to maintain a degree of social standing within rapidly modernizing western communities that seemed (to the reminiscers) increasingly disconnected from the world of their own pioneer experiences.[23]

Despite the heavy temptation to do otherwise, and the acknowledgment that the journey motif had been deeply embedded in the novel form for centuries, this study largely forgoes discussion of novels that adopted aspects of the travelogue form. One of those that might, for example, have merited inclusion is John Steinbeck's classic *The Grapes of Wrath* (1939). His narration of the Joad family's journey and the larger movement of displaced sharecroppers, tenants, and small landowners—from the dried-out and dust-blown southern plains to "[h]ighway 66 . . . the main migrant road . . . the long concrete path across the country . . . over the red lands and the gray lands, twisting up into the mountains, crossing the Divide and down into the bright and terrible desert, and across the desert to the mountains again, and into the rich California valleys"—was, unmistakably, the chronicle of an exodus that illuminated the state of things in the West and the nation. In that regard, the novel fit the contours of the travel book genre quite well.[24] However, Steinbeck's novel departed significantly from the traditional travel narrative form, which featured (and arguably necessitated) the author as traveler, commentator, and key protagonist, the person to whom things happen and who conveys their meaning to the reader, a role he later embraced in *Travels with*

Charley. Jack Kerouac's *On the Road* (1957) (discussed in the conclusion) is the only exception to the general rule of excluding novels in the study; but in the work Kerouac was unmistakably the key protagonist, and the end result (autobiography, with the names changed) constitutes as close a proximity to the travel book genre as the novel form can.

Readers will also find a virtual absence of discussion of the guidebooks produced by Baedeker's and other firms starting in the 1820s. These publications, while essential sources for the scholar of tourism, are for the most part a more commercial and less literary genre than the travel narrative form.[25] Yet there have been occasional moments in time when guidebooks have amounted to far more than the cataloguing of sites and directions to them. The Federal Writers' Project guidebooks to American states are a classic case in point. These works, generally marked by strong prose, keen insights, and the motivation to help highlight and even nurture a sense of place rather than just describe places, are closer to the travel book form in many ways than to the guidebook genre, and for this reason are examined in the study's closing chapter.

In addition to guidebooks, promotional works and works of reminiscence, government reports, and novels, I have largely avoided the broad genre of nature writing, being drawn more to cultural landscapes that natural ones; even John Muir makes only limited appearances (in chapter 3 and the conclusion). Moreover, I have limited my treatment largely to published works, for the simple reason that a main purpose of the project is to illuminate the significance of the travel writing genre to understanding popular perceptions of the American West in the nineteenth and twentieth centuries. The accounts of well-known travel writers reached large audiences initially and continue to do so in the early twenty-first century. The unpublished personal diaries of tens of thousands of other travelers to the West in these centuries certainly have great value as historical sources, and other scholars have mined them effectively in recent years, but they generally reached only the contemporary audiences that they merited (i.e., rather small ones at best) and thus are only peripheral to this study.[26]

However, I should emphasize that this choice to privilege the published travel writer over the unpublished author, the so-called "tourist," is anything but a reflection of my own sensibilities concerning the authenticity of the former and the artificiality of the latter category of journeyers. I have written previously about the "traveler-tourist dichotomy," namely the tendency of many academics and writers to denigrate the tourist as a pale modern or postmodern imitation of the traveler, and that of so-called "travelers" to elevate themselves above the derisively labeled "touring masses." (I explore this theme further in chapter 4 and the conclusion.) Such easy assumptions and generalizations, and such often rather shallow acts of self-promotion by self-defined travelers, reflect the cultural elitism of members of both groups and help explain my tendency in this study to give more space to those travel writers who seem to have been motivated by a desire to actually understand the peoples and places they experienced before attempting to assess their merits and shortcomings.[27] Mark Twain wrote in 1869 that "Travel is fatal to prejudice, bigotry and narrow-mindedness and many of our people need it sorely on those accounts." Twain was right for the most part, although one suspects that replacing his "is" (fatal) with the more measured "can be" would help account for the experiences and chronicles of the many travelers who have resisted any such positive self-transformations.[28]

Some travel writers, over the course of the past two centuries (and for centuries previous, too), managed to travel with their eyes and minds wide open, ready to experience *and* understand the peoples and landscapes they traveled in. Others, clearly, have been so thoroughly encumbered by the weight of their own cultural baggage, so closed minded that they need never have left home, that, indeed, staying home would only have been a kindness to the people they encountered along the way. Sinclair Lewis brilliantly encapsulated this latter type in the insufferable Nordic blowhard Lowell Schmaltz in the hilarious and caustically titled monologue "Travel Is So Broadening" (1928).[29] Schmaltz saw nothing on his travels, learned nothing from them, forgot or misremembered all the important details of the trips, and offended everyone he met. I am not suggesting that there are just two kinds of travelers—the unfailingly inquisitive and perceptive on the one hand, and the unremittingly judgmental and uninspired on the other. These tendencies do, however, seem to mark the opposite ends of the scale of traveling temperaments. *Global West, American Frontier* focuses largely on the inquisitive brand of traveler and devotes less space to those whom this author (and I suspect most readers) would least wish to travel with, although a few memorable representatives of the latter category do find their way into the pages.

The truly gifted and valuable travel writers are, I would venture, the ones who come to realize that they are not just traveling through other landscapes but through the landscapes of other people's lives; they are visitors who care to learn what a place means to the people who live there. They are the ones who live up to travel writer and novelist Paul Theroux's goal of enabling his readers to "see these people and places, to hear them and smell them."[30] Travel writers who seek experience on this level generally earn the trust of those they visit, as well as the reader's trust, and thus become the valued guides to a world of vicarious experiences. They journey in the tradition of Walt Whitman's "Song of the Open Road" (1856), "Listening to others, considering well what they say / Pausing, searching, receiving, contemplating."[31] If this study betrays my empathy for many of its subjects, then that is largely because they are the ones whose accounts I have found valuable and instructive, both as guides to the western past and sometimes as object lessons for the western and American present and future.

I have been especially drawn to the accounts of travelers whose global experiences enabled them to place the West into a larger comparative context in the nineteenth century, and to the accounts of twentieth-century travelers who sought to discover, or rediscover, to claim, or reclaim, or to bemoan the absence of the American frontier or the loss of a distinctive West. That I found quite easily the kinds of accounts I was looking for in both centuries, the kinds of travelogues I had imagined were out there from the very start of my reading for this project, underscores, I think, their ubiquity, far more so than any ability of my own to uncover the unusual in dusty archives and libraries. Nonetheless, I am certainly not claiming that there was an absence of popular travel accounts in the nineteenth century that accentuated the more fantastic aspects of the West and thereby contributed to its mythological status. Neither am I implying that there were no twentieth-century travelers who placed the region into global comparative context (rather than searching for its essential or imagined American "frontierness").

The point here is that the popular notion of the end of the nineteenth century as the watershed moment dividing a frontier nation from a postfrontier one conditions us to expect that travel writing about the West would be dominated by frontier-centric travel accounts in the frontier age and by more globally positioned ones during the "American Century," as the nation increasingly came to dominate the world stage. I am cautioning that we would do well to rethink such assumptions about how the West was presented to America and to the world in these two centuries. Furthermore, I suggest that there was an important counternarrative to the mythic West at the very time that amorphous entity was developing in the nineteenth century. Additionally, I am highlighting the role of travel writing in sustaining the notion of the West as frontier and as the most distinctively American part of the nation well into the twentieth century. In a sense, then, *Global*

West, American Frontier amounts to an inversion of common assumptions and expectations concerning the matter of how the nation and the world viewed the American West over time.[32]

The project amounts to a sort of intellectual homecoming after a quarter century as a British expatriate in America, working as an Americanist and specializing in the American West. On this level, it is a very personal study, one that, admittedly, features an unrepresentative number of British travelers trying to understand America.[33] I have myself spent a good deal of time traveling the nation's interstates and blue highways, particularly those in the West, and, if truth be told, have for many years, like so many others I am sure, thought about writing my own American travel book. This book about other travelers' books is a substitute of sorts, and one that led me on the trail of one of my subjects, Sir Richard Francis Burton, from the Huntington Library in San Marino, California, to an archive in Richmond and a tent-shaped tomb in Mortlake, both just a few miles away from the southwest London home where I was born and raised.

This study is itself part of a larger trend toward the globalization or internationalization of American history—the envisioning of America as a "transnational nation," to use Ian Tyrrell's phrase—and of the history of the American West, whose comparativists stretch across the generations from Herbert Eugene Bolton and Walter Prescott Webb to Howard Lamar and Walter Nugent to Patricia Limerick, Gunther Peck, and others who started in the West and ended up "going global."[34] Their work has smoothed the paths for globally positioned studies of the American West. I am a relative latecomer to those paths, but hope that my extension of them into the travel writing genre may be of some interest to students and scholars of the West in history and related fields such as American studies and literary studies.

Regarding the complicated matter of what constitutes a travel book, I think I have arrived at my own definition partly through the process of elimination outlined earlier. Travel books are generally not commercially produced guidebooks, promotional tracts, or retrospective tales of travel composed long after journeys were undertaken. Travel books are marked by their immediacy; they are written in the very course of journeys (and sometimes are published in serialized form during those journeys), or soon after their completion. Travel books are generally (not exclusively) the creation of nonresidents seeking to know unfamiliar places, and their greatest charm and insight, more often than not, stems from the sense of wonder of the traveler experiencing places and peoples for the first time, or from the traveler's ability to place his or her subjects into larger comparative contexts and thus better convey their characteristics. And that traveler stands at the center of the travel book, as the self-conscious narrator of personal experiences and impressions and the purveyor of information about cultures and landscapes.

While contemporary travelogues are usually catalogued today as nonfiction, travel narratives are often works of significant literary merit and can occupy that murky space between fiction and nonfiction. But take a trip along the stacks of any well-stocked western history library collection and you will find that travel books are interspersed with standard works of history. The pioneering western historian Earl Pomeroy recalled that in 1953–1954 when he was designing a course on the West, the second half of which was to focus exclusively on developments in the twentieth century, there was no established body of historical scholarship to draw on, but there were voluminous travelers' accounts on the library shelves. The result of Pomeroy's endeavors was *In Search of the Golden West* (1957), a superb study of visitors' writings about the region and the first significant work on western tourism, a subfield of western history that has been resurgent in recent decades. Pomeroy's book and his reflections also serve as an important reminder of the value of considering what was on the shelves for those interested in the West to read in earlier periods.[35]

Historians have drawn on travel writings frequently throughout the course of the twentieth century, and in the nineteenth century too, when travelers' accounts were among the only significant sources available. The general tendency of contemporary historians has been twofold. First, they have exhibited a penchant for using these accounts as vignettes to frame their theoretical arguments, or as memorable, albeit ill-informed, first-person narratives that highlight the prejudices and misconceptions of earlier ages. In this framing, the travel writings themselves generally fail to become the primary subjects of scholarly investigations. Historians have often treated travel writings as little more than garnish for the main fare they serve up. This is the case, I think, because travel writing is a form of expression that historians have had trouble trusting. Why place any stock in the observations of visitors who came laden down with cultural prejudices, spent comparatively limited time in any single location, and recorded their impressions for the benefit of readers in other places, and for the purpose of augmenting their own financial circumstances? Why put any faith in the historical significance or usefulness of writings that so often tell us as much, or even more, about their authors as they do about the actual places and peoples visited?

Surely there are better historical sources lying around: the letters and diaries of actual residents, the records of chambers of commerce, demographic data, official government correspondence and reports, legal records, church records, local newspapers. Such concerns are not unfounded. Yet, for the cultural historian who is interested in how the West has been envisioned by the reading public over the centuries, the travel book may be one of the very best archives to mine. Moreover, it is important to remember of course that all historical sources are in large part the products of their authors or preservers, and evaluating these creations of authorial subjectivity has always been the work of historians.[36]

The second and more recent tendency of scholars utilizing the travel book genre has been to make these sources the central subject of studies, and a voluminous body of scholarship about travel writing has developed in the last generation among cultural theorists, literary scholars, and historians. Much of this writing, as discussed in the opening chapter, has followed the general contours of postcolonial scholarship and has treated travel writers as agents of empire who played a pivotal role in presenting (and digesting the meaning of) the colonized world to the residents of those empire nations that were profiting from its natural and human resources. The present study departs from both of these contemporary trends: first, in treating nineteenth- and twentieth-century travel books and their authors as the central subjects, not the seasoning; and, second, in considering the possibility that travel writers of the nineteenth century, while undeniably always a part of the discourse of empire, might at times have offered a significant critique of empire and its consequences, one that would have been readily available to a large reading public, and might have actually shaped larger public perceptions and even policies.

In part 2, I consider how travel writings have remained important and popular sources of information about the West throughout the twentieth century. In these three chapters and in the conclusion, I examine how the travel book genre has helped sustain the frontier concept in the popular consciousness and how it can help illuminate discussions over the continuing vibrancy or impending death of western regional distinctiveness. In short, the travel narrative form has remained an important guide to western America even as new technological developments have compressed space and rendered the most faraway places more readily accessible. For this reason, the travel book can be deemed an unlikely survivor in the digital age. Then again, just as regions sustain themselves and maintain their distinctiveness partly in response to the forces of standardization and homogenization, the travel book may actually be more a beneficiary than a casualty of the new digitized world at our fingertips. The ability to pull up images of any place in the West or the world through Google Earth might actually make us more likely to want to visit in more than just a solitary, virtual capacity, albeit still vicariously but in the inherited company of Isabella Bird, Robert Louis Stevenson, or Theodore Roosevelt. Whatever the case, it is hard to imagine the American western past and present, or even to contemplate the region's future, without such important guides.

PART ONE

THE GLOBAL WEST
OF THE
NINETEENTH CENTURY

CHAPTER ONE

EXCEPTIONALISM AND GLOBALISM

Revisiting the Traveler

[T]he march of civilization is everywhere, as it is in America, a war of extermination, and that of our own species.

—George Catlin in London, *Adventures of the Ojibbeway and*
Ioway Indians (1852)

You shave my head in a severe winter, and then sell me a warm cap. Of course,
the cap keeps my head warm, and I need it from time to time; but I do not see
any reason why I ought to be obliged to you for it—the cap only keeps my head
as warm as my hair would have done; but why did you not leave it to me?—
only to sell me the cap.

—Friedrich Gerstäcker in Java, *Narrative of a Journey Round the World* (1853)

Exceptionalism and Empire

Since the publication of Edward Said's landmark study *Orientalism*
(1978), cultural historians have typically viewed travel writers within
the theoretical contours of the postcolonial framework Said helped
construct.[1] Travel writers have routinely been characterized as the archi-
tects of imperial visions, the exoticizers, commodifiers, and objectifiers of
colonized "others," the agents of empire who helped their readers in the
mother countries accept, consume, and digest imperial practices. While
travel writers certainly could and did serve this purpose, often portraying
other races and places as desperately in need of the civilizing hand of a
"higher" culture, scholarship on their work and significance has had the

effect of flattening the discourse about empire in travel writing. In the post-colonial framing, imperial advocates and critics, as well as those whose visions were marked by a great deal of ambiguity about empire, have been placed together, as if in concordance. However, when we examine the archive of nineteenth-century travelogues about the American West, we find more dissonance than harmony. Travel writers at times offered strong and influential criticism of the empires of rival nations as well as of their own nations' imperial projects.

In addition, the ubiquitous and enormously popular travel book genre offered readers an important countercurrent to the common notion of the American West as an exceptional place, one without parallel. Nineteenth-century travelers often placed the West in a broader, comparative global context, viewing it as one developing frontier among many and considering the United States as a colonizing power (like its European progenitors). Such observers were effectively putting the West into the world and thereby deemphasizing its exceptionalism. These global visions of travel writers can help us rethink our assumptions about western mythology and American exceptionalism, which has itself often rested on the matter of the significance of the nation's western frontier experience. The travel book is thus important for understanding how the West was envisioned by America and the world in the nineteenth century.

The tension between exceptionalism and empire stands today at the very heart of the American experience, as it has for more than two centuries. The idea of benign national distinctiveness, of republican purity and innocence, has continually collided with the notion of the United States as an empire, much like others that have risen and fallen in the course of human history.[2] From the earliest settlements in British North America, colonists viewed the western frontier within a wider context of global exploration, commerce, and imperial war. Rival empires traded, negotiated, and clashed on the western frontier before colonial subjects considered the path of independence from the mother country. Prior to the Revolutionary War, the issue of westward movement into the great interior of the continent sparked tensions between those colonists who wanted the freedom to expand their geographic and economic horizons and an anxious British empire that sought control over them and wished to reduce the potential for conflict with indigenous peoples on the frontier.

A generation after the end of the Revolutionary War, the Louisiana Purchase of 1803 doubled the size of the emerging American nation. The following year, Meriwether Lewis and William Clark went off to explore the lands that the new republic had just purchased from France. Two generations later, the admission of Texas and Florida as states (1845) and the settlement of the Oregon boundary question with Britain (1846) further expanded the geography of the young nation. The war against Mexico (1846–1848) added more territory with the spoils of victory of the Treaty of Guadalupe Hidalgo (present-day Arizona, California, Nevada, New Mexico, Utah, and portions of Colorado and Texas—an area totaling 1.2 million square miles). The postwar Gadsden Purchase from the recently defeated Mexican government in 1851 (the small piece of southwestern territory that Elliott West describes as "an after-dinner mint following the expansionist gorging") further enlarged the borders of the West into the familiar shape we know today.[3] In less than half a century, the new nation had tripled its size and its coastline. As Thomas Hietala notes, in less than a decade during the administrations of John Tyler (1841–1845) and James K. Polk (1845–1849), the country acquired "nearly eight hundred million acres of land" and pressed for "commercial and territorial advantages beyond the continent in . . . Hawaii, China, Cuba, and Yucatán."[4]

American history textbooks generally apply the term "imperialism" to the end of the nineteenth century—the period of the Spanish-American War and the acquisition of the Philippines, Puerto Rico, and other noncontiguous territories—the era immediately postdating the official closing of the frontier. The imperialist label is generally not applied so readily to the earlier part of that century, the era of continental or frontier expansion. So long as the United States had a western frontier to move into, that process of territorial growth seemed ostensibly, and retrospectively, nonimperialistic. This perspective implies that America had its fleeting imperial moment a century ago. But the nineteenth-century West, of course, was a stage for American foreign policy. The new territories entered the national body politic as full-fledged states, with all the rights and privileges of the existing states (a rather different practice from that of traditional empires with their tributary satellites). Their entry into the U.S. orbit nonetheless cannot be accounted for by providence alone.[5] These developments mark the process of nineteenth-century American expansion as a story of empire building, one characterized by the contending voices of self-described imperialists and anti-imperialists. Yet the story of westward imperial expansion has often paraded, in our historical memory, in far less aggressive clothing—as the "empire for liberty" that Thomas Jefferson championed in 1809 and that Stephen A. Douglas invoked in 1845, or an "empire of innocence," to use Patricia Nelson Limerick's irony-laden phrase of 1987, or it may best be described by Ian Tyrrell's 2007 phrase, "the empire that did not know its name."[6]

Evident for more than half a century, the global and comparative framing of western American history has gained momentum in recent years. Furthermore, the currently developing fields of Atlantic World and Pacific World history provide ample evidence of the heightened global emphasis among scholars of the United States today.[7] Nonetheless, consideration of the nation's nineteenth-century territorial growth as one imperialist story among many in the period has been obscured in our historical understanding by a far more popular and pleasing national narrative.[8] By moving into lands that it bordered, the United States' expansion into the West differed from the contemporary colonial ventures of the European powers by its contiguous nature, and advocates of American empire certainly emphasized that factor. Indeed, the pervasive hold of manifest destiny on the American imagination has had such strength that we still have to remind ourselves that the story of America's westward expansion really did take place on a global stage. The notion of a nation growing into its foreordained boundaries has such power that we can forget the foreign policy context of nineteenth-century western history. The myth of manifest destiny has endured so well because it provides such incredible comfort to the national psyche. Better for the national mental health to believe that the world's greatest democracy had grown naturally, providentially, into its God-given skin than to consider that it, like so many other nations, has a history of empire building. The West, so often declared the quintessential American region, has functioned as the primary stage for that imperial drama.

The story of national mission, God-given destiny, and American exceptionalism has not unfolded as the result of any great conscious design, at least no more so than the nurturing of myths of national exceptionalism in other countries.[9] Nations gradually create identities because they need them, and the process is generally rather unsystematic.[10] The United States provides a good case in point. Shortly after the conclusion of the Revolutionary War, Benjamin Franklin noted that the western frontier, the part of the new nation farthest removed from the European-influenced and tainted east coast, was the emerging heart of the nation.[11] In 1787, Thomas Jefferson wrote to James Madison: "Our governments will remain virtuous . . . as long as they are chiefly agricultural; and this will be as long as there shall be vacant lands in any part of America. When they [the people] get piled upon one another in large cities, as in Europe, they will become corrupt as in Europe, and go to eating one another."[12]

Thus, in a fascinating example of the inversion of the standard theory of center-periphery relations (an inversion that long predates postcolonial theory, which emphasizes the influence of the colonized on colonizers, and of colonies on empires), the western periphery—the frontier—increasingly came to be seen as the center of Americanism as it shifted farther from the physical center of real national power and federal infrastructure—the eastern seaboard. Here, on the periphery, a distinctive Americanism would emerge, as Franklin, Jefferson, and other contemporaries suggested. This observation occurred more than a half century before newspaper editor John L. O'Sullivan popularized the term "manifest destiny" in 1845, and more than a century before the historian Frederick Jackson Turner gave academic legitimacy to popular notions about the frontier's enormous significance.[13] While the particular concept of manifest destiny was clearly a creation of the moment by American expansionists seeking to justify an imperialistic course for their still new republic, the connection between the western frontier and the health of that republic had long been a staple in American thought.

Indeed, the development of a national consciousness in the nineteenth century depended partly on the notion that this new republic could somehow break the historical cycle of countries rising to greatness and then sinking and decaying. In this context, historian Dorothy Ross has explained, "the vast continent of virgin land that offered Americans an escape from republican decay assumed increasing, even mythic importance." The movement into the interior of the continent, into the heartland of the new country, could thus be viewed as a story of American escape from the world, of America discovering and expanding westward into itself. With its western safety valve, America could avoid the industrial violence, class division, and general social decline that had accompanied modernization in European countries; it could even escape the cycles of history and remain an Eden, suspended, as Ross notes, in "a position somewhere between the agrarian and commercial stages of development."[14] Having completed its ostensibly preordained continental expansion, America, with the closing of the frontier in the late nineteenth century, would have to decide whether to follow the course of imperial expansion, but not before then. But, of course, throughout the nineteenth century the new nation was not discovering itself or expanding into itself so much as constituting itself incrementally (in quite large chunks to be sure) on a world stage and displacing those residents who were already there—primarily Indians, Californios, Mexicans, and Tejanos.

The drama of national exceptionalism played out as the century unfolded, and the prairies, plains, Rockies, and Pacific coast were acquired, explored, conquered, and settled. The numerous critics of the process of empire building, particularly in the 1840s, include intellectual luminaries such as Henry David Thoreau (whose famous "Essay on Civil Disobedience" directly commented on citizens' rights in an age of empire) and an emerging young Whig politician, Abraham Lincoln (who worked hard to distance himself later in his career from his youthful anti-Mexican-American-War stance). Furthermore, the northeastern United States as a region generally opposed the mid-nineteenth-century imperial turn.[15] Expansionists dismissed the reservations of their anti-imperialist and sectional adversaries and argued for a "republican empire," one involving the acquisition and exploitation of "land not people" ("the myth of an empty continent"), which thereby did not diminish the nation's exceptionalism but actually enhanced it.[16]

Yet this complex story of clashing imperialists and anti-imperialists has been largely subsumed in the national memory by an infinitely simpler tale (in keeping with the imperialist rationale of the 1840s) in which continental expansion has been rendered natural, and only extracontinental expansion challenges the notion of national exceptionalism. More in the mainstream of national heritage construction were the young amateur and professional historians who told the story of the western frontier in stirring, grand narrative fashion, from Francis Parkman in *The Oregon Trail* (1849) to Theodore Roosevelt in *The Winning of the West* (3 volumes, 1889–1896), as well as Turner in his landmark essay "The Significance of the Frontier in American History" (1893) and in subsequent essays.[17] Writers, artists, performers, and, later, filmmakers all contributed to a national consciousness of the frontier West as the heart and soul of America. That consciousness became the core of a benign story of national growth, a story removed from the global stages where the imperial pursuits of presumably base, unenlightened European nations played out.

The great drama of the West became just the first of many stories of national exceptionalism that have sprung up because the nation needed them, and they have proven hard to purge from the national consciousness for the very same reason. We should include among these stories that of the Progressive era as an age of purely altruistically motivated reform, the absolute antithesis of (and corrective to) the Gilded Age; the story of the 1920s as a happy, colorful, carefree interlude; the Great Depression as a triumph of American cooperation, compassion, and perseverance; World War II as "the

Good War," with a wonderfully unified home front; and the Civil Rights movement as a great redemptive moment, a triumph of integration marked by a healthy national recognition of the country's shortcomings in the arena of race. All these memorable episodes were far messier, their contours less clearly, less dualistically defined, than the national collective memory has imagined. None of them quite qualify as the great morality plays and triumphs of America's better angels that the nation (including many of its historians) has remembered. Within the space of about thirty years, each of these purposeful interpretations of the past was challenged by professional historians; but like the story of the West and American exceptionalism, all continue largely intact in the broader public consciousness despite the weight of scholarly reservations.[18]

While the New Western History helped transform the history of the American West a generation ago, the contours of the story remained within an exceptionalist paradigm. Region sought to replace frontier as a theoretical framework (not that the frontier thesis held much weight for many scholars by that time); conquest replaced settlement as the key descriptor for what happened in the West; and tragedy replaced triumph in the trope department. The contours of this rejuvenating wave of scholarship were far more nuanced than an enthused media, hungry for stories of gunfights at politically OK corrals, implied. The story of the western past, in the media representation, went from being an exceptionally noble one, a mark of national pride, to an exceptionally ignoble one, a tale of national embarrassment. Whether a uniquely benign story (an oversimplification of Turner's thesis) or a thoroughly malign one (a similarly facile interpretation of the New Western History), whether resting on a thematic foundation of frontier or region, the print media presented the West as a unique place, a place apart from the rest of the world, rather than a part of it.[19]

The accounts of foreigners have often augmented this story of American exceptionalism. "What then is the American, this new man?" asked the French expatriate Hector St. John de Crèvecoeur in his *Letters from an American Farmer* in 1782. He declared that in the new continent, the European "leaves behind him all the ancient prejudices and manners ... [and becomes] a free man acting upon new principles."[20]

Alexis de Tocqueville, perhaps the most insightful of all foreign observers of American life, memorably emphasized the nation's uniqueness in his *Democracy in America* (vol. 1, 1835; vol. 2, 1840). The famed British observer Lord James Bryce's massive two-volume set of observations, *The American*

Commonwealth (1893–1895), is generally remembered by American western historians for its comment about the West as the most American part of America. These observers have stood the test of time (their works are still in print) not solely because they wrote wonderfully rich studies, full of insights and predictions that make us wonder, generations later, at their genius, but also because they tell a nation what it wants to hear: that it is benignly different, exceptional.[21]

Yet this positioning of Tocqueville's *Democracy in America* as a foundational text in the annals of American exceptionalism tells only a part of the story. As Jennifer Pitts has demonstrated in her recent analysis and translation of Tocqueville's writings on empire and slavery, Tocqueville advocated French empire building in Algeria. He visited Algiers in 1841 and 1846 and viewed U.S. efforts to address the "Indian problem" on its western frontier as a model for the French in dealing with the insurgent Algerian population.[22] This largely unknown side of Tocqueville's thinking leads us to another understudied counternarrative to the story of American and western American exceptionalism. Numerous nineteenth-century foreign travelers to America, as well as American travelers, described western places and peoples in a broader global context. Exploring this interplay of global visions and exceptionalist dreams in American thought complicates our understanding of how the American West and the theme of national exceptionalism were perceived by the American public in the nineteenth century. For many of these travel writers, the West was best understood in a global context, not as a quintessentially American frontier. Their global visions of the West would surely have prompted some readers to think about their nation comparatively, in relation to other expanding empires, rather than as a great benign exception or anomaly.

Such globally positioned accounts of American life, however, have not fully entered the national consciousness of the western American past, partly because of the enormous power of the notions of manifest destiny and "westward expansion."[23] Restoring those comparative narratives or at least underscoring the space that they occupied in the national imagination will not change the well-established fact that in the memory wars, these global visions were overwhelmed by exceptionalist dreams. However, resurrecting the globally contextualized West of the nineteenth century does remind us that the American and world publics were not fed a steady and unvarying diet of western exceptionalism, and this knowledge complicates our understanding of the contours of the western American past and of how that past has been remembered.[24]

Resituating the Traveler

Close to two thousand travel books were published in the United States between 1830 and 1900, and an even larger number were published in Europe in the same period.[25] Travel accounts, often serializations that later appeared as books, filled popular magazines and periodicals.[26] Travel writings were voluminous and vital to the public understanding or misunderstanding of place. Travelers' accounts helped meet the public need for information about faraway places in what was still an age of discovery. American travel writer Paul Belloni du Chaillu's *Explorations and Adventures in Equatorial Africa*, for example, sold nearly three hundred thousand copies in 1861, making it one of that year's best sellers.[27] Moreover, Mark Twain's travel books were his best-known writings and his primary source of income from the late 1860s through to the end of the century.[28] Twain's travel writings, along with those of hundreds of other popular and influential writers, constitute a wonderfully rich storehouse of ethnographic observations and commentary on the conquest of the West.[29]

Travel writing, however, has to some degree slipped through the cracks of our historiographical consciousness in much the same way that the genre naturally slips through the cracks between literature and history. Travel writings are neither novels about nor historical surveys of places.[30] They generally are, as Barbara Brothers and Julia Gergits note, "hybrids—drawing in part from other genres such as autobiography, history, natural history, anthropology, sociology, archeology, or geography."[31] Until the past few decades, the travel writing genre has not proven a fertile ground for literary scholars. As Brothers and Gergits suggest, while "Modernism dominated the academy . . . fiction, poetry, and drama" received the primary focus of critical attention, and more popular forms such as travel writing were generally forgotten or disparaged.[32]

Interestingly, though, as literary scholars largely ignored the travel book in the World War II and postwar years and as authors themselves declared it a dead form (see the conclusion), American historical scholarship experienced a moment of intense engagement with the earlier perceptions of visitors, largely of British origin, to America.[33] The "hands-across-the-ocean" sentiment that World War II inspired in Britain and the United States initiated a heightened emphasis on what Americans could learn about their past from the keen observations of previous generations hailing from America's current primary wartime ally.[34]

As Cold War tensions rose precipitously, Allan Nevins's *America Through British Eyes* was reprinted, in 1948. The following year, Oscar Handlin's *This Was America* appeared. Both works offer testimony to the nation's effort to "find itself" and define its national character in the postwar years.[35] In much the same vein, Robert Athearn's *Westward the Briton*, another analysis of the observations of nineteenth-century British visitors to the West, was published in 1953. A few years later, the *Mississippi Valley Historical Review* published Thomas D. Clark's "The Great Visitation to American Democracy" (1957), his presidential address delivered at the fiftieth annual meeting of that organization.[36] Within this climate of Cold War anxiety in the 1940s and 1950s, consensus history, intellectual and cultural history, and the related field of American studies all appeared on the American scholarly scene as the nation turned inward in an effort to better understand itself. Works in these fields sought to chart the sources of the nation's distinctiveness and generally emphasized the positive nature of the American national character and its democratic institutions, thus offering academic legitimacy to the efforts of politicians and statesmen to shore up the foundations of American exceptionalism.[37]

As the nation searched for and proclaimed what Arthur Schlesinger Jr. called "The Vital Center" (the hallowed middle ground of political democracy so distinguishable from totalitarian extremes of the right and left), scholars produced their studies of American exceptionalism. The various works of the 1940s and 1950s on travel writings about America and the West augmented that scholarly search for an exceptional national story and character.[38] In knowing how others had perceived America and American democracy, these historians presumably felt that they could more fully understand their nation's past and present. Uncoincidentally, this period rediscovered Tocqueville's *Democracy in America*, reprinted as one of the core texts of American exceptionalism.[39] However, and not surprisingly, no concurrent American "rediscovery" occurred at this time of Tocqueville's writings in support of French imperialism in North Africa.[40]

We can certainly distinguish this generation of scholarship from the 1940s and 1950s about foreign travelers to the United States by its generally positive tone. We can also distinguish it from the more recent trend, one influenced by the "formal end of European colonialism during the latter half of the twentieth century."[41] As noted previously, since the appearance of Said's *Orientalism*, scholars have mostly emphasized the ominous side of travel writing, viewing it as a "colonial discourse" marked by "the rhetorical strategies of debasement [of other cultures]" and the maintenance of "cultural hegemony in the postcolonial world."[42] Said, in *Culture and Imperialism* (1993), describes travel writing as a vital part of "the great cultural archive . . . where the intellectual and aesthetic investments in overseas dominion are made." "In your narratives, histories, travel tales, and explorations," he continues, "your consciousness was represented as the principal authority, an active point of energy that made sense not just of colonizing activities but of exotic geographies and peoples."[43] Said further explained that representational forms, including fiction, history, travel writing, and art, "depended on the powers of Europe to bring the non-European world into representations, the better to be able to see it, to master it, and, above all, to hold it."[44] Homi K. Bhabha made the point even more directly in *The Location of Culture* (1994), stating: "the objective of colonial discourse is to construe the colonized as a population of degenerate types on the basis of racial origin, in order to justify conquest and to establish systems of administration and instruction."[45] Bhabha went on to argue that "the effect of colonial power" works against itself and ends up producing "hybridization rather than the noisy command of colonialist authority or the silent repression of native traditions."[46]

Mary Louise Pratt's *Imperial Eyes: Travel Writing and Transculturation* (1992) was a landmark study in this more critical body of scholarship on travel writing. Pratt positioned her work as part of the academy's effort to "decolonize knowledge." She emphasized the "contact zones," the "social spaces where disparate cultures meet, clash, and grapple with each other, often in highly asymmetrical relations of domination and subordination." Emblematic of that asymmetrical relationship, Pratt argued, are the "travel books by Europeans about non-European parts of the world," which created the "'domestic subjects' of Euro-imperialism." Thus, she asked, "[h]ow has travel and exploration writing produced 'the rest of the world' for European readerships?" Pratt contended that the form, in conjunction with "enlightenment natural history," had nurtured a "Euro-centered form of global or . . . 'planetary' consciousness." She ventured that the travel writer embodied that privileged consciousness, viewing other cultures and landscapes as "the monarch of all I survey," the archetypal representative of empire.[47]

Clearly, in the postcolonial academic world, the visions of earlier generations of travelers have appeared increasingly less benign; indeed, increasingly sinister. Theirs is an imperial gaze. We see a shift, then, from the theme of American exceptionalism as confirmed through the eyes of white

European visitors, to that of the imperial visions and racial predilections of
white travelers, whether European or American, as they make others of the
"traveled upon."[48] In both cases, however, the possibility of knowing one's
own nation and culture better through travelers' eyes has motivated scholars. But as scholarship on travel writing has shifted from the first stage to
the second, the emphasis has increasingly illuminated the less laudatory
aspects of western civilization. The transition has been, then, from the
insightfulness of the travelers' vision to the harmfulness of the travelers'
gaze—from an emphasis on the positive validation of American democracy
that travelers offered to an emphasis on the cultural prejudices that they
exhibited.[49]

However, as we approach the massive body of nineteenth-century visitors' accounts of America and the West that line both the dusty shelves of
archives and, in surprisingly large numbers, the brighter shelves of contemporary bookstores, let us consider a theoretical framework that encompasses
both of these extremes of benign exceptionalism and the imperial gaze. Such
a framework must also include the more nuanced possible readings of travelers' visions of America and the American West that lie between those
extremes. For example, scores of popular nineteenth-century travel writers
offered critical accounts of the United States' conquest of its contiguous West
and compared it to the colonial ventures of European powers on other continents. Recovering the work of two mid-nineteenth-century travelers, the
American painter of Indians, George Catlin, who is well remembered today
(although not as a travel writer), and the German traveling and popular
adventure story–writing phenomenon, Friedrich Gerstäcker, who is nowadays hardly remembered at all, can illuminate the tension between empire
and exceptionalism and the relationship between a globally contextualized
American West and a quintessentially American frontier.

In Europe and Around the World

But first, a stop in Berlin, where in 1847 the American travel writer John
Lloyd Stephens and the legendary German scientist and traveler Alexander
von Humboldt met for the first time. Stephens was the author of some of the
best-selling travel books of the late 1830s and early 1840s, on Arabia, southern and eastern Europe, and Central America.[50] He had become the vice
president and director of the Ocean Steam Navigating Company and traveled from New York to Bremen on the line's inaugural voyage. After arriving

in Bremen, Stephens traveled to Berlin, hoping to gain an audience with Humboldt. Humboldt granted him an hour, and Stephens expected that the time would be devoted to a discussion of the mysterious decline of the ancient Mayan civilization, which both men had written extensively about. But Humboldt had no interest in dwelling on the distant American past; instead, he wanted to discuss the tumultuous American present as evidenced by the ongoing war between the United States and Mexico. The United States' imperial ambitions had clearly caught the attention of European observers.[51]

The following year, 1848, an American in Europe chronicled those imperial urges and their consequences for indigenous peoples in North America. George Catlin had traveled from the United States to England in 1839 to promote his famous Indian Gallery, which he opened to the public at London's Egyptian Hall in Piccadilly in 1840. The gallery itself resulted from Catlin's earlier eight years of travel among the Indians in the United States and its territories.[52] The Egyptian Hall, which housed cultural artifacts from Captain James Cook's South Sea voyages, provided an appropriately global setting for Catlin's work. The public obviously did not mind the housing of South Sea islands artifacts inside an Egyptian-inspired architecture or the addition of paintings and people of the American West. The hall functioned as a repository for the "exotic" from all over the world. The press described Catlin's public lectures there as a "journey into Indian country" for a public already familiar with travel accounts of the American West.[53]

Catlin discussed the manners, customs, and fate of the North American Indians with his paintings as the props, and he often became highly critical of his nation's actions, proclaiming that "fire-water," "small-pox," and the "exterminating policy of the United States government" doomed the Indians to extinction. Fortuitously for Catlin, as the crowds tired of his illustrated lectures by 1843, a group of nine Ojibways arrived from Canada. His gallery was soon filled not just with pictures but with real Indians. The Ojibways would soon leave Catlin to perform in another show, but a group of Iowas (men, women, a child, and an infant) soon arrived, and Catlin touted them as "wilder," more "primitive," and more authentically Indian than the Ojibways.[54]

Catlin recorded these observations about his indigenous attractions in promotional broadsides for the shows. He also gathered them into a compelling work of travel, the self-referentially titled *Catlin's Notes of Eight Years' Travels and Residence in Europe, with His North American Indian Collection* (1848), which he later republished with a new title, *Adventures of the*

Figure 1. The Egyptian Hall in Piccadilly, built in 1812 to house William Bullock's personal collection of artifacts from around the globe, including materials from Captain James Cook's South Seas voyages in the late eighteenth century, was demolished in 1905 and replaced with an office building (#170–173 Piccadilly). Courtesy of The British Library, London.

Ojibbeway and Ioway Indians in England, France, and Belgium: Being Notes of Eight Years' Residence in Europe with the North American Indian Collection (1852), thereby shifting the primary emphasis to the Indians.[55] He structured much of the book as a travel narrative about Europe through Native American eyes. Catlin recounted the observations of the Iowas as they traveled around London—to Lord's Cricket Ground, Vauxhall Gardens, and Windsor Castle, where they met Queen Victoria and Prince Albert. The reader is taken vicariously on a journey with the Iowas as they respond to white people and white institutions.

While Catlin's own ego provides the primary axis around which his Indian travelogue revolves, the Iowas' travel experiences in the early 1840s, even refracted through him, are revealing.[56] During a journey to London's West End, the Iowas told Catlin that they "had passed two Indians in the street with brooms, sweeping away the mud; they saw them hold out their hands to people going by, as if they were begging for money." Could they

UNPARALLELED EXHIBITION!

The 14 Ioway Indians!

AND THEIR INTERPRETER,

IN

CATLIN'S INDIAN GALLERY,

EGYPTIAN HALL,

Just arrived from the Upper Missouri, near the Rocky Mountains, North America.

"WHITE CLOUD,"

The Head Chief of the Tribe, is with this interesting party, giving them that peculiar interest, which no other party of American Indians have had in a Foreign Country; and they are under the immediate charge of G. H. C. MELODY, who accompanied them from their country, with their favourite Interpreter, JEFFREY DORAWE.

MR CATLIN, who is the writer of this, and who was acquainted with most of the men of this party, while sharing the genuine hospitality of this tribe in their own country, and who is to present them and their native modes to the English people, vouches for the fact that this party is chiefly composed of the most influential men in the tribe, and that they are by far the most pleasing and just representation of the North American Indians ever seen in England.

The vouchers which these people bring from the Indian Agents, and also from the President of the United States, whose written permission they possess, as the reward for instances of the most extraordinary individual merit, entitle them to much respect; and their personal appearance and purely native modes, to the attention of the curious.

THE DELEGATION CONSISTS OF:

CHIEFS

MEW-HU-SHE-KAW—(White Cloud) first Chief of the Nation.
NEU-MON-YA—(Walking Rain) third Chief.
SE-NON-TY-YAH—(Blister Feet) great Medicine Man.

WARRIORS AND BRAVES

WASH-KA-MON-YA—(Fast Dancer.)
NO-HO-MUN-YA—(One who gives no attention.)
SHON-TA-YI-GA—(Little Wolf.)
WA-TAN-YE—(One always foremost.)
WA-TA-WE-BU-KA-NA—(Commanding General.) The Son of Walking Rain, 10 years old.
JEFFREY—(The Interpreter.)

SQUAWS,

RUTON-YE-WE-MA—(Strutting Pigeon) White Cloud's wife.
RUTON-WE-ME—(Pigeon on the Wing.)
OKE-WE-ME—(Female Bear that walks on the back of another.)
KOON-ZA-YA-ME—(Female War Eagle sailing.)
TA-PA-TA-ME—(Sophia) Wisdom; White Cloud's daughter.
CORSAIR—(A Papoose)

This exceedingly picturesque group, with their "SHORN and CRESTED HEADS," will give their WAR and other DANCES, SONGS, GAMES, &c., all of which will be fully explained by Mr CATLIN, in his ROOMS in the EGYPTIAN HALL, each day and evening of this week, as follows:—

From Half-past 2 to 4 in the Day, and from Half-past 8 to 10 Evening.
Doors Open half-an-hour previous.

ADMITTANCE, ONE SHILLING.

1844   Printed by T. BRETTELL, 40 Rupert street.

Figure 2. Unparalleled exhibition: The 14 Iowa Indians and Their Interpreter, in George Catlin's Indian Gallery, Egyptian Hall, London, ca. 1844; promotional poster. Courtesy of the General Collection, Beinecke Rare Book and Manuscript Library, Yale University.

Nº 10.

Figure 3. Blistered Feet Addressing an Audience in the Egyptian Hall, from Catlin's
Adventures of the Ojibbeway and Ioway Indians in England, France, and Belgium
(1852). Courtesy of the Archives and Rare Books Library, University of Cincinnati.

really be Indians begging? the Iowas asked Catlin. He explained that they
were natives from the East Indies, Lascars, "left by some cruel fate, to earn
their living in the streets of London, or to starve to death." The Iowas, Catlin
noted, "seemed much affected by the degradation that these poor fellows
were driven to, and resolved that they would carry some money with them
when they went out, to throw to them."[57] Thus, the colonial subjects of one
empire come face to face with those of another on the streets of the nineteenth century's world capital of empire, London.

    Catlin traveled around England, Scotland, and Ireland with the Iowas,
and then to Paris in 1845; his Indian Gallery was displayed in the Louvre, and
King Louis Philippe and the French royal family visited.[58] He intended the
showcasing of living Indians to underscore his core message that Indians
were dying out. Then, tragically, some of the Iowas, including the infant boy
(Corsair) and his mother, O-kee-wee-me, died of disease. The remaining
Iowas returned to North America. But Catlin's living tribute to a dying race
continued. A new group of Ojibways arrived in Paris and joined Catlin's

Figure 4. Fourteen Iowa Indians, from Catlin's *Adventures of the Ojibbeway and Ioway Indians in England, France, and Belgium* (1852). Courtesy of the Archives and Rare Books Library, University of Cincinnati.

show, and he shamelessly marketed them as superior Indians to the Iowas. Then, in 1846, eight of those Ojibways contracted smallpox, and two of them died. The survivors returned to the United States. The representatives of a dying race, working in a living history exhibit designed to highlight their fate, were dying. The deaths brought the show to an end. Catlin never exhibited Indians again.[59]

Catlin had hoped in vain that his self-published and self-marketed account of the experience of his travels with the Indians in Europe would help retrieve some of the financial losses from his European ventures. He then returned to a fascinating and somewhat disquieting proposal he had first lectured on at the Royal Institution of London a decade earlier: a "Museum of Mankind." This ethnographic endeavor, Catlin explained, would "perpetuate the looks and manners and history of all the declining and vanishing races of man." What is more, he reminded his English audience, "Great Britain has more than thirty colonies in different quarters of the globe, in which the numbers of civilized men are increasing, and the native tribes are wasting away." Catlin then declared: "the march of civilization is everywhere, as it is in America, a war of extermination, and that of our own

Figure 5. Twelve Ojibway Indians, from Catlin's *Adventures of the Ojibbeway and Ioway Indians in England, France, and Belgium* (1852). Courtesy of the Archives and Rare Books Library, University of Cincinnati.

species." He even proposed that a ship would sail around the world exhibiting his museum of mankind.[60] Imagine the cruel irony of a vessel journeying to the far-flung reaches of the globe where indigenous peoples were in decline, displaying the human remnants of those and various other cultures from other continents and islands.

As Catlin was proposing his floating museum, a German, Friedrich Gerstäcker, embarked on the second great journey of his life, traversing the world and comparing colonial systems and demographic catastrophes. Gerstäcker's remarkable account of his global travels, *Narrative of a Journey Round the World*, was published in Germany, America, and England in 1853.[61] Born in Hamburg in 1816 to well-known opera singers, sent by his mother to live with an aunt and uncle after the death of his father, and then returned to his mother after his aunt's death, Friedrich Gerstäcker's wandering tendencies may well have been shaped by the transitory nature of his early years. He found literal inspiration in Daniel Defoe's *Robinson Crusoe* (1719) and James Fenimore Cooper's Leatherstocking Tales (1823–1841).[62] A cabin boy on his way to New York at the age of twenty-one, he worked at various jobs in the Arkansas and Texas-Louisiana borderlands in the late 1830s and early 1840s—hunter, fisherman, silversmith, cattle herder, and chocolate maker—traveling back to Germany in 1843. Upon returning, Gerstäcker found that a German magazine had published the journal entries he had sent to his mother from the western frontier. Gerstäcker quickly revised the entire journal of his American travels, and it was published as a book, *Adventures and Hunting Expeditions Through the United States of North America*, in 1844. In 1845, he published a novel, *The Regulators in Arkansas*, based on his American experiences. Three years later another of Gerstäcker's novels, *The River Pirates of the Mississippi*, appeared.

The California Gold Rush brought Gerstäcker back to the United States but as part of a larger world tour lasting from March 1849 to February 1852, with the official purpose of examining conditions in the German colonies in Brazil, Argentina, and Chile, and this time not as a cabin boy but with a small government grant and a publisher's advance. After crossing the Atlantic to South America, he traversed the Cordilleras in wintertime from Buenos Aires to Valparaiso accompanied by two Indian guides. From there he sailed on to California, then by whaling ship to the Hawaiian and Society Islands, and next to Australia (where he traveled two thousand miles by canoe up the Murray River), on to New Zealand and then Java before returning to Germany.[63]

Gerstäcker joined forty thousand maritime gold rushers who traveled via Cape Horn or across the Isthmus of Panama in 1849. Another forty-two thousand, historian Howard Lamar notes, went overland to California that year; however, their journeys occupy a far more familiar place in the national memory. (Six thousand more migrated to the California goldfields in 1849 from Mexico.)[64] Gerstäcker traveled to South America again in 1860–1861, to Egypt and Abyssinia in 1862, and to the United States once more, along with Mexico, the West Indies, Ecuador, and Venezuela, in 1867–1868. He died in 1872 after packing a great deal of traveling and writing into his fifty-six years of life.[65] Such was his fame in Germany that his own adventures were chronicled the following year in a travel book for German youth.[66]

Gerstäcker knew America. By the time he left the country in 1843, after his first visit, he had traveled extensively (largely on foot, for over six years) and had become more familiar with the landscapes and the people of the central and western United States and its territories than all but a few Americans. Gerstäcker also knew the world, having walked, ridden, and sailed across a good part of it over the course of thirty-five years. And the world knew Gerstäcker too; he was a tireless writer who produced

Figure 6. Friedrich Gerstäcker, author of *Narrative of a Journey Round the World* (1853). Courtesy of Friedrich-Gerstäcker-Gesellschafte V.

approximately 150 books of travel, adventure stories, and novels in the mid- to late nineteenth century. From the early 1850s until his death, Gerstäcker, a stranger to the modern literary and historical canons, was an enormously popular writer.[67] People would have read him without knowing it, as many of his stories were pirated and published as dime novels without acknowl-edgment of their author. While Gerstäcker's colorful western stories, such as *The Death Track; or, the Outlaws of the Mountain* (1879); *The Border Bandits; or, the Horse-Thief's Trail*; *The Bush Ranger; or, the Half-Breed Brigade*; and *The Outlaw Hunter; or, Red John, the Bush Ranger* (all 1881), may have sub-liminally entered the national consciousness, his travel writings, also widely known then, are virtually unknown today.[68]

In chronicling his travels, Gerstäcker placed the West into a world con-text; moreover, he put the world into the West, illuminating the deadly con-sequences of multicultural meetings on the western American frontier.[69] *Narrative of a Journey Round the World* was one of the most remarkable travel books of the century, and one that provided a powerful reminder that California was a global stage and its gold rush a world story, not just an

American western one. One example of this is Gerstäcker's chronicling of the story of an East Indian from Bombay who suddenly appeared in an American miner's camp at Douglas Flat in California's Southern Mines, claiming to have been robbed of nineteen hundred dollars in gold dust by local Indians. One group of miners gave chase, and in the process burned an Indian village and shot one of the fleeing Indians, who later died from the wound. But in the wake of the pursuit, others in the camp, Gerstäcker writes, determined "that they had proceeded a little too rashly in the affair, [and] they, therefore, arrested the Mohammedan." Then, another group of California Indians came to the miners' camp, providing evidence that the East Indian had lied about the events. It turned out that the California Indians had invited the East Indian into their village and that he had made inappropriate advances toward the women there and been thrown out, but had not been robbed. Thus, "the Mohammedan" was placed under the guard of "Indians and white men," and a party of Americans was sent to the Indian village to inform the original group of pursuers of this development. When this white deputation arrived, they found the California Indian dying from the bullet wound suffered in the encounter with the original group of American pursuers. The East Indian was subsequently held responsible for that man's death and "condemned to receive twenty-five lashes."

Gerstäcker vividly described the trial and execution of justice that took place on the Fourth of July. "The first thirteen lashes were given by the American sheriff—the others by an Indian; and it was a strange but picturesque spectacle, on the fine sunny day, to see, under the waving American flag, the wretched isolated Mohammedan, who, conducted by a gang of white men and Indians to the cattle yard of the butcher, was there tied to a post and flogged." Gerstäcker further noted that the offender was "surrounded in a wide circle by Yankees, French, Germans, Spaniards, Mexicans, and men of other nations; and whilst the copper-coloured Indians, in their fanciful attire, climbed on the fence, and half-triumphantly and half-anxiously looked at the infliction of chastisement, the Mohammedan in vain invoked his Allah."[70]

Thus, a German traveler described the flogging of a man from Bombay, for the death of a California Indian, while white Americans, various Europeans, Mexicans, South Americans, and North American Indians observed—all in the American West, that most American part of America, and on Independence Day. This was crime and punishment in the global West that was mid-nineteenth-century California. Audiences in America and Europe could read the account in their separate editions of the book.

Figure 7. Punishing "the Mohammaden," from Friedrich Gerstäcker, *Scenes of Life in California* (1942). Courtesy *of Montana The Magazine of Western History.*

Culturally diverse as the scene was, it was still very much a tragic land-scape of winners and losers, and Gerstäcker's writing forced readers to consider the larger context of Native American–white relations in California, particularly the acute indigenous population decline that accompanied that contact. Reflecting on the events, Gerstäcker wrote: "The Indians of California no longer exist in reality, though a few scattered tribes may wander about yet in the distant hills, looking toward the setting sun, down upon a country which was once their own, and where the ashes of their forefathers were given to the balmy breeze, or buried under the shady oaks of the plains."[71] But in recounting the story of the Bombay Indian, Gerstäcker was not prophesying and offering justification for the inevitable destruction of California Indians as a primitive race (a nine-teenth-century practice that scholars have rightly criticized); rather, he was explaining that process by emphasizing the consequences of white con-quest and the limitations of American democracy.[72] The Bombay Indian was held responsible for the death of the California Indian and punished.

But white Americans (likely inspired more by the prospect of procuring a nineteen-hundred-dollar prize than by any desire to assist the East Indian) did the actual killing and set fire to the Indians' village during the pursuit; they were not charged with any crime.

Gerstäcker visited the Indian camp after the attack and described how the wounded Indian had been shot in the back, remarking on the inevitability of his final demise: "death was written on his countenance."[73] While the wife wailed over her dying husband, Gerstäcker admitted, "I ran down the hill as fast as I could, to be out of hearing of those dreadful sounds. I was ashamed of being a white man at that moment."[74] He presented his shame as a microcosm of the collective guilt that he felt white people ought to have experienced on account of their inhumanity toward California Indians. Gerstäcker further noted that "while the natives of California resemble the Eastern tribes in stature and complexion, they do not most assuredly in warlike character, for they are really the most harmless tribes on the American continent," adding that they had "no offensive arms at all, except bows and arrows, and these are small and powerless," and had been "driven . . . to desperation" by "white people."[75]

The consequence of these differences between the California Indians and newly arrived white Americans, with respect to both martial inclination and capacity, was horrific. Gerstäcker proclaimed that "the whites behaved worse than cannibals toward the poor, inoffensive creatures, whom they had robbed of nearly every means of subsistence and now sought to trample underfoot."[76] His account of brutally violent acts committed with impunity by whites against Indians serves as a microcosm of the war of extermination that white settlers waged against California Indians. Historians John Faragher and Robert Hine note that California's indigenous population of around 150,000 in 1848 had fallen to 30,000 twelve years later.[77] Disease accounts only for a portion of this astonishing 80 percent loss. The numbers raise the issue of the applicability of the term "genocide" in America.[78] The topic of genocide, in turn, prompts the charting of moral equivalencies—the great counter to notions of benign American exceptionalism—thus rendering it perhaps the single most controversial topic for American historians. Gerstäcker's account reminds us that such difficult issues were very much in the American public eye a century and a half ago.

The observations of another European visitor, the Austrian woman Ida Pfeiffer, who visited the California goldfields in the fall of 1853, provide a

Figure 8. Ida Pfeiffer, author of *A Lady's Journey Round the World* (1850) and *A Lady's Second Journey Round the World* (1855). Courtesy of the Long Riders' Guild.

further reminder of travel writers' emphasis on and American public exposure to the awful human consequences of colonization in the Far West. Her popular account, *A Lady's Second Journey Round the World* (1856), included coverage of the plight of California Indians around Marysville. Pfeiffer noted that the Indians "who live in the neighborhood of the whites are said to die off much more rapidly than those who have taken refuge in the interior of the forests," and she pointed to the deadly impact of "spirituous liquors" and smallpox. But Pfeiffer was more explicit in her accounting of the factors behind Indian population decline among the Rogue River Indians of present-day southwestern Oregon, whom she visited that same fall (and two years prior to the outbreak of the Rogue River Wars of 1855–1856). She commented on how "these Indians are represented as treacherous, cowardly, and revengeful, and only attacking the whites when they found one alone," but then charged that "if the whites had suffered as many wrongs from them as they do from the whites, I rather think they too would have felt the desire of revenge." Pfeiffer observed "several burnt and devastated wigwams, whence the people had been driven out by force because they would not willingly give up their native soil to the stranger." She further commented on the seduction and often simply seizure and rape of Indian women by whites, and criticized the government for its "over indulgence towards the white settlers," noting that until there was a judicial system in place that would severely punish the perpetrators for their actions, "the poor Indian will remain the sport of the insolent white."[79]

Gerstäcker left California in 1851, two years before Pfeiffer arrived. He traveled from there to the Hawaiian Islands and then on to Australia. Here, in another white settler society, he again commented on race relations and more particularly the tendency of colonial masters to dehumanize their indigenous subjects for the purpose of legitimating their own acts of inhumanity against them. He reminded readers that "the devil is never so black as he is painted." Moreover, Gerstäcker concluded that the fate of Australia's aborigines seemed no brighter than that of California's Indians; they too, he declared, will be "swept from the face of the earth."[80] By this, Gerstäcker did not intend "ghosting the primitive"—positing indigenous extinction as a self-fulfilling prophecy—but rather to offer a more damning explanation for processes that were occurring in Australia, California, Hawaii, and all around the globe, one that ascribed culpability directly to those doing the killing. Worlds were being turned upside down by the discovery of gold, the introduction of European strains of disease, and the unrestrained actions of white militias, leading to dramatic losses among indigenous populations.[81] Gold and death went hand in hand. Entire races were declining so precipitously that they appeared headed for extinction, and Gerstäcker offered the genocidal acts of white people as a key cause.[82]

From Australia, Gerstäcker made one last stop on his global journey at the Dutch colony of Java, where he offered a stinging indictment of Dutch colonialism, adopting an indigenous voice for the purpose:

> You shave my head in a severe winter, and then sell me a warm cap. Of course, the cap keeps my head warm, and I need it from time to time; but I do not see any reason why I ought to be obliged to you for it—the cap only keeps my head as warm as my hair would have done; but why did you not leave it to me?—only to sell me the cap.

Gerstäcker then provided his readers with a comparative analysis of various

European colonial systems in which the Dutch came off quite well: "The Hollander leaves the native in his home, and to his gods, and does not trouble his soul as well as his body. Their households and their house-hold god are left to them." Gerstäcker further explained that the natives of Java "are not driven from the graves of their fathers by deeds and contracts, of which they understand nothing, and by persuasions and agreements closed with some chiefs, and enforced finally upon the whole nation, as English and Americans have done only too frequently."[83]

In May 1852, Gerstäcker arrived back in Germany after more than three years of travel. His *Narrative of a Journey Round the World* appeared the next year with its comparisons of the Californian and Australian gold rushes, European and American colonialism, and the catastrophic demographic decline of indigenous peoples on different continents.[84] His coverage of Gold Rush California made up one-fifth of the book, but illuminating parallels and contrasts between California and other places appeared throughout. America's West emerged as just one part of Gerstäcker's world, another developing frontier marked by violence against natives; it was not exceptional, not a world apart, but a global West. And Gerstäcker was hardly alone in positioning the West in this way.[85]

A year later, in 1854, George Catlin covered some of the same ground that Gerstäcker had traversed a few years earlier. Catlin, traveling in South America, hunted for gold in Brazil, explored the Amazon, crossed the Andes, and painted "vanishing" peoples.[86] The lives, works, and contradictions of these two chroniclers of the global West paralleled each other in interesting ways. Catlin died the same year as Gerstäcker, in 1872, although he had been born a generation earlier, in 1796. Gerstäcker's voluminous writings included many classic frontier tales, the kind of dime novel fare that nurtured notions of American western distinctiveness. But Gerstäcker was an insightful travel writer as well as a dime novelist. Scholars have often judged Catlin harshly, frustrated at his mythologizing of the theme of the vanishing Indian. Indeed, Catlin's own father noted in 1838 that the value of his son's pictorial record of Indian peoples would increase as his subjects decreased in number.[87] Catlin, for his part, was a complex character who exploited Indians for financial gain and yet knew their cultures better than most of his European or American contemporaries and loudly protested their mistreatment by his own nation's government. In the varied work and fascinating lives of just two individuals, we have a microcosm of the split or even multiple personalities housed within a national consciousness that could recognize global contexts yet still harbor exceptionalist dreams.

By recovering their work and the work of other travelers, we may better understand the global West of the nineteenth-century imagination as well as its exceptionalist counterpart, the American frontier. Their writings also suggest that the postcolonialist scholarly critique of the nineteenth-century traveler as an architect of empire could itself use some revision. Catlin and Gerstäcker, and Pfeiffer, too, are just a few of the many travel writers of their time who illuminated the awful consequences of European and U.S. imperialism for indigenous peoples. Their concerns cannot be dismissed as mere "imperialist nostalgia"—a sense of purported longing for that which has been lost by those who have played a part in its destruction.[88] Indeed, they voiced their criticisms of colonial policy during a time when there was no shortage of enthusiastic imperialists who expressed no such qualms over the destructive aspects of empire building.

No record exists of George Catlin and Friedrich Gerstäcker, two men who placed the fate of North American Indians into the global context of Western civilization's expansion, ever meeting, but they would surely have known each other's work. Like many other writers of their time, they positioned the American West within a world context in the nineteenth century, before later generations of Americans chose to separate it from those global moorings and "nationalize" it. Their travel writings formed part of a large body of observations about America that probably served as a brake on the unqualified acceptance of the rhetoric of exceptionalism by the American public and may have even acted on the conscience of the nation.

CHAPTER TWO

THE WORLD IN THE WEST,
THE WEST IN THE WORLD

Travels in the Age of Empire

If they were swept away to morrow not a trace of them except their metal work would be . . . found. Civilized as they are they don't leave any more impress on the country than a Red Indian would.
　　　—Isabella Bird on the Malay Peninsula, *The Golden Chersonese* (1883)

There are many humorous things in the world; among them, the white man's notion that he is less savage than other savages.
　　　—Mark Twain in South Africa, *Following the Equator* (1897)

From the African Continent to the Mormon Kingdom

When measured against the writings of many other nineteenth-century global travelers, Friedrich Gerstäcker's and George Catlin's accounts seem rather enlightened in their empathy for indigenous peoples and outrage over their mistreatment. Clearly, not every European or European American traveler viewed the world through blinkered imperial eyes. Nevertheless, there certainly was a disturbingly dark side to travel writing that we need to consider, and where better to begin than with an early publication from an Englishman who would later become the father of eugenic pseudoscience. Francis Galton's popular book *The Art of Travel; or, Shifts and Contrivances Available in Wild Countries* was first published in 1855 and reprinted in seven subsequent editions by 1893. A guidebook as well as a travel narrative, *The Art of Travel* has quite

48

a history. The book's material was drawn in part from the author's own exploration of South-West Africa in 1850–1852; he was the first European to explore the northern region of what is today Namibia, for which the Royal Geographical Society awarded him its Founder's Medal in 1854.[1] But in assembling the volume, Galton also made good use of the reports of various other explorers in the 1830s and 1840s, including Charles Sturt and F. W. Ludwig Leichhardt in Australia, John Palliser in the Canadian Rockies, and Colonel John C. Frémont in what was soon to become the United States' Far West. Galton also utilized Richard Francis Burton's reports of his adventures in Mecca in 1852–1853, the American Commodore Matthew Perry's chronicle of his arrival in Japan in 1853, and the Abbé Huc's account of his 1844–1846 journey from China to Lhasa, in Tibet (1850). In addition, he drew on his cousin Charles Darwin's *The Voyage of the Beagle* (1840), and in preparing the fourth edition of *The Art of Travel* (1867), also had at his disposal Darwin's *The Origin of Species* (1859).[2]

In his preface to the fourth edition of *The Art of Travel*, Galton complained that a reviewer of the previous edition (1860) had accused him of copying from Captain Randolph B. Marcy's *The Prairie Traveler* (1859), a similar kind of work—both travel narrative and guide to survival—about the western American frontier. Clearly irritated by the charge that a British writer would plagiarize from an American-authored book, Galton insisted that the passages in question were all taken from the second edition of his book, published in 1856, three years before Marcy's work. Galton proclaimed that he was the victim of intellectual theft, not the perpetrator. But for our purposes, the issue of who appropriated what from whom is of less significance than the fact that Galton *had* drawn on accounts from explorers across the globe, including those who traveled in the American West (even if Marcy's was not among them).[3] Likewise, numerous accounts of western American travel utilized Galton's book.

The mid-nineteenth-century world of exploration and travel writing was not composed of the individually distinct and disconnected experiences of sojourners on separated continents. Quite the contrary, the wide world of war, empire, trade, and travel brought continents together and into comparative view. Visitors to the American West could learn from the experiences of explorers in Africa and other "undeveloped frontiers," and vice versa. Moreover, there was nothing novel in the mid-nineteenth century about these processes of mutual edification among and between European travelers to the world's various frontiers and prospective colonies. It is

Figure 9. Swimming Horses, from Francis Galton, *The Art of Travel*, 2nd ed. (1856).
Galton wrote: "In crossing a deep river, with a horse or other large animal, drive him
in, or even walk him alongside a steep bank, and push him suddenly in; having fairly
started him, jump in yourself, and seizing him by the tail, let him tow you across."
From Richard Francis Burton's annotated copy of the work, Huntington Library,
HEH RB #BL 634262. Courtesy of the Rare Books Collection, Huntington Library.

worth remembering that the Scottish explorer Mungo Park's popular work
Travels in the Interior of Africa, recounting his remarkable journey to the
Niger River, had appeared a half-century earlier, in 1799. Indeed, by the
mid-nineteenth century readers had in all likelihood come to expect global
comparisons in travel accounts.

But, returning to Galton: what were the intellectual pearls of wisdom
whose ownership he had made such a concerted point of defending in his
1860 preface to *The Art of Travel*? In addition to providing practical advice
on how to pack food, pitch tents, and defend those encampments and supplies from hostile forces, Galton offered advice on the "Management of
Savages." "A frank, joking, but determined manner," he insisted, "joined
with an air of showing more confidence in the good faith of the natives than
you really feel, is the best." Galton further advised, "If a savage does mischief,
look on him as you would on a kicking mule, or a wild animal, whose nature

is to be unruly and vicious, and keep your temper quite unruffled." Then, if acute hostilities do arise and require retaliation, he further instructed, "recollect that it is not the slightest use to hit a negro on the head with a stick, as it is a fact that his skull endures a blow better than any part of his person."[4] As for women, Galton explained that "if some of the natives take their wives [on expeditions] it gives great life to the party . . . and a woman will endure a long journey nearly as well as a man and certainly better than a horse or bullock."[5] For supporting evidence of the physical endurance of native women, Galton offered the observations of the eighteenth-century British traveler Samuel Hearne, who claimed that his famous third expedition through Britain's Northwest Territory to the Arctic Ocean (1770–1772) was a success largely because of the presence of Chipewyan Chief Matonabbee's six wives, who did all of the heavy lifting and carrying on the trip.[6]

Galton also commented on the general untrustworthiness of "Natives," insisting that large numbers of them should never be permitted to enter one's camp at the same time, since their tendency was "to collect quietly in a friendly way, and at a signal to arise en masse and overpower their hosts." Moreover, Galton warned that natives "were not to be believed when they profess to have left their weapons behind," and noted that Captain Sturt "had known Australian savages to trail their spears between their toes, as they lounged toward him through the grass, professedly unarmed."[7] Clearly, for Galton, the indigenous inhabitants of different continents—Australia, the Americas, and Africa—were all alike enough for his advice and that of other travelers such as Sturt to be globally applicable.

Galton, of course, was a founder of the Social Darwinist movement and would go on to coin the term "eugenics" in 1883. Upon his death, in 1911, he left funds to establish the Galton Laboratory of National Eugenics at University College London (later renamed, less offensively, the Galton Laboratory, Department of Human Genetics and Biometry). He has been positioned within Holocaust studies as one of the direct progenitors of racial anti-Semitism and thus of the exterminationist policies of the Third Reich. There may be no more infamous example of the sinister side of global travel writing than Sir Francis Galton. Yet, surprisingly, scholars of the eugenics movement have had relatively little to say about Galton the traveler and travel writer, although the connection between those early experiences and his later work in eugenics seems clear. Galton's experiences in South-West Africa in the middle of the nineteenth century and his synthesis of writings by other white explorers about the far-flung regions and savage peoples of the globe surely

Figure 10. Richard Francis Burton, by Frederic Leighton (ca. 1872–1875, oil on canvas). The scar from the wound he sustained during the attack on his party in Harar is still clearly visible around twenty years later. Courtesy of the National Portrait Gallery, London.

helped shape his later theories of a world hierarchy of the human race.[8] *The Art of Travel* reads not just like a practical guide to survival in "savagedom" but like an enthusiastic invitation to vigorous Anglo-Saxon adventurers to take up the strenuous life, long before Theodore Roosevelt made the same call in 1899. Those in search of imperial visions constructed through travelers' eyes have in Galton an exemplar of that tradition. But our inquiries are complicated by the experiences and writings of another famed British adventurer of the period.

The same year that *The Art of Travel* was first published (1855), the first of three of the most thrilling travel accounts of the century appeared, all the work of a single traveler, Richard Francis Burton. Burton's *Personal Narrative of a Pilgrimage to El-Medinah and Meccah* (3 vols., 1855–1856) (which Galton had himself drawn on) recounted his 1852–1853 journey to Mecca disguised as a Pathan merchant named Mirza Abdullah and his entry into that hallowed site. *First Footsteps in East Africa* (1856) described Burton's dramatic exploits traveling in disguise as a Muslim merchant through Somalia to the "forbidden" city of Harar in 1855. Subsequently, in *The Lake Regions of Central Africa* (1860), Burton recounted his "discovery" of Lake Tanganyika (Africa's second-largest lake).

Burton's experiences were memorable to say the least. In advance of the first of those trips, to El-Medinah and Mecca, he was circumcised to further hide his white Christian identity and facilitate his entry into the sacred sites.

Figure 11. Richard Francis Burton in Arab dress around the time of his journey to El Medinah and Mecca, ca. 1852–1853. Courtesy of the Long Riders' Guild.

During the second trip, while in Harar, two hundred Somali warriors attacked Burton's small party, and during the course of the battle a spear was thrust through both his cheeks, "carrying away four teeth and transfixing the palate," as his wife Isabel later described it. Friends managed to extract the javelin and wired up his jaw, and he and the surviving members of his party, including John Hanning Speke, who had been captured and had endured numerous spear wounds before his dramatic escape from the Somalis, returned to England. When his jaw had healed, Burton went off to the Crimea, where a war was raging. On the third of these expeditions, to the central African lakes searching for the source of the Nile, Burton (accompanied by Speke) fell prey to numerous jungle diseases and nearly died. Isabel, who had a flair for the dramatic and a deep commitment in her biography of her husband to the shaping of his legacy, wrote that he "had suffered twenty-one attacks of fever, had been partially paralyzed and partially blind; he was a mere skeleton, with brown yellow skin hanging in bags, his eyes protruding, and his lips drawn away from his teeth."[9] Incidentally, Burton took along with him on the Nile adventure his very heavily annotated copy of the second edition of Galton's *The Art of Travel*.[10] He could have been accompanied also by the Austrian woman traveler Ida Pfeiffer, who had achieved public acclaim in the wake of her accounts of two trips around the world (published in 1850 and 1856) and had lobbied Burton to be included in the expedition, but he had refused.

Burton spent a good portion of his life engaged in these remarkable adventures and writing thrilling accounts of those exploits (thirty-nine volumes) for an eager public on both sides of the Atlantic Ocean. With knowledge of some twenty languages and an unparalleled understanding (among those in the western world) of the cultures of the Middle East and Africa, he was "the preeminent nineteenth-century British travel writer, a brilliant linguist and translator, a pioneer anthropologist, a poet, a civil engineer, a field cartographer, a soldier, one of Europe's best swordsmen, a diplomat, and a geologist."[11] But Burton is known to historians of the American West for his voluminous (six-hundred-page) account, *The City of the Saints, and Across the Rocky Mountains to California* (1861), which resulted from a nine-month visit to the United States in 1859, three weeks of which were spent in Salt Lake City.[12]

A month of Burton's time in America was spent traversing the Great Plains, and, not surprisingly, he presented his descriptions of the landscape within a global comparative framework: "Nothing, I may remark, is more monotonous, except the African and Indian jungle, than these prairie tracks," Burton wrote, adding, "As far as the eye could see the tintage was that of the Arabian desert." For a journey across the plains, Burton recommended that travelers carry a pistol (for protection against would-be robbers), a parasol (for protection against the sun), and a good supply of opium (for protection against the boredom of the journey). In the event of prairie fires, he advised, "the African plan of beating down with boughs might be used in certain places." To his mind's eye, Scottsbluff from a distance resembled the Arabian city of Brass, and Independence Rock seemed much like the Jiwe la Mkoa (Round Rock) in eastern Unyamwezi. Indeed, the physiographic makeup of the Utah Territory itself he compared to central equatorial Africa: "a trough elevated 4,000 to 5,000 feet above sea level, subtended on all sides by mountains 8,000 to 10,000 feet high, and subdivided by transverse ridges." He compared the region's climate to that of the "Tartar plains of High Asia," and the altitude sickness he experienced at the territory's highest elevations to what he felt "upon Mont Blanc and even in Tibet." Vast stretches of Burton's West, along with its distinguishing landmarks and climatic characteristics, seemed very much like other landscapes, landmarks, and conditions he had experienced across the globe.[13]

The one-hundred-page opening chapter of *The City of the Saints* is a tour de force of both comparative landscape and ethnographic analysis, encompassing the Indian subcontinent, the Middle East, the African continent, and the American West.[14] The native peoples of the West were, in Burton's estimation, neither nature's most distinctive noblemen nor the converse of that romanticized image, namely savages of unmatched cruelty and inhumanity. On the contrary, he paralleled the cultural practices of different American Indian groups with those of the whole range of peoples he had encountered on his global travels—Arab Bedouins, Hindustanis, African Somalis—and drew further global cultural comparisons through reference to the works of other Anglo explorers such as David Livingstone.[15] However, Burton's expansive comparative framework was often none too flattering to the victims of Anglo-American empire and quite laudatory when it came to the practices of the colonizing powers. For example, he paralleled the U.S. government's treatment of Native Americans with Great Britain's treatment of East Indians, praising both empires for their paternalism and for treating their respective indigenous subjects "as though they were a civilized people."[16]

Burton's estimation of the comparative lack of civilization in indigenous America was itself complicated by his own understanding of cultural differences among and between different Native American cultures. At one point in *The City of the Saints*, Burton did dismissively refer to all North American Indians as "savages"; yet, in the very same paragraph, he pointed to the failure of the 1853 reservation system to fully take into account the different cultural backgrounds from which various Indian groups sprang, and he listed by name thirty separate Indian peoples.[17] But, ultimately, and in spite of any purportedly assimilationist intentions on the part of the federal government, he concluded that "the westward gravitation of the white race" was destined to push the "few survivors . . . into the inhospitable regions north of the 49th parallel, or into the anarchical countries south of the 32nd."[18] Much like Catlin, Burton ultimately saw little hope for North American Indians, and certainly no hope for them within the contours of the United States' western empire.

Unlike Catlin, however, Burton went so far as to offer his American cousins some advice to facilitate the subjugation of indigenous opposition to their nation's westward expansion, advice based on his own personal experiences in Africa and India. As noted previously, Alexis de Tocqueville, in his "First . . ." and "Second Reports on Algeria" (1847), had suggested that the

French needed to learn from the example of the United States' subordination of Indian peoples and apply that lesson of colonial conquest and management of empire to their own possessions in Algeria, which were then in a state of rebellion.[19] Burton, in *The City of the Saints*, contended that the United States and Britain, in their respective western and eastern empires, could learn from the military example of the French in Algeria. He explained that the system of outposts maintained by the United States in the trans-Mississippi West and by the British in India was unworkable: he called for a more centralized system that would allow for the concentration of troops and weapons at the centers of military action, "making them pivots for expeditionary columns . . . that could be dispatched to wherever an attack or an insurrectionary movement required crushing."[20] Burton would have gained this military advice for empire consolidation from Marcy's famous work, *The Prairie Traveler*. Marcy, for his part, had actually drawn on the work the French colonel and military strategist A. Laure, who had used the very same phrase "pivots for expeditionary columns."[21]

Thus, a British traveler utilized an American-authored manual for western American frontiering, informed by the ideas of a French soldier, to facilitate the U.S. conquest of the plains Indians. It might seem that a clearer case of the travel writer—Burton—as a direct advocate or even agent of empire would be hard to find. Yet Burton's emphasis on the cultural diversity of indigenous America and his constant parallels between the spiritual lives of American Indian groups and those of indigenous peoples across the globe hardly constituted a firm intellectual foundation for those who advocated a genocidal approach to the Indian problem and who would have their way at Sand Creek, Colorado, a few years later (1864) and at other times during the Indian Wars of the 1860s and 1870s.

Incidentally, two years after the publication of *The City of the Saints*, as the Civil War raged, Marcy's book was republished (1863), with Burton as the editor and annotator of the volume; the two travelers had met during Burton's trip to Salt Lake City. Burton himself had relied heavily on the earlier edition of *The Prairie Traveler* in writing *The City of the Saints*. In his preface to Marcy's book, Burton indicated that what he had to offer was not expertise regarding travel and adventure on the American frontier that could rival Marcy's, but, rather, "a little collateral knowledge gained in other lands."[22] This "little collateral knowledge" amounted to an elaborate global comparative framework for describing nonwhite peoples and landscapes that emphasized similarities while at the same time recognizing significant cultural differences. While hardly a paragon of intercultural sensitivity, Burton exhibited a knowledge and understanding of other cultures that far exceeded that of Francis Galton, for example, a traveler whose cultural blinkers ensured that he would see only savagery in every distant corner of the world.[23]

Burton's study of the Mormons, like all of his works of travel and adventure, was a memorable one, but it did not present Great Salt Lake City as a truly exceptional or even particularly unusual place. Burton's global positioning of the West was evident in his stated rationale for taking the trip, which he offered at the beginning of the book: "I had long determined to add the last new name to the list of 'Holy Cities'; to visit the young rival (*soi-disant*) of Memphis [the ancient city of northern Egypt], Benares [in northern India], Jerusalem, Rome, Meccah."[24] Thus, the Mormons' promised land was for Burton one more important religious site and was best understood not in stark juxtaposition with the rest of the United States or the rest of the nation's West, but in relation to other world capitals of religion.

Indeed, Burton's coverage of western American cultures, from native peoples to Mormons, all needs to be considered within the much broader context of his world travels. As a lieutenant in the British army in India, he had demonstrated a rare ability to cut away the veil of cultural stereotypes of south Asians to better understand their cultures. Burton's reward for spending time with his Indian subcontinent friends was to have the contemptuous label "white Nigger" bestowed on him by his fellow officers.[25] In *The City of the Saints*, he was similarly able to move beyond the pervasive and damning stereotypes and view Mormonism on its own terms. He declared that there was nothing immoral or unnatural about polygamy—he had visited other polygamous cultures in the course of his world travels, particularly in Africa and the Near East—and he exhibited a lack of prejudice that contrasted sharply with the prevailing viewpoint that emphasized the licentiousness and depravity of those professing the Mormon faith.[26] Isabel Burton later insisted, and hoped, that her husband had not practiced what he preached concerning the normality of nonmonogamous relationships. Incidentally, Burton had left England for the Mormon polygamous kingdom before Isabel had consented to marry him, and had written her a note instructing her to make up her mind during the nine months that he would be gone.[27]

Recounting his arrival in Salt Lake City, Burton pointed to the "venomous" accounts of anti-Mormons and apostates, all of which, he explained, were readily available to interested readers in the city. The availability of

Figure 12. Portraits of Richard Francis and Isabel Burton at the time of their marriage, 1861, by Louis Desanges. Gouache, Burton Collection. Courtesy of the Richmond Borough Art Collection, Orleans House Gallery, London.

those works, Burton insisted, ran contrary to the popular claims of Mormon intolerance.[28] Moreover, while Burton found the Mormon settlements to be considerably different from other American settlements on the western frontier, and from those of the English in Australia or the Dutch at the Cape, he did find them similar to those of the French in Canada, where settlers also clustered around the Church.[29] Thus, in globally contextualizing Mormonism, Burton effectively normalized the religion and the culture, and even the physical space it occupied.

Filled with observations about the essential decency of Mormon society and packed with statistics, culled from census data and emigration reports, on the American state origins and British origins of the bulk of the Mormon population of the Utah Territory, *The City of the Saints* further contradicted the primary American current of anti-Mormon literature, which emphasized the aberrant and abhorrent nature of the religion. His discussion of the positive contributions of the Mormon Battalion to the U.S. military effort during the war against Mexico further mainstreamed the Mormons. His generally positive assessment of Brigham Young, whose company he enjoyed for rather longer than the typical sojourner to Salt Lake who was granted an audience with the Mormon prophet (and many were), further augmented the book's overriding message that Mormonism really ought to be understood

Figure 13. Sketch of Salt Lake City from Richard Francis Burton's *The City of the Saints, and Across the Rocky Mountains to California* (1862). Courtesy of *Montana The Magazine of Western History.*

prior to the passing of judgment on the faith and its adherents. This approach alone set Burton's observations apart from the travel accounts of most Americans who visited Salt Lake City in this period.[30]

Burton's global framework was not entirely absent from other mid-century accounts of travel to the Mormon kingdom. The French traveler and naturalist Jules Rémy's chronicle of his month-long trip to the Mormon capital in 1855 with British naturalist Julius Brenchley, *A Journey to Great-Salt-Lake City* (1861), was eventually published in book form the same year as Burton's study. Rémy's work, while (unlike Burton's) not absent of vitriolic criticisms of polygamy ("polygamy," he remarked, "is a baneful monstrosity, which would soon degrade men to the level of the most brutal monkeys"), nonetheless described the mix of people in Salt Lake City in a quite positive fashion, and found greater racial and ethnic diversity than Burton would four years later. He viewed the "English, Scotch, Canadians, Americans, Danes, Swedes, Norwegians, Germans, Swiss, Poles, Russians, Italians, French, Negroes, Hindoos, and Australians," who had come "to live more than brothers in perfect harmony," as quite inspirational. "There is," Rémy proclaimed, "something in this to induce one to believe in the possibility of a universal fusion, and the future unity of nations into one and the same great commonwealth."[31]

While certainly in the minority, Burton and Rémy were not the lone voices of partial tolerance among non-Mormon commentators on the Mormon faith, and were certainly not among the first to offer up a defense of the Saints. For example, in his 1852 account, *An Expedition to the Valley of the Great Salt Lake of Utah*, Captain Howard Stansbury of the U.S. Army's Corps of Topographical Engineers had praised the Mormons as thoroughly "fair and upright" "[i]n their dealings with the crowds of emigrants that passed through their city." Furthermore, Stansbury added, their "spiritual wife system" was marked by "[p]eace, harmony, and cheerfulness." He concluded that "a more loyal and patriotic people cannot be found within the limits of the Union," and added, like Burton, that this much was fully evidenced in the raising of the Mormon Battalion during the Mexican war.[32]

Nonetheless, Burton's measured assessment of Mormonism, along with those of Rémy and Stansbury, were a far cry from the scathing moral critiques typically offered in these years. For example, Jewish explorer Solomon Nunes Carvalho, in his 1857 account *Incidents of Travel and Adventure in the Far West*, concluded, after reviewing the Hebrew Bible for evidence in support of polygamy, that "Christian bigamists have but little cause for exultation," because "[i]n every view we take of polygamy, it is a false and vicious system, neither to be reconciled with revelation, with nature, or with reason. It is destructive to society, and to all human progress."[33] In her popular 1856 work *The Mormons at Home*, Mrs. Benjamin G. Ferris was considerably less reserved in her assessment, describing the Mormon community as "a society of fanatics . . . controlled by a gang of licentious villains," adding that "if the contents of Auburn's state prison, with females to match, could be isolated in a country by themselves, and induced to believe themselves a persecuted race, and that thieving and other crimes were virtues, such a community would furnish a faint counterpart of the worshippers of Beelzebub, in this secluded region."[34] Mark Twain, in his western travelogue *Roughing It* (1871), certainly avoided the moral vehemence of Carvalho and Ferris but nonetheless included a serious and damning appendix on the Mountain Meadows massacre of September 11, 1857, and an entire tongue-in-cheek chapter on the homely appearance of Mormon women and the strain that multiple wives were placing on Brigham Young's psychological well-being.[35]

Figure 14. Tomb of Sir Richard Francis and Isabel Burton, Saint Mary Magdalen's Church, Mortlake, London. Photo by David Wrobel (October 2011).

By the third quarter of the nineteenth century, accounts of life in Salt Lake City featured frequently in travel books about the West. While some of these assessments were quite positive or at least generally neutral, a great many more were negative, and many of those were absolutely scathing and condemnatory in tone. Burton's and Rémy's accounts are memorable not so much for their largely positive tone as for their effectiveness in placing the desert West's seemingly most peculiar institution into a largely normalizing global context.

From the Western Rockies to the Near and Far East

Burton and Galton, and Rémy, too, much like their contemporary Gerstäcker, viewed the American West (and, for that matter, everywhere else they visited) globally, but that perspective was by no means limited to men, as Ida Pfeiffer's memorable accounts of her journeys around the world demonstrate. Moreover, the remarkable experiences of another intrepid Briton, Isabella Lucy Bird, also illuminate the significance of the global West of the nineteenth century and illustrate how experiences in that region could provide a defining frame of reference for encounters all across the globe.

Figure 15. Isabella Bird, 1881
photograph, from Anna M. Stoddart,
The Life of Isabella Bird (1906).
Courtesy of *Montana The Magazine
of Western History.*

In 1856, the same year that Burton's account of his adventures in East
Africa appeared, Bird published her first travel book, a rather tame and for-
gettable record of a trip to Canada and the United States that she undertook
for the purpose of improving her health. Fortunately for lovers of good travel
writing, Isabella Bird would return to the West a decade and a half later and
write a series of letters home to her sister about her experiences that would
later be published as *A Lady's Life in the Rocky Mountains*, a fascinating
chronicle of her 1873 travels around Colorado. The book was published in
London and New York in 1879; it was in its seventh edition by 1882, its eighth
in 1912, and has remained in print to this day.[36]

Born in 1831, Isabella Bird was described by an acquaintance as "buck-
toothed, stout, sickly, and short (four feet, eleven inches tall)." Earlier in her
life, Bird's doctors "determined that her head was too large for her frame and
advised her to avoid holding it up. . . . Her family thought of her as an invalid,
apt to die young."[37] Yet Bird's descriptions in *A Lady's Life* of her ascent of the
14,700-foot Long's Peak in October 1873 (with the assistance of the archetypal
western desperado, one-eyed "Mountain Jim") and her winter horseback rides
across the Colorado plains and Rockies suggest a conquering of physical frailty
that more than rivals the better-known story of Theodore Roosevelt's transformation into muscular manhood. Moreover, it is worth remembering that

Figure 16. Isabella Bird, Home in the Rockies, from *A Lady's Life in the Rocky Mountains* (1879). Courtesy of *Montana The Magazine of Western History.*

Bird's ascent of Long's Peak was hardly a typical accomplishment of the period, whether for women or men. In the course of that journey, Bird found a pair of overshoes, which she wrote were "probably left by the Hayden exploring expedition" a few years earlier, and this may well have been the case, since few other nonnative people had ascended the mountain by that early date.[38]

On her Colorado trip, Bird came to the Rockies by way of the Hawaiian Islands, and then eastward from San Francisco. *A Lady's Life* is sprinkled with comparisons between the Rockies and the landscapes of Hawaii, and she compares her experiences herding cattle in Estes Park with her time as a *vachero* in Hawaii. In Perry Park, near Castle Rock, while riding with the daughter of John Perry, Bird remarks upon the young woman's "vivacious descriptions of Egypt, Palestine, Asia Minor, Turkey, Russia, and other countries" in which she had traveled. One wonders if those descriptions inspired Bird, or if the inspiration for global adventuring had come earlier. Whatever the case, Bird herself became a famous world traveler who climbed mountains, rode across deserts, and wrote book-length accounts (nine altogether) of her adventures in Japan (1880 and 1898), Malaya (1883), Persia and Kurdistan (1891), Tibet (1894), Korea (1897), and China (1899 and 1900), as well as the Hawaiian Islands (1875) and the American West.[39]

Figure 17. Bird among the lava beds at Long's Peak, from *A Lady's Life in the Rocky Mountains* (1879). Courtesy of *Montana The Magazine of Western History.*

Scholars of the American West have paid little attention to Bird's global travels, which is unfortunate, because some of the same issues that occupied her attention while in the western Rockies are evident in her later accounts of travel in the Near and Far East. While Burton's descriptions of western landscapes and cultures were very much shaped by his global experience, Bird's literal worldview was shaped in no small part by her time in the American West. Five years after she left the Rockies, Bird was in Japan, and upon arrival was driven almost immediately by an impulse to get away from the major cities and treaty ports to which most foreign visitors restricted their travels and explore the "unbeaten tracks" and "savage wilds" of the region.[40] In her aptly titled account of the trip, *Unbeaten Tracks in Japan* (1880), she discussed her journey to the island of Hokkaido to spend time with the Aino people, the original inhabitants of the Japanese archipelago. She offered a thoroughly dismissive and racist assessment of the Aino that paralleled her comments on California's Digger Indians in *A Lady's Life in the Rocky Mountains*, even if her opinions of the Aino were a shade more positive. She had described the Digger Indians as "perfect savages, without any aptitude for even aboriginal civilization . . . altogether the most degraded of the ill-fated tribes which are dying out before the white races." In similarly

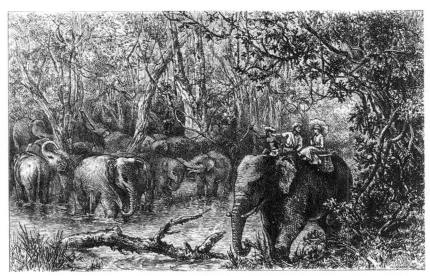

Figure 18. Isabella Bird in Perak, Malaya, from *The Golden Chersonese and the Way Thither* (1883). Courtesy of *Montana The Magazine of Western History.*

condemnatory fashion, she assessed the "savage life" of the Aino as one "not much raised above the necessities of animal existence, timid, monotonous, barren of good, dark, dull . . . though at its lowest and worst considerably higher than that of many other aboriginal races."[41]

A few months after her Japan trip, and just a few years since the publication of *A Lady's Life*, Bird was traveling across the Malay Peninsula, where no European steamers landed, a place generally believed to be "a vast and malarious equatorial jungle." In the resulting 1883 book, *The Golden Chersonese* (also, like *A Lady's Life* and *Unbeaten Tracks in Japan*, composed initially as a series of letters to her sister Henrietta in England), Bird commented on indigenous population decline on the Malay Peninsula, offering the damning observation, "If they were swept away to morrow not a trace of them except their metal work would be . . . found. Civilized as they are they don't leave any more impress on the country than a Red Indian would." Markedly less sensitive about the matter than some travel writers such as Friedrich Gerstäcker, she nonetheless exhibited the same tendency to place the demographic collapse of American Indians into a global context, albeit with the purpose of augmenting the expansion of imperial systems.[42]

Figure 19. Bird on horseback in Erzurum, a province of northeastern
Turkey, 1891, from Anna M. Stoddart, *The Life of Isabella Bird* (1906).
Courtesy of *Montana The Magazine of Western History.*

In 1891, Bird (who by this time had married and taken her husband's
name, Bishop) rode across Persia and Kurdistan. And then, in her late sixties,
she undertook another horseback trip on a black stallion, from Tangier a
thousand miles across Morocco to the Atlas Mountains. She fell ill after
returning to England and died in 1904, just short of her seventy-third birthday. Her adventurous life of travel and her voluminous printed accounts of
those journeys serve as a good example of how western American experiences could shape the experience of world travel, just as global travels could
shape perceptions of the West. While Burton placed the world in the West,
Bird placed the West in the world. The writings of both, and of many other
renowned travelers and writers of their century, illuminate an American
West very much connected in the popular consciousness to other developing
frontiers, and very much a part of the nineteenth-century world of empire.

Across the Plains, Around the World, and Back to Africa

Bird, Burton, Galton, Pfeiffer, and Gerstäcker are just a few of the hundreds
of nineteenth-century global travelers who viewed the West within that

larger world context. In placing the drama of the American West on a global stage, these travel writers reminded Americans that they were thoroughly connected to the world of empire building and that their western frontier served as the primary stage for imperial endeavors, not an escape from them. Additionally, as Ian Tyrrell reminds us, "the U.S. was principally a maritime nation through to the Civil War," and this reality also nurtured a "global vision."[43] In 1866, when the first successful transatlantic telegraph cable was put into service (an earlier effort had been made in 1858, but the cable had broken), and even more so in 1869, with the completion of the American transcontinental railroad, the nation became more firmly connected to that wider world. In fact, the effort to link Europe and North America by cable gave rise to another important and popular travel book, George Kennan's *Tent Life in Siberia* (1870). Kennan recounted his remarkable journey with three other men across the Russian frontier of Siberia in the employ of the Western Union Telegraph Company in 1865–1867. Their efforts to survey the route across Siberia and the Bering Strait were rendered redundant by the success of the transatlantic cable effort in 1866. But Kennan, a distant relative of the primary architect of American Cold War containment policy George F. Kennan, received some fame for his account of the exploratory effort, in which he drew parallels between the landscapes and indigenous peoples of the "frontiers of our western States and Territories" (66) and those of the Russian hinterlands.[44]

The previous year, 1869, Jules Verne made reference to the transatlantic cable in his novel *Twenty Thousand Leagues Under the Sea*, and that same year the completion of the first transcontinental railroad across North America closed the final link in a global transportation chain; it was now possible to travel all the way around the world on trains and ships. Three years later, Verne's novel *Around the World in Eighty Days* (1873) appeared. In the book, the chief protagonist, Phileas Fogg, travels to Bombay, Calcutta, Hong Kong, Yokohama, and Shanghai, and then on to San Francisco, across the United States—with a three-hour delay on the Central Pacific Railroad in the Humboldt Range of northeastern Nevada, courtesy of a lumbering herd of bison, and a thrilling ride on a sail-powered sled from Fort Kearney to Omaha, Nebraska—to New York, across the Atlantic to Liverpool, and down to London, arriving just in time to win his bet that he could make the trip in eighty days.[45] And in 1872, British tour operator Thomas Cook, the father of modern mass tourism, led his first personally conducted, 222-day world tour. In 1889, the American journalist and travel

Figure 20. Robert Louis Stevenson, aged thirty-five. Photograph by Lloyd Osborne, 1891. From *The Letters of Robert Louis Stevenson*, vol. 1, edited by Sidney Colvin (1901).

writer Nellie Bly completed a much-publicized trip around the world in just 72 days, following the Fogg/Cook route, which became the standard for world travelers in the late nineteenth century. Indeed, Cook's itinerary created a travel infrastructure that in turn helped create a new mountain of travel books in the late nineteenth century.[46]

That public would also have been exposed to the work of British traveler Robert Louis Stevenson, whose literary fame today stems largely from his novels *Treasure Island* (1883), *Kidnapped* (1886), and *The Strange Case of Dr. Jekyll and Mr. Hyde* (1886). But Stevenson, like so many of the notable novelists and short story writers of his day, was a widely renowned travel writer, too. For romantic reasons, he traveled from Scotland to California in 1879, taking a train across the United States.[47] An abridged account of the trip, "Across the Plains," was published in *Longman's Magazine* in 1883, and the full version finally appeared in book form in 1892. The delay in publication can be explained in part by his publisher's and family's nervousness over the gritty realism of the account. In that year Congress renewed the Chinese Exclusion Act, and while Stevenson's work clearly did not significantly impact the political debate, it may well have given American readers some cause for reflection in the years that followed.

In a section of his travelogue titled "Despised Races," Stevenson declared: "Of all the stupid ill-feelings, the sentiment of my fellow-Caucasians towards our companions in the Chinese car was the most stupid and the worst." He then proceeded to undermine popular stereotypes about the Chinese, most notably their presumed lack of cleanliness, noting that they "were the cleanest people on the train." Stevenson further explained, "the Chinese are considered stupid because they are imperfectly acquainted with English. They are held to be base, because their dexterity and frugality enable them to underbid the lazy, luxurious Caucasian." Moreover, after criticizing white Americans for their inordinate levels of prejudice, Stevenson highlighted "the gulf between America's rhetoric of freedom and the failure of Americans to match that rhetoric in their actions."[48]

Stevenson next turned his attention to the actions of his fellow passengers toward an impoverished Indian family at a railroad station. "The silent stoicism of their conduct, and the pathetic degradation of their appearance," he wrote, "would have touched any thinking creature, but my fellow-passengers danced and jested round them with a truly Cockney baseness," which made Stevenson "ashamed for the thing we call civilization." And, he added, in language that might inform contemporary debates, "We should carry upon our consciences so much, at least, of our forefathers' misconduct as we continue to profit by ourselves."[49] He then proceeded to outline the injustices of the American conquest of the continent for native peoples. "If oppression drives a wise man mad," Stevenson asked rhetorically, "what should be raging in the hearts of these poor tribes, who have been driven back and back, step after step, their promised reservations torn from them one after another as the States extended westward, until at length they are shut up into these hideous mountain deserts of the centre—and even there find themselves invaded, insulted, and hunted out by ruffianly diggers?" He pointed to "[t]he eviction of the Cherokees (to name but one instance), the extortion of Indian agents, the outrages of the wicked, the ill-faith of all, any, down to the ridicule of such poor beings as were here with me upon the train," as the lamentable constituent parts of "a chapter of injustice and indignity such as a man must be in some ways base if his heart will suffer him to pardon or forget."[50]

The 1883 *Longman's Magazine* version of Stevenson's illumination of the reprehensible shortcomings of U.S. federal Indian policy came two years after Helen Hunt Jackson's controversial damning of the same in *A Century of*

Dishonor (1881). Indeed, Stevenson's voice of protest was just one among many, rather than the cutting edge of that particular countercurrent to the romantic vision of westward expansion depicted by artists of the period. Nonetheless, Stevenson's searing critique of late-nineteenth-century American racism warrants consideration as a manifestation of both the anticolonial and the antimythic nature of travel writing on the West in this period.

Some readers of Stevenson's travelogue might conclude that the work is just one of many by British travelers that exhibit the scolding, "holier than thou" attitude of representatives of that empire nation toward another, rival empire nation—an "our colonialism is more benign and beneficent than yours" outlook. But whatever Stevenson's motivation, Anglo-Americans (after 1895, at least, when the account was posthumously published in book form in America, as *The Amateur Emigrant*) were fully exposed to his criticism of their racial attitudes and their nation's racial policies. This interesting and often accusatory dialog between colonizing nations has not, to date, been the subject of postcolonial theorists; yet it seems to constitute an interesting variant of Homi Bhabha's notion of hybridity. In criticizing another aspiring empire nation, British travel writers (and readers) may have become increasingly cognizant of the shortcomings of their own colonial systems, while American readers (of the very same texts) became more aware of the embarrassing incongruence between racial attitudes and rhetoric on the one hand and democratic aspirations on the other, in their own country.

By the late 1880s, in the wake of the publication of his best-known novels between 1883 and 1886, Stevenson was experiencing significant fame but also increasing ill health, and he sought warmer climes to combat his respiratory ailments. Under the sponsorship of American syndicator (and later, magazine editor) S. S. McClure, Stevenson and his wife Fanny made three voyages to the South Seas between 1888 and 1890 and, by arrangement with McClure, sent letters about these travels back to the United States for publication in the *New York Sun* and other English-language newspapers around the word, including *Black and White* in Britain. The practice was a common one for travel writers of the period—serialized letters followed by a book compiled from the very same materials, often completely unedited. However, Stevenson was tiring of the conventions of the travel book, such as the careful recording of port landings and the provision of dates for every stage of a journey. The thirty-seven pieces he sent to the newspaper seem to have failed to capture the imagination of readers. This was partly because they belied convention— Stevenson was no longer interested in taking an autobiographical approach, despite public interest in him—but partly, too, because of the ambivalence of the accounts. His South Seas writings lacked the fascination with the exotic that had become a standard feature of the travel book and exhibited instead an anthropologically engaged approach to the native peoples of the islands that eschewed high drama and privileged careful observation.[51]

In writing about the Marquesas Islands (previously visited by Herman Melville and the subject of that writer's popular 1846 work, *Typee*), for example, Stevenson charted the dramatic decline of the native population in the wake of contact with white explorers and colonizers and the smallpox and syphilis they brought with them. He also reported on the growing "despondency and depression" of the islanders in the wake of French colonial oppression, which had also been a target of Melville's ire nearly a half-century earlier.[52] "The Marquesan," Stevenson wrote, "beholds with dismay the approaching extinction of his race . . . he lives and breathes under a shadow of mortality awful to support; and he is so inured to the apprehension that he greets the reality with relief."[53] He then examined the culture of cannibalism that had once existed on the islands, accounting for it as a product of group dynamics and the scarcity of animal foods.[54] "[T]o cut a man's flesh after he is dead," Stevenson wrote, "is far less hateful than to oppress him whilst he lives; and even the victims of their appetite were gently used in life and suddenly and painlessly despatched at last."[55]

In a sense, Stevenson was offering the kind of careful treatment of cannibalism as a product of certain conditions rather than an essential characteristic of a debased nonwhite culture (which was the a common assumption at the time), paralleling Burton's coverage of white Mormon polygamy thirty years earlier. Both travelers sought to understand the cultures they came into contact with rather than rushing to judge them.

However, Stevenson was not slow to hold the British responsible for their role in the opium trade in the South Seas, or the Germans for their meddling in the Samoan Islands (where he would settle in 1890 and die in 1894).[56] While not quite the kind of fully developed critical comparative analysis of colonial systems and their impact on indigenous peoples that Friedrich Gerstäcker had produced in the middle of the century, Stevenson's *In the South Seas*, posthumously published in 1896, amounted to one more voice—and a particularly eloquent one—in the growing chorus of concern toward the close of the century over the consequences of imperial activities around the globe.[57]

America's most renowned nineteenth-century writer, Mark Twain, was also a contributor to that chorus. Another beneficiary of the wide world of

Figure 21. Robert Louis Stevenson and family (in Samoa), by J. Davis, albumen
print, ca. 1891. Left to right, unknown woman; (Samuel) Lloyd Osbourne; Margaret
Stevenson (née Balfour); Isobel Stuart Strong (née Osbourne); Robert Louis
Stevenson; Austin Strong; Fanny Stevenson (née Van de Grift); Joseph Dwight
Strong. Courtesy of National Portrait Gallery, London.

travel engineered by Thomas Cook, Twain eventually became a critic of
American empire. It is important to consider, as Twain scholar Jeffrey Melton
reminds us, that "[f]or the readers of the late nineteenth century, Samuel
Clemens was first and foremost a travel writer, not a novelist," a reality that was
clearly reflected in his book sales.[58] Twain is best known to American audiences today for his novels, particularly *The Adventures of Huckleberry Finn*
(1884) and *The Adventures of Tom Sawyer* (1876), and for his American travel
books *Roughing It* (1872) (which includes material drawn from his four-month
visit to the Hawaiian Islands in 1866) and *Life on the Mississippi* (1883). But
Twain's best-selling work during his lifetime was his second book and first
overseas travel narrative—which chronicled a five-month trip to Europe, the
Near East, and the Holy Land—*The Innocents Abroad, or the New Pilgrim's
Progress* (1869). The book, which lampooned the enormously popular

Figure 22. Mark Twain, "Carte de visite, [photo by] Charles Watkins, Chancery Lane [London]," ca. 1873. Courtesy of the Barrett Collection, University of Virginia Mark Twain Print Collection.

midcentury customs and manners school of travel writing, sold over 70,000 copies in its first year (and 125,000 in its first decade).[59] It was sold by subscription, with traveling salesmen and women peddling the book. Subscription publishing was enormously popular at the time, and several more of Twain's books were sold in this way.

A decade after the appearance of *The Innocents Abroad*, Twain set sail for Europe to revive his flagging financial fortunes by writing a second European travel book, *A Tramp Abroad* (1880), a sequel of sorts to the earlier book. The new work was also widely popular; it sold 62,000 copies (by subscription) in its first year. *A Tramp Abroad* begins with Twain musing, in his inimitable fashion, about travel: "One day it occurred to me that it had been many years since the world had been afforded the spectacle of a man adventurous enough to undertake a journey through Europe on foot." "After much thought," he continued, "I decided that I was a person fitted to furnish mankind the spectacle." Twain would be a true traveler, climbing the tallest peaks and descending into the deepest valleys. But he employed Mr. Harris, an

Figure 23. Sketch of Mark
Twain by True W. Williams,
from *A Tramp Abroad* (1880).

assistant, to accompany him, and at the last moment the two decided "for
private reasons" to change the program: they "took the express train"—the
act of true tourists.[60] Then, deciding that the Furka Pass, the Rhone Glacier,
the Finsteraarhorn and the Wetterhorn, "etc." were essential elements of any
pedestrian tour of Europe, and insisting that "I never allow myself to do
things by halves, or in a slurring, slipshod way . . . I called in my agent and
instructed him to go without delay and make a careful examination of these
noted places, on foot, and bring me back a written report of the result, for
inclusion in my book."[61] Twain was parodying "authentic" traveling, or
adventure travel, travel beyond the beaten path. Twain's travels in Europe
would present no physical challenges and unearth no great discoveries of
geography or culture. In short, *A Tramp Abroad* is the quintessential example of Twain the irreverent iconoclast, unimpressed with Europe's great cultural treasures or its renowned landscapes. It is an antitravel narrative, yet
perhaps the funniest travel book ever written.[62]

    In 1895, after various failed financial ventures left him bankrupt, Twain

Be good + you will be lonesome.
Mark Twain

Figure 24. Mark Twain at sixty, aboard a ship during his global tour in 1895, from *Following the Equator* (1897), Pageant of America Collection. Courtesy of the Photography Collection, Miriam and Ira D. Wallach Division of Prints and Photographs, New York Public Library, Astor, Lenox, and Tilden Foundations.

decided to undertake a world lecture tour and write a world travelogue, *Following the Equator* (1897; sold by subscription in America and republished later that year as *More Tramps Abroad*).[63] Unlike the majority of other travelers treated in this study, Twain went on his journey around the world for no significant reason other than to make money. The trip began in July 1895 and took Twain and his family to a hundred cities. It proved to be an awfully tragic one. In April of that year his youngest daughter, fifteen-year-old Jean, suffered the first of a series of epileptic seizures that would later result in her being confined to a sanatorium. As Twain reached the end of his journey, in London (where he wrote the book) in August 1896, he learned that his eldest daughter Susy had died from spinal meningitis, at the age of twenty-four.[64] *Following the Equator* has a harsh tone, far removed from the playful comedy of his earlier travel books; the humor of the younger Twain is replaced with dark irony and searing cynicism.

During the course of the thirteen-month journey, Twain lectured to every English-speaking audience he could find—the bulk of his global trip falls largely within the broad geographic contours of the British Empire. But the resulting book was no glorification of British imperialism. Quite the contrary, Twain commented on the consequences of colonization for people around the world, and in doing so he questioned the very concept of imperialism, which was enormously popular at the end of the nineteenth century as various European powers and the United States seemed to be in a race to acquire as many overseas possessions as possible. Twain let loose his incomparable skepticism in writing about the natives of the Fiji Islands in *Following the Equator*: "Only sixty years ago they were sunk in darkness; now they have the bicycle."[65] In Australia he commented on the same indigenous population decline that had alarmed Catlin and Gerstäcker a half century earlier: "The white man knew ways of reducing a native population 80 per cent in twenty years."[66] He then remarked on the absence of Australian aboriginal people from that country's museums and on the application of the word "native" "to Australian-born whites only"—the aborigines were referred to as "blackfellows." Then it struck Twain (whose treatment of Native Americans in *Roughing It* is lamentable, to say the least) that American Indians had suffered the same fate of erasure from U.S. museums.[67]

Twain devoted a chapter to the savage campaign of extermination against the natives of Tasmania (Van Dieman's Land).[68] Of the brutal regime in South Africa, he wrote: "There are many humorous things in the world; among them, the white man's notion that he is less savage than other savages."[69] He declared that the Boers' treatment of black Rhodesians "is slavery, and is several times worse than was the American slavery which used to pain England so much; for when the Rhodesian slave is sick, superannuated or otherwise disabled he must support himself or starve—his master is under no obligation to support him."[70] Moreover, as literary scholar Larzer Ziff emphasizes, the horrors of colonization and the brutal imposition of racial hierarchies that accompanied it reminded Twain of the awful mistreatment of slaves in the Old Southwest (the region west of the Appalachians and south of the Ohio River) during his Missouri boyhood. After watching a German hotel proprietor strike an Indian employee in Bombay, Twain experienced the painful memory of his father hitting "our harmless slave boy" and recalled witnessing another slave being killed by a white man. Twain's whole life came to make more sense as a result of his last global journey.[71] It was not just his personal past but the racial landscape of the American present, too, that became clearer to Twain because of

Figure 25. The White Man's World, by Daniel Carter Beard. Illustrations for Mark Twain's *Following the Equator* (1897), original drawings courtesy of the Henry W. and Albert A. Berg Collection of English and American Literature, New York Public Library, Astor, Lenox, and Tilden Foundations.

his last travels. The experience of his global journey made him critical of America's thrust toward empire in the wake of the Spanish-American War of 1898, and he became an important anti-imperialist voice.

America's quest for empire had been justified in part by those such as Theodore Roosevelt, Albert Beveridge, Josiah Strong, and Alfred Thayer Mahan who argued that the nation had lost its contiguous western frontier and needed new overseas frontiers if it was to retain its vigorous spirit.[72] American imperialists were literally putting the West into the world in support of empire. In *Following the Equator*, Twain, the anti-imperialist, reminded Americans of the consequences of empire for the conquered and colonized. He surely hoped that his American readers would learn from this global context. It might seem a long journey from the Far West of *Roughing It*, the creation of a brilliant

Figure 26. Mary Kingsley, portrait from *West African Studies* (1899). Courtesy of the Royal Geogographical Society, London.

young cynic and comic, to the sage and tragic observations of a global traveler a quarter century later. But is it worth remembering that in that first American travel book, which included a reworking of the letters he had written from Hawaii in 1866, Twain had exhibited the seeds of his later anti-imperialism. In *Roughing It*, Twain had observed that "contact with civilization and the whites has reduced the native population from *four hundred thousand* (Captain Cook's estimate) to *fifty-five thousand* in something over eighty years!" Moreover, Twain viewed the Hawaiian Islanders' violent action against their colonizer, Captain James Cook, in 1779 a fitting response to his injustices against them. "Small blame," he wrote, "should attach to the natives for the killing of Cook. They treated him well. In return, he abused them. He and his men inflicted bodily injury upon many of them at different times, and killed at least three of them before they offered any appropriate retaliation."[73] Twain was considerably more conflicted in *Roughing It* when it came to the matter of the United States' potential colonization of the islands, and to the impact of

Christian missionaries on the islanders.[74] Still, it would be hard to find a suitable place for him, at any stage in his literary career, in the travel-writing-as-empire-building school.[75]

In the very same year that Twain's *Following the Equator* appeared, the first of two popular and influential works by British traveler Mary Henrietta Kingsley was published, *Travels in West Africa* (1897); the second work, *West African Studies* (1899), appeared soon thereafter. There was no shortage of travel writing advocates of British imperialism at century's end, but Kingsley, like Twain, did not fit that mold. In the first of her books, recounting her travels in the region in 1893 and 1894–1895, she criticized British missionary endeavors for their insensitivity to the continent's cultures and derided their efforts to ensure that readers of missionary reports and financial contributors to the cause "not get any foolishness into their heads about obtaining an inadequate supply of souls for their money."[76] She also offered ardent and convincing defenses of indigenous cultural practices, including polygamy.

In a letter to the renowned Oxford anthropologist E. B. Taylor, written in the midst of the controversy that accompanied the publication of *Travels in West Africa*, Kingsley championed the benefits of living among the people one wrote about rather than relying on the misassumptions and stereotypes about Africans perpetuated in the popular press and by politicians. She caustically referred to "missionaries, stockbrokers, good intentions, ignorance, and maxim guns" as the "old toys" of British empire building.[77] Then, in *West African Studies*, which included coverage of her time among the Fang people (purported cannibals), Kingsley referred to the "maladministration of West Africa" as "a disgrace to my country," adding that "[w]e have killed down native races in Australasia and America, and it is no use slurring over the fact that we have profited by doing so" and warning that the pattern ought not to be repeated on another continent.[78]

Kingsley, to be clear, was not a thoroughgoing critic of the principle of British empire, but rather of the policies and practices (such as the Crown Colony system) used to establish and govern it; she favored an informal imperialism based on commerce.[79] Nonetheless, her effectiveness in illuminating the essential humanity of Africans and the complexity and variety of their cultural systems certainly cut against the grain of official pro-empire attitudes in the British government and press, which held that the peoples of "darkest Africa" were barbarous and much in need of a firm white civilizing hand. And, interestingly, Mary Kingsley's empathetic treatment of African societies and emphasis on colonial Britain's misguided policies may have resulted from the influence of her father, Dr. Charles George Kingsley, a personal physician to several British aristocrats and ardent critic of the United States' Indian policies. Charles Kingsley had accompanied Lord Dunraven on his travels in North America in the first half of the 1870s and had been invited to join George Armstrong Custer on his fateful trip into the Montana Territory in the early summer of 1876, but bad weather proved his good fortune by preventing him from doing so.

Charles's daughter Mary would die in a war zone, in 1900, after contracting typhoid fever while working for the British government nursing Boer prisoners of war in South Africa. Before her fateful end, though, Kingsley met the champion of "The White Man's Burden," (1899), Rudyard Kipling, in South Africa, and offered a public response to his advocacy concerning the responsibilities of empire for "superior" peoples. Kingsley proclaimed that:

> [I]t is the black man's burden that wants singing . . . for the poor [African] has to put up with a lot of windy-headed fads and foolishness no good to him or to the white man, and a jest for the Gods.[80]

Mary Kingsley's life, like Twain's, further elucidates the anti-imperialistic strain in some of the most significant travel writings that appeared just as European powers and the United States were racing to acquire colonial possessions across the globe; in the four decades between 1876 and 1915, these countries gained an additional quarter of the world's land mass.[81] The likely influence of father on daughter—of the brutal subjugation of native peoples in the United States' West as an object lesson for the British in how not to manage empire and treat subject peoples in Africa—serves as another example of the American West's interconnectedness with the wider world at the close of the nineteenth century.[82] The two empires were deeply entwined parts of the same global picture, a picture that was illuminated both by the critiques of imperial policies and actions offered by some travel writers and by the support offered by others.

These travelers, Catlin, Gerstäcker, Pfeiffer, Galton, Burton, Bird, Stevenson, Twain, and Kingsley, remind us of the need to step outside of the confines of postcolonial academic discourse surrounding the "other" and recognize the variety of perspectives on conquered and conquerable peoples that were offered by travel writers in the nineteenth century.[83] As a group, these commenters on the global West offered a diversity of perspectives that ranged from the unbridled advocacy of empire and brutal management of "savage" peoples to impassioned criticism of imperial projects and their harrowing consequences for the colonized, with much ambivalence in between. It would be naïve to suggest that the critique of empire in the writings of the period rang louder than the chorus of those who were advocates of empire, even among those working within the travelogue genre. For every Stephenson or Twain there was a Richard Harding Davis, quick to judge other peoples as fit for colonization, as he did in his 1896 work *Three Gringos in Venezuela and Central America*. Perfectly encompassing the notion of travel writer as imperial scribe, Davis disparagingly wrote:

> The Central American citizen is no more fit for a republican form of government than he is for an arctic expedition, and what he needs is to have a protectorate established over him, either by the United States or by another power; it does not matter which so long as it leaves the Nicaragua Canal in our hands.[84]

The point, though, is that the American public, like people all across the globe, would have seen and heard these conflicting visions and voices as they considered the nation's imperial pathways.[85] How this cacophonous symphony of imperial praise and condemnation would have sounded to that public can only be a matter of speculation.[86] However, it is clear that nineteenth-century readers would not have experienced any kind of harmony or consistency in travel writers' descriptions and assessments of imperial practices and purposes. The travel writings of the era would certainly not, as a collective whole, have facilitated the easy acceptance of those imperial initiatives among the residents of nations with empires.

To view travel writing as one great imperial archive and all its practitioners as mere imperial scribes, describing and cataloging the fruits of empire for home consumption, is to render the genre more monolithic and less discerning than was the case. Some of the most insightful and popular travel writings of the century are best considered as a counternarrative to American imperialism and to nationalistic, frontier-centered notions of American exceptionalism. Similarly, one suspects that Americans in the nineteenth century were hardly so smitten with the mythic West of romantic artists, dime novelists, and unoriginal and imitative travel writers that they collectively and unreservedly viewed western America as exceptional, incomparable, and unparalleled. For them to have done so would have meant ignoring the many popular travel accounts that centered on or included the United States' West and suggested a messier set of realities, including a wealth of global connections and comparisons.

The notion of a distinctive American frontier was in fact nurtured by the sense that the far-flung recesses of the earth were now closer than ever because of steamships, railroads, telegraphs, and, by 1876, telephones. The frontier concept served as an antidote of sorts to "globalization," to use a more contemporary term. The growing emphasis in the second half of the nineteenth century on the exceptional nature of the western frontier experience—the continued construction of a mythic West—provided a kind of nationalist escape from an emerging global reality in which the immense geography of the United States was just another stage of an integrated journey around the world, a single page in a Thomas Cook book of tickets. Meanwhile, visitors from all over the globe traveled more easily across the United States in the transcontinental railroad age, sometimes reminding Americans, as Stevenson did, of the failure of the majority culture to echo the nation's democratic rhetoric in their treatment of those peoples who fell outside of the white mainstream. What is more, as the century drew to a close, the newly developed transportation networks and the confinement of pacified indigenous people on reservations rendered travel to the American frontier a less thrilling prospect, leading some of America's most adventurous citizens to seek adventures beyond their nation's borders on what they imagined as the final global frontiers of that shrinking world.

PART TWO

THE AMERICAN FRONTIER
OF THE
TWENTIETH CENTURY

CHAPTER THREE

"NO, ADVENTURE IS NOT DEAD"

Frontier Journeys in the Last Great Age of Exploration

No, adventure is not dead, and in spite of the steam engine and of Thomas Cook and Son.

—Jack London, *The Cruise of the* Snark (1911)

There is a universal saying to the effect that it is when men are off in the wilds that they show themselves as they really are.

—Kermit Roosevelt, *The Happy Hunting-Grounds* (1921)

Global Frontiers

Notions like the closing frontier—and with it the passing of the "real," "authentic," old, Wild West—the death of regionalism, the end of "real" travel, and the loss of uncharted space, are all connected. Twentieth-century travel writers, in searching for the last supposed remaining vestiges of authentic old westernness, have in fact helped keep the western frontier alive in the public consciousness, thereby fortifying the storehouse of American western exceptionalism in the face of the forces of first modernization and then globalization. While the tendency among many of the more insightful and engaging nineteenth-century travel writers was to view the American West within a broader and largely deexceptionalized global context, their twentieth-century counterparts often, in contrast, looked persistently inward while searching for a distinctively American frontier, a place like nowhere else on earth.

The chronological divide between travel writers' envisioning of a global West and then, subsequently, of an American frontier, comes somewhere between the end of the nineteenth century and the start of the twentieth, but it is not rigid. Like all such efforts at periodization it bleeds at the edges. The motivation to search in the American Far West for the final traces of what had been or was being lost is generally more evident in twentieth-century travel books about the region, just as the tendency toward global contextualization of the West is more characteristic of the travel accounts of the previous century. The completion of the transcontinental railroad in 1869 marked for some the end of the old frontier West and the beginning of the new modern West. Moreover, concern over the perceived closing of the American frontier was a well-established strain in American thought by the 1880s.[1] Richard Harding Davis's book of train travel observations, *The West from a Car Window* (1892), constituted a search for the remnants of the Old West, yet using the very conveyance that symbolized the end of an earlier era.

In the early twentieth century, both Jack London and Theodore Roosevelt (in the wake of his presidency) searched for new frontiers of adventure well beyond the geographic borders of their newly frontierless nation. London's and Roosevelt's dramatic global adventures were in no small part manifestations of the urge to find the American frontier, or at least a fitting set of substitutes for the hardships, dangers, and discoveries it had afforded. In a sense, they were looking for the West in the world. Yet at the same time they were part of a larger landscape of frontier adventuring that brought the North and South Poles, Mount McKinley, and other far-flung peaks, rivers, and even peoples more fully within the purview of the Euro-American world.

From Hawaii to Africa

As the twentieth century unfolded, the much discussed closing of the frontier and attendant end of rigorous, dangerous, and memorable journeying experience hit such a nerve with London that he boldly declared in his 1911 work *The Cruise of the* Snark that the purported demise of adventure was premature, and that was so, he added, "in spite of the steam engine and of Thomas Cook and Son." London recounted how, when he made the announcement that he and his wife Charmian would be building a vessel and sailing it around the world, "young men of 'roving disposition' proved to be legion, and young women as well—to say nothing of the elderly men and women who volunteered for the voyage." After highlighting the deluge of

Figure 27. Jack London, photographing the *Snark* while
under construction. Courtesy of the Jack London Collection,
Huntington Library, JLP 456 Alb 18 #05808.

letters of inquiry from eager prospective journeyers, London announced
again, "I know Adventure is not dead, for I have had a long and intimate correspondence with Adventure."[2] London had thought long and hard about the
intersections of the frontier, adventure, and ideology.

In 1903, Jack London published two essays, "The Class Struggle" and "How
I Became a Socialist," which linked the end of the frontier era in the United
States to the development of class conflict in the country and to his own con-
version, as a nineteen-year-old, to socialism. "[T]he day of an expanding

frontier is passed," he wrote. "Farthest West has been reached. The gateway of opportunity after opportunity has been closed, and closed for all time."[3] That same year he also published *The People of the Abyss* (1903), a sociological exploration of the terrible squalor and degradation of the underclass of London's East End in which he utilized aspects of the travelogue form.[4] Most likely inspired by Jacob Riis's account of New York slum life in *How the Other Half Lives* (1890), yet more depressing and less hopeful and displaying a rare mixture of empathy and antipathy, London proclaimed in *The People of the Abyss*, "No more dreary spectacle can be found on this earth than the whole of the 'awful East,'" and described its half a million residents as being "as dull and unimaginative as its long gray miles of dingy brick," and home to "[a] new race . . . a street people." London argued that the opportunities for advancement provided by the far-flung colonies and former colonies of the British Empire—"the fresher and freer portions of the globe"—siphoned off what little cream there was of the East End crop, thereby exacerbating the process of racial degeneracy in London, the imperial heartland, which in turn, he suggested, would precipitate the empire's decline.[5]

In early 1904, London was in Korea reporting on the Russo-Japanese War for the Hearst syndicate. He had personally chartered a small boat and crew to sail from Pusan in southern Korea up Korea's Yellow Sea coast, in freezing and stormy conditions, to reach the front lines. A British correspondent remarked that London had arrived there "with the halo of adventure around his head." His adventures in Korea included several arrests by the Japanese military and a threatened Japanese court martial, which he escaped because of the interventions of another American correspondent and travel writer, Richard Harding Davis, who contacted President Theodore Roosevelt on London's behalf, enabling him to return to California that summer.[6] In the spring of 1906 he was in San Francisco, reporting on that city's terrible earthquake and planning to build a sailboat and embark on a seven-year voyage around the world. London was arguably the most famous author in the world by this time, and in 1907 he published *The Road*, his recollections of a trip he made across the United States in 1894, from west to east, Oakland, California, to Hannibal, Missouri, with the Industrial Army of the Unemployed (nicknamed Kelly's Army).[7] That same year, 1907, Jack and Charmian, with five additional adventurers, departed from the dock in San Francisco on their remarkable, albeit much abbreviated, two-year voyage.

The *Snark* set sail during a heady moment in the history of global adventuring, one that has been labeled the "last great age of exploration."[8] That

Figure 28. Charmian and Jack London on the deck of the *Snark*, wearing
lava lavas. Courtesy of the Jack London Collection, California
Department of Parks and Recreation.

year, 1907, the American explorer and anthropologist George Byron Gordon
embarked on an expedition to central Alaska, reaching Lake Minchumina
(near Mount McKinley), source of the Kuskolwim River.[9] The American
journalist and adventurer Robert Dunn's *The Shameless Diary of an Explorer*
was published that year, too. Dunn's was a fascinating account of his party's
unsuccessful effort in 1903 to reach the summit of Mount McKinley (Denali).
They did achieve the first known circumnavigation of North America's highest peak, at 20,320 feet; the first successful ascent of Denali was not achieved

until 1913.[10] On that 1903 expedition, Dunn accompanied the soon-to-become-controversial American explorer Dr. Frederick Cook (no relation to the tourism promoter Thomas Cook), to whom he referred somewhat contemptuously throughout his account as "the professor." Cook would falsely claim to have made a successful ascent of Mount McKinley on a second expedition in 1906.

Cook would later achieve massive fame, then infamy, in the wake of his grandest claim of all. He insisted that he had reached the jewel in the crown of exploration and adventure, the North Pole, on April 22, 1908.[11] Notably, in that year, "nine major exploratory expeditions from Europe and America" were underway or about to be launched, to the Brazilian Amazon, the Himalayas, the Australian interior, and the Antarctic.[12] Cook's account of his expedition, *My Attainment of the Pole* (1911), was a best seller and in its third edition by 1913. The public interest in Cook's polar expedition was sparked in part by the equally controversial claim of U.S. Navy engineer Robert Peary to have set foot on the pole on April 6, 1909, an assertion made in his book *The North Pole* (1910). In the preface to the second edition (1912) of *My Attainment of the Pole*, Cook proclaimed: "The Pole has been honestly reached—the American Eagle has spread its wings of glory over the world's top."[13] (In the 1920s, Cook would spend five years in federal prison for mail fraud).[14] Meanwhile, a small group of Norwegian explorers led by Roald Amundsen were racing to the South Pole, which they finally reached in mid-December 1911, a month ahead of British explorer Robert Falcon Scott's second Antarctic expedition. Scott and his party of four all perished from hunger and cold on their journey home, and their tragic ending was recounted a decade later by Apsley Cherry-Garrard, a member of the expeditionary team that discovered their bodies, in one of the most renowned of all modern adventure chronicles, *The Worst Journey in the World: Antarctic, 1910–1913* (1922).[15]

The reading public was fascinated by these adventures, and London played into this fascination in his proclamation that adventure was not dead. Jack and Charmian headed to considerably warmer climes on the *Snark*, first to Hawaii, then on to the Marquesas, the Paumotus, Tahiti and the other Society Islands, Samoa, Fiji, the New Hebrides, the Solomons, the Gilbert Islands, and finally to Australia, where Jack's ill health brought the global voyage to a premature close; he had such painfully acute swelling and psoriasis of the hands that he feared he had contracted leprosy.[16] The *Snark* adventure is particularly memorable because of the heightened cultural sensitivity that Jack displayed in his encounters with Pacific Island peoples; indeed, *The*

Cruise of the Snark might well be considered the absolute antithesis of travel writing as empire building, just as Cook's proclamation about the American eagle spreading its glorious wings seems the fullest embodiment of it. Like Mark Twain on his global tour and in his resulting critique of imperialism, *Following the Equator* (1897), London traveled more as a cultural ambassador than as an agent of empire. His remarkable photographic record of the journey, like his published account, is a model of empathy for the island peoples he encountered. Unlike Twain's comfortable steamship journey, though, London's was fraught with danger. Members of the crew, including Jack and Charmian, contracted tropical diseases. In truth, given their collective lack of nautical experience (Jack actually learned to navigate from books he brought on board the *Snark*) and the limitations of the vessel, all the participants in the Londons' adventure were lucky to survive it.

Jack London, like Robert Louis Stevenson two decades earlier, put himself at great risk, at least in the estimation of the popular press around the globe, by visiting the leper colony on the island of Molokai with its eight hundred residents.[17] The first case of leprosy in Hawaii occurred in 1848, and as the disease spread in the 1850s and 1860s, the Kalaupapa community on Molokai was established as a colony for the afflicted in 1866. A thirty-three-year-old Catholic missionary priest, Father Damien de Veuster, arrived seven years later to care for those living in isolation on the island. Father Damien fell victim to the disease in the mid-1880s and died from it in 1889. Stevenson wrote an impassioned tribute to the priest in response to the Reverend Dr. Hyde of Honolulu's charges that Father Damien was a bigot who had impure relations with women and contracted leprosy because of his own vices. (Father Damien was canonized and thus vindicated by the Catholic Church in 2009; and Stevenson's estimation of the man thereby received official corroboration.)[18]

Stevenson's travel writings about Molokai serve as a memorable precedent to London's. Like Stevenson, Jack and Charmian London spent time with the island's residents, and London wrote a powerful account of his experiences wherein he chided the "sensationalists" for shamelessly disseminating tales about the horrors of the island and of leprosy without ever visiting, and attacked American newspapers for publishing such lurid and uninformed accounts. A seasoned traveler to some of the remotest and most lightly peopled parts of the North American West and the globe, as well as to the leading centers of industrial capitalism, London wrote that if forced to choose a residence for the remainder of his life, and the options were limited to Molokai, the East End of London, the East Side of New York, or the

Figure 29. Leper nurses on Molokai, 1908. Courtesy of the Jack London Collection, Huntington Library, JLP 493 Alb 55 #06899.

stockyards of Chicago, "I would select Molokai without debate." He added, "I would prefer one year of life in Molokai to five years of life in the above-mentioned cesspools of human degradation and misery."[19]

In January 1909, Jack and Charmian London were in Sydney, Australia; Jack was recovering from his illness. He issued a statement to the press asking that his friends "please forego congratulating us upon the abandonment of the voyage. We are heart-broken."[20] The Londons had failed to complete the greatest adventure of their life together, although they looked back on it as two of the very best years of their lives. The enormous promise of the *Snark* journey, as well as the spirit of adventure and the concluding despondency, were all captured in London's account, which appeared a few years later, and in Charmian's own book, *The Log of the* Snark (1915; also published in London as *Voyaging in Wild Seas: A Woman Among the Head Hunters*).[21] That sense of adventure, along with a heavy emphasis on the exotic and erotic

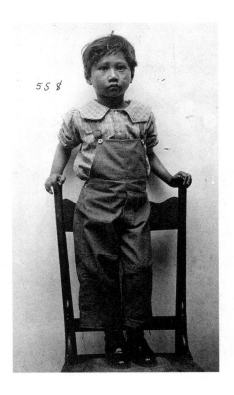

55 8

Figure 30. Young boy leper on Molokai, 1908. Courtesy of the Jack London Collection, Huntington Library, JLP 493 Alb 55.

elements of the South Sea islands experience, was also kept before the public for a good number of years after the voyage by Martin Johnson, a *Snark* crew member (officially the cook, although his culinary experience upon embarkation matched Jack London's nautical expertise). Johnson developed a series of lectures illustrated with his and Jack and Charmian's photographs of the peoples and landscapes of the islands. These performances, labeled travelogues (which occasionally included "men only" shows featuring numerous images of topless native women), were given at theaters all across the country, including Johnson's own aptly named Snark Theater in Independence, Kansas, built in the shape of a boat, and in European cities, too, during much of the second decade of the twentieth century.

For a brief time in 1913, and without first securing Jack and Charmian's permission, Johnson titled his show (or at least allowed his manager to name it) "Jack London's Adventures in the South Sea Islands."[22] That same year, Johnson's own written account, *Through the South Seas with Jack London,* was published. Johnson began the account much as Jack London had introduced

Figure 31. Wheelchair-bound woman leper on Molokai, 1908. Courtesy of the Jack London Collection, Huntington Library, JLP 493 Alb 55.

his earlier chronicle of the *Snark*, writing: "Through all my twenty years I had been in pursuit of Adventure. But Adventure eluded me . . . [but now] Adventure would be mine!"[23] Five years later, Johnson and his wife, Osa, would earn fame in their own right as filmmakers, creating travelogue movies much in the tradition of Johnson's earlier adventures with the Londons, including *Among the Cannibals of the South Sea Islands* (1918) and *Jungle Adventures* (1922), which recounted their travels in Africa. Osa later titled her book about their life and travels together *I Married Adventure* (1940).[24]

In her account of the *Snark*'s journey, Charmian London wrote that Jack had "thirsted for Marquesan exploration" ever since he had "happened upon Melville's *Typee* as a small boy."[25] Meanwhile, with the *Snark* adventure very much in the public imagination in 1911–1912, largely because of London's travel account and to a lesser degree because of Johnson's illustrated lectures on the topic, another famous American writer completed a solo journey to South America and Africa that he had dreamed of since he was a young man in the 1860s. At the end of the trip, America's most revered and influential naturalist, John Muir, triumphantly proclaimed: "I've had the most fruitful

Figure 32. Charmian London watching a rodeo on Molokai, 1908.
Courtesy of the Jack London Collection, Huntington Library, JLP 432 97a.

time of my life on this pair of hot continents." Muir's trip lasted from August
1911 to March 1912. He covered forty thousand miles in seven and a half
months, "sailed for 109 days, crossed the equator six times, and studied . . .
rivers, jungles, forests, plains, mountains, and rare trees." He traveled "a
thousand miles up the Amazon . . . crossed the continent into the Chilean
Andes . . . re-cross[ed] the pampas to Buenos Aires . . . [then] traveled through
south and central Africa to the headwaters of the Nile." He arrived home in
California on his seventy-fourth birthday.[26]

Muir's global journey, much like those of Isabella Bird and Mark Twain,
has been largely overlooked by historians of the West and even by most Muir
aficionados. His eloquent and passionate exhortations from the 1908–1913
period (including *The Yosemite*, 1912) against the damming of the Hetch
Hetchy Valley are naturally viewed as the pinnacle of his remarkable career
in California nature; his 1894 collection *The Mountains of California* has
meanwhile become a classic of American nature writing. Not surprisingly,
his journals and correspondence from the trip to South America and Africa,
unpublished until 2001, have left little impression. American nature writing,
as would be expected, has been "America-centric" and has found little place,

Figure 33. John Muir, portrait, ca. 1912, by Underwood and Underwood, after his return from a trip to South America and Africa. Courtesy of the John Muir Papers, Holt-Atherton Special Collections, University of the Pacific Library.

or use, for Muir's writing about other landscapes across the globe. Furthermore, it is the youthful, vigorous Muir, the tireless hiking, mountain-and-glacier-conquering, tree-climbing phenomenon that graces the pages of his best-known writings and of most writings about him, not the old man seeking to make one last journey into nature before his time expires.[27]

Moreover, as Muir's most recent and finest biographer, Donald Worster, notes, Muir's keen powers of perception and naturalist instincts led him to the evergreen coniferous trees (*Araucaria*) that he sought in South America and to the baobob tree (*Adansonia digitata*) that he sought in Africa, but he seemed less fully aware of the darker realities that marked the landscapes in which he traveled near the end of his life (he died less than three years after his return from South America and Africa). In the Amazon, he was hosted by English-speaking rubber exporters who were building a railroad into the rainforest, but he offered no commentary on the attendant natural destruction. In Africa, he said nothing about the brutalities that accompanied British imperial expansion, not to mention the expansion of other European powers on the continent. As Worster notes, "[h]e had only trees in mind."[28]

Nonetheless, Muir's global journey does add an important dimension to our understanding of his life and career, particularly since he had intended his famous thousand-mile hike from Indiana to the Gulf of Mexico in 1867 as a much longer journey that would take him into South America and the Amazon basin; ill health had cut that earlier journey short.[29] At that time, he had been inspired in part by the Scottish explorer Mungo Park's classic work *Travels in the Interior Districts of Africa* (1799).[30] More than four decades later, he made the trip to South America and Africa, thereby finally placing himself in that long tradition of travelers considering the West within larger global contexts, one that stretched back long before even Alexander von Humboldt at the turn of the eighteenth century and was continued by Friedrich Gerstäcker, Richard Francis Burton, Isabella Bird, George Catlin, and others in the nineteenth century. Robert Underwood Johnson, editor of *Century Magazine*, corresponded with Muir in an effort to get three or four articles drawn from Muir's observations of the flora and fauna of South America and Africa. Muir had originally hoped for at least this much, and perhaps a whole travel book devoted to those last major explorations in nature. But as Muir's energies declined in his final years, he was unable to complete these and other writing projects. One can only wonder whether his legacy as one of the clearest voices and advocates of American nature might have been a little different had his global observations seen the published light of day a century ago.[31]

While Muir sought the kind of adventure beyond the North American West that accompanies the first sight of species of trees in wild nature, one of his great admirers, Theodore Roosevelt, had just a few years before sought a rather different sort of experience in wild frontiers. Indeed, in a letter penned in June 1912, just a few months after his return from South America and Africa, Muir described the itinerary of his journey, noting that he had traveled by rail "up through the game region where Roosevelt hunted."[32] In early 1909, just seven weeks removed from his successful presidency, Theodore Roosevelt departed with his son Kermit for Africa with a $50,000 advance from *Scribner's Magazine* and a lucrative book publishing contract from Charles Scribner's Sons for the accounts of his African adventures. He also traveled under the sponsorship of Andrew Carnegie and other wealthy American entrepreneurs, all to the tune of $75,000. The safari concluded in March 1910. In the course of a year or so, Theodore and Kermit had killed more than five hundred animals between them, including lions, elephants, hippos, rhinos, giraffes, zebras, wildebeest, and antelope.[33]

Roosevelt's trip continued a pattern that had begun with his flight to the Dakota Territory in 1884 in the wake of the tragic loss of his first wife and his mother on the same day (February 14, Valentine's Day). Those experiences on the western frontier provided the subject matter for Roosevelt's books *Hunting Trips of a Ranchman* (1885), *The Wilderness Hunter: An Account of the Big Game of the United States and Its Chase with Horse, Hound, and Rifle* (1893), and *Ranch Life and the Hunting Trail* (1896). But a quarter century later, in the wake of the perceived closing of the American frontier, adventures in wilderness now had to be found outside of the nation's borders. On the continent of Africa, Roosevelt noted in the book's preface (written in Khartoum at the end of the trip), one could once more find "delight in the hardy life of the open, in long rides rifle in hand, in the thrill of the fight with dangerous game."[34]

Roosevelt's written installments of his African adventures were a runaway success for *Scribner's*. The handsome and expensive two-volume collectors' edition of *African Game Trails* appeared in 1910 and was quickly followed by a single-volume trade edition.[35] Roosevelt's safari was also adapted into a picture book for young readers, *Roosevelt's Thrilling Experiences in the Wilds of Africa*.[36] Also, in 1910, two documentary films about Roosevelt's trip were released, one featuring real footage from the expedition and the other a fake documentary shot in California with a lookalike actor playing the role of the ex-president.[37] Among the young Americans inspired by Roosevelt's African adventures was Ernest Hemingway, who had met Roosevelt when he was a young boy, followed his hero's African adventures in serialized form in *Scribner's*, watched the documentary film coverage of the African expedition, and later traveled there himself, with the same guide who had led Roosevelt's expedition a quarter century before. Hemingway's journey was the inspiration for his nonfiction book *Green Hills of Africa* (1935).[38]

Roosevelt's description of British East Africa in the early twentieth century must have reminded some readers of his historical descriptions of the American West in the late eighteenth and early nineteenth centuries in *The Winning of the West* (4 vols., 1889–1896). "Again and again, in the continents new to peoples of European stock," he condescendingly wrote in *African Game Trails*, "we have seen the spectacle of a high civilization all at once thrust into and superimposed upon a wilderness of savage men and savage beasts."[39] Roosevelt's racialized assessment of societies, much in keeping with that of most of his European and American contemporary thinkers, was globally

Figure 34. Theodore Roosevelt, holding a dead bustard and standing next to a dead rhinoceros, photograph by Kermit Roosevelt, 1909–1910. Courtesy of the Theodore Roosevelt Collection, Houghton Library, Harvard University, Photographs, African Safari, 1901–1910. Undated, #560–61, no. 1 of 221.

comparative. But more than that, the African trip clearly afforded Roosevelt the opportunity to escape modernity and embrace what was deemed to be primitive, and the imperial tone that had marked his earlier work on the American West was very much evident in the African chronicle.[40] The first volume of *The Winning of the West* appeared just one year after Belgian king Leopold II (1865–1909) had set policies in motion (contrary to the stipulations of the Berlin Conference of 1884–1885) that would result both in brutal indentured servitude of the Congolese and horrifying retribution against their resistance to this repression over the course of two decades, leaving as much as half of the Congolese population, ten million people, dead.[41]

Figure 35. First bull elephant killed by Theodore Roosevelt, photograph by R. J. Cunninghame, September 16, 1909. Courtesy of the Theodore Roosevelt Collection, Houghton Library, Harvard University, Photographs, African Safari, 1901–1910. Dated, #560–61, no. 69 of 95.

African Game Trails appeared after King Leopold's death in 1909 but made absolutely no mention of the terrible tragedy in the Congo, a territory bordered on two sides by Britain's East African possessions. Indeed, Theodore and Kermit, after landing in Mombasa and traversing Britain's possessions with their party of 250 porters and guides, actually entered the Congo (with the permission of the Belgian government to hunt there) before heading back to the Nile. Joseph Conrad's influential novella *Heart of Darkness* had appeared in 1902.[42] Sir Arthur Conan Doyle's popular pamphlet *The Crime of the Congo*, with its disturbing photographs of Congolese men, women, and children with their hands cut off, appeared in November 1909 (after Roosevelt's return from his African safari).[43] Of course, Roosevelt would have been thoroughly familiar with the atrocities in the Congo since they had been making headlines internationally for a decade. Moreover, Roosevelt, in September 1904, had received Edmund Dene Morel, one of the chief crusaders against Leopold II's Congo atrocities, in the White House.

Mark Twain had lobbied the Congolese cause in the nation's capital after meeting Morel and had lunched with Roosevelt to discuss it. Roosevelt's secretary of state, Elihu Root, had met with Leopold II and had reported back to the president.[44] A far cry from his earlier pro-imperialist travelogue *Three Gringos in Venezuela and Central America* (1896), Richard Harding Davis's 1907 travel account *The Congo and the Coasts of Africa* offered a blistering assessment of Leopold II and the rubber trade and included his unforgettable description of the "little, roughly rolled red balls, like pellets of coagulated blood, which had cost their weight in blood, which would pay Leopold their weight in gold."[45] But clearly, these genocidal consequences of colonialism were not the ex-president's concern in *African Game Trails*. It is worth noting that Roosevelt overtly insisted that politics, whether domestic or foreign, not intrude in his African experience.[46] Contemporary political issues were conspicuously absent from his narrative, although the matter of colonialism was certainly present.

In Roosevelt's account, Britain was to Africa as the United States had been to its own western frontier. Moreover, the coming of the railroad, "the embodiment of the eager, masterful, materialistic civilization of to-day," spelled order, progress, and ultimately salvation.[47] He was crystal clear in his opinion that the peoples of Africa were ultimately the beneficiaries of colonialism. *African Game Trails* is as clear an embodiment of the travel writer/ adventurer as agent of empire as perhaps any other work in the travelogue canon. But such issues were not in the foreground of Roosevelt's recounting of experiences in Africa; his personal experience as a hunter was. Most importantly, for Roosevelt in 1909–1910, East Africa's role was akin to that of the western frontier a quarter century earlier in the Dakotas, one that offered the opportunity for "plunging into the wilderness" and reliving the early American frontiersman's "unending struggle with the wild ruggedness of nature," as he described that process in *The Winning of the West*'s coverage of early American frontier expansion.[48]

Of course, the "unending" nature of that struggle, to reassert a globalizing virility, in the reckoning of Roosevelt and others, could be maintained only through risk-laden adventures in new frontiers worldwide. What is more, Roosevelt contended, "roughing it" in equatorial Africa was actually a more dangerous proposition than doing so in "the Rockies or the North Woods" (of New England, New York, and Quebec) had ever been. Early western pioneers, he insisted (indeed, he had made a publishing career of such insistence), "were as hardy as bears, and lived to a hale old age, if Indians and accidents permitted." However, "in tropic Africa a lamentable proportion of the early explorers paid in health or life for the hardships they endured"; one simply could not rough it for long in Africa "with impunity," he observed.[49]

Indeed, a little over a century earlier, in 1805, at the very same time that Meriwether Lewis and William Clark were traveling up the Missouri River seeking a route to the Pacific and exploring the recently acquired lands of the Louisiana Purchase, Scottish explorer Mungo Park was searching for the mouth of the Niger River and assessing the prospects for the expansion of the British empire there. Of Park's party of forty-four, thirty-nine fell prey to malarial diseases; Park and the four other remaining men drowned while trying to escape an attack by local villagers.[50] A half century later, in 1854, Richard Burton's small party barely escaped the East African holy site of Harar with their lives after an attack; and four years later, after becoming the first European to see Lake Tanganyika, Burton nearly died from disease.[51] Paul du Chaillu, in his popular account *Explorations and Adventures in Equatorial Africa* (1861),[52] claimed to have suffered "fifty attacks of the African fever" during his three years in the western part of the continent. And, of course, in one of the most legendary moments in the history of European and American exploration of Africa, Henry Morton Stanley found a weakened David Livingstone in Ujiji, on the shores of Lake Tanganyika, in 1871; Livingstone remained in Africa and died from malaria and dysentery less than two years later.[53] Thus, equatorial Africa, with its storied legacy of dangers for European explorers, became a worthy proving ground for the maintenance of the ex-president's frontier fortitude in the wake of the Old West's passing.[54]

But Africa for Roosevelt was more than a mere substitute for the western frontiering experience. Throughout his account, Roosevelt was reminded of the West and saw the possibilities for this new African frontier through the comparative lens of his western experiences. The Kitanga Hills, within sight of Mount Kilimanjaro, brought to mind "the great plains of the West, where they slope upward to the foot-hills of the Rockies. . . . I might have been on the plains anywhere, from Texas to Montana," he remarked. Roosevelt went on to explain that a "Westerner" could see the possibilities of the highlands of East Africa far better than an "Easterner." "No new country is a place for weaklings," Roosevelt ventured in a fashion typical for him and for promoters of settlement in white territorial possessions across the globe (from the American West and Canada to New

Zealand, Australia, and Africa), adding that "the right kind of man, the settler who makes a success in similar parts of our own West, can do well in East Africa."[55]

Yet, for all these direct comparisons, including occasional commentary on the stages of civilization of African and American Indian peoples, *African Game Trails* did not reach or aspire to the levels of comparative ethnographic and topographic analysis that marked Burton's trip across the western plains a half century before. Roosevelt's book, at its core, was about the thrill of the hunt, and the list of species and numbers killed, with separate columns for Theodore's and Kermit's respective achievements, took up a full three pages of the account (and a good many of the book's illustrations); most of the chapters in the two volumes were devoted to the hunting of particular kinds of big game. Well aware that more sensitive readers might demonize his African safari and the resulting book as a chronicle of wanton bloodletting, he insisted that father and son between them "did not kill a tenth, nor a hundredth part of what we might have killed had we been willing." He and Kermit "kept about a dozen trophies," but Theodore insisted that aside from those prizes, "we shot nothing that was not used either for museum specimen [many of which went to the Smithsonian] or for meat—usually for both purposes."[56] In offering this justification, Roosevelt underscored a driving reality of his African adventure: it was a collecting trip, not a journey of discovery; and while there were dangers in hunting large game to be sure, his traveling party resembled a small military force, and those numbers brought a measure of safety.

On the River of Doubt

Just a few years later, in the wake of his failed bid for the presidency as the candidate of the Progressive Party in the 1912 election, Roosevelt repeated the pattern once more, again moving swiftly from the public sphere to the wild frontier, journeying almost a thousand miles through the Brazilian rainforest down the uncharted Rio da Dúvida, the River of Doubt, and this time nearly losing his life. A major departure from the largely unadventurous South American trip Roosevelt had originally envisioned—traveling down well-charted portions of the Amazon and other rivers—the journey he and his son Kermit eventually undertook at the beginning of 1914 became one of the greatest and most dangerous adventures of their lives. The Expedição Científica Roosevelt-Rondon, as it came to officially be titled, was a joint

Figure 36. Map of Brazil, 1914, showing the route of the Roosevelt-Rondon Expedition. http://www.theodorerooseveltcenter.org/Research/Digital-Library/ Record.aspx?libID=0284968. Theodore Roosevelt Digital Library, Dickinson State University, North Dakota.

venture between New York's American Museum of Natural History and the Brazilian government and was co-led by Roosevelt and the distinguished Brazilian explorer, engineer, and commander Colonel Cândido Mariano da Silva Rondon, who knew the country as well as anyone from his experience laying telegraph lines across its vast expanses.[57] The expeditionary group was composed of Rondon's party of eleven Brazilians, Roosevelt's party of seven "norte Americanos," including Kermit, and about a dozen local hired hunters, carriers, paddlers, and cooks.

As the expedition began, Roosevelt concurrently recorded his experiences and sent them back to *Scribner's* prior to their publication in book

Figure 37. Roosevelt-Rondon Expedition. Courtesy of the Harvard College Library.

form. Readers of his previous travel adventures, while transported geographically from East Africa to South America, would have had little difficulty making the transition. Roosevelt the hunter was still the centrifugal force of the narrative, but the subjects of his attention were now jaguars rather than lions, and the hunting of the former was discussed with much the same relish that had characterized his descriptions in *African Game Trails*. In addition, the standard dangers of the Amazon rainforest and river system were catalogued for readers—mosquitoes and other bloodsucking and flesh-eating insects, vampire bats, piranha fish (described by Roosevelt as "the embodiment of evil ferocity"), a variety of venomous snakes, caimans and crocodiles, dysentery, skin infections, and tropical fevers. In addition, the expedition would experience unpacified (indeed, even formerly unencountered) indigenous peoples, fatal accidents, and an act of murder within the party.[58]

When the expedition approached its first dangerous stage, on the Rio da Dúvida itself, the narrative, mirroring Roosevelt's experience, shifts from safari mode to the chronicling of real adventure. Roosevelt made a point of emphasizing that the region his expedition would be moving through was uncharted territory and that he was no mere "ordinary traveler" but rather an "explorer." "Danger" and "privation" had to be endured, and "exceedingly trying experiences" had to be undergone in order for the "ordinary traveler" to be able to subsequently traverse the trails "with little discomfort and no danger." The person "who never goes off the beaten route and who on this beaten route is carried by others, without himself doing or risking anything," Roosevelt declared for effect, "does not need to show much more intelligence than an express package." Moreover, he added, "[i]f this kind of traveler is a writer, he can of course do admirable work . . . but the value comes because he is a writer and observer, not because of any particular credit that attaches to him as a traveler."[59]

To drive the point home and give it an American western corollary, Roosevelt explained: "When a man travels across Arizona in a Pullman car, we do not think of him as having performed a feat bearing even the most remote resemblance to the feats of the first explorers of those waterless wastes." But this was not the western frontier of Roosevelt's earlier days, but rather South America a generation later, a place where, and here he echoed his own earlier African assertions, "[t]here yet remains plenty of exploring work to be done . . . as hard, as dangerous, and almost as important as any that has already been done." And it was the ex-president (now in his mid-fifties), who presented himself as the very quintessence of the pioneering qualities he claimed were still essential to the exploration of the world's last remaining far-flung frontiers, as "the true wilderness wanderer . . . a man of action as well as observation," who was the co-commander of the expedition. In this regard, his account was reminiscent of Burton's accounts of his African explorations more than a half century earlier. Roosevelt presented himself as both travel writer and adventurer, and time and again gave short shrift to the former occupation when it was not accompanied by the adverse circumstances experienced in unknown terrain. "Let me make it clear that I am not deprecating the excellent work of so many men who have not gone off the beaten trails," he wrote, adding, "I merely wish to make it plain that this excellent work must not be put in the same class with that of the wilderness explorer."[60] Moreover, given the dangers and privations that the expedition members were to experience, and those he would personally endure, Roosevelt's self-definition as a wilderness explorer, while certainly self-congratulatory, hardly seems inaccurate.

Figure 38. Theodore Roosevelt, Colonel Rondon, and a group of Nhambiquara Indians; from Theodore Roosevelt, *Through the Brazilian Wilderness* (1914).

In mid-February, as the expedition moved through the lands inhabited by the Nhambiquara Indians, Roosevelt drew on his various travel experiences to engage in some comparative ethnographic analysis: "Nowhere in Africa did we come across wilder or more absolutely primitive savages, although these Indians were pleasanter and better-featured than any of the African tribes at the same stage of culture." He added that among the Nhambiquara "there was no male brutality like that which forms such a revolting feature in the life of the Australian black fellows and, although to a somewhat less degree, in the life of so many negro and Indian tribes."[61] The Nhambiquara (later a subject of anthropologist Claude Lévi-Strauss's famous 1930s travels, recounted in *Tristes Tropiques*, 1955), Roosevelt noted, had been largely pacified—a prelude to the next stage of development in their homeland. "The country when opened," he predicted, "will be a healthy abode for white settlers," but added that in the meantime "pioneering in the wilderness is grim work for man and beast." He then remarked on the failed pioneering efforts of those who had previously explored the region: "Continually, as we journeyed onward, under the pitiless glare of the sun or through the blinding torrents of rain, we passed desolate little graves by the roadside. They marked the last resting-places of men who had died by fever, or dysentery, or Nhambiquara arrows."[62]

The same fate nearly befell Roosevelt himself. "On February 27, 1914, shortly after midday, we started down the River of Doubt into the unknown." So begins the final segment of Roosevelt's account of the most remarkable journey of his life, one that saw him endure both malaria and a bacterial infection, and concluded with the successful mapping of a nearly thousand-mile long tributary of the Amazon River. A week later, as the expedition performed the slow and difficult work of portaging around the Navaïté Rapids—"two and a half days of severe and incessant labor [and] damage to the canoes"—Roosevelt returned again to what was for him a "subject of perpetual wonder," namely "the attitude of certain men

Figure 39. Roosevelt and Rondon at the post marking the renaming of the Rio da Dúvida as Rio Roosevelt, subsequently renamed the Rio Téodoro by the Brazilian government. http://www.theodorerooseveltcenter.org/Research/Digital-Library/Record.aspx?libID=0284968. Theodore Roosevelt Digital Library. Dickinson State University, North Dakota.

who stay at home, and still more the attitude of certain men who travel under easy conditions, and who belittle the achievements of the real explorers of, the real adventurers in, the great wilderness." These "imposters and romancers among explorers or would-be explorers and wilderness wanderers . . . are fit subjects for condemnation and derision," he insisted, while reporting on the slow progress of his party along the river—twelve kilometers one day, nineteen the next.[63]

On March 10, as the party continued its portaging efforts to avoid impassable rapids, they advanced a kilometer and a half.[64] The very next morning, they discovered that the heavy canoes they had expended so much energy dragging overland had escaped their moorings and washed away. So they undertook the toilsome task of building new canoes. A few days later, as the party sought to navigate the rapids in these new vessels, one of Rondon's men, Simplicio, drowned, "his life beaten out on the bowlders beneath the racing torrent."[65] Kermit Roosevelt (whose marriage was scheduled for the end of the trip) nearly suffered the same fate. Soon thereafter, Colonel Rondon, much to Theodore Roosevelt's proclaimed surprise, and certainly to his great delight, erected a large post to signify the renaming of the Rio da Dúvida as the Rio Roosevelt.

By late March, the party had been on the river for a month but had traveled only around 160 kilometers of its course and had used up over half of their provisions. As the expedition advanced at a perilously slow pace, portaging the canoes, cutting new trails, and lowering the canoes down narrow gorges with ropes, Roosevelt sustained a serious cut on his right leg and began to fall ill, showing signs of coronary stress.[66] To facilitate their advance, the expedition members had to discard all but their most essential items. They managed to kill the occasional monkey and various birds to help feed themselves and their dogs as the supplies dwindled. Conditions were becoming desperate by the last days of March and the first days of April. Heavy rains deluged the weary group. Roosevelt's health began to worsen, and he contracted Cuban fever (a form of malaria) and dysentery. For a time, the ex-president had to be carried in a litter. He begged his son and the rest of the party to leave him behind and devote their energies to saving themselves; indeed, he had packed a lethal dose of morphine prior to embarking on the adventure, aware that he might be faced with circumstances as harrowing as these.

Kermit refused the earnest request for abandonment, and his steadfastness seemed to inspire his father to carry on.[67] But then, in the early morning

hours of April 5, delirious from fever, Roosevelt pleaded with Rondon to
move the expedition forward without him; Roosevelt came close to death
before the fever broke. Circumstances were becoming increasingly desperate
for the group as a whole. One member of the expedition, Julio, murdered
another, Paishon, and then fled. Kermit also fell ill with malarial fever, and
most of the other members of the party were suffering from fever and some
from dysentery.[68] But by the middle of the month the expedition had cleared
the worst of the river's descent and entered calmer waters, faced less inclem-
ent weather, and found more abundant fish and game; yet they were still
some distance from safety.

By the middle of the month, the expedition finally reached the farthest
settlements of the *seringueiros*, rubber tappers. Theodore Roosevelt's leg wound
had become badly infected, and he faced the very real danger of the infection
leading to blood poisoning, which in turn could most certainly kill him, particularly given his generally weakened state at this stage of the long and punishing journey. The pain intensified, and Roosevelt consented to an operation
on the leg, performed by the expedition's physician, Dr. José Antonio Cajazeira,
on the bank of the river, without anesthetic. On April 16, Dr. Cajazeira drained
the infected fluid from the leg, saving the ex-president's limb and life alike.[69]
After ten more days on the river and portaging, the expedition saw the flags of
the United States and Brazil adorning the tent of one of Rondon's men,
Lieutenant Antonio Pirineus de Sousa, who had been sent to explore a water-
way (which Rondon assumed to be the Rio da Dúvida) from the other direction. Lieutenant de Sousa, with supplies in hand for the beleaguered expedition,
had been waiting for over a month in the vicinity of the seringueiros for his
commander's arrival.[70]

Thus, members of the expedition had escaped the worst ravages of the
River of Doubt and found their salvation in the outposts of "civilization" that
marked the advance of an extractive industry, which in turn accompanied the
great new symbol of modernity, the automobile. Henry Ford's introduction of
the Model T in 1908 had precipitated an explosion in rubber harvesting, and
the Amazon had become the major source of the precious commodity, out-
pacing the Congo, home to Leopold II's atrocities. But by 1913 the British were
harvesting as much rubber in Malaya and Ceylon as the Brazilian government was in the Amazon.[71] Still, the shifting balance of the global rubber
trade could not undermine the significance of the seringueiros in Roosevelt's
estimation: "These are real pioneer settlers," he wrote. "They are the true

wilderness-winners." Then, linking his exploits to theirs, he added: "No continent is ever really conquered, or thoroughly explored, by a few leaders, or exceptional men, although such men can render great service. The real conquest, the thorough exploration and settlement, is made by a nameless multitude of small men . . . contented to live in the wilderness." "[T]hese men, and those like them everywhere on the frontier between civilization and savagery in Brazil," Roosevelt continued, "are now playing the part played by our backwoodsmen when over a century and a quarter ago they began the conquest of the great basin of the Mississippi." Their efforts, he further explained, were the parallel of those of Boer farmers in South Africa and Canadians in the Northwest. Moreover, he added, the "last frontier" was far more evident in Brazil than in Canada or Africa, "and decades will pass before it vanishes."[72] Having played a role in the settlement of the American western frontier during his time in the Dakotas in the 1880s, Roosevelt now placed himself, at the end of a journey that had brought him near to death (and certainly took years off his life, and fifty-seven pounds off his frame), at the center of a new story of frontier exploration and settlement.[73]

By April 27, 1914, after two months of further river travel and portaging, the Expedição Científica Roosevelt-Rondon, benefiting from smoother waters in the last weeks of the journey, had traveled a distance of close to eight hundred kilometers along the Rio Roosevelt (subsequently renamed the Rio Téodoro by the Brazilian government), although the often winding course of the previously unmapped river constituted a journey of closer to fifteen hundred kilometers, almost a thousand miles. (Thirteen years later, the English explorer, Commander George Miller Dyott, traversed the same route and confirmed the accuracy of the Expedição Científica's charting of the river's course.)[74] The age of frontier exploration was not quite yet over, even as the Great War was about to begin. Moreover, a new subgenre of frontier travel writing—the transcontinental automobile narrative—was well underway, markedly less thrilling than Roosevelt's remarkable Amazonian adventure but equally illustrative of the continued desire of its practitioners to experience and report on faraway peoples and places, and for readers to experience them vicariously. In a way, then, it was the automobile, the conveyance that inspired this new genre, and necessitated the expansion of the rubber industry in the Amazon and beyond, that had effectively saved the former president's life by providing a safe haven for his expedition prior to its rendezvous with de Sousa.

Coda: In Asia

But first a quick detour. Theodore Roosevelt died in the first days of 1919, and Kermit recounted his adventures with his father in Africa, Brazil, and closer to home, in *The Happy Hunting-Grounds* (1920). Kermit began the book by noting: "There is a universal saying to the effect that it is when men are off in the wilds that they show themselves as they really are," and by reflecting on how much this was the case for his father, and, by implication, for himself.[75] A decade after Theodore and Kermit survived the Rio da Dúvida, Kermit traveled with his brother, Theodore Roosevelt Jr., or Ted (as he was known), across the Himalayas and along the Silk Road to China. Their journey was undertaken in the wake of Ted's defeat as the Republican candidate to the Democrat Alfred E. Smith in the New York gubernatorial election of 1924, a failure that was at least partly attributable to his role, while serving as assistant secretary of the navy (a post his father had held), in the Teapot Dome scandal that had plagued the Warren G. Harding administration.[76]

Under the sponsorship of Chicago's Field Museum and James Simpson (president of the Marshall Field and Company department stores), the Roosevelts' expedition amounted to a quest for adventure and animal specimens, particularly the legendary Asian bighorn sheep (*Ovis poli*), "[c]onceded by sportsmen all over the world," Theodore Roosevelt Jr. wrote, "to be one of the finest of all game trophies." The two recorded their exploits in alternating chapters in their book *East of the Sun and West of the Moon* (1927).[77] In outlining perhaps the larger underlying motive behind their trip, Roosevelt Jr. echoed Jack London's earlier insistence that "adventure is not dead," and chronicled a public response to the announcement of their pending expedition which echoes that which followed London's announcement of the *Snark*'s voyage. "There are those who say that Americans have lost the pioneer spirit," Roosevelt Jr. declared, adding, "I doubt if they would maintain this had they seen the flood of letters that were received by the museum. . . . Literally hundreds of people from all over the country wrote asking to go on the expedition." Men, and some women, from all walks of life volunteered their free service to the Roosevelt brothers, but all applications were refused: "[I]n a country where every additional ounce of baggage counts against you, it is necessary to cut personnel to the bone," Roosevelt Jr. explained.[78]

In the early summer of 1925, the Roosevelt expedition successfully completed a twenty-five-day climb over the Himalayas—including the nineteen-thousand-foot Karakoram Pass ("nearly half again as high as

Pike's Peak," Roosevelt Jr. reminded readers)—losing thirteen pack ponies but no men along the way. From there, the group moved across the plains of Turkestan at the beginning of July. With the real dangers of the journey now behind them, the rest of the expedition turned into a hunting trip, much like Kermit's African safari with his father in 1909. The brothers' trip lacked the near death drama of the earlier South American adventure as well as the keen comparative ethnographic and landscape observations that had featured so heavily in both *African Game Trails* and *Through the Brazilian Wilderness*. Nonetheless, while the James Simpson–Roosevelts–Field Museum Expedition, as it was officially named, made no cartographic contributions to parallel those of the Roosevelt-Rondon expedition, theirs was the first American expedition to explore the region, and they traversed previously uncharted parts of the Himalayas.

Moreover, the Roosevelt brothers' efforts served as a reminder of the persistence of the adventure travel genre in the modern age and the enduring tendency to search for proving grounds for the pioneer spirit in the world's last "great stretch[es] of wilderness." In Kashmir at the end of their central Asian expedition, Kermit Roosevelt wrote: "After seven months we were back in the land of motor transport, but to us it seemed outlandish to make in an hour what had been for so long the distance of a long day's march"; in the wake of their pioneering exploits, the trappings of the modern world of tempo seemed momentarily alien.[79] Meanwhile, as the Londons (husband and wife) and the Roosevelts (father and son, then sons together) explored final global frontiers and measured them against the backdrop of their own national frontier experience back in the North America, a new generation of travel writers was using motor transport to explore what it imagined remained of the western American frontier in order to keep it, or at least the idea of its imminent disappearance, at the center of the public imagination.

CHAPTER FOUR

THE END OF THE WEST?

Automotive Frontiers of the Early Twentieth Century

I do not like Americans as a whole. . . . The towns which he constructs are encampments; the houses which he raises are inns; the family which he creates is a partner, a companion for life and fortune.

—Antonio Scarfoglio, *Round the World in a Motor Car* (1909)

But what is the good of talking about it all? The Indians are losing too, in the long race. They too prefer to sit passive at the moving pictures, now. Their form of entertainment is nearly finished. The dollar is blotting the mystery out for ever, from their race as from ours.

—D. H. Lawrence in Taos, "Indians and Entertainment" (1924)

The Pioneering Strain

As the twentieth century dawned and the automotive age began, the American transcontinental motor journey constituted a challenge and an adventure for drivers. Horatio Alger Nelson made the first successful trip across the continent, from San Francisco to New York City, with his mechanic, Sewall K. Crocker, in a Winton touring car in 1903.[1] The pair experienced multiple breakdowns on their sixty-four day journey, but celebrity status too. For Nelson and Crocker, and anyone else intrepid enough to try it, driving was particularly difficult outside of cities because roads were truly awful. In 1904 there were 2,152,000 miles of rural roads in the nation, but only 154,000 of them (around 7 percent) were surfaced, and most of those with just a gravel mix and binding agent. Then the number of automobiles on the nation's roads began to grow at an astonishing rate, from ten thousand in 1900 to two hundred thousand by 1908 (approximately one car for every 450 Americans), close to half a million in 1910, nearly two and a half million by 1915, and over nine million by 1920 (one car for every 11 Americans).[2] Little wonder then that a "Good Roads" movement began to develop in this period. Nonetheless, even as automobile ownership became more common, transcontinental automobile journeys in the early decades of the century were still such a comparative novelty—especially so prior to the completion of the 3,389-mile-long Lincoln Highway from New York City to San Francisco in 1913—that the chronicling of experiences on the road became almost a prerequisite for undertaking them.

Hundreds of transcontinental automobile travel narratives appeared in book form and in popular magazines in the early decades of the new century, many of them authored by drivers (and passengers) who presented themselves as authentic pioneers, opening up the West's automotive frontiers, much in the tradition of their covered wagon predecessors.[3] Given the near total lack of decent roads between cities and towns early in the new century and the comparative fragility of the vehicles, there was at least a little truth to such self-perceptions.[4] Historian Anne Hyde notes that the first automobile to reach the South Rim of the Grand Canyon, in 1902, took three days to get there from Flagstaff, at a time when the same journey by train took just a few hours. Moreover, she adds, automobiles were banned from Yellowstone National Park that same year because of a series of accidents resulting from the mismatch between the park's primitive roads and the delicacy of the machines, and because the cars frightened horses. Fast forward less than two decades to 1919, and Yellowstone was receiving more than sixty thousand visitors annually, with two-thirds of them arriving in cars.[5] Even in that short span of time, what had been tough journeying became relatively undemanding leisure travel.[6] Nonetheless, the transcontinental automotive travel book genre continued to grow in size and significance during the twenties, when it became increasingly common for drivers and passengers to publish their impressions of the West from a car window.[7]

Philip Delaney, author of one of the earliest of these accounts, a short piece in *Outing Magazine* in 1903, titled it "Frontiering in an Automobile." Delaney ventured that while "Romance is fast being crowded out of the life of the pioneer," the automobile, "the latest pathfinder of the plains," might restore "the thrill of earlier days." He explained that "the machine" was literally "conquering the old frontier" by facilitating encounters with the "wildest and most natural places on the continent," making possible in days what used to take months. "The trails of Kit Carson and Boone and Crockett, and the rest of the early frontiersmen, stretch out before the adventurous automobilist," Delaney proclaimed, encouraging adventurous Americans to engage with history, be inspired by it, and even make some of their own.[8] In a similar vein, other intrepid travelers of the period, including the irrepressible Ezra Meeker (from 1906–1908) and the less renowned David and Viola MacFadyen (in 1911), sought to sustain the spirit of the western pioneers and memorialize their endeavors by journeying across the American continent at a much slower pace in covered wagons pulled by teams of oxen.[9] Such efforts at historical reconstruction and reengagement sought to promote the old pioneer West through anachronism, the unchanging nature of their conveyances purposefully contrasting with the metamorphosis of the landscapes they slowly passed through. The automotive continent crossers, on the other hand, sought to utilize the tools of modernity to encounter peoples and places in their premodern condition; or at least, that was the purpose they claimed at the outset of their journeys.

Most of the motorists who recorded and published their transcontinental experiences, especially those who traveled in the early years of the century, had significant financial means and leisure time; and the more accomplished ones, in the tradition of Theodore Roosevelt on his African and Brazilian adventures, embarked with publishers' advances to finance their journeys. Most authors of these travelogues journeyed from east to west, and almost all of them made a dramatic point of emphasizing where the West began—generally at the first sight of the Rockies, or somewhere between the 98th and 100th meridian in western Kansas or Nebraska, where the hue of the landscape shifted from green to yellow and brown.[10] Notably, these automotive chroniclers sometimes emphasized the privations and hardships of their journeys, presenting themselves as pathfinders of sorts. More significantly, they generally claimed at least to be motivated by the desire to search for any frontier distinctiveness that might remain in the westernmost far-flung corners of the nation.[11]

By the 1910s and 1920s, however, this travelers' quest for the "real" or premodern West was marked by an increasing expression of disillusionment on the part of its practitioners, who, more often than not, found a West despoiled by modernity, with the last traces of frontier authenticity fast fading away. But their discoveries should come as no great surprise, since their imaginations seem to have been fueled by an antimodernist vision before their journeys even began. In a sense, they found what they came for, even if it was at times the polar opposite of what they claimed to be seeking. By way of contrast, as the Great Depression worsened during the thirties, writers influenced by a different set of conditions rediscovered the distinctiveness of both the West and of all the nation's regions. It is on that shift away from the West in the world and toward the American frontier that we now focus our attention, via the observations of transcontinental automotive travelers in the first three decades of the twentieth century and the remarkable New Deal state guidebooks that followed them (the subject of chapter 5).

The Great Race and the Acids of Materialism

In 1907, a small group of motorists raced more than nine thousand miles from Peking to Paris. The following year, as nine major European and American expeditionary teams were exploring parts of four separate continents, six teams of automotive racers from four nations (France, Germany, Italy, and the United States) were participating in "The Great Race," the first round-the-world competition. The course amounted to a six-month, twenty-thousand-mile trek, departing from New York City on February 12 and heading across North America via Chicago, Wyoming (where the American team met with old frontier legend and showman Buffalo Bill Cody), Utah, and Nevada, and across the Sierras into California. From San Francisco, the teams traveled to Valdez, Alaska, by ship, and were then supposed to drive to the Bering Strait and from there across to Siberia. The ambitious and exceedingly unwise original plan had been to drive across the fifty-mile strait before the ice melted in early May—although the strait had not frozen over completely in twenty years. The proposed route had also included a drive from Valdez to Fairbanks, then across the Alaska Mountain range and up the frozen Yukon to the strait (more than 750 miles of remarkably rugged terrain). When the American crew, in the lead and well ahead of its competitors, found the Alaska leg impossible, they expected that they would have to abandon the race. But the organizers decided that all the participants would skip this leg and instead travel by boat to Japan, then drive across much of the length of the island's landmass to the Sea of Japan, ferry across to Vladivostok, and resume the race by car across Manchuria and Siberia.[12]

From Siberia, the teams crossed the European continent, driving through Russia, Germany, and into France. By this point, the German and American teams had separated themselves completely from their

118

competitors (most of whom had already abandoned their efforts). Technically speaking, the final days of the competition in the last days of July to the finish line in Paris hardly amounted to a race, since the Germans, who arrived a day ahead of the American team, had earlier been subjected to a fifteen-day penalty (for transporting their vehicle by train across much of the American Northwest), while the Americans had received a fifteen-day credit (for their efforts to drive their vehicle, the Thomas Flyer, across Alaska). The American team arrived on July 30, a day after the Germans, but twenty-nine days ahead, technically speaking.[13]

While the anticipated climax of the race was certainly less dramatic than its followers would have hoped for, the exploits of the driving teams received extensive press coverage across the globe, particularly in the *New York Times* and the French newspaper *Le Matin*, the primary sponsors of the event. The high level of interest was hardly surprising; the Great Race was viewed within the larger context of frontier adventuring and global exploration, and what the six teams were attempting was truly ambitious and dangerous. Only nine automobiles had successfully crossed the United States prior to 1908. What is more, the racers were circling the North Pole around the time that Frederick Cook was racing toward his controversial claim of attainment, and the media drew the comparison between the two efforts and highlighted the "spirit of adventure" that fueled both.[14] But for all the drama of the Great Race, its most memorable remnant, at least for historians of the West and America, may be a travelogue composed by a member of the three-man Italian team that successfully completed the marathon course in their vehicle, the Züst, albeit arriving in Paris on September 17, more than a month and a half after the Thomas Flyer and the German car, the Protos.[15]

Better known for his reporting on the Armenian genocide in Turkey in June 1909, the young Neapolitan journalist and writer Antonio Scarfoglio (then just twenty-two years of age) received payment from the British newspaper the *Daily Mail* for his reportage on the Great Race, in which he was participating. Those dispatches were then published in book form under the title *Round the World in a Motor Car* (1909). The lengthy account included an absolutely scathing critique of the American character. As he chronicled the New World leg of the race from the vantage point of Chicago, site of the famous Columbian Exposition of 1893 with its many testaments to technological innovation in the host nation, Scarfoglio contrasted the "smooth and harmonious life" of Europeans, composed of "innumerable pleasures" that combined to form "an organic whole," with the American "conception of life

Figure 40. Antonio Scarfoglio, portrait from *Round the World in a Motor-Car,* translated by J. Parker Heyes (1909). Courtesy of the Rare Book Collection, Huntington Library.

. . . naked, rigid, skeletonic, like a spear held upright." Scarfoglio was merely warming up to the task of lambasting his current hosts and their cultural shortcomings. "I do not like the Americans as a whole," he next proclaimed, "just as I do not like the cheesemonger whom a prize in a lottery or a sudden rise in the price of potatoes has made wealthy." He proceeded to rail against the rising American middle class, whose "coarseness irritates and wounds us" and whose purported legacy of English refinement and education "has been destroyed and suffocated by the mountains and the forests." Turning Frederick Jackson Turner's by then well-known frontier thesis and, more broadly, America's frontier heritage on their heads, Scarfoglio lamented that contact with (and conquest of) nature had nurtured a uniquely reprehensible American character and concluded that the process had "destroyed in one century the work of fifteen."[16]

As Scarfoglio raced further west, his jeremiad on the decline of culture in America became even more vitriolic. "The American, as a rule," he ventured from Omaha, Nebraska, while his crew "yawned with ennui and

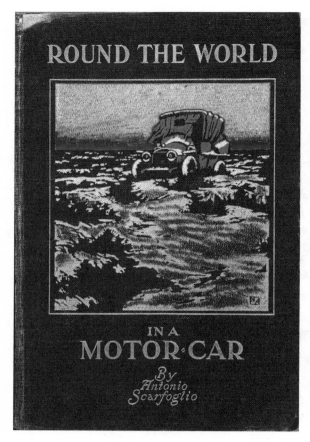

Figure 41. Cover of
*Round the World in a
Motor-Car.* Courtesy
of the Rare Book
Collection, Huntington
Library.

dejection" waiting for the rain to stop and the muddy road to harden up, "does not love the land; he does not care for the wealth which is acquired by slow, regular labor"; quite the opposite, Scarfoglio posited, "he is a man of adventure, a man of the sudden, of the unexpected. He is a gold-seeker to-day as he was a hundred years ago, and his joy is in the mine discovered by chance, conquered in a day, worked out in a month, exhausted in a year." Even worse, Scarfoglio suggested that the American's "well-being cannot be the fruit of labour; it must be the outcome of conquest and strife." The Italian race car driver–cum–cultural critic then concluded that "[t]he towns which [the American] constructs are encampments; the houses which he raises are inns; the family which he creates is a partner, a companion for life and for-tune."[17] The whole process of rapid settlement of the American continent unnerved and enraged him, not because of its consequences for indigenous peoples in the wake of westward expansion but because of that movement's impact on the core values he professed to revere: love of the land and of community, and of life lived at a pace at which it can be truly savored. It was in a sense ironic then that Scarfoglio's judgment on a whole nation and its culture was rendered without much reflection as he raced across its geography in pursuit of media glory and a cash prize.[18]

The fifty-two-day cross-continental journey only got worse with respect to Scarfoglio's assessments of America and Americans as he crossed the plains and the desert and raced through "the blinding sun, the sand, the infernal [Death V]alley," until he finally emerged in the Mediterranean climate of southern California—"Behold the Land of Promise!"—to once again "breathe the perfume of our own houses and our own country."[19] Scarfoglio's account, as we will see, echoed John Muir's and Rudyard Kipling's criticism of American tourists, which in turn was part of a long tradition, and expanded it to the American nation as a whole, particularly its mad rush toward materialism. If the frontier period had indeed come to a close, then Scarfoglio might have happily bid it good riddance, since its deleterious influence was keeping the nation in a state of cultural infancy as it raced forward (or backward) in a state of commercial overdrive. But then again, his unrelenting condemnation of the American character left no room for redemption, no possibility that the nation could overcome the legacy of its frontier past.

Scarfoglio's condemnation of America's frontier heritage, although marked more by vitriol than careful balance, might nonetheless be deemed quite prescient, at least in one regard: his idea that the process of frontier settlement had nurtured a lamentable process of cultural regression would be more famously expressed some years later by various American intellectuals, including Van Wyck Brooks in *America's Coming of Age* (1915), Waldo Frank in *Our America* (1919), and John Dewey in his essay "The American Intellectual Frontier" in the *New Republic* (1922).[20] Such criticisms were echoed in dramatic fashion a generation after Dewey by American expatriate writer Henry Miller, whose *The Air-Conditioned Nightmare* (1945) recounted his transcontinental automotive travels in his former homeland, which he observed was suffocating under the weight of consumerist excess: "Everything that was of beauty, significance or promise has been destroyed and buried in the avalanche of false progress."[21] Scarfoglio's condemnation of America, which appeared two generations before Miller's, while interesting (like Miller's) for its emphasis on what we might call the "acids of materialism," was in a way actually quite representative of the bulk of works in the western travel genre in the early twentieth century, which tended to focus on what Walter Lippmann labeled the "acids of modernity."

The Acids of Modernity

There were growing fears in the early twentieth century, particularly in the post–World War I years, that regional distinctiveness was dissipating in the face of the forces of modernization. Modernity, it seemed, was imposing a sterile American sameness on the landscape and the people living on it, dissolving the distinctive cultural traits that accompanied adherence to ethnic or religious traditions. In *A Preface to Morals* (1929), Lippmann lamented that "[t]he acids of modernity are so powerful that they do not tolerate a crystallization of ideas which will serve as a new orthodoxy into which men can retreat;" in short, those acids seemed to constitute a virus for which there was no antidote.[22] In searching for frontier distinctiveness in the West, the automotive travel writers of the teens and twenties were expressing their concern over the "acids of modernity" as they sought landscapes and peoples "untouched" by those forces and could imagine no road back to cultural purity and authenticity once the proverbial snake had entered the garden.

Of course, these chasers of the primitive performed their quest in a particular form of conveyance that was the very quintessence of modernity's arrival on the scene. While today's readers might find some irony in this aspect of their search, the automotive chroniclers of regional change and decline certainly did not. For those travel writers, the clearest sign that modernity was damning and dissolving the cultural distinctiveness of the nation's western peoples and places was not their own presence, borne by modern machines, but the presence of the tourist trade. It was, in their estimation, modern mass tourism that was responsible for all of the other visitors who were considerably less authentic travelers than themselves. The tourist-traveler dichotomy (discussed at greater length in the conclusion)—the juxtaposition of the former as unknowledgeable and inauthentic trespassers with the latter as well-informed and legitimate guides to people and places—remained at the very heart of the early-twentieth-century transcontinental automotive travel narrative genre, a full century after the emergence of the class prejudices that had created the dichotomy in the first place.

Writer and etiquette authority Emily Post's memorable 1916 book *By*

Figure 42. Photograph of the author, Emily Post, in her automobile in the Southwest,
from *By Motor to the Golden Gate* (1916).
Courtesy of the Rare Books Collection, Huntington Library.

Motor to the Golden Gate, although one of the earlier transcontinental auto-motive accounts (and journeys) by a woman and marked by considerably stronger prose than that of most driver chroniclers (female or male), was quite typical of the transcontinental auto traveler's search for remaining frontiers of western authenticity.[23] Post, who had already acquired extensive motoring experience in Europe, including a drive from the Baltic to the Adriatic in 1898 (a decade before the Great Race), traveled across the United States with her cousin Alice and her college-aged son Edwin.[24] The party left New York in April 1915 and arrived in San Francisco a month later. Ten days into the journey, when they reached Omaha, she wondered: "Where, Oh, where, is the West that Easterners dream of—the West of Bret Harte's stories, the West depicted in the moving pictures? Are the scenes no longer to be found except in the pages of a book, or on a cinematograph screen?" She then declared, and with no small disappointment: "We have gone half the distance across the continent and all this while we might be anywhere at home." The comforts and conveniences along the route—hotels, restaurants, and stores in modern downtowns—seemed so familiar that they amounted to a symbolic postponement of the real start of her adventure. Nearly 450 miles further west along the recently completed Lincoln Highway, in Cheyenne,

Wyoming, her search for the Old West was still unsuccessful. "If you think Cheyenne is a Buffalo Bill Wild West town, as we did," Post declared, "you will be much disappointed . . . the West of yesterday was no longer to be found in Cheyenne!"—except for one day a year during the "Frontier Days Celebration."[25]

A little further on, just west of Pueblo, Colorado, Post's party did finally encounter a few remnants of an earlier era—three "white-topped wagons," a lone "cowboy galloping over the plains swinging a lariat," "a herd of cattle driven by three cowboys." But by the time they reached Trinidad, modern-world realities reemerged in the form of "our first companion motor tourists." Another encounter with a quintessential western cowboy type near Las Vegas, New Mexico, confirmed for Post that "cow-punching was not what it used to be. Cattle were getting tame and the ranches were enclosed in wire fences and life was so soft and easy, that cattle raising was no more exciting than raising sheep."[26] She entitled the chapter "A Glimpse of the West that Was."

Emily Post did at first seem to find a world of difference in the Southwest and admonished herself for knowing the ancient wonders of the world, from the Pyramids to Pompeii, and yet not knowing those in this exotic corner of her own country. However, closer observation revealed a more sobering set of realities. The real thrust of Post's account was the theme of the passing of the primitive, consumed by the voracious appetite of tourists. She described the almost surreal experience of dining in the Santa Fe Railroad's Harvey Houses as a nonrailroad traveler. It was "very like being behind the scenes at a theater. The hotel people, curio-sellers, and Indians are the actors, the travelers on the incoming trains are the audience." Her small group became invisible as the staff and the Indians turned their attentions fully to the dining and purchasing passions of the latest group of disembarking passengers with no time to lose before they reboarded the train. After driving from Santa Fe to Albuquerque, Post described "another comedy" playing out at the railroad station. Ten minutes before the train was due to arrive, there was not an Indian in sight, but suddenly, "[o]ut of nowhere appear dozens of vividly costumed Navajos and Hopis . . . their headbands and beads and silver ornaments fill the platform with color like a flower display"; and when "the first passenger alights," the chorus "Tain cent! Tain cent!" begins.[27]

It was quite fitting that Post, toward the end of *By Motor to the Golden Gate*, recounted her visit to the Panama Pacific Exposition in San Francisco, during which she commented on "the lovely statues of [Solon] Borglum's

Figure 43. Emily Post, "The Indian Pueblo of Taos," *By Motor to the Golden Gate
(1916):* "To See the Sleeping Beauty of the Southwest."
Courtesy of the Rare Books Collection, Huntington Library.

'Pioneer' [and James Earle] Fraser's 'End of the Trail,'" the former depicting
an aged white pioneer on horseback with rifle and axe in hand and the latter
an equestrian Indian, body slouched forward, spear pointing down; both
have become iconic images of the passing of the Old West. For all the wonders of the Southwest and the rejuvenating "spirit-awakening" that Post
experienced in traversing the country, her account is marked more by her
realization that the frontier era, the great age of western and southwestern
distinctiveness, had passed away as the crush of commerce and modernity
arrived.[28] The sentiment was a common one in automotive travelogues of the
early twentieth century.[29]

Like Post, many travelers of the period at least began their journeys hoping to encounter the last vestiges of that passing age. Hugo Taussig, for example, expressed great disappointment in his 1910 account, *Retracing the
Pioneers: From East to West in an Automobile*, "that we met no Indians on
our way across the Continent, and that the country harbored no such people
as our interesting California '49'er, the ubiquity of the railroad having made
the entire people as one, and the numberless hotels mitigating against meeting with the old time hospitality of the farmer."[30] Taussig's account, despite

four-thousand-plus miles of generally unremarkable encounters, nonetheless reflects well the efforts of the authors of early-twentieth-century transcontinental auto narratives to unveil the final remnants of the old frontier, and their tendency toward dramatic pronouncements of its end and with it the passing of authentic westernness.

Winifred Hawkridge Dixon, who traversed the western United States a decade later with her friend Katherine in a Cadillac Eight (steadfastly avoiding overhyped California), felt she had found a glimpse of the disappearing frontier in Kayenta, Arizona, in the heart of Navajo country. Dixon recorded her impressions of the West in one of the most engaging of all the early-twentieth-century transcontinental travel accounts, *Westward Hoboes: Ups and Downs of Frontier Motoring* (1921). In a moment of global comparison not common to the travelogues of the early twentieth century (indeed, one reminiscent of Burton's observations during his trip across the western plains—see chapter 2 of this study), Dixon compared the Navajos on horseback to "the fierce Mongolian horsemen" of the "Thibetian plains," and Kayenta as "a gateway, like Thibet, to the Unknown." It is, she declared, "a frontier, perhaps the last real frontier in the States," where "[o]nly Piutes and Navajos brave the stupendous Beyond." But for the most part, what Dixon experienced amounted to just glimpses, fleeting moments when "all traces of civilization drop out of sight, and you are living the Day after Creation," amid the larger backdrop of how "Harveyized [i.e., commercialized] these picturesque creatures [Indian peoples] have become."[31] Nonetheless, it is important to note that in taking such automotive journeys, women travelers such as Dixon and Post were asserting a degree of independence from conventional norms that paralleled the efforts of Isabella Bird and other women travelers in the previous century.[32]

Soon after Dixon traversed the West and expressed her disappointment at the region's commercialization, an adventurous young Englishman found even less in the way of frontier remnants. In the wake of the Great War, veteran C. K. Shepherd wondered "what form of dissipation would be best suited to removing that haunting feeling of unrest, which as a result of three or four years of active service was so common among the youth of England at that time." He concluded that rather than plunging into marriage (a course of action far too fraught with danger in his estimation), a motorcycle trip across the United States was the answer. Shepherd was hardly the first to accomplish this feat. George Wyman made the 3,800-mile trip from New York City to San Francisco in fifty days in 1903, and the Van Buren sisters, Augusta and Adeline, became the first women to cross the country on motorcycles, covering 5,500 miles (of non-directly traversed terrain) from New York City to Los Angeles in just over two months in 1916. Shepherd does, however, seem to have been the first to publish a book-length account of such a trip, his fascinating *Across America by Motor-Cycle* (1922). Shepherd's westward solo adventure covered nearly 4,500 miles in three months, with about a month of that time actually on the bike, and a fair amount of time off it for the purposes of rest and recovery—he noted, "I was thrown off 142 times, and after that I stopped counting! Apart from that I had no trouble."[33] Shepherd did, however, have some difficulty addressing the great divide between his heady visions of the American western frontier and the less grandiose realities that he experienced. As he left Kansas City, Shepherd asked rhetorically, "Now, instead of the prosaic, the conventional and the luxurious, are we to find the unique, the heterodox and the primitive[?]" He continued, in rather effusive fashion:

> After the tainted breath of huge cities and the seething, crushing, maddening turmoil of wealth and modernism are to follow the pure unbounded atmosphere of the giant plains, the mystic call of the great mountains, the vastness, the fearfulness and the rapture of the scorching deserts. What shall it be for me?

The more somber reality, it turned out, was "500 miles of perfectly flat and uninteresting country," and then after entering Colorado, "another 200 equally flat, equally drear, to be crossed before the Rockies loomed into sight.[34]

Numbed by the topography of the plains—"[s]even hundred miles of endless weary prairie, stretching always, everywhere, as far as the eye can see"—much as Burton had been sixty years earlier—Shepherd was also a little chagrined by the pervasive presence of modern conveniences even in the West's seemingly most remote frontier locations. He bemoaned the fact that he had not seen a single "petrol tin" anywhere on his travels, noting that even in the remotest parts of New Mexico, Arizona, Nevada, and California, "even in the terrible 'Death Valley'" and in the Mohave, gas stations could be found, and carrying extra supplies was not necessary.[35] To not be burdened with the responsibility of carrying extra fuel and other supplies amounted, in Shepherd's estimation, to being robbed of the possibility of encountering true adventure on his travels.

Shepherd lamented, too, that the Indians of the Southwest did not live up to the expectations nurtured by popular stereotypes: "He that goes to the

Figure 44. C. K. Shepherd,
Across America by Motor-Cycle
(1922), "Portrait of the Author."
Courtesy of the Rare Book
Collection, Huntington Library.

West and expects to see the landscape decorated with Indians dressed in multicolored garbs of picturesque pattern," the increasingly disillusioned motorcyclist wrote, "is doomed to disappointment." Lingering memories from "childhood's days," Shepherd continued, "when one read with ceaseless delight of stalwart Indians with huge muscles and painted bodies galloping along, bow and arrow in hand, on a fiery white mustang in pursuit of an unfortunate 'pale face,'" failed to find an echo in contemporary reality, or at least the reality of his own ethnocentric vision. In his less than empathetic judgment, the Indian peoples of the region, "having had the gentle arts of civilization thrust upon [them], and being naturally of a lazy disposition, [were] content to loaf around chewing shag and disfiguring the landscape with [their] presence." Moreover, Shepherd ventured: "all are agreed that the Indian of to-day is in a far lower stage of civilization than when the early settlers first drove him from his rightful property."[36]

Shepherd's particular mode of transportation for a cross-country trip was fairly unusual for the time, and as a consequence his levels of privation and inconvenience exceeded those of most transcontinental automobile travelers in the period.[37] But his motivations and observations were not dissimilar from those of other motorists, whether foreigners or Americans, in the early twentieth century. Shepherd was searching for the kind of distinctive American frontier westernness that had been marketed to Americans and Europeans for more than a century (concurrent with nineteenth-century travel writers' tendency toward envisioning a global West), and which found its quintessence in notions of the noble vanishing Indian, suspended in Old West time. The actual indigenous peoples of the Southwest and other western American regions of course failed, in the eyes of many travelers and travel writers, to live up to those imaginings, and their ostensible inauthenticity as "Indians" seemed to confirm that there was no longer a frontier.[38]

Of Tourists and Travel Writers

Confirmation of the frontier's absence could, in the blinkered vision of the supercilious travel writer, be found also in the very presence of tourists. In this vein, the American Frank Trego began his automotive narrative *Boulevarded Old Trails in the Great Southwest* (1929) with the observation that "[t]he romance of the Old [Santa Fe] Trail is past . . . the vast herds of buffalo . . . the hordes of Indians which infested the Plains and the great prairies, devoid of civilization, have all passed into the mists of antiquity." At the Isleta Pueblo, near Albuquerque, Trego was "overjoyed" that "[a] little Indian boy danced for me," and he proceeded to take pictures of the Indian residents who "seemed pleased to pose before the camera." A brief amateur anthropological analysis of the clan structure of the pueblo led him to the conclusion that these were "the best governed communities in North America." All boded well, then, the reader might imagine, for a fuller discussion by Trego of the far from anomalous place of these communities in modern America, a kind of counternarrative to the vanishing American discourse so prevalent in the 1920s (and for generations previous), an examination of modern Indians adapting to a postfrontier nation, and that nation and its other residents coming to terms with the continued presence of native peoples.[39] But conventional wisdom (blinkered as it was) trumped the promise of originality, and Trego resorted to the standard narrative wherein the last authentic holdouts of indigenous culture come under threat from modernity and all its accompanying discontents.

"Tourists," Trego proclaimed, and with all the self-obsessed conviction of a British aristocrat from the mid-nineteenth century, "have invaded the

Indian country of the *Southwest*." "Over roads once traveled by the conquis-
tadores," he angrily declared, "the sight-seeing buses now 'honk' their way;
and into even the remote fastnesses of the pueblos penetrate these curious
'city-folk.'"Adopting the by then well-established (and well-worn) trope of
exasperated irony to convey the tourists' uninformed expectations, their
appetite for the "wild," the "outlandish," and the "uninhabited," Trego mused
that "what mark the ever-increasing hordes of tourists will leave upon these
Original Americans with their ancient and strange customs, is impossible to
estimate at this time." The older Indians, Trego explained, "eye [the tourists]
from a distance, shake their heads, and turn their backs upon the cameras
pointed in their direction." However, "the younger generation," he added,
"soon took advantage of this condition and may be found putting on the
desired 'side-shows' and displaying all sorts of hastily made pottery and
blankets (woven in Connecticut)" for purchase by eastern tourists "who
know little about their own country west of the Mississippi River."[40]

Trego presented readers with four basic types that emerged in two
dualistic pairings: the traveler and the tourist, and old authentic Indians
and young inauthentic Indians. Trego, in the role of the informed travel
writer, created space between himself and the uninformed and uninspired
tourists, who were the primary target of his ire. Meanwhile, he explained,
older generations of indigenous residents exhibited a wise resistance to
change and to the shallow acquisitiveness of tourists, while their own progeny—younger generations of Indians—exhibited the same undignified
characteristics of crass materialism as the tourists, "commercializing their
arts, their customs and their ceremonies" to meet visitor demand. Trego
further regretted that "[t]he dignity, the reverence for ancient ceremony,
the skill and patience in their arts, are rapidly being pushed aside for the
gathering of the dollar." But the real loss, it turned out, was a personal one
for Trego and other self-described actual travelers who presumed to truly
understand and appreciate indigenous culture. He emphasized the "sadness" that overcame people like himself who properly appreciated the
authenticity of elderly Indians. He described such enlightened observers as
"the lover[s] of the remarkable history and romance of these [old] people,"
who in turn were still "living to-day practically as they were long before the
discovery of America by Columbus, and perhaps almost like this when the
kings of Egypt were in the height of their glory." But Trego did not blame
the younger generations of Indians for their descent from the cultural high
ground of their forbears; rather, it was "the wealthy tourists [who] scatter

money among them with a free hand" who bore responsibility for the new conditions that he abhorred.[41]

That Trego, not unlike the commodifying tourists he disparaged and dismissed, had paid to take pictures of the Isleta Indians (and proudly said as much in the account) does not seem to have struck him as unusual or hypocritical; as a true traveler, he could presumably experience such commercial transactions on a higher, more spiritual plane than other visitors. Most significantly, though, *Boulevarded Old Trails*, while presented as a guidebook for fellow travelers, served more as a eulogy for the frontier, with all its indigenous cultural authenticity, that was being squashed out of existence by the weight of touristic commerce. In 1926, three years before his travelogue appeared, the Atchison, Topeka and Santa Fe Railroad had introduced its "Indian Detour," which afforded travelers on transcontinental trains the opportunity to disembark and take a three-day auto tour "through the storied heart of the Indo-Spanish Southwest." Taos, Santa Fe, Santo Domingo (Kewa) Pueblo, Bandelier National Monument, Carlsbad Caverns, Rainbow Bridge and Monument Valley, Canyon de Chelly, and the Hopi Snake Dance were among the treasured sites and attractions now easily accessible to wealthy tourists in the Fred Harvey Company's Packard Eight touring cars.[42] In fact, the railroad and the Harvey Company had been selling the Southwest to the American public since the 1890s.[43]

Trego's frustration at the arrival of the touristic hordes (as he described them) in the Southwest certainly echoed (as we will see) the dismissive superciliousness of the British upper class a century earlier toward the first mass market tourists. His antitourist ire was also thoroughly unoriginal in its own day, reflecting a then increasingly common strain in Anglo-American thought. Aldous Huxley had expressed this trend quite memorably in his 1925 collection of essays on travel, *Along the Road*. The book's opening piece, titled "Why Not Stay at Home?," had painted tourists as "a very gloomy-looking tribe" who did not actually enjoy traveling but felt compelled to engage in the practice "out of a kind of snobbery." Huxley explained that "[t]o justify this snobbery a series of myths has gradually been elaborated" and proclaimed that "[f]ew things are more pathetic than the spectacle of inexperienced travelers, brought up on these myths, desperately doing their best to make external reality square with fable." Huxley was pointing to travel as a kind of conspicuous consumption on the part of people who "travel, not for travelling's sake, but for convention's."[44] This was a theme that Huxley would take to its farthest extreme in his famous anti-utopian novel *Brave New World* (1932), which featured tourism at a New

Mexico Indian pueblo, where savagery was openly on display, as a periodic palliative to offset the limitations of life in the strictly governed World State.[45] For its part, Trego's *Boulevarded Old Trails* not only fed into the popular practice of tourist disparagement but actually contributed in some way to the very process of tourism expansion, much as the promotional literature of national parks of that period (and later ones) helped to attract the visitors whose presence in turn placed such a strain on park ecologies.[46]

Trego's core message to readers of the "true traveler" variety was that they should attempt to see these southwestern places, and particularly their Indian residents, before the forces of modernity, manifested in the arrival of tourists, changed all of them forever. He presumed, like so many travel writers and other observers of his day and since, that the indigenous cultures of the Southwest had been unchanging, and thus culturally pure and authentic, prior to the advent of tourism. In doing so, Trego perpetuated a set of stereotypes of the antimodern Indian in the modern world that were no less unrealistic than those that some mass tourists might have adhered to. As historian Philip Deloria notes, according to such sensibilities, "imagined Indians had to be protected from the contamination of the modern." Moreover, as Deloria explains, such acts of "[i]magining Indians as technological primitives empowered an equal and opposite reaction—a celebration of the mechanical advantages of a distinct white modernity."[47] Moreover, such implicit celebrations of cultural superiority could be articulated concurrent with lamentations over the impact of the acids of modernity on indigenousness. More than a decade earlier, Emily Post had concluded that the changes Trego bemoaned had already been effected. Katharine Fullerton Gerould, in her popular account of the postfrontier West, *The Aristocratic West* (1925), offered the same opinion. Gerould suggested that there had been a "chance of preserving [the Pueblo Indian's] semi-civilization unimpaired, of co-existing with him in a dignified manner. [But t]hen came the tourist, who always ruins an alien peasantry." The Pueblo Indians had "learned to sell their wares . . . and learned . . . to beg," and their pride and their art had henceforth been "subtly corroded by the traveller."[48]

Hoffman Birney, in *Roads to Roam*, his account of a car journey in 1928 through seven western states, was similarly convinced that the age of authentic travel in the Southwest had long since passed. He complained that "the Pueblo Indians of New Mexico are woefully over-civilized and commercialized" thanks to the Harveycars that introduced them to the "great and gullible" American tourists. Birney bemoaned the new realities of this touristic exchange whereby visitors' requests for photographs met with the Indians' expressions of concern over the loss of their souls, but then "American money makes [the Indian] a heterodox agnostic that delights in posing before clicking shutters." He added facetiously that "the cost of making the noble red man see the light of progress varies."[49] Gerould commented, too, on "the Indian who will not let himself be photographed except at an exorbitant price," but (like Trego) took some comfort in the presence of a few "older inhabitants of Laguna pueblo" who had managed to retain their "uncompromising but quite unaffected Indianness."[50] The presence, or presumed discovery, of such final remnants of indigenous authenticity amid so much degeneracy was momentarily uplifting for Gerould, but the persistence of real Indianness only among the aged in a sense merely confirmed for readers the fate of the Pueblo Indians as victims of the acids of modernity.

Not every automobile-bound traveler of the period failed to appreciate the rich regional culture of the Southwest by virtue of participating so readily in the antimodernist fashion of bemoaning its demise. Indeed, some of the writers more instrumental to the development of an antimodernist outlook in America, including Mary Austin and D. H. Lawrence, offered travelogues that underscored the vitality of the Southwest's landscapes and Indian peoples. Austin, in *The Land of Journey's Ending* (1924), a work that drew on her experiences in the course of a 2,500-mile road trip across the desert Southwest, ventured that the land "[b]etween the Rio Colorado and the upper course of the Rio Grande" would in fact become home to America's greatest cultural achievements in the future, rather than a mere touristic playground for experiencing the shadows of its primitive past.[51] She urged her readers to go to the Southwest to experience "the inspiriting stir of native rhythms," to sense "Art Becoming," to witness the "ultimate American expression in dance and drama," and to feel "the beat of the pulse of race-beginning." These were the things "you cannot afford to miss," Austin implored; and she insisted that this was so because those things were so essential, so powerful, and not because they were passing away.[52]

Lawrence, who at the invitation and partial sponsorship of Mabel Dodge Luhan had visited Taos Pueblo in 1923 and 1924, never achieved the kind of stirringly and unerringly positive vision of the Indian Southwest that Austin did and that Dodge Luhan had hoped he would.[53] Nonetheless, there are moments in his collection *Mornings in Mexico* (1927) of keen perception and reflection that celebrate the vibrancy of southwestern Indian cultures, regardless of the presence of tourists.[54] His essay "Indians and Entertainment," for example, ends with what Lawrence ventured was the only positive Indian commandment, "Thou shalt acknowledge the wonder." (The only negative Indian commandments that Lawrence surmised were: "Thou shalt not lie" and "Thou shalt not be a coward.")[55] Lawrence certainly acknowledged the wonder in his own writings on the Southwest, and in doing so prompted his readers to do the same.

Austin and Lawrence, in large part because they were better observers of the world around them than most of their travel writing peers, paid more attention to what was still there in the Southwest than to what had presumably passed. Yet, for all of the sense of wonder they both still found, they were unmistakably part of the antimodernist anxiety about the indigenous future. Lawrence, for example, after providing a breathtaking description of an Indian track race in "Indians and Entertainment"—"they are putting forth all their might, all their strength, in a tension that is half anguish, half ecstasy, in the effort to gather into their souls the creative fire, the creative energy which shall carry their tribes through the year"—concluded, with considerably more eloquence than most others, but along essentially the same lines:

> But what is the good of talking about it all? The Indians are losing too, in the long race. They too prefer to sit passive at the moving pictures, now. Their form of entertainment is nearly finished. The dollar is blotting the mystery out for ever, from their race as from ours.[56]

The acids of materialism and modernity fueled the western travel writer's imagination from Antonio Scarfoglio's Great Race in 1908 to Lawrence's *Morning in Mexico* and the end of the twenties.

As the new decade dawned and the Depression began to unfold, Americans were still traveling around the country in large numbers, but more often than not as job seekers rather than mass tourists. Travel writers, like other observers of the nation in crisis, found more pressing concerns than the culturally deleterious impact of tourism to fuel their imaginations. Even in the darkest depths of the thirties, indeed, especially then, regions came to have profound meaning, and the search for distinctive western frontiers continued, with greater earnestness than was exhibited by most automotive chroniclers of the western scene in the twenties, and with considerably greater success. Indeed, it was a series of guides for travelers (as well as residents and general readers), commissioned and directed by the New Deal

government, that emphasized most memorably the varied regional characteristics that still marked the United States.

Furthermore, and despite the massive transformation in the nation's
transportation infrastructure since the beginning of the twentieth century,
along with the greater durability of the vehicles themselves, the "frontiering"
strain in American automotive travel writing has long endured (see the conclusion). Even in much later road books such as Jack Kerouac's *On the Road*
(1957), John Steinbeck's *Travels with Charley* (1962), William Least Heat-
Moon's *Blue Highways* (1982), and Dayton Duncan's *Miles from Nowhere*
(1993) (which explores those counties in the West with a population of less
than two persons per square mile), we find the persistence of a kind of topographical nostalgia manifested through the search for remaining vestiges of
the frontier and last examples of presumed regional authenticity.[57] So, from
the announcement of modernity's end of the frontier to the postmodern
present, we see the search, sometimes sincere, sometimes not, for a distinctive American West, for last American frontiers, last authentic places, last
most dangerous places that might serve as proving grounds for latter-day
Jack Londons and Theodore Roosevelts seeking to resurrect the past, or as
measures of the perceived shortcomings of contemporary society.

CHAPTER FIVE

REDISCOVERING THE WEST

Regional Guides in the Depression Years

As far as the eye could see there was not a tree, or a blade of grass, or a fence, or a field; not a flower or a stalk of corn, or a dog or a cow, or a human being—nothing at all but gray raw earth and a few far houses and barns, sticking up like white cattle skeletons on the desert.

—Ernie Pyle in western Kansas (mid-1930s)

Here in this Western American wilderness, the new man, the man of the future, has done something, and what he has done takes your breath away. . . . Here is the soul of America under socialism.

—J. B. Priestley at the Hoover Dam, in *Midnight on the Desert* (1937)

If hunger and hardships and uncertainty are the essences of the pioneer tradition . . . these latter-day American pioneers may strengthen that cohesion and make their own distinctive contribution to the state.

—*WPA Guide to Oregon* (1940), on the northern plains dust bowl migration to the Pacific Northwest

The Promise of the West

In 1935, the same year the Works Progress Administration (WPA) and the Federal Writers' Project (FWP) were established, newspaper columnist Ernie Pyle began crisscrossing America with his wife Jerry ("That Girl," as he affectionately called her), taking the pulse of the nation and reporting his findings in daily columns in the Washington *Daily News* (and

Figure 45. Ernie and Jerry Pyle, ca. mid-1930s. Courtesy of the Indiana State Museum and Historic Sites.

subsequently in other Scripps-Howard newspapers). His journeys between 1935 and 1940 resulted in the composition of a million and a half words, a remarkable chronicle of the nation struggling with the Depression and one that made him a household name before he went on to even greater fame as a World War II correspondent. Pyle, as much as any writer in the period, was the voice of American democracy. In the same year that he set out, the British writer J. B. Priestley undertook a winter's-long journey around the Southwest, publishing his observations in *Midnight on the Desert* (1937). Priestley, for his part, was the voice of British social reform. His previous travelogue, the influential *English Journey* (1934), explored the economic problems in his home country and appealed for socially progressive policies to alleviate the hardships of the working class. The book perhaps even helped pave the way for the Labour Party's electoral victory in 1945.[1] Priestley's western American travelogue went so far as to present parts of the New Deal reforms being implemented in the West as a model for Britain's (and more broadly for Europe's) socioeconomic policies.

Pyle and Priestley might be considered precursors of sorts of the FWP American Guide Series, a set of book-length guides to each state as well as

Figure 46. J. B. Priestley in
Wickenburg, Arizona, ca. 1936.
Courtesy of Special Collections,
University of Bradford.

books and pamphlets on various American cities and towns and even
routes, such as *U.S. One: Maine to Florida* (1938) and *The Oregon Trail*
(1939).[2] Both writers found and emphasized the kinds of place-centered
distinctiveness that would characterize the American Guides. An American
and an Englishman exploring the country at the same time, they both discovered in their separate journeys a remarkable tapestry of regional characteristics; for both of them, the West was still very much alive and
culturally vibrant in the Depression years. That place-centered vitality was
manifested most clearly for Pyle in the presence of unmistakably western
characters such as Josie Pearl, whose cabin could be found off the beaten
path and "amidst the knee-high sagebrush" thirty-five miles from
Winnemucca, Nevada. "Josie Pearl," he wrote, "was a woman of the West"
who wore "a farmer's straw hat . . . mismatched men's shoes, and . . . six
thousand dollars' worth of diamonds"; she was "a sort of Tugboat Annie of
the desert." A gold prospector since the age of nine and a miners' boardinghouse operator at various times, "playing a man's part in a man's game,"
she was an exemplar of "the Old West—one day worth one hundred thousand dollars, and the next day flat broke."[3] Virginia City, Nevada, resident

Jimmy Stoddard was another such quintessential old westerner and "the Comstock's only living bridge between the distant past and the present."[4] Stoddard had arrived in the town as a thirteen-year-old in 1864, the year after Samuel Clemens, then a local reporter for the *Territorial Enterprise*, had coined his pen name Mark Twain, and five years after the Comstock Lode silver rush had begun. Stoddard had worked in the mines from his arrival in town until the age of seventy-one, fifty-eight years of labor, and was still prospecting around in the hills in the mid-1930s at the age of eighty-four when Pyle interviewed him.

In late 1937, the Pyles sailed to the Hawaiian Islands, and during the visit Ernie spent four days at the leper colony of Kalaupapa on the island of Molokai, which resulted in a thoroughly engaging and endearing sketch of life there, much in the tradition of Robert Louis Stevenson's and Jack London's sympathetic writings about the place and its patients. Pyle wrote to a friend of his time there: "Of all the places I've ever been, Kalaupapa to me is the most powerful and dramatic experience."[5] From the island where lepers went to die, Ernie and Jerry headed to Hollywood, where expectant stars go to be born, and interviewed two of the giants of the film industry, Walt Disney and Gene Autry.[6] Next, they headed northeast to the southern edge of Death Valley, where Mrs. Ira Sweetman and her cousin, Adrian Egbert, both in their mid- to late sixties, lived in a three-room cottage connected to a series of caves that Egbert, a former mining engineer, had drilled and blasted for habitation. Sweetman had lived in South Dakota's Black Hills and still owned stock in a mine in that state, had been active in politics in South Dakota and Arizona, and had been a postmistress in California. She occasionally drove to Los Angeles to a banquet of the Black Hills Pioneer Society: "I never knew I was a pioneer till they started making me over a few years ago," she told the Pyles. The couple had resided at Death Valley since the mid-1920s, when a doctor had prescribed a desert climate to alleviate Sweetman's influenza (first contracted in 1918, during the Spanish influenza pandemic). After constant driving and hauling of lumber and other materials in his Ford Model T during the early years of cave and cottage construction, Mr. Egbert had settled into a more sedentary retirement, but Sweetman was certainly no hermit. She drove sixty miles to and from Barstow once a week for the mail, a hundred and fifty miles to San Bernardino for supplies every other week, and to Los Angeles on occasion, and she was about to leave for a three-month Central American cruise.[7]

All across the West and America, Ernie Pyle managed to paint the landscapes of other peoples' lives in a few captivating pages, and sometimes just the landscapes themselves: "Western Kansas, in the middle 1930's, was the saddest land I had ever seen. . . . You might honestly say there was nothing left. . . . As far as the eye could see there was not a tree, or a blade of grass, or a fence, or a field; not a flower or a stalk of corn, or a dog or a cow, or a human being—nothing at all but gray raw earth and a few far houses and barns, sticking up like white cattle skeletons on the desert."[8] Pyle in a sense returned to the Depression as he and Jerry drove east into western Kansas. Evidence of the economic downturn had not been entirely absent from his reportage on the far western states, but the remarkable cast of western characters he encountered made it a faint backdrop. Likewise, for Priestley in *Midnight on the Desert*, the Depression was also very much present in the background, but it was the grand landscapes of the region and the Roosevelt administration's response to the economic crisis that took center stage.

Priestley knew the face of a society in economic despair; his *English Journey* was arguably the most harrowing depiction of British working-class suffering since Jack London's *The People of the Abyss* (1903). Priestley was not so blinded by the mythology of the Old West that he failed to see abject poverty in Arizona and other parts of the desert Southwest. Yet he found in the western cowboy a "figure who seems to have escaped the economic slavery and universal degradation of our time," one who seemed to offer others a strangely amorphous and indefinable respite from the economic depredations that surrounded them. Priestley was careful to explain both the power of western mythology and the severity of the backlash against it, particularly its emphasis on unbridled individualism, in the Depression years, when a more cooperative ethos seemed more appropriate. He recognized that "the cowboy and his West, the whole sunlit legend, have been cynically distilled into what the more impatient and austere critics of our society call 'dope.'" He explained that for such cynics "the heroic free man [the cowboy] . . . has been used to stupefy the enslaved masses." But Priestley suggested that the cynics had missed the point and that even in a promised future society where industrial labor was meaningful and appropriately rewarded, "some wistfulness" for the cowboy "would remain."[9] This was partly because the cowboy occupied a land of abundant space. For Priestley, the wide-open spaces of the West were its greatest distinguishing feature: "Anybody who is under the impression that the world is becoming too crowded should move into Nevada," he wrote, adding that "[i]f the whole of Great Britain were inhabited by the people of Oxford, there would still be more folk about than there are in Nevada."[10] The real contrast for Priestley of course was not between comparatively idyllic and uncrowded places such as Oxford and the West's wide-open spaces, but between the latter and England's cramped, damp, polluted, and impoverished industrial cities.

But Priestley discovered something even more deeply uplifting in the West than its vastness and emptiness. At Boulder (now Hoover) Dam, he found what he hoped might be the future of modern life. "Here in this Western American Wilderness," he wrote, "the new man, the man of the future, has done something, and what he has done takes your breath away." Compared with the dam, Priestley declared, "the recent skyscrapers seem like toys. The shining towers of New York merely express the new man in his initial playful mood. With Boulder Dam he has really set to work. This is what he can do when given a real job." For Priestley, the dam offered "a first glimpse of what chemistry and mathematics and engineering and large-scale organization can accomplish when collective planning unites and inspires them." "Here," he earnestly proclaimed, "is the soul of America under socialism. This is the reply to the old heedless, wasteful individualism." To Priestley, the dam symbolized "the new man, a new world, a new way of life," and marked America's passage from "the adolescent frolics of individualism" to the "sober adult task of cooperation."[11]

Priestley was similarly awestruck by the wonder of western American geological formations unaltered by human hands. His description of the Grand Canyon is one of the most memorable of all writers' efforts to capture the grandeur of the place: "We seemed to be witnessing, within a few hours, all the mad prodigality of Nature. One stupendous effect was piled on another; veils of mist and broken rainbows were caught in forests hanging in midair . . . to one hand, across the gulf, was a vertical Egypt, and to the other a perpendicular Assyria." Priestley noted that he had "heard rumors of visitors who were disappointed," concluding that these "same people will be disappointed at the Day of Judgment," and described the canyon as "a revelation." So profoundly moved by what he saw, Priestly wrote, "[i]f I were an American, I should make my remembrance of it the final test of men, art, and policies. I should ask myself: Is this good enough to exist in the same country as the Canyon?" Priestley went further still in his description, adding a sacred dimension: "I felt wonder and awe, but at the heart of them a deep rich happiness. I had seen His handiwork, and I rejoiced."[12]

A few hours' drive from the canyon, in Sedona, Arizona, Priestley found "within a morning's walk . . . all the climates worth having, with the Highlands of Scotland and Canada within waving distance of Africa and Australia . . . a charm as deeply romantic as that of any South Sea islands I have seen. . . . Here was the perfect haven." Priestley's impression was confirmed when he encountered a Civilian Conservation Corps camp and the "fortunate young men" whom it housed. "[T]hey had some decent work to do for the good of their community, and they were being reasonably well sheltered and fed and paid in one of the most enchanting places on earth." He contrasted these "brown, husky lads" in the employ of the CCC with the "unemployed English youths who stand outside our labor exchanges and slushy street corners, just miserably kept alive by the dole," and concluded, "I could not see that we could teach the Americans much about social services."[13]

Portrait of a Nation and a Region

During the 1932 campaign, Franklin D. Roosevelt had highlighted the role the federal government would have to play in providing a safety net to replace the safety valve of the western frontier, thereby ensuring "everyone an avenue to possess himself of a portion of that plenty sufficient for his needs, through his own work." Other key New Dealers such as Rexford G. Tugwell and Henry A. Wallace had made the same kinds of arguments for enlightened government as a substitute for the "free lands" of the frontier, and a few years later, with the New Deal programs in full operation, Priestley commented glowingly on the presence of that safety net of American government-created and administered jobs.[14] The Federal Arts Projects—Writers', Music, Theater, and Art—were administered under the Works Progress Administration (WPA; created in 1935 and renamed the Work Projects Administration in 1939) and were among the most innovative of the New Deal social programs. While the Music Project promoted the remarkable diversity of musical forms across the nation—from folk music and Negro choirs to Mexican *orquestas típicas* as well as traditional symphonic arrangements—and the Art Project highlighted the regional richness and variety of art forms, the Federal Writers' Project (FWP) produced approximately four hundred books and an additional six hundred pamphlets, amounting to literally tens of thousands of pages of striking confirmation of the regional richness of the nation.[15] The FWP achieved what Harry Hopkins, director of the WPA, described in 1938 as its "ambitious objective of presenting to the American people a portrait of America, its history, folklore, scenery, cultural backgrounds, social and economic trends, and racial factors."[16]

Part of the larger American Guide Series, the FWP's western state guides, like the guides to the states in other regions, were being compiled by the mid-1930s and began to appear in the latter part of that decade; all of the state guides were in print by the early 1940s.[17] The individually authored automotive travel books (discussed in chapter 4), and the almost exclusively team-produced and federally overseen guidebooks, were quite different in their respective forms; the WPA guides, for example, lacked "the presence of a self-conscious narrator," one of the key elements of the travel book form. Nonetheless, the two sets of roadmaps to western lives and landscapes were marked by purposes that were often quite similar.[18] The automotive accounts and the state guides all sought to describe places and peoples to prospective visitors in a fashion markedly different from that of promotional writings and typical guidebooks. While they followed a government-prescribed format, the FWP state guides were anything but mere catalogs of what to do and see. They were rich cultural inventories of life as it was lived in each place, compiled by writers who traveled the roads and experienced firsthand the landscapes and people they described, as any self-respecting travel writer should do. Moreover, as architectural historian Gwendolyn Wright points out, the administrators in Washington, D.C., who oversaw the guides (as well as the writers themselves, it should be added) focused on "the problematic present of each state, as well as its illustrious past," and this probing and nonboosterish emphasis constituted "a revolution in the field of guidebooks."[19]

The commonly shared format ensured that each of the state guides was composed of three kinds of material: general background information, a section on cities and towns, and another, generally accounting for half or more of the volume's pages, devoted to tours through the state, designed for automotive travelers. The first section included chapters on the contemporary setting, the state's history, ethnic groups and folkways (distinctive cultural traditions), Indian history and Indian life (a subject that, not surprisingly, received its fullest coverage in the western state guides), agriculture, labor, industry and commerce, transportation, education and religion, the arts and architecture, and recreation and tourism. All of the guides were generously illustrated with photographs of scenic treasures, buildings and monuments, and residents at home, at work, and at play. All of the state projects provided employment for unemployed writers, who could be found in abundance in many states but were often a more precious commodity in the more sparsely populated and unmetropolitan western states such as North and South Dakota and Wyoming. But beyond those similarities, the state guides varied significantly in quality and emphasis.

The coverage of the guides provided here mimics their tours format and divides the seventeen western states and Alaska (there was no WPA guide to Hawaii) into four regions: the greater southwestern borderlands, extending from the California coast to the Texas-Louisiana border; the second tier of trans-Mississippi western states (the northern and southern plains) running from Oklahoma to North Dakota; the Rocky Mountain and Great Basin, or intermountain, West, stretching south from Montana to Colorado, west into Nevada and then north into Idaho; and the Pacific Northwest (of Oregon and Washington), and Alaska.[20] But for all of the significant regional differences all across the West, from the Pacific coast to the second tier of trans-Mississippi states, the guides generally emphasized the western frontier heritage and pioneering tradition. In that regard, they collectively amounted to a clear statement about where the West began and ended in the public consciousness and in the estimation of the guides' writers in the 1930s. Moreover, and not surprisingly, in their attention to such themes, they differed from the WPA guides to states in other regions of the country.

Indeed, most of the western guides, contrary to the Roosevelt administration's many public pronouncements concerning the passing of the frontier, actually devoted a good deal of space to highlighting those aspects of the frontier heritage that *had* survived into the present across the varied landscapes of the West. For the guidebook writers in some of the western states, the frontier spirit seemed very much alive; indeed, in several of the guides it seemed to be the very essence of the western character, even in the modern age of enlightened government intervention. In fact, in California, the guide's authors went so far as to advocate government action for the purpose of keeping alive the promise of the western frontier.

Tour 1: California Coast to the Lone Star State

(1940: CA 6,907,387; AZ 499,261; NM 531,818; TX 6,414,824; total 14,353,290).[21]
(2010: CA 37,253,956; AZ 6,392,017; NM 2,059,179; TX 25,145, 561; total 70,850,713).
(U.S. Census Bureau)

Figure 47. California: A Guide to the Golden State, 1939. Courtesy of Special Collections, University of Rochester Library.

The L-shaped region stretching from the California coast across Arizona and New Mexico to the east Texas line encompassed the whole of the U.S. border with Mexico, although the guides provided surprisingly little discussion of its significance or of migration back and forth across it. These four states, with a combined population of over fourteen million, also accounted for more than half the total population of the seventeen western states and Alaska, including a good portion of its Hispanic, Asian, and Native American residents. A journey from the far northwestern corner of California down through the state to San Diego and eastward to the Texas-Louisiana line covers over two thousand miles. With close to seventy-one million residents in 2010 (a nearly 500 percent increase over 1940), the region has been the fastest-growing part of the West and the nation (just edging out the intermountain West states) in the seven decades since the guides appeared.

The California guide (1939) began with an introductory essay titled "El Dorado Up to Date," which made a point of emphasizing that "[t]he days when the American people finally reached land's end on the Pacific are almost completely within the memory of living men." The year before the guide was published, John Steinbeck's short story "The Leader of the People" appeared in his collection *The Long Valley* (1938) and conveyed the poignant story of old Grandfather Tiflin, a pioneer who had led wagon trains across the old frontier and now bemoaned the end of the "westering" process, lamenting that "there is no place to go. . . . Every place is taken," sadly declaring that "westering has died out of the people."[22] The California guide did not fully share the fictional Tiflin's fatalism, not to mention that of his creator, Steinbeck, whose novel *The Grapes of Wrath*, which appeared the same year as the guidebook, powerfully highlighted contemporary California's failure to live up to its frontier promise. With an initially more positive tone, the guidebook proclaimed that "[t]he restlessness of the men who made the westward trek persists in the unquenchable wanderlust with which their descendants have taken to the automobile, thronging the highways with never-ending streams of traffic bound for seashore, deserts, forests and mountains." Unusual, one might think, to find the frontier spirit manifested in the presence of traffic. Still, the California guide went on to suggest that the "sturdy instinct for independence" that characterized the mining camps nearly a century before still inspired Californians to democratic action (a rather selective memorializing of the spirit of those camps to be sure), and concluded that the state's residents still perhaps hoped that "the stubborn search for better land that brought their grandfathers here to the shores of the Pacific has not spent itself . . . that they can yet make of El Dorado the promised land that fired men's imaginations for years."[23]

Further underscoring the significance and the endurance of the frontier spirit in the Golden State, the main text of the California guide opened with John Bidwell on the crest of the Sierra Nevada in 1841, leading the first white emigrant train to that promised land and looking back at "the dry wilderness of the Great Basin behind them" and westward "toward the Great Valley of California."[24] Such a triumphalist opening might suggest that the California guide would be an unambivalent chronicle of the blessings of white settlement, but this was certainly not the case. The volume charted indigenous population decline in California, placing the blame, much as Friedrich Gerstäcker had done nearly a century before in his *Narrative of a Journey Round the World* (1853), on disease, starvation, and the genocidal acts of white settlers and militias. The failures of federal Indian policy were also clearly highlighted, and in a critical tone reminiscent of Helen Hunt Jackson's *A Century of Dishonor*

(1881). But in addition to charting demographic decline—"For every seven or eight Indians living in California before the white man came to stay, only one remained 14 decades later. . . . a decline of about 90 percent"—the guide also pointed to the resurgence in the state's Indian population since 1910 (up from just over sixteen thousand to around twenty-four thousand). Moreover, the work emphasized the recent revival of Indian cultural ceremonies under the influence of the Bureau of Indian Affairs, but lamented that "this policy of encouragement has succeeded that of persecution too late to save more than a tiny remnant of Indian culture."[25]

A similarly realistic tone marked the California guide's coverage of the state's very recent history, which included discussion of Upton Sinclair's 1934 gubernatorial campaign and his EPIC platform (End Poverty in California: a production for use, not profit, system, which proposed to open up shuttered factories and farm fallow land to provide labor for all the state's unemployed people), Dr. Francis Townsend's pension initiative ($200 a month to those sixty and older), and Robert Noble's "Ham and Eggs" plan (to provide $25 per week to every unemployed man and woman over the age of fifty). That section of the guide concluded with an account of the arrival of hundreds of thousands of migrants from the southern plains. Their stories around the wayside campfires where they parked their "latter-day prairie schooners," the authors observed, "resembled not at all the stories of the earlier pioneers: 'the dust was drifted high as the window sills' . . . 'The cattle died a-lookin' at you' . . . 'Wouldn't a blade of grass grow anywhere in the valley.'" The California guide quoted the National Labor Relations Board's 1934 description of one of the districts where California's latest pioneer migrants were having to reside, amid "filth, squalor, an entire absence of sanitation, and a crowding of human beings into totally inadequate tents or crude structures built of boards, weeds, and anything that was found at hand to give a pitiful semblance of a home at its worst." The guide's authors then went on to describe the failure of workmen's compensation laws to protect these laborers, agribusiness's practice of ignoring minimum wage laws for women and minors, the denial of medical aid to desperately ill people, and the corrupt practices of labor contractors.[26]

The WPA Guide to California, in its treatment of California migrant labor, echoed Steinbeck's tone of condemnation of the state's failure to treat its migrant workers fairly, or even humanely, as expressed in *The Harvest Gypsies*, a series of newspaper articles he published in the leftist *San Francisco News* in 1936, as well as Carey McWilliams's lambasting of California agribusiness in *Factories in the Field* (1939).[27] Moreover, the guide, much in line with the postfrontier pronouncements of FDR and the New Dealers, arrived at the conclusion that "Californians could look forward neither to the opening up of new lands nor, probably, to the discovery of new resources." Like Steinbeck, the guide's authors advocated government intervention on the migrant workers' behalf and praised the sanitary camps that had been established across the state by the New Deal's Farm Security Administration (FSA).[28] The guide concluded that the state's future would be marked by "an intensive struggle to solve the social and economic problems which are the inevitable heritage of California's four centuries of development."[29] With its emphasis on the complicated and often lamentable history of California race relations and on the contemporary mistreatment of migrant worker families, the work was a far cry from the simple boosterism of previous guides to the state and its resources and one of the most compelling of the WPA guides.

The legacy of the Old West was also very much a feature of the Arizona guide (1940), although contemporary social and economic problems were not center stage as was the case in its more engaging California counterpart. The Arizona guide actually began with a hint of skepticism regarding the "'another-redskin-bit-the-dust' type of reminiscence" as well as the role of the annual pioneer reunion and the Arizona Historical Society (which evolved from the Society of Arizona Pioneers) in perpetuating pioneer memories that were "perhaps embellished" and that made up "a unique, if not altogether accurate chronicle" of the state's past. The guide also noted that the state "tries to live up to its cowland reputation for the benefit of tourists." But the work then hinted at an enduring aspect of the frontier democratic tendency to "judge every man by what he is and does, rather than by what he owns." Unfortunately, this advice was not followed terribly closely in the guide's coverage of the Mexican quarters of Arizona's towns—"squalid . . . but picturesque" and characterized by "[t]he drowsy plunk of a guitar"— which relegated a significant portion of the state's population to the category of mere adornment, "part of the exotic charm that is Arizona's." Its coverage of Arizona's Indian peoples was similarly uninspired and uncomplimentary—"[They] become natural to their surroundings only on the reservations . . . [and] wear a bastard dress half Indian and half western"—although the guide did acknowledge the role that Arizona's Anglo population had played in "undermining and destroy[ing]" Indian culture.[30]

Less attentive to the complexities of the state's past or present than the California guide, the Arizona guide was certainly more attuned to its cowboy culture and heritage. "The Sunburnt West of Yesterday" (the title of one of the guide's sections) received extensive coverage, and special attention was devoted to the cowboy and his saddle, with the reader learning that while a cowboy might part with "his boots, his bankroll, and even his best girl," no cowboy in an uninebriated state would part with his saddle; without it he was "but a man," yet "with it and his mount he is a veritable centaur."[31] Just a few generations removed from their pioneer past, Arizonans, the guide noted, were "remarkably aware of some aspects of their frontier heritage" and insisted that "[t]he drama of the pioneers is the classic saga of the state." The guide's descriptions of parts of the state, such as Globe ("its crooked Broad Street is crowded with cowboys, Apaches, and old prospectors with drooping mustaches and sharp faded eyes"), Prescott (with its Home for Arizona Pioneers and State Hospital for Disabled Miners, founded in 1909 and still in existence today), Phoenix, Tombstone, and State Route 95 from Quartzsite to Yuma, amounted to a grand tour through an old wild western heritage that seemed alive and well in the Arizonan present.[32]

The New Mexico guide (1940) did a markedly better job of illustrating the rich cultural landscape of that state. Indeed, the lengthy "Annual Calendar of Events" that opened the volume drew attention to the remarkable variety of Indian and Mexican festivals that crowded out the Anglo celebrations of Pioneer Days and Cowboy Reunions in every month except for July. The guide's coverage of New Mexico's tricultural heritage was sophisticated and deeply attentive to the state's regional heterogeneity. The work was overly dramatic at times, such as when it emphasized those differences: "Suddenly and without forewarning, from almost any point in the State, one may step from modern America into Old Spain, or into aboriginal Indian territory, within the space of a few miles." Nonetheless, the guide provided careful and extensive coverage of Mexican folk songs and religious dramas, and Indian dances and celebrations, making it clear that the fearful pronouncements of so many transcontinental automotive travel writers during the previous decades concerning the disappearance or impending death of authentic southwestern regional culture were largely unfounded. Moreover, the New Mexico guide presented the Anglo frontier heritage of cattle trails and Billy the Kid as a legacy that certainly "help[ed] to swell the volume of New Mexico folklore," but did not stand at its center.[33]

The same could not be said for the Texas guide (1940; supervised by the writer James Francis Davis), which, for all its occasional nods to the state's multicultural demography, was as clear a paean to the Anglo-pioneer past and its pervasive influence in the present as could be found in any of the western state guides. "The West of ranch and rodeo, big hats and handsome riding boots remains," the authors explained, "but it is not violently 'wild and woolly' as of old." However, they added that "the customs of the frontier have not fully vanished, even in the large cities," and went on to explain, rather proudly, that "the six-shooter still arbitrates many a dispute, urban as well as rural," adding that "juries are likely to be lenient as regards the resulting homicides if womenfolk are involved in the cause, if certain expletives are spoken unsmilingly, or if a self-defense plea seems to have justification."[34]

While the Lone Star State guide declared that "Texas folk cultures are generally expressing themselves in new forms instead of dying," it offered little evidence of vibrant folk cultures aside from those of Anglo and other whites. The reader learned that "[i]nnumerable feast days are observed by the Mexicans, with all the colorful pageantry that is part of the racial tradition," but those events received considerably less empathetic coverage than was the case in the California and New Mexico guides. In a similar vein, the reader was informed that "nature myths and proverbs" were common among "Texas Negroes," but also that "[t]his folk culture" was retreating in the face of economic and educational development, although "Negroes of the old plantation type," barefoot and superstitious, could still be found in parts of East Texas. What had endured, in the estimation of the guide's authors, was the spirit of white pioneer democracy, which "removed class barriers." And to that end, the volume declared: "A man's past mattered not in early Texas. What he was *did* matter." Extensive coverage of "typical social groups" such as the Pioneers' Association, the Old Trail Drivers' Association, and various old settlers' reunions, and of the prevalence of "[p]ioneer customs" in the Texas backcountry, drove home the point that the Old white West was very much alive in this state's present. The Texas guide emphasized the cattlemen's "chivalry, courage, and hospitality that remain as patterns for their descendants," the "hardy ranchers who dared to push their herds out into Indian country," and the "[w]olves and sandstorms, droughts and occasional Indian raids [as late as the 1870s] [that] failed to daunt the hardy few who, largely of Anglo-Saxon stock, ventured into this frontier."[35] At more than seven hundred pages, the Texas guide was, like California's, among the longest of the state guides; however, unlike its Golden State counterpart, it was a veritable catalogue of

Anglocentrism and Anglo-Saxonism, and of frontier-rooted state-level exceptionalism.

Tour 2: Southern Plains to the Northern Border

(1940: OK 2,336,434; KS 1,801,028; NE 1,315,854; SD 642,961; ND 641,935; total 6,738,212).
(2010: OK 3,751,351; KS 2,853,118; NE 1,826,341; SD 814,180; ND 672,591; total 9,917,581).
(U.S. Census Bureau)

Moving from the greater southwestern borderlands region north through the second tier of trans-Mississippi western states (from Oklahoma to the Dakotas, a distance of approximately thirteen hundred miles), a traveler in 1940 would have traversed the second most densely populated part of the

Figure 48. Nebraska: A Guide to the Cornhusker State, 1939. Courtesy of Special Collections, University of Rochester Library.

West, but one where population size dropped from state to state as one moved from the southern plains into the far northern plains. More significantly, the population of each of the five plains states had declined during the 1930s—collectively by around 300,000, and by approximately 60,000 in Oklahoma and Nebraska, 80,000 in Kansas, and 50,000 in North Dakota and South Dakota. These were the only five states in the nation to lose population during the 1930s. And because natural population growth (achieved through an excess of births over deaths) continued during the thirties at a healthy rate in all five states, the figures for population decline do not come close to matching the actual volume of emigration from each state. During the Depression decade, more than 269,000 residents (over 11 percent of the population) left Oklahoma, and more than 100,000 departed each of the other plains states (72,000 residents migrated from Texas).[36] The region then grew to nearly ten million people between 1940 and 2010, with Oklahoma's population increasing at a steady rate and that of the other four states somewhat less impressively; North Dakota hardly grew at all during those seven decades.[37] As a whole, these plains states have expanded at the slowest rate of all four western regions, and they currently constitute the least densely populated part of the West (with the exception of Alaska).[38]

The traveler with the WPA guides in hand would have seen a similar pattern in coverage to that of the southwestern guides, with all of the plains guides emphasizing the distinctive regional cultures within their respective states, but some doing a better job than others of highlighting cultural diversity. In this regard, the Oklahoma guide (1941) echoed the tone and coverage of the California and New Mexico guides more closely than it did the Arizona or Texas guides. The Oklahoma guide benefitted significantly from being directed by Angie Debo, the state's and probably the nation's leading scholar of American Indian history during that period.[39] The volume also bore the mark of historian Edward Everett Dale, who a generation earlier in a 1923 essay, "The Spirit of Soonerland," had offered no sugarcoating in his assessment of the realities of westward expansion, writing that "Anglo-Saxon greed and the lust for land drove the red man westward."[40]

In his essay in the guide, "The Spirit of Oklahoma," Dale emphasized Oklahoma's status as the "last frontier," one that "lies in a point of time very near to pioneer society." But he also offered a full accounting of the centrality of the state's Indian people not only to its past but to its present and future as well.[41] While Dale and other contributors to the guide made a point of noting that a significant number of the state's white residents could date their arrival to the land openings that began in 1889 and continued until right before the granting of statehood in 1907, they also emphasized that this pioneer tradition was no more significant than Oklahoma's Indian heritage.[42] This balancing act concerning competing cultural legacies was a delicate one, but the Oklahoma guide perhaps succeeded better in this regard than any of the other western state guides.

This balance was evident particularly in the tours section of the volume. The Oklahoma tours provided as much coverage of Pioneer Day celebrations and other manifestations of the enduring white frontier heritage as most other western guides, but considerably more detailed and informed treatments of Indian communities, tribal councils, and museums (such as those of Pawhuska, population 5,443) than was the norm. The tour along U.S. Route 70 from the Arkansas line to the Texas line, running north of the Red River (and largely unpaved prior to 1939), introduced readers (and travelers) to the Choctaw and Chickasaw communities as well as to the descendants of slaves freed from Indian masters during the Civil War, and to families of cotton pickers—"Indians, Negroes, and whites"—near Broken Arrow (population 2,367). The U.S. Route 69 tour, from the Kansas line to the Texas line, roughly paralleling the old Texas Road, was similarly effective at illuminating the interactions of Osage, Cherokee, Creek, Choctaw, Chickasaw, and Caddoe Indian cultures with white traders, trappers, emigrants, and settlers. This tour also included coverage of Washington Irving, whose travels to the region, recounted in his book *A Tour on the Prairies* (1835), included a visit to the area that later became the modestly named town of Okay, OK (population 322). Even in their description of the tour along U.S. Route 81 (Kansas to Texas) along the old Chisholm Trail, the guide writers resisted the temptation to devolve into romantic reveries about the cowboy heritage and the cattle drives and included careful treatment of Indian communities in the present and white-Indian conflict in the past. The tour along U.S. Route 283 (also Kansas to Texas), the guide noted in critical fashion, ran "near the timbered breaks of the Washita [River] where the massacre of Black Kettle's band in the dawn of a freezing winter day helped to establish the military glory of General Custer."[43] Passages such as this are indicative of Angie Debo's firm and knowledgeable hand throughout the Oklahoma guide.

The backdrop of the Great Depression was very much a part of the California guide, but if readers had traveled vicariously with the FWP western state guides, surveying their coverage of the economic hardship of the period, they would have found surprisingly little evidence of its presence as they moved in a generally eastward direction through the pages of the Arizona, New Mexico, and Texas guides. The same would have been the case for readers turning north into Oklahoma, whose state guide briefly acknowledged that the northwestern counties and the Panhandle had "become for a time part of the Dust Bowl," but did not dwell at length on the matter. The Oklahoma guide briefly charted the downturn in the value of agricultural lands during the 1930s and more generally acknowledged the "pinch of economic depression." But the authors added that these conditions brought "a feeling of pessimism and discouragement" only to a few people and explained that this limited impact was attributable largely to the "pioneer spirit, compounded of courage, optimism, and faith" that was "still strong among a people so close to the frontier of yesterday." The Oklahoma guide also surmised that while union organization had progressed in the state, such efforts had to "reckon with the essentially individualistic psychology of a state that is close in time to its pioneer period."[44]

The Kansas guide (1939) also provided quite strong coverage of the history of the region's Indian peoples, including the Kansa, Osage, and Pawnee, as well as the native nations that were moved into the region, including the Shawnee, Wyandot, and Delaware; but it did not integrate Indian history and culture into the tours section as effectively as the Oklahoma guide. The volume did, however, note in categorical fashion that Indians had been "repeatedly deceived by meaningless promises of the Government."[45] The Kansas guide was a little less insistent and effusive than its Oklahoma counterpart concerning the persistence of the pioneer spirit in the Sunflower State, and considerably more forthcoming with regard to the magnitude of the Depression. The authors stated that three quarters of the state's territory, roughly forty million acres, had "been damaged in varying degrees by erosion," and the productivity of the land across the state had as a result been significantly reduced. "By 1935," the volume noted, confirming the observations of Ernie Pyle, "almost nine million acres of once green farmlands [in western Kansas] had been scraped and gouged by wind erosion," and a Farm Security Administration photograph of farm buildings surrounded by a desert-like landscape accompanied the discussion. But the guide, like California's, also highlighted state and federal efforts to alleviate the agricultural depression and improve land quality, and concluded its coverage of conservation efforts by quoting a federal official who declared that "[h]armonious adjustment to the ways of nature in the Plains must take the place of attempts to 'conquer' her."[46]

In short, the Kansas guide was the very antithesis of state boosterism, noting, for example, and with unmitigated honesty, that while average rainfall across the state might have been twenty-six inches (comfortably above the twenty-inch minimum necessary to sustain traditional modes of agriculture), "it is very unevenly distributed." Furthermore, while the authors suggested that Kansas's reputation as a "tornado State" might be a little unfair since the frequency of tornadoes was no greater than in other plains states, the volume's discussion was accompanied by a reproduction of John Steuart Curry's famous 1929 painting *Tornado Over Kansas*.[47] Moreover, editor, author, and famous Progressive voice William Allen White, then in his mid-seventies, in his introductory essay in the guide entitled "Contemporary Scene," painted a picture of a state marked by a stark sectional divide between its eastern and western parts. He described eastern Kansas farmers as "thrifty, cautious, diligent descendants of the New England Puritan, physically and spiritually"; their western counterparts, on the other hand, were "gambler[s]" and "go-getter[s]." In the political arena, White insisted, the state's eastern and western parts "often find antagonistic interests, honest and deeply divisory differences," adding that "Western Kansas, in politics, is inclined to be clannish."[48] Later in the volume, in a section entitled "Journalism and Journalists," the guide highlighted several figures including White and declared that "[t]he indomitable spirit of the pioneer editor still prevails in Kansas journalism" and that the state's press was undaunted by "[r]ecent years of unprecedented drought and agricultural depression." White's short essay in the guide certainly demonstrated that over the course of more than four decades he had lost none of his earlier enthusiasm for charting "What's the Matter With Kansas."[49]

An automotive traveler in this period heading north from Kansas and across the state line with the accompaniment of the Nebraska guide (1939) would have found multiple echoes of its Kansas FWP counterpart, including very close attention to the severity of the Depression.[50] Indeed, the Nebraska guide was another thoroughly unboosterish work, presenting the place where "the Middle West merges with the West" in unerringly honest fashion as a hard land marked by harsh extremes of temperature, droughts, blizzards, and grasshopper plagues in the late nineteenth century and, in more recent years, continued droughts (in 1934 and 1936) and severe winters (1936), falling agricultural prices, rising farmer indebtedness, and the growth of farm tenancy and sharecropping. The guide also illuminated the severity of the economic downturn on the Great Plains in the 1920s; at the beginning of that decade, approximately 35,000 of the state's more than 124,000 farms were mortgaged (a little more than 30 percent), but by 1930 almost 100,000 of them (approximately 80 percent) were mortgaged and almost 50 percent were tenant managed, and the situation grew more desperate still during the thirties.[51]

Nonetheless, for all these acute hardships, there was an admirable endurance in the state's farm sector, which the guide also highlighted: "debt-ridden farmers seed their land again. It is this determination to remain on the land, this never-ending struggle of human strength and will against natural forces, that characterizes the Nebraska temperament." And that temperament, forged by the legacy of "the trials and triumphs of Nebraska pioneer life," it seemed was expressed most fully in the western Sandhills region of the state. The Nebraska Homestead Act of 1904 (the Kincaid Act) had expanded the allowable size of homesteading tracts from a quarter section to a full section (640 acres), prompting a new round of agrarian boosterism, captured in the effusive optimism of the "Kincaider's Song":

> The corn we raise is our delight,
> The melons, too, are out of sight.
> Potatoes grown are extra fine
> And can't be beat in any clime

But Sandhills residents, the guide noted, had "spared neither truth nor feelings" in their parodies of the song:

> I've reached the land of drought and heat,
> Where nothing grows for man to eat.
> For wind that blows with burning heat,
> Nebraska land is hard to beat.

The guide also reprinted the grim lines that had been carved into the door of a shack near the Sandhills town of Chadron in the 1890s and recorded by Mari Sandoz in her remarkable account of her father's tireless efforts to settle the region, *Old Jules* (1935):

> 30 miles to water
> 20 miles to wood
> 10 miles to hell
> And I gone there for good.[52]

However, the state's comparative lack of natural resources and good weather, not to mention its highlighted lack of architectural originality, were offset, the authors insisted, by this cultural storehouse of enduring pioneer spirit. Indeed, the work suggested a Nebraska regional identity forged through collective resilience and adversity. One suspects, though, that the various Indian peoples—including the Pawnee, Otoe, Omaha, Ponca, Cheyenne, Arapaho, and Sioux (Oglala and Brule)—who had contributed so vitally to the region's history and remained an important part of its cultural landscape, might have been better incorporated into the narrative (as they were in the Oklahoma guide, due to Angie Debo's influence) had Mari Sandoz been a formal contributor to the volume rather than just an informal adviser.[53]

The South Dakota WPA guide (one of the first to be published, in 1938) presented a state that had witnessed large-scale white settlement a generation later than its southern neighbors Nebraska and Kansas (not to mention much of the Far West), and thus, the authors suggested, "offers one of the few remaining opportunities to see frontier life." But the pattern of the guide was not dissimilar from those of its neighbor states, with its emphasis on the hardships endured by the "famous homesteading cavalcade of the eighties" (namely, drought and grasshoppers) and by contemporary South Dakotans (to wit, dust storms, drought, and the Depression), and on the lingering "spirit of the pioneers," which ensured that the state's hardy residents (from "back East" as well as from Germany, Sweden, and Norway) would endure. The guide's main distinction was a photo essay entitled "Pioneer Trails," which included the 1874 Custer wagon train, gold panning, a stagecoach, the Sioux Sun Dance, and Sioux "maidens."

When it came to direct references to the "pioneer character" of the state, the South Dakota guide may well have outdone all its western counterparts.[54] In keeping with the volume's opening portrait of the state's character, the cities and tours sections also played up South Dakota's "Wild West" heritage, with extensive coverage of Deadwood (population 3,362) and its famous "Days of '76" celebration, and of smaller communities such as Dupree (population 364), which had "lost little of its Western color"; Faith (population 564), "typically a town with western flavor, dominated by ranchers [and] cowboys and colored by a mixture of Indians who come from the nearby reservation to trade"; Buffalo Gap (population 150), which "has never quite lost the glamour of cowboy days"; Gregory (population 1,185), where "the frontier spirit of the West still dominates"; Winner (population 2,136), also "one of the most typically Western in color"; and Martin (population 942), the "metropolis of the Pine Ridge Reservation country," whose residents—"Indians, inter-spersed with cowboys, farmers, and white-collared men—make a composite picture that is truly Western and colorful."[55]

But while uncomplicated in its reverence for the state's pioneering heri-tage and authentic westernness, the South Dakota guide was considerably less clear in its coverage of the resident Sioux Indian population, a reflection per-haps of the varied perspectives of multiple contributing authors. For the most part, the work presented the state's Indian residents, such as those in the town of Martin, in rather innocuous fashion, as an essential element of its backdrop of Western color. But when it came to describing Indians in the present, the authors struggled at best, and periodically gave in to the prejudices common in the state and elsewhere. Readers would have learned that "[f]ew Indians on the Pine Ridge Reservation are successful farmers, virtually none of them producing enough from their tracts to support their families," but not about the wide range of factors contributing to the Sioux's failure or reluctance to embrace Euro-American agriculture, or the marginal nature of much of the land on the reservation. Coverage of the famous 1890 Wounded Knee battle-field site presented the Sioux's ancestors as victims and described the affair as "nothing short of a massacre in which non-combatants—squaws with infants on their backs, boys and girls, were pursued and relentlessly shot down by maddened soldiers long after resistance had ceased and nearly every warrior lay dead or dying on the field." But the guide's treatment of the tragedy also emphasized the famous Ghost Dance, referring to it disparagingly as "the Messiah craze, which for months had been deluding Indians and terrifying white residents," hardly the kind of language that nurtured empathy for the victims as thinking people.[56] In a sense, the South Dakota guide exemplified the difficulties that the authors of the western state guides faced in trying to weave the Native American past and present into the cultural fabric of the nation, although other state guides, such as New Mexico's and Oklahoma's, demonstrated that the enterprise could also be undertaken quite successfully.

Moving across the state line into North Dakota, the reader of the western state guides would have found no significant departures from the overriding theme of the presence of the pioneer heritage that characterized all the second tier of trans-Mississippi western states. Indeed, the authors of the North Dakota guide (1938) emphasized that in their state "[r]uts left by the wagon trains of early explorers, military expeditions, and home seekers have not yet been effaced from the prairies," and they titled a section of the history chapter of the volume "On the Frontier," covering the period from the first white colonization efforts to the surrender of Sitting Bull's forces in Canada, marking the end of the Indian Wars in 1881. Regarding North Dakota's people—"Norwegians, Germans, Russians, Poles, Czechs, Icelanders"—the authors emphasized that, through the trials and tribulations of settlement, they were all now "Americans"; a classic expression, and one echoed in many of the western state guides, of Frederick Jackson Turner's notion of the "formation of a composite nationality for the American people . . . [forged] [i]n the crucible of the frontier." Indeed, the North Dakota guide encapsulated the spirit of the state's residents, "still a new people—pioneers," in verse:

Brave spirits stirred with strange unrest
They found broad waters and new lands,
And carved the empires of the west.[57]

The reader would also have found that frontier spirit exemplified in a character whose legacy helped define the state's identity—the former Rough Rider, president, African big game hunter, and Amazon River expeditionary Theodore Roosevelt. Not surprisingly, Roosevelt, although he had graced the Dakota Territory with his presence for just a few years, received more coverage than any other person or place in the volume.[58] North Dakota's authentic frontier heritage was validated by the very presence of contemporary residents, "[r]ed men and white men," still alive to tell their tales of contact with Roosevelt in the Badlands. Visitors to the state, and residents too, were encouraged to stop at the state capital of Bismarck (population 11,090) to visit the "Roosevelt Cabin," where "Teddy" had resided in the mid-1880s, as well as Roosevelt Park in Minot (population 16,099), the Roosevelt Regional State Parks (North, and South, the former accessible via the Roosevelt Bridge) in the Badlands of the Little Missouri, and Marmouth (population 721), the town closest to where Roosevelt killed his first grizzly bear and his first buffalo.[59] Roosevelt had been dead for a generation by the time the North Dakota guide was published, but he was clearly the volume's central character, with his exploits and the sites and structures that marked his legacy collectively receiving about as much coverage as that devoted to all the state's Indian peoples—Mandan, Hidatsa, Cheyenne, Assiniboine, Sioux, Arikara, and Chippewa (Ojibway)—and their histories.[60]

The automobile-bound traveler, or the vicarious traveler, with the FWP guides in hand, moving west from North Dakota into Montana would have done so with a clear understanding that the residents of the northern plains (Nebraskans and Dakotans) were of hardy pioneer stock and molded through adversity. The guides to those states readily admitted that their residents had suffered a great deal as a result of the drought conditions from 1929 to 1936 (the year that witnessed "the driest, hottest weather ever recorded in the region") and the accompanying Depression resulting from both crop failures and record low prices. But the underlying message in the guides was that those people had persevered. Readers would have gained no sense from the Nebraska, North Dakota, or South Dakota guides that approximately three hundred thousand people had abandoned the northern plains during the 1930s and headed to the Pacific Northwest, a regional migration pattern on a scale that paralleled the migration from the southern plains to California. Steinbeck would burn the latter exodus into the national consciousness with *The Grapes of Wrath*; the former exodus has had no great literary chronicler and has remained largely outside of American collective memory.[61]

Tour 3: Rocky Mountains and Great Basin

(1940: MT 559,456; WY 250,742; CO 1,123,296; UT 550,310; NV 110,247; ID 524,873; total 2,893,256).
(2010: MT 989,415; WY 563,626; CO 5,029,196; UT 2,763,885; NV 2,700,551; ID 1,567,582; total 13,614,255).
(U.S. Census Bureau)

The six intermountain West states averaged fewer than half a million residents each in 1940, with Colorado at a little more than a million and Nevada with just over one hundred thousand marking the opposite ends of the demographic scale. The region as a whole was the least densely populated part of the West (again, with the exception of Alaska). A tour from northeastern Montana down to Trinidad in the southeastern corner of Colorado (approximately one thousand miles), westward across that state and Utah to Las Vegas, Nevada (another eight hundred plus miles), and from there up to Idaho's border with Canada (approximately twelve hundred miles), covers around three thousand miles of mountain, basin, and range landscape that is among the most spectacular in the world. Seventy years later, the region's rugged beauty and economic vitality, as well as its much vaunted "quality of life," had attracted well over ten million additional residents, a rate of population growth of over 470 percent for the period, only just behind that of the greater Southwest, but higher than that of the Pacific Northwest and well ahead of the rate for the nation as a whole. (From 1940 to 2010, the U.S. population grew from just under 132 million to nearly 309 million, a demographic increase of 234 percent.)

The Montana guide (1939) emphasized the physiographic contrast between the dryland farming eastern two-thirds of the state and the mountainous western portion, but, unlike its Kansas counterpart, did not dwell on sectional divisions among Montanans. Instead, the guide highlighted three aspects of the state's history and character: its "fairly warlike tradition," strong labor movements, and Wild West past. Readers learned that "[m]any of the state's pioneers were veterans of the Civil War or had fought Indians," and the guide also commented on the military accomplishments of Montanans in the Philippines at the turn of the century, patrolling the Mexican border in 1916–1917, and in France during the Great War, making special mention of the famous war cry of the Ninety-First Montana Regiment in the Argonne, "(We're from) Powder River; let 'er buck!"[62] Indeed, the guide's general history section drew attention to the "action and color" of the state's history as evidenced through conflict, ranging from "Indian battles" to the "war of the copper kings" to "the dryland farmer's struggle against the elements."[63] Moreover, the coverage of the history of labor in the state was not just more extensive than that in all the other western guides with the exception of California's, but emphasized how "a consciousness of the community of interests of all types of workers" is "woven into the intellectual fabric of the whole state."[64]

Unfortunately, the guide's coverage of the state's indigenous residents was not so effectively woven into the pages of the narrative. To a greater degree than in most of the western guides, Indians were confined to the past in Montana. The short chapter devoted to the Blackfoot, Crow, Flathead, and numerous other peoples is titled "Before the White Man Came." These groups received additional coverage in the tours section of the volume, which devoted a page or two to each of the state's reservations. But readers would have searched in vain for visual evidence of the growing Indian population of the state; the guide featured just three pertinent photographs: an elderly Flathead Indian chief, an elderly Flathead woman, and Crow tepees.[65] By way of contrast, the state's white pioneer and cowboy heritage took center stage in the Montana tours, from "the 'boots and saddle' country of eastern Montana" along U.S. Route 10 (from the North Dakota line to Billings), where "the cowpuncher lingers" and "the man who cannot travel fifty miles in the saddle without discomfort is felt to have missed the most important part of a citizen's education," and all the way across the state. The "rowdy vigor of the West" was "manifest . . . in the banter of cowpuncher, townsman, and farmhands" in Terry (population 779), to the stretch of land running from Miles City (population 7,175) to the Wyoming line along State Route 22, "the sort of region that cowboys dream about" and where old pioneers still lamented the onset of dryland farming three decades earlier and immortalized their sadness in song:

> I've hung up the saddle and turned out ol' Buck;
> I'm feelin' right solemn and blue.
> I'm a bowlegged puncher whose shore outa luck,
> and I reckon my punchin' is through. . . .
> But my program is set and I can't back out now,
> though I squirm in my grief and my sorrow,
> for I just bought a rake and a second-hand plow,
> and I starts in at farmin' tomorrow.[66]

Travelers and readers following the eastern slope of the Rockies south into Wyoming with the WPA guides in hand would have experienced a smooth transition from one state that celebrated its pioneer and cowboy heritage to another that did the same and in more unabashedly boosterish fashion. The Wyoming guide (1941), which was completed in 1940 during the course of the state's celebration of its fiftieth anniversary, was the least restrained of all the western state guides in its promotional tone. The opening line declared that "Wyoming was, and continues to be, the land of the cowboy," and what followed in virtually all the guide's sections amounted to hundreds of pages of confirmation of the ubiquity and vitality of the pioneer heritage. The guide explained how tourists could tap into that heritage on dude ranches—where "the hospitality of the Old West is paramount"—and at rodeos, such as Cheyenne's by then famous Frontier Days, as well as in Yellowstone National Park, which received excellent detailed description. Even arguable shortcomings, such as the state's near record-low population density, were presented as absolute benefits—"Wyoming is a land of great open spaces with plenty of elbow room," the authors declared, and with a population of 2.1 persons per square mile, it was indeed virtually a frontier according to the Census Bureau's definition (of two people or fewer per square mile). "Wyoming is a land of opportunity," they continued, where "[f]ew questions are asked the newcomer concerning his past or his ancestry. It is not

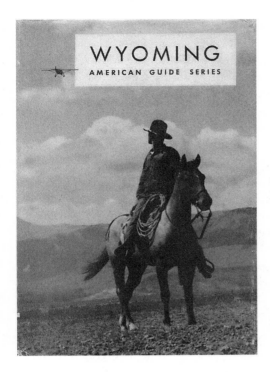

Figure 49. Wyoming, 1941.
Courtesy of Special Collections,
University of Rochester Library.

altogether rhetoric to say that a man is accepted for what he is and for what he can do."[67]

The Wyoming guide thus echoed its Texas and Arizona counterparts in its emphasis on white pioneer democracy and more generally reflected the positive aspects of historian Turner's declarations concerning the frontier heritage, first expressed nearly a half century earlier, and insisted that "[i]n Wyoming men are still exploring and building."[68] The guide devoted considerable space to "original cowboy songs—the folk music of the Plains," and to Buffalo Bill Cody's contributions to the frontier legacy.[69] One wonders whether the volume's positive, even celebratory tone concerning the frontier characteristics of the state's residents was in part a response, or acquiescence of sorts, to what FWP historian Jerre Mangione has described as "the hostility of the [Wyoming] citizenry to the WPA and the Writers' Project." Indeed, those who worked on the project often hid their WPA affiliation in an effort to secure interviews from New Deal–hating Wyomingites.[70]

However, the Wyoming guide's treatment of Indian peoples in the state was superior to that in the Texas guide and the majority of the other western state guides. The volume emphasized the presence of a wide range of cultural groups in the lands that would become Wyoming—Crow, Blackfoot, Sioux, Ute, Bannock, Flathead, Cheyenne, Arapaho, Shoshone, Modoc, Nez Perce, and Kiowa—and the fierce resistance that some of them put up to white migration across the region to Oregon, California, and Utah starting in the 1840s. In addition, the guide provided useful coverage of the state's contemporary Indian residents, the Shoshone and Arapaho dwellers on the Wind River Reservation. And, particularly impressive in retrospect and perhaps surprising to readers at the time, the guide included a range of photographs of Cheyenne and Arapaho people across the generations, adorned in a wide range of attire and engaged in a similarly expansive range of activities; the photos included children in traditional costume, members of the tribes' Joint Business Council, and women tanning hides. The cumulative impression provided by these images was one of cultural survival among Indian peoples of all ages in the present, and their effective adaptation to modernity—hence a more complex visual history that would certainly have surprised the transcontinental automotive travelers of the twenties with their inflexible antimodernist approach to presumably "vanishing" Indians.[71] In addition, the Wyoming guide's detailed coverage of Yellowstone National Park, which included a series of striking William Henry Jackson photographs from the Hayden Survey in the 1870s (including one of Shoshone Chief Washakie), was among the best parks coverage of any of the western guides.[72]

The Colorado guide (1941) was less focused on the significance of the state's pioneer heritage than were those for Wyoming, Montana, and most of the rest of the western states for that matter. Gardner (population 125), in south-central Colorado, was described as "typical of the old Southwest," a place that "retains the spirit of the frontier"; and "a [further] glimpse of what remains . . . [of] the old West [that] has largely vanished" could be found, according to the authors, in western Colorado along State Route 90, from Montrose to the Utah line.[73] But these were rare and occasional references when compared with the ubiquitous frontier allusions in many of the other guides that were clearly marked by their attention to and insistence upon the pervasive presence of the western pioneer past, all as a means of lauding the strength of character necessary for westerners to combat the challenges of the Great Depression.[74] The Colorado guide certainly emphasized the state's quintessential westernness—its ranching economy, its buffalo and big horn rams, its rodeo events (the guide's calendar listed nine separate ones)—along with its mining and milling sectors, agriculture, national forests and parks, cities and towns, and historic characters and sites, in striking photo essays that included the work of FSA photographer Arthur Rothstein. But despite these extensive and excellent visual accompaniments and the opportunity they provided for extended discussion of the significance of Colorado's frontier heritage, that legacy was confined to the past in the guide.[75]

While the Colorado guide's visual support for its coverage of Indian peoples was almost entirely absent (confined to William Henry Jackson's famous portrait of Chief Ouray and other Southern Ute subchiefs in 1870), its textual coverage was quite strong, with extensive space devoted to a thoroughgoing condemnation of the role of Colonel John Chivington and the Volunteer Militia of the Colorado Territory in the Sand Creek massacre (in the far east-central part of the state, near the Kansas border): "The majority of the victims were old men, women, and children, who were shot down indiscriminately." In addition, the history section of the work included a lengthy discussion of the Ute, Comanche, Kiowa, Cheyenne, Arapaho, and Pawnee presence in the nineteenth century, although that section ended with the unfortunate pronouncement that "[l]ike the buffalo that was the mainstay of his existence, the Indian has all but vanished from Colorado." But the volume's later coverage (in the tours section) did not confine Indians to the past, noting the steady increase in the Ute population residing in the Consolidated Ute Agency in the southwestern part of the state and the vibrancy of their cultural life.[76]

A source of controversy concerning the Colorado guide was its detailed and painfully honest description of the conditions and wages of Mexican American and Russian field workers in eastern Colorado's sugarbeet fields. The guide printed wage figures for workers that were provided by the U.S. Department of Agriculture and were considerably lower than those that had been forwarded to FWP workers by Colorado agribusiness interests; an average family income of $400 was projected for 1940. The labor was described as "backbreaking" and the participation of "minors in the worker's family" was emphasized, as was the federal prohibition against the employment of children under the age of fourteen and the restrictions on the length of the working day for those between fourteen and seventeen. The guide also featured a series of images by FSA photographers Rothstein and Jack Allison of Mexican American beet field workers and their families, including one of a union meeting and another of children (albeit in the doorway of a rudimentary abode rather than working in the fields), the collective effect of which would surely have generated empathy for those working families among readers of the volume.[77]

Moving from southwestern Colorado across the border into Utah, the guidebook reader would have found a state dominated by both Mormonism and the consciousness of a pioneer heritage. "The Mormon habitat has always been a vortex of legend and lie," the Utah guide's (1941) dramatic opening line declared. The authors, whose efforts were supervised by western historian Dale L. Morgan, then noted that "[m]any still journey to Utah to see a Mormon," but suggested that there were now "fewer outward stigmata to a Utahn" and that "[m]ost visitors now betray no disappointment at finding Mormons hornless." The guide pointed out that approximately 60 percent of Utah's population was Mormon and that "the particular quality of Utah life is almost wholly Mormon," but also noted that the word "gentile" had almost lost its significance and that "[t]he violent days of struggle between Mormon and anti-Mormon, polygamist and anti-polygamist, have faded almost to nothing." Indeed, while the Utah guide did not attempt to completely normalize and mainstream Mormonism—it emphasized the larger size of Mormon families, the presence of a more "acute . . . religious consciousness" than in "probably" every other state, and the homogeneity of the Church's racial stock (then approximately 99 percent Anglo-Scandinavian)—it did effectively downplay any contemporary controversies. While the work also provided extensive coverage of the Mountain Meadows massacre of 1857 and the culpability of the Mormons in the slaughter of the white emigrant party, it also pointed to the failure of generations of non-Mormons to write about the Church in an unbiased fashion, singling out Richard Francis Burton's *The City of the Saints* for coming as close to the goal of balanced observation and reflection as any other visitor account and commenting on its author's "background of world travel."[78]

Part of the process of deexceptionalizing Mormonism involved playing up the "pioneer distinctiveness that survives in Utah life," emphasizing that "the stamp of a pioneer culture is everywhere manifest," including in the built environment where even structures built of wood and mud "stand up indomitably to the years," thus "retain[ing] their pioneer flavor of accomplishment," and where the state's spaciously planned cities reflect "the grand sweep of pioneer planning." Indeed, the Utah guide was replete with grandiose claims about the character of the state and its residents, and the shaping role of the frontier heritage. "In Utahns," readers learned, "there is universally a consciousness of the earth, in part because of the recency of its pioneering." Moreover, the guide suggested, "[p]erhaps some of the especial flavor of Utah comes from [the] quality of things coming hard." Thus, "the

Mormon struggle with the earth," the spirit of "Mormon enterprise" displayed in a "hostile environment," forged a character much like that of other hard frontier lands in the West. In this way, the Utah guide echoed the tone of those for Nebraska and South Dakota, and the state appeared as a natural part of the larger western pioneering process rather than an aberration from it.[79] Moreover, much like several other western guides, including Montana's, the volume's contributing authors devoted little effort to writing the state's Indians into its present. A mere six pages of the Utah guide were devoted to the Ute, Shoshone, Navajo, and Paiute, and the coverage concluded with an uncomplimentary and stereotypical cartoon image of an Indian warrior and the dismissive declaration that "Utah Indians have retained little of their original culture."[80]

Heading west from Utah into Nevada and then down to the southern tip of the Silver State, the traveler would experience the emerging town of Las Vegas, an economic and demographic beneficiary of the legalization of gambling in 1931 and the building of Hoover Dam (1931–1936; officially Boulder Dam until 1947). The contemporary reader of the Nevada guide (1940) would be struck by the description of today's metropolitan poster child for adult entertainment, consumerism, place branding, and architectural simulacrum run amok:

> Relatively little emphasis is placed on the gambling clubs and divorce facilities—though they are attractive to many visitors. . . . No cheap and easily parodied slogans have been adopted to publicize the city, no attempt has been made to introduce pseudo-romantic architectural themes, or to give artificial glamor and gaiety. Las Vegas is itself—natural and therefore very appealing to people with a very wide variety of interests.[81]

Before Bernard-Henri Lévy jumped on the Vegas-bashing bandwagon in the 2000s, his French compatriot Jean Baudrillard, in his critically acclaimed travelogue *Amérique* (1986), had lambasted Sin City's unnaturalness—its "phosphorescent lights" and its "[g]ambling . . . a desert form, inhuman, uncultured, initiatory, a challenge to the natural economy of value, a crazed activity on the fringes of exchange."[82] More recently, Timothy Egan chose to title his scathing indictment of the place "Chaos or Cancer" (1998), drawing on Edward Abbey's warning that "[g]rowth for growth's sake is the ideology of the cancer cell" and Southern Nevada Water Authority head Patricia

Mulroy's warning that "[i]f you tried to slow growth around here, you'd have chaos." Egan determined that the movers and shakers of the desert metropolis were "creating the Los Angeles of Blade Runner" in Las Vegas, concluding that the place represented both chaos and cancer.[83]

But in 1940, with just over 110,000 residents in the whole state of Nevada and only 8,422 of them in Las Vegas, the exponential demographic growth of the place (Clark County, which encompasses the Las Vegas metropolitan area, had two million residents in 2010) and its iconic cultural significance as a global center for gaming and mass entertainment were things of the future. No other state in the West or the nation had fewer residents or a more sparsely settled landscape than Nevada in the 1930s (of all U.S. possessions, only the Alaska Territory was more sparsely populated). The guide, not surprisingly, devoted more space to the state's cattle and cowboy culture—"brands and the branding of cattle are subjects of inexhaustible interest in the range country"—than it did to the contemporary scene in Reno or Las Vegas, and also played up Mark Twain's literary beginnings in Virginia City and devoted a section to "Mining and Mining Jargon." However, the Nevada guide, unlike so many of the other western guides, did not offer any bold statements about the significance of its pioneer past to the contemporary character of the state. The authors mentioned Las Vegas's annual Helldorado Days celebration of the Old West (inaugurated in 1935 and still a major civic event today), but commented that the various rodeo and other events "intended to recreate the early spirit turn Las Vegas into a rollicking hybrid of two vastly different eras." They noted, too, that Reno's annual rodeo was "underwritten by the merchants" and promoted in part through the mayor's ultimatum decreeing "western dress" and its "kangaroo court" to enforce the edict. If the spirit of the Old West was alive in Nevada, it was a relatively recent imposition, manufactured for the express purpose of meeting the expectations of others.[84]

But if the legacy of the frontier West was conspicuously absent from the Nevada guide, seemingly overlooked by a group of writers who felt no compulsion to play up the pioneer past, the traveler heading northeast from Reno through Elko across to Winnemucca and up into southern Idaho in possession of the Idaho guide (1937) would have been hard pressed to avoid finding that Anglo frontier spirit unceremoniously attacked. The very first of the guides to appear—to the great chagrin of FWP bureaucrats, who would have much preferred to see the Washington, D.C., guide as the first in the much-anticipated series—*Idaho: A Guide in Word and Picture* was largely the work of a tireless and thoroughly opinionated novelist, Vardis Fisher.[85] The volume featured the most dramatic opening lines of any of the state guides:

> After three centuries of adventurous seeking, the American conti-
> nent has been explored and settled, and the last frontier is gone. The
> lusty and profane extremes of it still live nebulously in the gaudy
> imbecilities of newsstand pulp magazines and in cheap novels. . . .
> But these villains with their Wild Bill mustaches, these apple-
> cheeked heroines agog with virtue . . . are shoddy sawdust counter-
> feits who would have been as much out of place in the old West as
> Chief Nampuh with his huge feet would have been among the the-
> atrical ineptitudes of a Victorian tea.

In language that would surely have offended many readers (while ringing true to many others), Fisher lambasted nineteenth-century western mission-aries for their internecine struggles for the procurement of new Christian souls, remarking that "[i]t is difficult to believe that men so far from the meaning of God themselves could have brought to the Indians a larger vision of humanity and fellowship." He then attacked the generation of pioneer set-tlers for their part in the proceedings: "These simple-minded red men heard the Sermon on the Mount one day and on the next were got drunk or robbed or attacked by persons from that race with which the Sermon had been a byword for nineteen centuries." Fisher then concluded: "It is folly, on the one hand, to grow sentimental over the Indians. They were not noble savages. They were not thriftless vagabonds. It is folly, on the other hand, to pretend that the early missionaries, no matter how well-intentioned, were able to achieve more good than harm."[86]

Fisher's opening essay was a powerful reaction against frontier trium-phalism and the role of "some historians" in perpetuating the popular ste-reotypes of a West heroically won, rather than brutally conquered. "An attack by Indians," they will tell you, "was an outrage, a treachery, or a plain and terrible massacre," but on the other hand, "attacks by white warriors were courageous stands against howling and bloodthirsty maniacs." Fisher lamented the persistence of the popular perception that "the whites, fighting to possess land what did not belong to them, were splendid soldiers of God," while the Indians "were yelping and unvarnished assassins." Reflecting on the experience of the Coeur d'Alene, Spokane, and Nez Perce with white settlers and troops in Idaho, Fisher described it as a "shameful history of warfare against Indians." He then proceeded to retell the narrative of Chief Joseph and the flight of the Nez Perce from the imagined perspective of an Indian historian, who described "[t]he white invaders with their terrible ghostly faces and brutal instruments of death." In addition to the extensive coverage of white-Indian relations in the volume's opening essay, Fisher also devoted separate chapters to the history and anthropology of Idaho Indians.[87]

Fisher's Idaho guide was unconventional. He dismissed the popular stereotypes about the miners who rushed into the region in the early 1860s with the same raw cynicism that he directed at the mythmakers who had creatively reimagined and inverted the history of white-Indian relations. He described them as "petty thieves and shysters," "a feverish and floating horde," "organized gangs," "banded packs," and "an army of hell-roaring and money-mad men." Fisher lambasted the early governors of the Idaho Territory for their corruption, inaction, and ineptitude, and castigated the legislature for forcing the Chinese to pay a residence tax and for prohibiting their marriage with whites. He referred to the state's ghost towns as "the decaying monuments of twenty violent years" during the territorial period. He declared again that Idaho's "frontiers are gone" and expressed great relief at their passing, devoting a chapter to the theme of the state's "emerging from the frontier." He welcomed that emergence with enthusiasm, remarking that Idaho "is still so close to the frontier that its social development is still for the most part in its formative stages."[88] The Idaho guide was not a departure from the other western guides in its marked absence of a boosterish tone (its Kansas and Nebraska counterparts were just as candid in their respective assessments of state shortcomings). However, in its thoroughgoing rejection of the western pioneer heritage, or at least of the colorful, romantic, and uncritical fashion in which that heritage had been constructed over time, Fisher elevated the Idaho contribution to the American Guide Series to another level.

Tour 4: Pacific Northwest to the Last Frontier

(1940: OR 1,089,684; WA 1,736,191; AK 75,524; total 2,901,399).
(2010: OR 3,831,074; WA 6,724,540; AK 710,231; total 11,265,845).
(U.S. Census Bureau)

Driving north across Oregon from Medford to Portland (274 miles) and then across Washington from Vancouver to Lynden (266 miles), and then traversing

Figure 50. Oregon: End of the Trail, 1940. Courtesy of Special Collections, University of Rochester Library.

much of Alaska, from Juneau in the southeast to Seward (973 miles), north to Fairbanks (484 miles), and on up to Prudhoe Bay on the Arctic Ocean (another 500 miles), covering a total distance of nearly 2,500 miles, would take the traveler from some of the West's most dynamic emerging metropolitan places (Portland and Seattle) to its most wide-open spaces, and from one of the Far West's oldest states, Oregon (1859), to the nation's second newest, Alaska (admitted a whole century later, in 1959, just months before Hawaii). The vast bulk of the region's population in 1940 was in the two Pacific Northwest states, just as it is today, and the region would see an impressive 389 percent demographic increase by 2010, while Alaska witnessed a remarkable growth rate of close to 1,000 percent, although still remaining a frontier in the technical sense of the word, with a population density of just 1.26 persons per square mile of its massive geographic expanse.

The armchair or actual traveler, after the chastening experience of the Idaho guide, would have returned to the familiar mental territory of the western state guides' tendency toward positive pioneer memorialization in *Oregon: The End of the Trail* (1940). But that reader would also have recognized a sense of anxiety over the passing of the frontier and a fear that Oregon in the modern age might become like everywhere else, which echoed the transcontinental automotive travel narratives of the previous generation. The preface to the Oregon guide presented the state as "still the most unspoiled and most uncluttered spot in America—partly because the gold rushes of California and Alaska left it undisturbed." The authors' laudatory descriptions of the state's National Forests—"The woods of Oregon are a wonderland of overwhelming proportions"—reinforced the image of Oregon as a natural paradise. But the "coming of [hydroelectric] Power"—the Grand Coulee and Bonneville Dams—along with the "inrolling of immigration from the dust bowl, the devastation of timber cutting and forest fires, and the boosting activities of chambers of commerce" ran the risk of transforming "this peaceful beautiful land . . . into a network of highways clogged with cars and defaced with hot dog stands, the groves littered with tin cans and papers, the hills pock-marked with stumps, and the cities cursed with the slums that seem to accompany industrial progress." Moreover, in a dramatic commentary on the intersections of physiography and racist physiognomy, the Oregon guide wondered whether the state's "tall and sturdy" sons and "native rose" complexioned daughters, whose impressive stature and good looks had been nurtured in the "pleasant outdoors," would, in the "impending industrial age[,] be shorter and shrewder, and the daughters dependent for their beauty upon commodities sold in drug-stores." Would "Oregonians become less appreciative of nature and rooted living and more avid and neurotic in the pursuit of wealth?"[89]

But if the state's physical stock and natural grandeur were under threat in the face of commerce, modernity, and new in-migration, the Oregon guide's busy "Annual Calendar of Events" featured a plethora of pioneer heritage activities that might at least sustain the spirit of earlier and simpler times. Old Timers' Reunions and Picnics, Pioneer Picnics, Oregon Founders' Day, '62 Gold Rush, Oregon Pioneer Association, Paul Bunyan, Frontier Days, and Territorial Days celebrations, the annual meetings of the Sons and Daughters of Oregon Pioneers, the Oregon State Pioneer Association, and sixteen separate county-level Pioneer Associations, along with the state's various Round-Ups, Stampedes, and Rodeos, suggested that the state at the end of the Oregon Trail was purposefully connected to its frontier past. The guide celebrated the "epochal journey of Lewis and Clark into the wild country," but its praise for the pioneer phase of the state's history was not absolute. The authors noted that while the "great overland migration to Oregon has been sanctified by tradition it seems foolish to presume that covered wagons carried nothing but animated virtues into Oregon." Still, these few minor qualifications concerning the benign character of the pioneering past in Oregon hardly echoed the tone and content of Fisher's assault on Idaho's frontier era.

The Oregon guide described the "successful efforts" of Oregon's cattlemen "to wring livelihoods from the hostile land" as "an unwritten epic of the frontier." Moreover, the authors offered "two symbols for Oregon: a pioneer of the covered wagon epoch, and beside him likewise grim and indomitable, the plodding figure of a modern farmer driven from middle-western soil by years of drought." Noting that thousands of "dust-bowl refugees" had moved to Oregon during the 1930s (an exodus that did not receive discussion in those WPA guides to the northern plains states that the migrants left), the Oregon guide drew as direct a connection between the pioneering past and the present as any of the western state guides:

> If hunger and hardships and uncertainty are the essences of the pioneer tradition, they are a part of it already; and as the bearded early immigrants brought a first cohesion to the territory, these latter-day American pioneers may strengthen that cohesion and make their own distinctive contribution to the state.[90]

There was little in the guide's limited coverage of Oregon's Indian peoples— beyond a perfunctory listing of the population sizes of the Klamath, Warm Springs, and Umatilla Reservations and of the Siletz River district—to suggest that their significance to the state's history and heritage came anywhere close to matching that of either the early or the contemporary generation of white pioneers. Indeed, in its coverage of Indian-white settler hostilities in the 1840s, the Oregon guide's choice of language—including mention of "Indian outrages" and the Indians' "frenzy of resentment" in the wake of the white response to the Cayuse's killing of Marcus and Narcissa Whitman and twelve other white settlers in 1847 ("they appeared everywhere, killing the settlers and driving off their cattle")—does in fact bring to mind Fisher's highlighting of biased white histories of the frontier era.[91]

The volume's chapter on pioneer food recipes was almost as long as its chapter on Indians, whose presumably peripheral place in Oregon was underscored in the illustrations (which were few in number and relegated native peoples to the distant past) as well as the text.[92] The tours section also played up the white pioneer heritage, in Klamath Falls (population 16,093), where "[t]he old West rubs elbows with the new"; in Pendleton (population 6,621), home of the famous September Round-Up; in the aptly named and sparsely peopled town of Remote (population 15); in Prairie City (population 438), home of the annual Round-Up and Jamboree; and along Oregon State Route 54 from Vale (population 922) near the Idaho border, 370 miles across the state to Albany (population 5,325) in the Willamette Valley in the northwest, "a comparatively unsettled country, about which cluster the traditions of the Old West, when the range was free, herds uncounted, and ranches small principalities, with the latch-string out for strangers."[93] Leaving Oregon, the traveler in the company of the western state guides would have had the impression of the halcyon days of the pioneer past still alive and pertinent in the present, after taking a very different mental journey, for the most part, from the one Fisher had mapped out for Idaho.

Entering Washington State near the end of a tour through the West with the WPA guides would have seemed quite fitting at the time. The Washington guide finally appeared in late 1941, just ahead of its Oklahoma counterpart (the very last of the American Guides to be published).[94] The delay was largely due to poor direction of the Writers' Project at the state level but also to the political controversy that surrounded the Washington State FWP office, which was accused of being "a hotbed of Communists."[95] The resulting volume (nearly seven hundred pages long—along with those of Texas and California, the biggest of the western guides) bore no overt traces of particularly radical hands, although it did adopt a tone toward the frontier heritage that distinguished it from most of its counterparts. The tone was softer and less confrontational than Fisher's assault on the popular memory of the pioneer past, but nonetheless memorable in its own right. The authors began with the popular conception of the state "as virtually a frontier wilderness, accessible only to the rugged and adventurous," and admitted that "[s]omething of this primitive condition still remains today" in the state's "magnificent virgin forests," mountains, lakes, and shores. But the real emphasis was on responsible conservation of resources in the wake of the toll that the "haphazard development of the country has taken."[96]

Subtitled *A Guide to the Evergreen State*, the Washington guide was probably the "greenest" of the western state guides. The authors commented on the "vast scarred and denuded areas" left after clear-cutting in forest areas and championed more recent "[s]elective logging methods," reforestation programs, and the establishment of national forests as important steps in the state's march toward responsible environmental stewardship. The guide welcomed the new Bonneville and Grand Coulee Dams and other power projects, and understandably so in an era before the great debate over whether the negative consequences of dams would outweigh their benefits. The authors presented the dams, along with the withdrawal of lands from commercial use and their preservation for "enjoyment and inspirational needs of man," as "measures expressive of a people with broad vision and with the capacity for significant long-range planning." However, they were aware of the impact of dams on fishing runs and soil erosion. Indeed, the Washington guide devoted a section to resource conservation in which it celebrated the state's departure from its former acquiescence to the "cut-up-and-get-out" logging methods that had characterized the timber industry, and discussed the cooperative efforts between the United States and Canada, and among federal and state agencies, the University of Washington, and other involved parties to improve salmon runs. It even included a photo essay on lumbering that included a disturbing image of "Cutover Land." The volume emphasized the state's natural beauty as a magnet for tourists, but more generally exhibited a commitment to effective resource management and preservation achieved through progressive cooperative initiatives; hardly communistic, it was eminently sensible and responsible.[97]

The Washington guide's section on Indian history and cultures began with a reminder that echoed Fisher's narrative in the Idaho guide, although in gentler fashion: "American history written in terms of the white man is a story of his triumphant march westward. . . . For the Indian, however, this never-ceasing advance into his lands has meant the end of his way of life." While the Washington writers overemphasized the idea of the "vanishing" of authentic Indian culture, they nonetheless provided informed discussion of contemporary Indian cultures in the state, including the Colville, Yakima, Snohomish, Muckleshoot, Tulalip, Puyallup, and Makah. The volume also provided a more balanced discussion of the Indian Wars of the 1850s in the Oregon Territory than did the Oregon guide, and, like a number of the western guides—echoing the observations of Friedrich Gerstäcker in the mid-nineteenth century—it highlighted the connection between gold rushes and conflict with indigenous peoples.[98] The Washington tours featured occasional nods to the pioneer past, and the guide's calendar of events listed a few pioneer society gatherings, along with the Ellensburg (population 5,944) Rodeo and the Colfax (population 2,853) Roundup, but the guide on the whole focused more on the progressive present, celebrating technological advances and commercial growth as well as natural grandeur while still advocating a cautious path toward a sustainable future, and finding a central role for government in the endeavor.[99] In this way, the Washington state guide encapsulated the Washington, D.C., New Deal emphasis on enlightened government as the substitute for the frontier opportunities of generations past.

Our WPA western tour concludes with *A Guide to Alaska: Last American Frontier* (1939), which appeared three years before the completion of the Alaska Highway, running from Dawson Creek, British Columbia, to Delta Junction in far northwestern Alaska; a distance of 1,700 miles when the highway was first constructed, but that has since shrunk to 1,387 miles as a result of road straightening and rerouting.[100] John W. Troy, the governor of the territory, wrote in his foreword to the guide that while "Alaska may be the United States' 'last frontier,'" its technological prowess (including its "revolutionary use of air transportation") along with the "energy and inventiveness of its citizens" merited the title "the United States' 'foremost frontier.'"[101] Largely the work of a single author, Merle Colby, the Alaska guide is one of the most compelling of the western guides, with an eye to regional differences, illuminated by the division of the territory into "the Six Alaskas" (southeast, south central, southwestern and Bristol Bay, interior, Seward Peninsula, and Arctic Slope) and by its attention to the coexistence of the industrial present and indigenous cultural life: "A plane circles down and comes to rest beside a skin kayak, its design unchanged for a thousand years. A Tlingit Indian carves his 'family tree' with an adze on a forty-foot totem pole—but works 'on the line' in a cannery buzzing with the best of modern automatic machinery." Similarly, Eskimo children who had never seen a car or a horse "hardly looked up when a plane roared down." Alaska was far removed geographically from the southwestern Land of Enchantment that had so disenchanted the antimodernist transcontinental travel book authors of the teens and twenties, and its WPA guide was a polar opposite in approach from their lamentations over the loss of authentic regional cultures.[102]

Nonetheless, for all its attention to the dramatic natural beauty of the Alaska Territory and its rich indigenous presence harmoniously aligned with the trappings of modernity, the guide was anything but an exercise in regional boosterism. Colby discussed the individualistic character of Alaska's white pioneers but did not celebrate it, and he also emphasized their "distrust of Orientals and natives" while devoting considerable space and a positive and empathetic tone toward the Athapascans, Aleuts, Tsimshains, Tlingits, and Haida Indians. He also addressed the impact of the gold rush at the turn of the century (gold was discovered on the beach at Nome, on Alaska's Seward Peninsula coast, in 1899) and the disease epidemic (a combination of measles and pneumonia, or smallpox and typhoid) that decimated the Eskimo communities there, and included the territorial governor's description of diseased natives who "become stupefied and utterly helpless and lie down to die."[103] The Alaska guide was far removed from the Oregon guide's unhelpful paean to vanishing Indians, which was in part a reflection of the larger size of the indigenous populations of Alaska and the considerably higher proportion of the population they constituted (Alaska's indigenous peoples made up about half the territory's total demography), but the guide was also a marker of authorial attitudes—Colby simply cared more about Indians' cultures and needs than did his Oregonian counterparts or those involved with the guides to various other western states, including Arizona, Montana, and Texas.

Colby pointed out that between 1867 and 1890, Alaska's first decades under U.S. control, "little was done for the Natives," and then proceeded to outline the serious health problems they suffered in the present, including high rates of tuberculosis. He called for economic independence for Alaska's natives to secure their well-being but also advised that this end could only be attained with the assistance of the federal government in the areas of "health, education, and social welfare, as well as economic aid and guidance." Colby also discussed the advantages enjoyed by the Metlakatla Indians in southeastern Alaska, whose reserved fishing rights protected them from competition with whites, while the Haida and Tlingit Indians in the same region were disadvantaged by their lack of reserved rights. He called for consideration of whether similar reserved areas might work to the advantage of the Indians and Eskimos of the interior and northern Alaska. In addition, Colby noted the extensive participation of natives in the territory's industrial economies and advocated further expansion of industrial labor opportunities for them.[104]

Alaska was part of the nation's last homesteading frontier. The two-hundred-farm Matanuska Colony, established in 1935 in southeastern Alaska's Matanuska Valley (northeast of Anchorage), was one of several agricultural colony initiatives undertaken by the New Deal's Division of Rural Rehabilitation of the Federal Emergency Relief Administration. The national media played up the homesteading effort on "America's last frontier," painting the participating families as part of the nation's long pioneering tradition.[105] The Alaska guide itself devoted an entire photo essay to the Matanuska Colony.[106] But in the last analysis, the guide to the "last frontier" tended to downplay, rather than overplay, the state's pioneering heritage, in favor of careful coverage of Alaska's indigenous peoples, the territory's history, geography, and natural grandeur, and its place in the postfrontier present. Like its Washington counterpart, the Alaska guide was a memorable testament to what a strong federal government could and should do in the West, as well as a deeply informative introduction to a culturally vibrant group of regions and residents. It was an appropriate complement to a set of western state guides that celebrated the regional richness of a geographic expanse stretching from the Great Plains to the Pacific that, with the inclusion of the massive Alaska Territory (and its 75,000 or so residents), constituted approximately two-thirds of the nation's geographic expanse.

Coda: Returning to Native Grounds

In his landmark work *On Native Grounds* (1942), published as the Federal Writers' Project was winding down and the last state guides were appearing, the emerging literary critic Alfred Kazin proclaimed that the guides' authors had collectively "recovered an American sense of history and began to chant the rich diversity and beauty of the country as if America had never really been known before." From their efforts, Kazin added, "there emerged an America unexampled in density and regional diversity."[107] The New Deal western state guides were filled with examples of regional distinctiveness and were often characterized by their highlighting of persisting frontier characteristics in the West, and even parts of the Midwest, too.[108] By way of contrast, the auto-bound travel writers whose works appeared earlier in the century purposefully announced that they were searching for such place-centered distinctiveness and authenticity, but their claims seem rather unconvincing, and the disappointment they expressed over what they found (or failed to find) appears contrived in retrospect. Had they, like later travelers, been fortunate enough to carry the FWP western state guides with them on their journeys, one suspects that they might have been prompted to see more of and presume less about the places and the people they experienced on their travels. But that, of course, would have been impossible; the earlier generation of traveling chroniclers missed the regional richness of the West in large part because they were motivated more by the need to express an antimodernist disillusionment than by any real search for regional diversity.

The New Deal guides, on the other hand, were part of the larger rediscovery of America during the Depression years that another of the nation's
most talented literary critics and cultural commentators, Malcolm Cowley,
had described in *Exile's Return: A Literary Odyssey of the 1920s* (1934), published before the guides initiative had even begun. Cowley's landmark
work described a generation of American expatriate writers (including
T. S. Eliot, John Dos Passos, F. Scott Fitzgerald, and Hart Crane) disillusioned by the condition of a post–World War I society they felt powerless
to change, one dominated by the forces of materialism, Puritanism, and Ku
Klux Klanism, a society culturally drained by the acids of modernity and
anti-intellectualism. Upon their return, those writers discovered America
again through their empathy with the "common man" suffering through
the hardships of the economic collapse. With renewed energy and confidence in their capacity for facilitating change, they "allied themselves"
with the cause of social change on behalf of the underclass, and "they
ceased to be exiles." Cowley continued, "they had acquired friends and
enemies and purposes in the midst of society, and thus, wherever they lived
in America, they found a home."[109]

Cowley's assessment, in contrasting the so-called Lost Generation
American writers with the socially engaged and empowered intellectuals
who found a home in 1930s America, offers an interesting parallel with the
automotive travel writers of the early decades of the century and the FWP
state guide writers. The former, especially by the 1920s, were describing a
West that they imagined to be increasingly nondistinct, devoid of regional
character and absent of frontier influences. Their concerns over the creeping
conformity that accompanied modernity paralleled those of the expatriate
writers. By way of contrast, the state guides that came later were packed with
the particularities of region, including the pervasive presence of frontier legacies. Yet the guides presented a more positive regional vision that was just
starting to develop in the 1920s. Indeed, they constituted the realization of
Frederick Jackson Turner's vision for America, expressed in his 1922 essay
"Sections and Nation," that "we shall find the strength to build from our past
a nobler structure in which each section [read *region*] will find its place as a
fit room in a worthy house."[110] That vision of national strength through
regional diversity was echoed that same year by the editors of *The Nation*,
who declared it "Better [to] have the States a little rowdy and bumptious, a
little restless under the central yoke, than given over to the tameness of a
universal similarity," and commissioned a series of articles on the essential

character and particularities of each state, published in the magazine (in alphabetical order) between January 1923 and January 1924.[111]

The New Deal guides described home, wherever it happened to be in America, as the kind of place where the formerly disillusioned, even the expatriate, would feel a sense of belonging.[112] The western guides (much like those to states in the other regions) also described places that were culturally vibrant and thus well worth visiting, while their auto-bound traveling predecessors had described ones that were virtually dead (with respect to cultural authenticity), and so not really worth the trip.

But both of these genres of writing about the West did share one important commonality: they underscored how travel writing in the first four decades of the twentieth century constituted a movement inward, toward the national, and regional, and away from the global.[113] This trend was further marked by a tendency to search for and to sometimes find those aspects of the West that were unique, and thus distinctly American. The travel writers who came to the West in this period (including those who visited from other countries), along with those such as the FWP state guide authors who gathered their material by traveling within the states where they resided, all shared the tendency to envision the twentieth-century West through considerably less global lenses than their nineteenth-century predecessors. The modern West, for all the despair and lamentation over the loss of regional distinctiveness that characterized the antimodern sensibility, was for these observers still in a sense a quintessentially American frontier (even if that frontier was perceived to be disappearing), or at least a place best explained within the context of the nation, not the world. This nation-centric tendency would continue to characterize travel writing about the West in the second half of the twentieth century, too, and into the twenty-first.[114]

CONCLUSION

Enduring Roads

To-day I am in Yellowstone, and I wish I were dead.
> —Rudyard Kipling, *From Sea to Sea: Letters of Travel* (1899)

I could see Denver looking ahead of me like the Promised Land, way out there beneath the stars, across the prairie of Iowa and the plains of Nebraska, and I could see the greater vision of San Francisco beyond.
> —Jack Kerouac, *On the Road* (1957)

Premature Endings: The Presumed Death of the Travel Book

In 1937, Canadian writer Stephen Leacock declared: "All travel writing and travel pictures in books are worn out and belong to a past age. It is no longer possible to tell anyone anything new about anywhere."[1] Two years later, *Journey to a War*, Christopher Isherwood's and W. H. Auden's account of their 1938 visit to China during its war with Japan, was published.[2] For some critics, *Journey to a War* serves as a profound marker of "the end of an era in travel writing."[3] In this vein, cultural historian and literary critic Paul Fussell has suggested that the golden age of British travel writing, which began after World War I, was over by the time of World War II, effectively laid waste by the twin forces of technological progress and martial destruction. Writing just after the end of World War II, amid numerous such pronouncements, novelist Evelyn Waugh noted that he did not "expect to see many travel books in the future. . . . Never again, I suppose, shall we land on foreign soil with a letter of credit and passport . . . and feel the world wide open before us."[4] How, indeed, could travel hold out the promise of adventure and discovery after the misadventures of global warfare, the loss of world frontiers, and the new speed of air travel?[5]

The observations of Fussell, Waugh, and Leacock seem logical enough. Travel writing had thrived for centuries as a genre because it offered the reading public a glimpse of largely, or at least relatively, unknown people and places. Could there really be any geographic or cultural discoveries to be made, any news of the unfamiliar to be conveyed, in the modern world? Well, it turns out that such rumors and pronouncements concerning the death of the travel book were not only part of a much larger tradition of lamentations over "true" travel's end but have been, to use the words of America's most renowned travel writer, Mark Twain (in reference to his own death), "greatly exaggerated."[6] Indeed, a decade after publishing *Journey to a War*, Isherwood himself wrote another classic of the genre, *The Condor and the Cows* (1948), recounting his travels in South America in 1947–1948.[7]

The travel book, of course, is no nearer extinction because of the development of travel networks and speedier conveyances than is regionalism as a consequence of the forces of standardization and homogenization that have accompanied modernity and globalization.[8] Regions and localities as units of human consciousness will persist not merely in the face of those forces, but because of and in response to them. People will seek to retain, and even create, place-based exceptionalism as an anchor to stem the seemingly ominous drift toward cultural sameness.[9] And so with the travel book: nagging concerns that the globe has become a single, uniform place, rather than a world of rich cultural and physiographical differences, are partly alleviated by travel writing that sparks the imagination of even (or, perhaps, especially) the vicarious traveler who only flips pages and boards no planes, trains, or ships. Two-thirds of a century after the warnings of the doomsayers, the travel book is still not dead; there is no postmortem to perform. What is more, the American West has, throughout the twentieth and into the twenty-first century, remained a favored destination for travel writers despite the purportedly crushing weight of regional uniformity in the United States.[10] Indeed, the travelogue in the modern period has at times even acted as a counterweight to assumptions about the death of regionalism (the WPA guides' "Tours" sections are a memorable case in point).[11]

Nonetheless, people in general, and intellectuals especially, have always worried about endings and changes, and we can connect mid-twentieth-century pronouncements concerning the end of meaningful travel and travel writing with late-nineteenth and early-twentieth-century concerns over the passing of the American western frontier and the death of distinctive regional landscapes and identities. When Frederick Jackson Turner declared the end of the frontier in 1893, his definitions, as critics have often noted, were quite fluid: "the outer edge of the wave," "the meeting point between civilization and savagery," and, more literally, "the margin of that settlement which has a density of two or more to the square mile."[12] Still, this definitional fluidity actually reflected quite accurately the contemporary thinking in the western world about frontiers. The frontier anxiety expressed by Turner and hundreds of other American intellectuals around the same time was about far more than the absence of available and affordable farmland. These nervous observers were bemoaning what they presumed to be the accompanying loss of democracy, of a peculiarly pragmatic American character and a vigorous American manhood, all nurtured by the special trials and tribulations of conquering a continent, taming wilderness, and triumphing (in the name of civilization) over savagery. Such frontier concerns were about nothing less than the end of American innocence (loosely conceived, to be sure), the end of a great American adventure, the drying up of the great wellspring of American exceptionalism.[13] As Turner declared at the end of his essay, "now, four centuries from the discovery of America . . . the frontier has gone, and with its going has closed the first period of American history."[14]

When, two generations after Turner lamented the passing of the frontier, Leacock, Waugh, and others declared the death of the travel book, they were insisting that no significant frontiers of travel remained. All such adventurous horizons had been obliterated as distance shrank into meaninglessness in the face of technology's power to enable mere mortals to "look down on the earth as if [they] were moonlighting gods," as Pico Iyer has put it.[15] True discovery was no longer possible for the traveler; modernization had taken the "journeying" out of travel, just as conquest and settlement had taken the frontier out of the West and the nation. All that remained was tourism, which, we are so often told, is a pale substitute for real travel, just as Walt Disney's "Frontierland" is a pale (albeit fascinating) substitute for the old western frontier.[16]

Old western pioneers expressed a parallel sentiment when they referred disparagingly, in the late nineteenth and early twentieth centuries, to those new settlers who came west on the railroad as "Pullman pioneers." The derisive label actually mirrored closely the infrastructural reality of the time. The original Pullman Pioneer sleeping car, built during the Civil War, was too lavish, too ornate and well appointed, and just too plain big to be able to run—it was inordinately heavy and too high to pass under standard-height railway bridges. The absolute antonym of the little engine that could—a metaphor that old pioneers would have found characteristic of their struggle in an earlier era and against ostensibly insuperable odds to journey across and conquer western frontiers—the Pullman was the big carriage that could not.[17] Hence, these new, Pullman-assisted arrivals in the postfrontier era were not true western settlers in the estimation of generations of old westerners. Those pioneer settlers, through purposeful remembrance of the great national story, viewed the trials and tribulations of actual frontier travel and the transformation of howling wildernesses into blossoming Edens as the work of a hardier, braver, more virtuous breed—namely, themselves.[18]

Thus, the Pullman pioneer was to the "real" pioneer as the tourist was to the "true" traveler, at least in the estimation of self-identified "real" pioneers and "true" travelers. Indeed, self-defined travelers were making jokes at the expense of tourists as early as the end of the Napoleonic Wars in 1815. By the middle of the nineteenth century, Thomas Cook was offering packaged tours to Italy and other parts of the European continent, and coming under criticism from British "travelers" for doing so. Such dichotomizing of tourist and traveler was clearly class driven, a defense mechanism of European elites against the disparagingly described "teeming masses" of middle-class culture seekers who were rendering the elite's hallowed vacationing terrain less exclusive. Typical of this sentiment was an 1848 article in Britain's conservative *Blackwood's Magazine* that disparagingly described the tourists as "everywhere" in Europe, "all pen in hand, all determined not to let a henroost remain undescribed," mercilessly foisting their writings on the "reading public . . . without compassion or conscience."[19] In *Pictures from Italy* (1846), Charles Dickens commented caustically on the group of British tourists who could be found "in every tomb, and every church, and every ruin, and every Picture Gallery" in Rome. A decade later, John Ruskin bemoaned in memorable fashion the presence of tourists in previously pristine natural landscapes: "Our modern society in general goes to the mountains, not to fast, but to feast, and leaves their glaciers covered with chicken-bones and egg shells."[20]

That tourists, the great unwashed, visited and by their very presence polluted the privileged traveling grounds of the social elite was painful enough to those defenders of the leisure high ground. That those unwanted visitors actually had the temerity to describe their experiences in writing seemed to mark the absolute end of an era of exclusive travel and the end of travel's authenticity. We should not then be surprised at the proclamation of one especially supercilious British observer in 1870 that "of all noxious animals the most noxious is the tourist."[21] Or that two years later America's beloved nature writer, John Muir, in a letter to a friend, referred to tourists as "sticks of condensed filth" and dismissively commented on how they were "content with what they can see from [railway] car windows or the verandas of hotels, and in going from place to place cling to their precious trains like wrecked sailors to rafts."[22] By the late 1870s, Richard Francis Burton, by then a British consul posted in Trieste, was expressing similar sentiments in his published works, conveying, in the words of his most recent biographer, Dane Kennedy, an "antagonism towards the tourist industry [that] was fueled by his regret at the passing of the age of exploration."[23] Another British military man and travel writer, William Francis Butler, author of travel books ranging from the North American West to Afghanistan and southern Africa, expressed the same concern. While in Muir's beloved Yosemite Valley, Butler lamented, in the tradition of Ruskin, that the tourists' picnic remnants now lay "amid the cones that hold the seeds of thirty centuries."[24]

Such sentiments were well entrenched by this time, on both sides of the Atlantic, and more generally were expressed by those whose travels (unlike Burton's) had not been much marked by adventure.[25] They were encapsulated most memorably at the close of the century by Rudyard Kipling in *From Sea to Sea: Letters of Travel* (1899), in which he proclaimed, in response to the pervasive presence of busy journal- and diary-writing tourists, "To-day I am in Yellowstone, and I wish I were dead." In accounting for his own morbidity, Kipling explained that "[i]t is not the ghastly vulgarity, the oozing, rampant Bessemer-steel self-sufficiency and ignorance of the men that revolts me, so much as the display of these same qualities in the women-folk." He then added, hopefully, in regard to "[t]he tourists," "may their master die an evil death at the hand of a mad locomotive!" Barely a step up the ladder of humanity from the common tourist, in Kipling's estimation, was the wealthy traveler and would-be travel writer, whom he dismissively described as the "Globe-trotter," "the man who 'does' kingdoms in days and writes books upon them in weeks."[26] Kipling's real fear, and more generally that of upper-class Britons and other Europeans who directed their ire at the touring masses, was not tourism in and of itself (i.e., the process of visiting places and peoples beyond the realm of one's day-to-day experience), but the democratization that tourism stood for as manifested in an expanding middle class whose abilities to travel and tour, spend and consume, and even write and publish thus increasingly invalidated the achievements of the old elite.[27]

Authenticity, then, was the proclaimed key both to true pioneering and to true traveling, although the matter of *exclusivity* is the real key to understanding the sentiments directed against tourists and Pullman pioneers. The presumed death of the travel book in the mid-twentieth century paralleled the earlier perceptions of the closing of the frontier in the late nineteenth century, which in turn echoed in interesting ways the British elite's fears, beginning early in that century, over the rise of tourism and the consequence of now having to share its travel experience with the British middle class. Old western pioneer memoirists emphasized the trials and tribulations of their journeys to western places and laid claim to the true soul and spirit of those locales in part because they saw their social status being undermined by later arrivals; thus, they reminisced about the Old West to bolster their standing in the New (contemporary) West. Such paralleling of the sentiments of old western American pioneers in the late nineteenth and early twentieth centuries with those of stodgy British conservatives in the mid-nineteenth hardly bolsters common notions of the West as an exceptional place marked by uniquely democratic attitudes. Indeed, through this comparison, the West's old pioneers seem more like the intellectual progeny of Old World elitism and exclusivity than its antithesis.

All of these chroniclers and commentators of course were engaged in a self-legitimating endeavor, one that privileged their own experience as authentic while denigrating the experience of others for being contrived or artificial. Pico Iyer nicely captured this sentiment and the purpose behind it (albeit in gender-specific language) when he wrote in 1986, "It is the first conceit of every voyager to imagine that he alone has found the world's last paradise. It is the second to believe that the door has slammed shut right behind him."[28] We see this sentiment still firmly manifest even in late-twentieth-century travel books such as William Least Heat-Moon's best seller, *Blue Highways* (1982), in which authentic places are generally to be found at the end of unpaved roads, as far away as possible from the trappings of franchised civilization, and thus to be experienced only by the legitimate traveler willing to eschew the interstates with all their accompanying comforts and conveniences. Heat-Moon, in his converted half-ton Ford Econoline van, which he named *Ghost Dancing*, set out on his land voyage much in the cultural tradition of Jack London's maritime adventures on board the *Snark* seventy years earlier.

During the course of the century explored in this study, from the 1840s through the 1930s, the pace of life and travel in the United States moved from that of a horse or horse-drawn carriage to hundreds of miles per hour on transcontinental flights.[29] The emergence of the railroad and then the automobile might each have sounded the death knell of "true" travel and hence the travel book, just as jet travel seemed to do a few decades later. But each new technological turn was accompanied by premature pronouncements in this regard. The travel book lives on, oblivious to the assumption that its time should long since have passed. Perhaps this is because the particular means of transportation, or, more broadly, the comparative difficulty of a journey is hardly the sole key to the authenticity of the travel experience. Indeed, as we have seen, the authenticity factor is something of a red herring with respect to "true" travel writing, the stop sign that the ostensibly more pedigreed traveler, beginning in the early nineteenth century, held up in protest against those people who were the beneficiaries of the democratization of transit.

The real authenticity or value of the genre surely lies in the expansiveness of the vision of its practitioners. This is why the travel book has persisted for nearly two centuries since its death was first announced and for more than three-quarters of a century since its demise was dramatically reproclaimed, and why today it seems as vital as ever, even though getting to almost anywhere in the world in next to no time at all is now more a chore than a challenge. The ease of travel does not restrict the vision of the observant travel writer in the postmodern age any more than the difficulty of travel guaranteed smart observation in the premodern or modern periods. The most talented travel writers of today would in all likelihood have been talented in any period (so long as they had the financial means to travel in the first place), just as those of earlier eras would be effective today, despite the comparative ease of travel. It is the ability of the traveler to experience and reflect on what is encountered along the way that is most important. And the West certainly continued to beckon a steady stream of travel writers in the post–World War II years.

Enduring Western Roads

At the midpoint of the twentieth century, Jack Kerouac wrote to a prospective publisher about his new work, one he envisioned being of epic proportions, "a novel whose background is the recurrence of the pioneering instinct

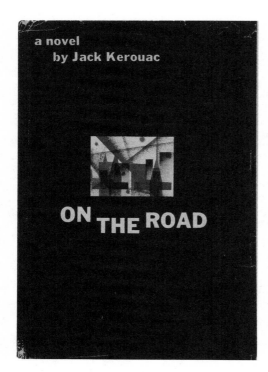

Figure 51. Jack Kerouac,
On the Road (1957).

in American life and its expression the migration of the present generation";
a book provisionally entitled *On the Road.*[30] Seven years later, Kerouac's literary tour de force, a hybrid of the novel and travel book forms, was finally
published. The Benzedrine-fueled account of Dean Moriarty and Sal
Paradise's (Neal Cassady and Kerouac, respectively) racing back and forth
across the country became a vital accompaniment to many thousands of
post–college graduation American road trips after its publication in 1957.
Still, it is worth remembering Kerouac's novelistic travelogue also for the
theme he outlined when he first envisioned the work: the search for the western frontier that weaves its way through the entire narrative.[31]

"I'd often dreamed of going West to see the country," Sal Paradise
announces in the fourth sentence of *On the Road,* explaining that Dean was
"the perfect guy for the road because he was actually born on the road" (in
1926, while his parents passed through Salt Lake City on their way to Los
Angeles). His first impression of Dean "was of a young Gene Autry. . . . a
sideburned hero of the snowy West . . . a western kinsman of the sun." Before
departing on his first hitchhiking trip across the continent, Sal notes that he

had been "reading books about the pioneers and savoring names like Platte and Cimarron." By the time he reached Iowa City, Sal's imagination sailed: "I could see Denver looking ahead of me like the Promised Land, way out there beneath the stars, across the prairie of Iowa and the plains of Nebraska, and I could see the greater vision of San Francisco beyond." The weight of anticipation was so great, it was unnerving: "I was half way across America, at the dividing line between the East of my youth and the West of my future." At Council Bluffs, near the Nebraska line, Sal recalls that he had been reading all winter about "the great wagon parties that held council there before hitting the Oregon and Santa Fe trails." He passes through Cheyenne, Wyoming, during the Frontier Days celebration, and on to Denver, where he meets up with Dean. Sal Paradise's experience in Denver fails to match his high expectations, and, spurned in love and friendship, he moves on to Hollywood, "the ragged promised land, the fantastic end of America." But when he arrives at the bus station, he finds the place no different from "where you'd get off a bus in Kansas City, or Chicago or Boston . . . the hopeless dawn, the whorey smell of a big city." Los Angeles, it turns out, "is the loneliest and most brutal of American cities."[32] Sal, thoroughly disillusioned, returns home to the East. Subsequent trips to the West end with the same disappointment, and a final trip with Dean southbound ends with Sal suffering from dysentery in Mexico City. The backdrop of western promise and anticipation is genuine in *On the Road*, just as it is for the Joads in Steinbeck's *The Grapes of Wrath*, and the crushing weight of failed dreams, the noncordance of hopes and realities, drives Kerouac's narrative just as it sets the tone for much of the travel writing about the West in the more than half century since *On the Road*'s publication.

Not all travel books about the modern West, to be sure, have adopted the frame of anticipation (for frontier authenticity or western promise) turned to disappointment. J. B. Priestley returned to the American Southwest (from Houston to Mesa Verde) in the 1950s with his wife, the archeologist Jacquetta Hawkes. The two ventured down different investigatory paths upon their arrival in the region, with Priestley heading to Texas's booming cities, "the newest triumphs of civilisation," and Hawkes to New Mexico's, Arizona's, and Colorado's "ancient and primitive cultures." The end result, *Journey Down a Rainbow* (1955), was an insightful set of observations conveyed through individually authored essays and letters to each other conveying their respective experiences. In one of her letters, Hawkes wrote to Priestley to express her annoyance at "how the very same people who rejoice at being

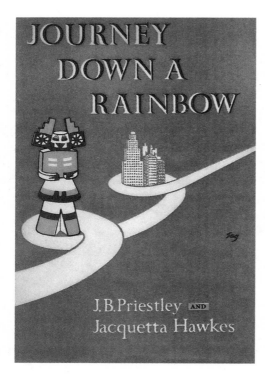

Figure 52. J. B. Priestley and
Jacquetta Hawkes, *Journey Down
a Rainbow* (1955). Copyright
© 1955 by John Boynton Priestley
and Jacquetta Hawkes.
Reprinted courtesy of
HarperCollins Publishers.

able to do a journey in one morning which before would have taken three
days, groan and complain when they find their favourite scenery spoilt and
Indian villages and ruins seething with tourists."[33]

At Taos, Hawkes found "the genuine life of the Pueblo . . . holding out
against tremendous odds," an observation that was a departure from the fatal-
istic assessments of transcontinental auto travelers and chroniclers who visited
the place earlier in the century. She also expressed some confidence that even
in the wake of uranium discoveries on Pueblo lands, those cultures would
remain intact. Hawkes explained, "I am not so inane as to imagine a return to
[primitive life] to be either possible or desirable," but then added, "[b]ut can we
not, like the Pueblos, make some conscious refusals?" In response to those who
insisted that "Indians cannot hold out much longer" against the forces of
change, she replied: "There is in the world today some spirit rising against the
huge forces of uniformity."[34] Priestley, for his part, was not charmed by the
Lone Star State's cities in the way he had been by the New Deal's works projects
and the Southwest's dramatic scenery a generation earlier, but neither was he
by any means inclined toward wholesale rejection of those centers of rapid

metropolitan growth and innovation. *Journey Down a Rainbow* leaves the sensible impression that the premodern and modern were vital and not necessarily incompatible parts of the same world.

Another British travel writer, James Morris, arrived at much the same conclusion in *Coast to Coast* (1956), his account of seventy thousand miles of travel in the United States during a series of trips in 1953 and 1954, including time among the Pueblo, Navajo, and Sioux. Morris described the Indian peoples of the West collectively as "an odd, anachronistic part of the American body politic, in an uncomfortable state of half-integration," while also detecting "a lingering spirit of frontier freedom" in the geographic expanse from Texas to Montana. At the same time he marveled at the modern network of dams, bridges, and roads that was springing up across the region. But, like Priestley and Hawkes, Morris found the old and new, the anachronistic and the futuristic, coexisting in ways that seemed natural enough.[35]

The more common course, though, in travel books about the modern West has been to search for vestiges of the frontier and regional authenticity, and to end up largely disappointed, finding the old submerged and suffocated by the new. Such is the case with John Steinbeck's *Travels with Charley in Search of America* (1962), one of the most widely read American travel books of the twentieth century. During his travels, Steinbeck experienced "a definite regional accent unaffected by TV-ese, a slow-paced warm speech" in Montana, found the state pleasantly unaffected by "the frantic bustle of America," and promptly fell in love with it. But, while insistent that he was not bemoaning an earlier time, "the preoccupation of the old," or "cultivat[ing] an opposition to change . . . the currency of the rich and stupid," Steinbeck, when he arrived at the Pacific coast, was nonetheless nostalgic for the Seattle he had once known and was repulsed by the city's "frantic . . . carcinomatous growth" at the expense of nature. "The tops of hills are shaved off to make level warrens for the rabbits of the present. The highways' eight lanes wide cut like glaciers through the uneasy land." He complained that "[b]ulldozers rolled up the green forests and heaped the resulting trash for burning" and wondered "why progress looks so much like destruction."[36]

Returning to his native California and the beautiful Monterey Peninsula, site of some of his most memorable work, including the novel *Cannery Row* (1945), Steinbeck wrote ruefully that "[t]hey fish for tourists now, not pilchards, and that species they are not likely to wipe out." Expressing disappointment befitting his age (he was in his late fifties), not Kerouac's despair over youthful dreams crushed by hard reality, Steinbeck wrote: "The place of

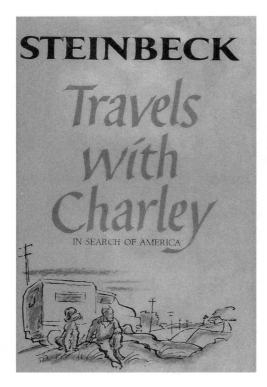

Figure 53. John Steinbeck, *Travels with Charley in Search of America* (1962).

my origin had changed, and having gone away I had not changed with it." He added, "Tom Wolfe was right. You can't go home again because home has ceased to exist except in the mothballs of memory." Nonetheless, Steinbeck then drove eastward from California and returned to his home on Long Island, New York, and did so via the greater Southwest. In Texas, he ruminated on the sense of exceptionalism that marked residents of the state, manifested in their occasional threats to secede from the Union. In flippant response, he formed "an enthusiastic organization—The American Friends for Texas Secession." But finding no reciprocal enthusiasm for his efforts, Steinbeck concluded: "They want to be able to secede [from the Union] but they don't want anyone to want them to."[37] For the most part, though, Steinbeck viewed sectional differences in America to be in decline and Texan separateness as an anomaly.

The demise of western authenticity is similarly evident in Robert D. Kaplan's disappointed conclusion in *An Empire Wilderness: Travels into America's Future* (1998) that Santa Fe and Taos "are yet another theme park where Americans can dress up and play new roles." The same sentiment drives William Leach's jeremiad against the death of regionalism in *Country of Exiles: The Destruction of Place in American Life* (1999). It is apparent, too, in Richard Grant's wandering reflections in *American Nomads: Travels with Lost Conquistadors, Mountain Men, Cowboys, Indians, Hoboes, Truckers, and Bullriders* (2003). Grant finds his authentic subjects, but they are outliers residing on the margins rather than representative types illuminating the mainstream.

Other recent western travelers, including Dayton Duncan in *Out West: An American Journey* (1987), Ian Frazier in *The Great Plains* (1989) and *On The Rez* (2000), Jonathan Raban in *Bad Land: An American Romance* (1996) and *Old Glory: An American Voyage* (1981), and Kathleen Norris in *Dakota: A Spiritual Geography* (2001), have found more to celebrate in the way of western regional distinctiveness.[38] Larry McMurtry, in *Roads: Driving America's Great Highways* (2000), his book of engaging observations during his travels along the interstates (not the blue roads that enchanted Least Heat-Moon), offers, in his words, a "counterargument to the often expressed view that because of the chain businesses, America all looks the same. But it doesn't," McMurtry insists, "and it won't, no matter how many McDonald's and Taco Bell's cluster around the exits. . . . Place will always be distinct . . . [and] America is still a country of immense diversity."[39]

Whether celebrating the regional diversity of the West or bemoaning its passage—whether more in the tradition of the WPA state guides that described 1930s America, or of the transcontinental automotive travel narratives of the early twentieth century—authors of travel books have continued in recent decades to view the West more often within the context of the nation rather than the world. Their travels are best considered American frontier journeys rather than global ones. Whether the global orientation that characterized so many nineteenth-century western travelogues will see a return in the twenty-first century is uncertain, but the longer history of the genre certainly has significance. That history is unlikely to reach a terminal point in the foreseeable future. The West's cultures and landscapes remain as enduring roads for new generations of travel writers and will do so for as long as the region and its storied legacies remain a barometer of national health and identity.

Similarly, songwriters and filmmakers will continue to draw on the travel narrative form, embedding the great American road, with all its promise and peril, into their sonic and celluloid creations. From John Ford's adaptation of

Steinbeck's *The Grapes of Wrath* (1940) to *Easy Rider* (1969), *Rain Man* (1988), *Powwow Highway* (1989), *Thelma and Louise* (1991), *Smoke Signals* (1998), and *Borat, Little Miss Sunshine*, and the Disney Pixar animated movie *Cars* (all 2006), to name just a very few examples, the road journey across the national landscape for purposes of escape and self-discovery has become a staple of American film.[40] In popular music, from the 1960s through the 1980s, the road song was ubiquitous, from Bobby Troup's classic "(Get Your Kicks) on Route 66" (first recorded in 1946 by Nat King Cole, and covered by Chuck Berry in 1961 and the Rolling Stones in 1964), Hank Snow's "I've Been Everywhere" (1962; later recorded by Johnny Cash, 1996), Bob Dylan's "Highway 61 Revisited" (1965), Simon and Garfunkel's "America" (1968), and Janis Joplin's posthumous number one hit "Me and Bobby McGee" (1971), to the Grateful Dead's "Truckin'" (1970) and Little Feat's paean to the indomitable American trucker, "Willin'" (1971), the Eagles' "Take It Easy" (1972) and "Life in the Fast Lane" (1977), Jackson Browne's "Running on Empty" (1977), Bruce Springsteen's "Born to Run," "Thunder Road" (both 1975), and "The Promised Land" (1978), Willie Nelson's "On the Road Again" (1980), Dire Straits' "Telegraph Road" (1982), Bob Dylan and Sam Shepard's "Brownsville Girl" (1986), U2's album *The Joshua Tree* (1987), and Tom Petty's "Runnin' Down a Dream" (1989), to mention just a handful of the highlights. In the past quarter century, the American road song, like the road film and the travel book, has continued to endure, with Tom Cochrane's "Life Is a Highway" (1991) and the Red Hot Chili Peppers' "Road Trippin'" (2000) among the better-known examples.[41] The great American road trip, drawing on travel books and novels, film, and music, also became a memorable educational endeavor in Douglas Brinkley's efforts to facilitate his students' discovery of their national heritage (in all its regional variation). In his course An American Odyssey: Art and Culture Across America, Brinkley took his Hofstra University class on the road and recounted their experiences in engaging fashion in *The Magic Bus: An American Odyssey* (1993), itself now a recognized part of the American road book canon.[42]

Legacies of the Global West and the American Frontier

There are lessons for the present in a reexamination of nineteenth- and twentieth-century travel accounts. Clearly, we live in another age when the exceptionalist rhetoric of U.S. policy makers would be well served by a healthy dose of global contextualization and comparative analysis. In the early years of the twenty-first century, the George W. Bush administration struggled to maintain an exceptionalist framework for the war in Iraq by emphasizing America's role in bringing freedom and democracy to the Iraqi people. The administration downplayed the growing concern about strategies of preemptive war and unilateralism, rendition, torture, and Orwellian oversight on the home front. Such strategies led the world and eventually the American public to question the United States' motives and purposes, and to highlight imperialistic tendencies, thus echoing the criticism of the nation's actions in Vietnam two generations earlier. This tension between exceptionalism and imperialism is becoming increasingly taut and fraught even as the United States has officially pulled out of Iraq and is withdrawing from Afghanistan.[43] Indeed, during the administration of Barack Obama, the Republican Party has made the belief in American exceptionalism a litmus test of conservative pedigree and patriotic conviction.

While the struggle between notions of national exceptionalism and the realities of American imperialism is highlighted today in a wide array of electronic media outlets, in the nineteenth century it was global travel writers—including George Catlin, Friedrich Gerstäcker, Richard Francis Burton, Isabella Bird, Robert Louis Stevenson, and Mark Twain—who reminded the American public of that tension. The road maps of a globalized, comparative West that those writers provided remain valuable today. Their accounts remind us that when we as scholars of earlier ages place the regions of our respective expertise into global comparative context, we are not necessarily doing something that the residents of those times and places could not do, or providing them with parallels they could not have conceived of, or seeing the world more clearly for them than they could have seen it for themselves.[44] Quite the contrary, in the case of nineteenth-century Americans, we are continuing their work of seeing themselves, and thus seeing ourselves, within the larger world. That is an enterprise which seems particularly useful in this challenging moment in the American present, when trade wars and distressed global financial markets, undocumented residents and border anxieties, the threat of foreign and home-grown terrorism, "dirty" bombs and nuclear proliferation, wars and genocides, and environmental challenges force us to think more deeply about America's place in the world, and the world's place in America.

The nation, born on the stage of worldwide conflict between European powers, had, in the wake of the Louisiana Purchase of 1803 and certainly by the end of the Napoleonic Wars, the War of 1812 (in 1815), and Spain's cession of Florida in 1819, set itself on a path of continental expansion that would involve wars of conquest against Mexico and a range of indigenous peoples as settlement surged westward.[45] What in retrospect and to many at the time seemed like the playing out of destiny was, of course, a process of conscious expansion of the nation's geographic borders: empire building. That process differed in some important ways from those of other contemporary imperial powers. For example, new western territories were incorporated into the body politic as full-fledged states, not as satellite states or colonies, although most of the conquered peoples did not share the citizenship rights of the majority population. Travel writers during the nineteenth century, both Americans and foreign visitors, commented on American expansion and were more likely than not to place it into that larger global context of empire building.

During the twentieth century, or "the American century," the nation's travel writers turned inward in their efforts to present their nation to the world, following much the same course as historians, economists, political scientists, sociologists, literary critics, philosophers, and theologians, particularly from the 1930s to the 1950s, as they constructed the intellectual underpinnings of modern American exceptionalism.[46] The process by which these cultural foundations and the edifice of exceptionalism were built also included, as we have seen, the rediscovery of the works of foreign travelers to America in the nineteenth century, such as Alexis de Tocqueville, whose impressions could be read selectively to serve as celebrations and confirmations of a benign American character and polity. Any such confirmations of a Jeffersonian American empire, an empire of liberty, were destined for inclusion in the annals of exceptionalism. But the process did not have space for the rediscovery of the more critical works by European visitors, such as Gerstäcker's *Narrative of a Journey Round the World* (1853). Such travelogues, by contextualizing American empire globally and underscoring the harrowing intersections of expansion and genocidal acts against indigenous populations, firmly planted the United States within the world; but it was a world that remained outside the intended purview of many American legacy builders of the twentieth century. We still have much to learn both from what nineteenth-century travelers decided to include in their analyses of the global West, and from what their twentieth-century counterparts decided to leave out of the picture in envisioning that geographic space as an exceptionally American frontier.

NOTES

Introduction

1. John White, *Sketches from America: Part I.—Canada; Part II.—A Pic-nic to the Rocky Mountains; Part III.—The Irish in America* (London: Sampson Low, Son, and Marston, 1870), 230. The work is now available in a British Library Historical Print Edition, 2011. White used "lions" as a synonym for attractions; the four massive lion statues that grace London's Trafalgar Square, the work of sculptor Sir Edward Lanseer, were erected in 1868 and were almost certainly the inspiration for White's use of the term.

2. Ibid., 231–32.

3. Ray Allen Billington, *Land of Savagery, Land of Promise: The European Image of the American Frontier in the Nineteenth Century* (New York: W. W. Norton, 1981).

4. The notion that travel writers contributed in a significant way to the body of western mythology that developed in the nineteenth century is certainly evident in Billington's *Land of Savagery* as well as in Robert G. Athearn's *Westward the Briton: The Far West, 1865–1900, as Seen by British Sportsmen and Capitalists, Ranchers and Homesteaders, Lords and Ladies* (New York: Charles Scribner's Sons, 1953; reprinted, Lincoln: University of Nebraska Press, Bison Books, 1962), 7–8.

5. See, for example, Ray Allen Billington's influential textbook *Westward Expansion: A History of the American Frontier* (New York: Macmillan, 1949); Henry Nash Smith's *Virgin Land: The American West as Symbol and Myth* (Cambridge: Harvard University Press, 1950); and two anthologies of nineteenth-century European travelers' descriptions of the United States: Allan Nevins's *America Through British Eyes* (New York: Oxford University Press, 1948); and Oscar Handlin, *This Was America: True Accounts of People and Places, Manners and Customs, as Recorded by European Travelers to the Western Shore in the Eighteenth, Nineteenth, and Twentieth Centuries* (Cambridge: Harvard University Press, 1949). For more on the manifestations of early Cold War American exceptionalism in a range of academic disciplines, including history, see John Diggins,

The Rise and Fall of the American Left (New York: W. W. Norton, 1992), 187–200.

6. Helen Hunt Jackson, *A Century of Dishonor: A Sketch of the United States Government's Dealings with Some of the Indian Tribes* (New York: Harper and Brothers, 1881); Josiah Royce, *California, from the Conquest in 1846 to the Second Vigilance Committee in San Francisco: A Study of American Character* (Boston: Houghton Mifflin, 1886).

7. Frederick Jackson Turner used the metaphor of the frontier as "the outer edge of the wave"; see "The Significance of the Frontier in American History" (1893), in *Rereading Frederick Jackson Turner: "The Significance of the Frontier in American History" and Other Essays*, ed. John Mack Faragher (New York: Henry Holt, 1994; reprinted, New Haven, CT: Yale University Press, 1998), 31–60, 32; page references from the 1998 edition.

8. Regarding the great volume of nineteenth-century travel accounts, Mary Suzanne Schriber notes that 1,765 books of travel were published in the United States between 1830 and 1900; see her *Writing Home: American Women Abroad, 1830–1920* (Charlottesville: University of Virginia Press, 1997), 2. Lynne Withey, in *Grand Tours and Cook's Tours: A History of Leisure Travel, 1750–1915* (New York: William Morrow, 1997), 234, states that at least 1,044 travel books about the Middle East were published in the nineteenth century. Max Berger, in *The British Traveller in America, 1836–1860* (New York: Columbia University Press, 1943), 14, notes that 230 accounts by British travelers to America were published between 1836 and 1860. For a good introduction to a wide range of the better-known nineteenth-century travelers' accounts of the West, see John Francis McDermott, ed., *Travelers on the Western Frontier* (Urbana: University of Illinois Press, 1970); Billington, *Land of Savagery*; and, most recently, Roger L. Nichols, "Western Attractions: Europeans and America," *Pacific Historical Review* 74 (2005): 1–17.

9. There is an abundance of writing about travel writing that tries to chart the contours of the genre, or determine the degree to which it is a genre at all. Among the most useful entrées into these debates are: Michael Kowalewski, "Introduction: The Modern Literature of Travel," in his edited collection *Temperamental Journeys: Essays on the Modern Literature of Travel* (Athens: University of Georgia Press, 1992), 1–16; Peter Hulme and Tim Youngs, introduction to their coedited volume *The Cambridge Companion to Travel Writing* (Cambridge: Cambridge University Press, 2002), 1–17; Jan Borm, "Defining Travel: On the Travel Book, Travel Writing and Terminology," in *Perspectives on Travel Writing*, ed. Glen Hooper and Tim Youngs (Aldershot, England: Ashgate, 2004), 13–26; Barbara Korte, "Charting the Genre," in her *English Travel Writing: From Pilgrimages to Postcolonial Explorations*, trans. Catherine Matthias (London: Macmillan, 2000), 5–18; and Alfred Bendixen and Judith Hamera, "Introduction: New Worlds and Old Lands; The Travel Book and the Construction

of American Identity," in their coedited collection *The Cambridge Companion to American Travel Writing* (Cambridge: Cambridge University Press, 2009), 1–9.

10. Bernard-Henri Lévy, *American Vertigo: Traveling America in the Footsteps of Tocqueville* (New York: Random House, 2006). There is nothing original in the book's concept; South African and British writer David Cohen's travelogue *Chasing the Red, White, and Blue: A Journey in Tocqueville's Footsteps Through Contemporary America* (New York: Picador, 2001) is more insightful, although it includes only a single chapter on the West, "California: The America Tocqueville Never Knew," 218–65. American political commentator Richard Reeves's popular work *American Journey: Traveling with Tocqueville in Search of Democracy in America* (New York: Simon and Schuster, 1982) is more hopeful than either Cohen's or Lévy's Tocqueville-inspired accounts.

11. Alexis de Tocqueville, *Democracy in America*, trans. and ed. Harvey C. Mansfield and Delba Winthrop (Chicago: University of Chicago Press, 2000). See chapter 1, note 39 for the various editions that appeared in the 1940s and 1950s.

12. For more on the stigmatization of Las Vegas and other urban centers, see Jonathan Foster, "Stigma Cities: Dystopian Urban Identities in the United States West and South in the Twentieth Century" (PhD dissertation, University of Nevada, Las Vegas, 2009).

13. Louis Theroux's *The Call of the Weird: Travels in American Subcultures* (London: Macmillan, 2005; reprinted, Boston: Da Capo Press, 2007) is in many ways a more satisfying travelogue than Lévy's *American Vertigo*. Theroux's primary intention was to take a walk on the weird side and explain why there is so much weirdness in American culture; secondarily, he wished to use that set of subcultural experiences to illuminate aspects of the American mainstream. The approach is considerably more transparent than Lévy's. Lévy's ostensible goal is to examine all the strands of the American cultural fabric, but he more often than not uses extraordinary people as his cultural yardsticks. Tocqueville, of course, understood that the new country's penitentiary system could serve as a window onto the mainstream of American democracy, and Lévy's time with a Nevada death row inmate might be deemed as being within that tradition of emphasizing the margins to illuminate the mainstream, but the echo is faint at best.

14. Readers seeking explorations of this nature might consider, in addition to Theroux's *The Call of the Weird*, Melanie McGrath, *Motel Nirvana: Dreaming of the New Age in the American Desert* (New York: Picador, 1996).

15. Selections from the better known of these earliest accounts are gathered together in Edward Watts and David Rachels, *The First West: Writings from the American Frontier, 1776–1860* (New York: Oxford University Press, 2002). Larzer Ziff devotes a chapter to John Ledyard in his excellent study *Return Passages: Great American Travel Writing, 1780–1910* (New Haven, CT: Yale University Press, 2000).

16. The term "travelogue" was actually coined by the American world-traveling photographer and filmmaker Burton Holmes, who used it as the descriptive label for his illustrated presentations on parts of the Americas and the rest of the world from the late nineteenth century into the late 1930s. For more on Holmes's life and work, see Genoa Caldwell, ed., *The Man Who Photographed the World: Burton Holmes Travelogues, 1886–1938* (New York: Harry N. Abrams, 1977).

17. For a superb examination of von Humboldt's influence on American explorers, see Aaron Sachs, *The Humboldt Current: Nineteenth-Century American Exploration and the Roots of American Environmentalism* (New York: Viking, 2006). Also useful are Alain de Botton's insightful chapter on von Humboldt, "On Curiosity," in his *The Art of Travel* (London: Penguin Books, 2003; first published, London: Hamish Hamilton, 2002), 103–25; and Nigel Leask's chapter "Alexander von Humboldt and the Romantic Imagination of America: The Impossibility of Personal Narrative," in his *Curiosity and the Aesthetics of Travel Writing, 1770–1840: "From an Antique Land"* (Oxford: Oxford University Press, 2002). Von Humboldt's *Personal Narrative* was originally published in French between 1814 and 1825, translated by Thomasina Ross and published in English in three volumes (London: H. G. Bohn, 1852).

18. From Reuben Gold Thwaites's centennial edition of *The Original Journals of the Lewis and Clark Expedition, 1804–1806* (1904) to the surge of scholarly and public interest surrounding the recent bicentennial commemorations (2004–2006), most particularly the outstanding work of James P. Ronda, this topic has been so well traveled that my own coverage here would be redundant. See James P. Ronda, *Lewis and Clark Among the Indians* (Lincoln: University of Nebraska Press, 1984; Bison Books First Printing, 1998; Bison Books Centennial Edition, 2002). A good example of the excellent work on Lewis and Clark that accompanied the bicentennial is Carolyn Gilman, *Lewis and Clark: Across the Divide*, with an introduction by James Ronda (Washington, D.C.: Smithsonian Books, 2003).

Similarly, to have included in this study the nineteenth-century government-sponsored expeditions of Zebulon Montgomery Pike (1806–1807), Stephen Harriman Long (1820), Charles Wilkes (1838–1842), John Charles Frémont (throughout the 1840s), and John Wesley Powell (1869 and 1872)—all of which resulted in published accounts of the journeys and important descriptions and discussions of the West's landscapes and peoples—would have added little to the well-developed historiographical record. The landmark work on these government-sponsored expeditions remains William H. Goetzmann's Pulitzer Prize–winning study *Exploration and Empire: The Explorer and the Scientist in the Winning of the American West* (New York: W. W. Norton, 1966). For a particularly insightful treatment of John C. Frémont's observations during his explorations of the West, see Anne Farrar Hyde, *An American Vision: Far Western Landscape and National Culture, 1820–1920* (New York: New York University Press, 1990), 1–11. Two other U.S. government-sponsored expeditions that warrant a mention but do not find their way into the main coverage of this study are naval lieutenant William Hearndon's *Exploration of the Valley of the Amazon, 1851–1852* (1854), available in a new edition edited by Gary Kinder (New York: Grove Press, 2000); and John L. Stephens's *Incidents of Travel in Central America, Chiapas, and Yucatan*, 2 vols. (New York: Harper and Brothers, 1841; reprinted, Cambridge: Cambridge University Press, 2010).

Austrian Prince Maximilian of Wied-Neuwied provides another potential point of entry into the topic. Wied journeyed to Brazil in 1815–1817 and then to North America from 1832 to 1834, and compared the landscapes, plant and animal life, and Indian peoples of the New World (accompanied on the latter of the two trips by the artist Karl Bodmer). Prince Maximilian's account of the second trip, published in German (2 volumes, 1839–1841), in French (3 volumes, 1840–1843), and in an abridged English translation, *Travels in the Interior of North America, 1832–1834* (1843), includes some wonderfully detailed examples of comparative ethnographic observation and remains a vital source of information on the West and its Indian peoples in the early 1830s. But the work's initial appearance in English, almost a decade after the conclusion of its author's travels (and then, only in truncated form), renders it less central to the current study, which tends to focus on travelogues that appeared quite shortly after the conclusion of their authors' journeys (and sometimes even during them, in serialized form). A beautifully designed and illustrated three-volume edition of the work is now available: *The North American Journals of Prince Maximilian of Wied*, vol. 1, *May 1832–April 1833*; vol. 2, *April–September 1833*; and vol. 3, *September 1833–August 1834*, edited by Stephen S. Witte and Marsha V. Gallagher, translated by William J. Orr, Paul Schach, and Dieter Karch (Norman: University of Oklahoma Press, 2008, 2011, and 2012). For a comparative ethnographic analysis of the Blackfoot Indians and Brazilian Indians, see volume 2, 422–23.

Other potential points of departure for this study that have themselves become classics of the American travel writing genre include Washington Irving's *A Tour on the Prairies* (London: John Murray, 1835) and Richard Henry Dana's *Two Years Before the Mast* (New York: Harper and Brothers, 1840).

19. Walter Nugent, *Habits of Empire: A History of American Expansion* (New York: Alfred A. Knopf, 2008).

20. Elliott West, *The Last Indian War: The Nez Perce Story* (New York: Oxford University Press, 2009).

21. While Friedrich Gerstäcker (see chapter 1) received a small grant from the new provisional government in Germany, that support hardly shaped his observations of peoples and places and colonizers and the colonized around the world.

22. Indeed, during the late nineteenth and early twentieth centuries, a wide range of writers whose work spanned both the fiction and nonfiction forms often found that the best route to publishing a collection of shorter pieces—essays, letters, ruminations—was to place them in the form of a travel book.

23. I have treated the promotional and reminiscence genres in another book, *Promised Lands: Promotion, Memory, and the Creation of the American West* (Lawrence: University Press of Kansas, 2002, 2011).

24. John Steinbeck, *The Grapes of Wrath and Other Writings, 1936–1941*, ed. Robert DeMott and Elaine A. Steinbeck (New York: Library of America, 1996), 334.

25. For more on these sources, see Nicholas T. Parsons, *Worth the Detour: A History of the Guidebook* (Gloucester, England: Sutton Publishing, 2007); and Robert Foulke, "The Guidebook Industry," in *Temperamental Journeys: Essays on the Modern Literature of Travel*, ed. Michael Kowalewski (Athens: University of Georgia Press, 1992), 93–106.

   Also absent from this study are extended discussions of the development of travel networks in the West. Readers interested in transportation in the West are directed to the Center for Transportation Studies at the University of Missouri–Saint Louis, directed by Carlos Arnaldo Schwantes (http://www.umsl. edu/~cts/index.html), and to Schwantes's books, including *Long Day's Journey: The Steamboat and Stagecoach Era in the Northern West* (Seattle: University of Washington Press, 1999); *Going Places: Transportation Redefines the Twentieth-Century West* (Bloomington: Indiana University Press, 2003); *Railroad Signatures Across the Pacific Northwest* (Seattle: University of Washington Press, 1996); and, with James P. Ronda, *The West the Railroads Made* (Seattle: University of Washington Press, 2008). Works on the history of automotive transportation in the West are cited in chapter 4 of the present study.

26. John Muir's recently published letters and diaries pertaining to his trip to South America and Africa in 1911–1912 are briefly discussed in chapter 3. For a good example of recent utilization of unpublished western travel accounts, see Robert Campbell, *In Darkest Alaska: Travel and Empire Along the Inside Passage* (Philadelphia: University of Pennsylvania Press, 2007).

27. See David Wrobel, "Introduction: Tourists, Tourism, and the Toured Upon," in *Seeing and Being Seen: Tourism in the American West*, ed. David Wrobel and Patrick Long (Lawrence: University Press of Kansas, 2001), 1–34.

28. Mark Twain, *The Innocents Abroad, or the New Pilgrims' Progress* (Hartford, CT: American Publishing Company, 1869; reprinted as *The Innocents Abroad* and *The New Pilgrims' Progress*, 2 vols., London: Hotten, 1870). Cited in Paul Theroux, *The Tao of Travel: Enlightenments from Lives on the Road* (New York: Mariner Books, 2012), 13.

29. Sinclair Lewis, "Travel Is So Broadening," in *The Best American Humorous Short Stories*, ed. Robert N. Linscott (New York: Random House, 1945), 186–206. The piece first appeared in Lewis's *The Man Who Knew Coolidge: Being the Soul of Lowell Schmaltz, Constructive and Nordic Citizen* (New York: Harcourt, Brace, 1928). See also Aldous Huxley, "Why Not Stay at Home?" in his *Along the Road: Notes and Essays of a Tourist* (London: Chatto and Windus; New York: George H. Doran, 1925), 3–14.

30. Paul Theroux, introduction to *The Old Patagonian Express: By Train Through the Americas* (Boston: Houghton Mifflin, 1997; first published, 1979).

31. Walt Whitman, "Song of the Open Road," in *Leaves of Grass*, 2nd ed. (Brooklyn, NY: Fowler and Wells, 1856).

32. There is, of course, an extensive scholarship on the processes by which western mythology was constructed and disseminated in the twentieth century; see, for example, Richard Slotkin, *Gunfighter Nation: The Myth of the Frontier in Twentieth-Century America* (New York: Atheneum, 1992); and Robert Athearn, *The Mythic West in Twentieth-Century America* (Lawrence: University Press of Kansas, 1989).

33. The extensive scholarship on British observers of American life includes Louise Mesick, *The English Traveler in America, 1785–1835* (New York: Columbia University Press, 1922); Allan Nevins, *American Social History as Recorded by British Travellers* (New York: Henry Holt, 1923; reprinted as *America Through British Eyes*); Max Berger, *The British Traveler in America, 1836–1860* (New York: Columbia University Press, 1943); Athearn, *Westward the Briton*; and Richard L. Rapson, *Britons View America: Travel Commentary, 1860–1935* (Seattle: University of Washington Press, 1971).

34. Ian Tyrrell, *Transnational Nation: United States History in Global Perspective Since 1789* (New York: Palgrave Macmillan, 2007). See also Thomas Bender, *Nation Among Nations: America's Place in World History* (New York: Hill and Wang, 2006); and Gary W. Reichard and Ted Dickson, eds., *America on the World Stage: A Global Approach to U.S. History* (Urbana: University of Illinois Press; Bloomington, IN: Organization of American Historians, 2008). For a full listing of the works on the West cited and others that have taken the field in a global direction, see chapter 1, note 7.

35. See Earl Pomeroy, "Foreword: Still Searching for the Golden West," in Wrobel and Long, *Seeing and Being Seen*, ix–xi; see also Earl Pomeroy, *In Search of the Golden West: The Tourist in Western America* (Lincoln: University of Nebraska Press, 1990; first published, New York: Alfred A. Knopf, 1957). Pomeroy's preface to the 1990 edition discusses his research for the book (v–xiv, esp. vi–vii).

36. E. H. Carr's essay "The Historian and His Facts," in his book *What Is History?*, 2nd ed. (London: Penguin Books, 1987; first published, 1961), remains the most compelling brief discussion of the matter of historical sources and subjectivity. See also John Lewis Gaddis, *The Landscape of History: How Historians Map the Past* (New York: Oxford University Press, 2002); and Joyce Appleby, Lynn Hunt, and Margaret Jacob, *Telling the Truth About History* (New York: W. W. Norton, 1994).

Chapter One

1. Edward Said, *Orientalism* (New York: Pantheon Books, 1978).

2. Thomas R. Hietala explores this tension in the chapter "American Exceptionalism, American Empire," in his *Manifest Design: Anxious*

Aggrandizement in Late Jacksonian America (Ithaca, NY: Cornell University Press, 1985), 173–214. Other useful global contextualizations of American empire include Paul Kennedy, *The Rise and Fall of the Great Powers: Economic Change and Military Conflict from 1500 to 2000* (New York: Random House, 1987); Walter Nugent, *Habits of Empire: A History of American Expansion* (New York: Alfred A. Knopf, 2008); Shelley Streeby, *American Sensations: Class, Empire, and the Production of Popular Culture* (Berkeley: University of California Press, 2002); James Belich, *Replenishing the Earth: The Settler Revolution and the Rise of the Anglo-World, 1783–1939* (Oxford: Oxford University Press, 2009); and Bruce Cummings, *Dominion from Sea to Sea: Pacific Ascendancy and American Power* (New Haven, CT: Yale University Press, 2009).

3. Elliott West, "Thinking West," in *The Blackwell Companion to the American West*, ed. William Deverell (Malden, MA: Blackwell, 2004), 25–50. For more on the travel narratives about Mexico during the Mexican-American War, see Howard R. Lamar, foreword to Susan S. Magoffin, *Down the Santa Fe Trail and Into Mexico: The Diary of Susan Shelby Magoffin, 1846–1847*, ed. Stella M. Drumm (Lincoln: University of Nebraska Press, 1982; originally published with the Lamar foreword, New Haven, CT: Yale University Press, 1962; originally published, New Haven, CT: Yale University Press, 1926), ix–xxxv.

4. Hietala, *Manifest Design*, 2.

5. Fred Anderson and Andrew Cayton, *The Dominion of War: Empire and Liberty in North America, 1500–2000* (New York: Viking, 2005), xv, emphasize how the realities of territorial acquisition undermine the rhetoric of exceptionalism.

6. Jefferson had used the phrase "empire of liberty" as early as 1780. On Stephen A. Douglas's use of the phrase "Empire for Liberty," see John Mack Faragher and Robert Hine, *The American West: A New Interpretive History* (New Haven, CT: Yale University Press, 2000), 199. See also Patricia Nelson Limerick, "Empire of Innocence," in her *The Legacy of Conquest: The Unbroken Past of the American West* (New York: W. W. Norton, 2006; first published, 1987); and Ian Tyrrell, "The Empire That Did Not Know Its Name," in his *Transnational Nation: United States History in Global Perspective Since 1789* (New York: Palgrave Macmillan, 2007), 134–54.

7. Henry Nash Smith's *Virgin Land: The American West as Symbol and Myth* (Cambridge: Harvard University Press, 1950), which emphasizes early Anglo exploration of the West as a search for trade routes to the Orient, and Walter Prescott Webb's *The Great Frontier* (Boston: Houghton Mifflin, 1952) are classic examples of the early global contextualization of western American history. See also Howard Lamar and Leonard Thompson's pioneering anthology, *The Frontier in History: North America and South Africa Compared* (New Haven, CT: Yale University Press, 1981); Walter Nugent's broad comparative piece, "Comparing Wests and Frontiers," in *The Oxford History of the American West*, ed. Clyde A. Milner II, Carol A. O'Connor, and Martha Sandweiss (New York:

Oxford University Press, 1994), 803–33; Gunther Peck, *Reinventing Free Labor: Padrones and Immigrant Workers in the North American West, 1880–1930* (Cambridge: Cambridge University Press, 2000); Patricia Nelson Limerick's presidential address to the Western History Association, "Going West and Ending Up Global," *Western Historical Quarterly* 32 (Spring 2001): 5–23; and Stephen Aron's "Returning the West to the World," in *America on the World Stage: A Global Approach to U.S. History,* edited by Gary W. Reichard and Ted Dickson (Urbana: University of Illinois Press; Bloomington, IN: Organization of American Historians, 2008), 85–98. Richard White's *Railroaded: The Transcontinentals and the Making of Modern America* (New York: W. W. Norton, 2011) is a brilliant example of how transnational themes (the study covers Canada and Mexico as well as the U.S. West) can be seamlessly woven into western history. For an excellent example of the successful forays of a historian of the U.S. West into Pacific World history, see David Igler, "Diseased Goods: Global Exchanges in the Eastern Pacific Basin, 1770–1850," *American Historical Review* 109 (June 2004): 693–719. World historians have comfortably incorporated the story of U.S. expansion into the global contexts of their works. See, for example, J. M. Roberts, *The New Penguin History of the World* (New York: Penguin Books, 2004; first published, 1976). Roberts writes: "there was much that was barely distinguishable from imperialism in the nineteenth-century territorial expansion of the United States, although Americans might not recognize it when it was packaged as a 'Manifest Destiny'" (827–28). One of the most recent efforts at globalizing western American history and culture is Neil Campbell's *The Rhizomatic West: Representing the American West in a Transnational, Global, Media Age* (Lincoln: University of Nebraska Press, 2008).

8. The obvious imperial parallels include the British colonization of India (under a policy of "Dual Control" from 1784, followed by the formal assumption of control in 1858), the French conquest of Algeria (1830–1847), and the European nations' carving up of the African continent at the West African Conferences of Berlin (1884–1885). Algeria's two most prominent leaders and resistors of French colonial authority, Abd al-Qadir and Ahmad Bey, surrendered to the French in 1847, the same year that American forces entered Mexico City.

9. For more on American exceptionalism, see Michael Kammen, "The Problem of American Exceptionalism: A Reconsideration," *American Quarterly* 45 (March 1993): 1–43; Ian Tyrrell, "American Exceptionalism in an Age of International History," *American Historical Review* 96 (October 1991): 1031–55; David Noble, *Death of a Nation: American Culture and the End of Exceptionalism* (Minneapolis: University of Minnesota Press, 2002); and Deborah L. Madsen, *American Exceptionalism* (Jackson: University Press of Mississippi, 1998).

10. Richard Slotkin, in *Regeneration Through Violence: The Mythology of the American Frontier, 1600–1800* (Middletown, CT: Wesleyan University Press, 1973); *The Fatal Environment: The Myth of the Frontier in the Age of*

Industrialization, 1800–1890 (New York: Atheneum, 1985); and *Gunfighter Nation: The Myth of the Frontier in Twentieth-Century America* (New York: Atheneum, 1992), contends that there was a more conscious construction of the national identity on a foundation of frontier mythology.

11. Benjamin Franklin, "The Internal State of America: Being a True Description of the Interest and Policy of that Vast Continent," in *The Writings of Benjamin Franklin*, ed. Albert K. Smythe, vol. 10 (New York: Macmillan, 1907), 117–18. See also James Paul Hutson, "Benjamin Franklin and the West," *Western Historical Quarterly* 4 (October 1973): 425–34.

12. For the Jefferson quotation, see Gilbert Chinard, *Thomas Jefferson: The Apostle of Americanism* (Boston: Little, Brown, 1929), 80–82; James C. Malin, *The Contriving Brain and the Skillful Hand in the United States* (Ann Arbor, MI: Edwards Brothers, 1955); and H. A. Washington, ed., *The Writings of Thomas Jefferson*, vol. 2 (Washington, D.C.: Taylor and Maury, 1854), 332.

13. John L. O'Sullivan's article "Annexation," addressing the opposition of European powers to the annexation of Texas, appeared in *Democratic Review* 17 (July–August 1845): 5–10. His later, more famous expression of the concept of manifest destiny appeared as an editorial in the *New York Morning News*, December 27, 1845. For more on manifest destiny, see Hietala, *Manifest Design*; David M. Pletcher, *The Diplomacy of Annexation: Texas, Oregon, and the Mexican War* (Columbia: University of Missouri Press, 1973); Robert W. Johannsen, "The Meaning of Manifest Destiny," in *Manifest Destiny and Empire: Antebellum American Expansionism*, ed. Sam W. Haynes and Christopher Morris (College Station: Texas A&M University Press, 1997), 7–20; and Julius Pratt, "The Ideology of American Expansion," in *Essays in Honor of William E. Dodd: By His Former Students at the University of Chicago*, ed. Avery Craven (Chicago: University of Chicago Press, 1935), 335–53. Pratt is also the author of two other useful articles, "The Origin of Manifest Destiny," *American Historical Review* 32 (July 1927): 795–98; and "John L. O'Sullivan and Manifest Destiny," *New York History* 14 (July 1933): 213–34. See also Frederick Jackson Turner, "The Significance of the Frontier in American History" (1893), in his *The Frontier in American History* (New York: Henry Holt, 1920), 1–38.

14. Dorothy Ross, "Historical Consciousness in Nineteenth-Century America," *American Historical Review* 89 (October 1984): 909–28.

15. For good coverage of the American debate over the war with Mexico, including Lincoln's "Spot Resolutions," see chapter 10, "Conquest and Controversy, 1846–1850," in Ray Allen Billington and Martin Ridge, eds., *Westward Expansion: A History of the American Frontier*, 6th ed. (an abridgement) (Albuquerque: University of New Mexico Press, 2001), 215–36, esp. 220–21. For an excellent discussion of regionalism and American foreign policy in this period see Joseph A. Fry, "Place Matters: Regionalism and the Formation of American Foreign Policy," with commentaries and author response, *Diplomatic History* 36 (June 2012): 451–514.

16. Hietala, *Manifest Design*, 173.

17. Francis Parkman, *The Oregon Trail: Sketches of Prairie and Rocky-Mountain Life* (Boston: Little, 1872; first published, 1849); Theodore Roosevelt, *The Winning of the West*, 4 vols. (New York: G. P. Putnam's Sons, 1889–1896). Turner's essays were collected in *The Frontier in American History*.

18. Among the more notable New Western History critics of Turner's frontier thesis are Limerick's "Introduction: Opening the Frontier and Closing Western History," in *The Legacy of Conquest*; and various essays by Limerick, Richard White, Donald Worster, and others in Patricia Nelson Limerick, Clyde Milner II, and Charles Rankin, eds., *Trails: Toward a New Western History* (Lawrence: University Press of Kansas, 1991).

19. The leading New Western historians, Limerick, White, and Worster, all viewed the West within a broader context of imperialism. The titles of Limerick's *The Legacy of Conquest* and Worster's *Rivers of Empire: Water, Aridity, and the Growth of American West* (New York: Oxford University Press, 1985) speak to a comparative global contextualization. Richard White's seminal textbook, *"It's Your Misfortune and None of My Own": A New History of the American West* (Norman: University of Oklahoma Press, 1991), also parallels American empire building in the West with the efforts of other empires around the globe.

20. Hector St. John de Crèvecoeur, *Letters from an American Farmer* (New York: Fox, Duffield, 1904; first published, 1782), 41, 43–44.

21. Alexis de Tocqueville, *Democracy in America*, Henry Reeve text as revised by Francis Bower, ed. Phillips Bradley, 2 vols. (New York: Macmillan, 1945); James Bryce, *The American Commonwealth*, 2 vols. (New York: Macmillan, 1893–1895).

22. See Jennifer Pitts's introduction to *Alexis de Tocqueville: Writings on Empire and Slavery*, ed. and trans. Jennifer Pitts (Baltimore: Johns Hopkins University Press, 2001), ix–xxxxviii, esp. xxi. The pertinent Tocqueville writings in the volume are: "Essay on Algeria" (October 1841), 59–116; "First Report on Algeria" (1847), 129–73; and "Second Report on Algeria" (1847), 174–98.

23. I refer here to the broad concept of westward expansion and to Ray Allen Billington's textbook, *Westward Expansion*, which first appeared in 1949 (New York: Macmillan) and has played an influential role in sustaining the notion that the story of the West is the story of white movement into the West.

24. An example of this placement of the West within the wider world in the genre of travel writing can be found in the *Western Journal and Civilian*, published in Saint Louis. In volume 11 of this publication, subscribers could read about "Aubrey's Journey from California to New Mexico" (no. 1, October 1853, 84–96), a fast-paced, blood-filled, and highly questionable account of white endurance against Indian attacks; just a few months later, subscribers could read Man Butler's "Exploration of the River Amazon: A Sketch from Lieutenant Herndon's Travels," a U.S government–sponsored expedition to the Amazon that began in May 1851 (no. 5, February 1854, 342–49).

25. Sarah Bird Wright, "Harriet Beecher Stowe (1811–1896)," *Dictionary of Literary Biography*, vol. 189, *American Travel Writers, 1850–1915*, ed. Donald Ross and James J. Schramer (Detroit: Gale Research, 1998), 305–20, 307; hereafter referred to as *DLB*.

26. Later in the century, in 1888, *National Geographic Magazine* first appeared to satiate the public's hunger for knowledge about far-flung places; for more, see Robert M. Poole, *Explorer's House: National Geographic and the World It Made* (New York: Penguin Press, 2004).

27. Mary K. Edmonds, "Paul Belloni du Chaillu (1831?–1903)," in *DLB*, vol. 189, 109–31.

28. Jeffrey Alan Melton, "Samuel Langhorne Clemens (Mark Twain), 1835–1910," in *DLB*, vol. 189, 65–78.

29. For a good overview of these archives, see Introduction, note 8.

30. James Schramer and Donald Ross, in their introduction to *DLB*, vol. 183, *American Travel Writers, 1776–1864* (Detroit: Gale Research, 1997), xxv, explain that "the basic mimetic impulse in travel writing is sociological or anthropological rather than psychological—a major difference between travel literature and the novel." Generally classified today as nonfiction, the best travel writings are far more literary than the average book of essays in the nonfiction genre but are nonetheless very different from the novel and short story traditions.

31. Barbara Brothers and Julia M. Gergits, introduction to *DLB*, vol. 204, *British Travel Writers, 1940–1997* (Detroit: Gale Research, 1999), xv–xxi, xviii.

32. Ibid.

33. This particular vein of historical scholarship was first mined long in advance of the World War II years. We can go back all the way to the Civil War and find Henry T. Tuckerman's *America and Her Commentators: With a Critical Sketch of Travel in the United States* (New York: Charles Scribner, 1864); this seems to be the earliest secondary work available on the topic of travel writers' perceptions of America. John Graham Brooks, *As Others See Us: A Study of Progress in the United States* (New York: Macmillan, 1908), appeared during the Progressive era; and Allan Nevins's *American Social History as Recorded by British Travellers* (New York: Henry Holt, 1923) was published another decade and a half later.

34. For example, Max Berger's *The British Traveller in America* appeared in 1943, at a time, the author noted, "when Americans are observing their English ally more closely and more critically than ever before" (5).

35. Allan Nevins, *America Through British Eyes* (New York: Oxford University Press, 1948; first published as *American Social History as Recorded by British Travellers*). See also Oscar Handlin, *This Was America: True Accounts of People and Places, Manners and Customs, as Recorded by European Travelers to the Western Shore in the Eighteenth, Nineteenth, and Twentieth Centuries* (Cambridge: Harvard University Press, 1949).

36. Robert G. Athearn, *Westward the Briton: The Far West, 1865–1900, as Seen by British Sportsmen and Capitalists, Ranchers and Homesteaders, Lords and Ladies* (New York: Charles Scribner's Sons, 1953; reprinted, Lincoln: University of Nebraska Press, Bison Books, 1962, 1969); Thomas D. Clark, "The Great Visitation to American Democracy," *Mississippi Valley Historical Review* 44 (June 1957): 3–28. That same year also saw the publication of Earl S. Pomeroy's *In Search of the Golden West: The Tourist in Western America* (New York: Alfred A. Knopf, 1957), which included a commentary on the observations of travel writers as well as of tourists.

37. This post–World War II search for an American character helps explain the appearance of various works that we tend to lump together as examples of the "myth and symbol school." Henry Nash Smith's classic *Virgin Land* and John William Ward's *Andrew Jackson: Symbol for an Age* (New York: Oxford University Press, 1955), are particularly notable examples. In the field of American intellectual history, Henry Steele Commager's *The American Mind: An Interpretation of American Thought and Culture Since the 1880s* (New Haven, CT: Yale University Press, 1950) stands as the most significant example of the postwar explorations of a distinctive Americanism. Likewise, another body of works that are generally defined as "consensus history" can be understood within the context of the post–World War II effort to define the national character and include Richard Hofstadter, *The American Political Tradition and the Men Who Made It* (New York: Alfred A. Knopf, 1948); Daniel Boorstin, *The Genius of American Politics* (Chicago: University of Chicago Press, 1953); David M. Potter, *People of Plenty: Economic Abundance and the American Character* (Chicago: University of Chicago Press, 1954); and Louis Hartz, *The Liberal Tradition in America: An Interpretation of American Political Thought Since the Revolution* (New York: Harcourt, Brace, 1955).

38. These works were not simply paeans to a benign national distinctiveness, to be sure (Smith's *Virgin Land*, e.g., offered a highly cautionary tale), but they are all marked by their efforts to chart the sources of the nation's distinctiveness and generally emphasize the benign nature of the national character and democratic institutions. Nevins's collection *America Through British Eyes* and Handlin's *This Was America* both contained a number of very critical assessments of the American character and American institutions. Clark, to offer another example, concluded his Mississippi Valley Historical Association presidential address, "The Great Visitation," with criticism of American materialism and of the nation's failure to live up to its vaunted purpose as outlined in the Declaration of Independence and the Bill of Rights (27). Yet, characteristic of the time when it appeared, Clark carefully added that even the most "malicious comments" of some foreign travelers "have never provoked a desire [among Americans] to deny free visitation to America and its institutions" (28).

39. The Henry Reeve text of Tocqueville's *Democracy in America* was published in New York by Alfred A. Knopf in 1945 and reprinted in 1945, 1946, 1948, 1951, 1953, and 1957. Oxford University Press also reprinted the Reeve text in 1947 and 1959.

40. Tocqueville, *Democracy in America*, Henry Reeve text, xxi.

41. David Spurr, *The Rhetoric of Empire: Colonial Discourse in Journalism, Travel Writing, and Imperial Administration* (Durham, NC: Duke University Press, 1993), 1. Spurr's book begins with a chapter titled "Surveillance: Under Western Eyes," emphasizing the privileged nature of the writer's gaze that renders him or her as an objectifier but never as an object. Subsequent chapters on "Appropriation," "Aestheticization," "Classification," "Debasement," "Negation," "Affirmation," "Insubstantialization," "Naturalization," and "Eroticization," and a final chapter titled "Resistance," leave no doubt as to where the author stands vis-à-vis the nature, purpose, and consequences of the imperialist gaze. For more on this topic, see Steve Clark, ed., *Travel Writing and Empire: Postcolonial Theory in Transit* (London: Zed Books, 1999).

42. Spurr, *The Rhetoric of Empire*, 4.

43. Edward Said, *Culture and Imperialism* (New York: Vintage Books, 1994; first published, New York: Alfred A. Knopf, 1993), xxi. David Cannadine offers a different perspective on the British empire and the ways in which it was perceived. He argues that "pace Edward Said and his 'Orientalist' followers, the British Empire was not exclusively (or even preponderantly) concerned with the creation of 'otherness' on the presumption that the imperial periphery was different from, and inferior to, the imperial metropolis: it was as least as much (perhaps more?) concerned with what has recently been called the 'construction of affinities' on the presumption that society on the periphery was the same as, or even on occasions superior to, society in the metropolis." *Ornamentalism: How the British Saw Their Empire* (New York: Oxford University Press, 2001), xix.

44. Said, *Culture and Imperialism*, 99.

45. Homi K. Bhabha, *The Location of Culture* (New York: Routledge, 1994), 70.

46. Ibid., 112.

47. Mary Louise Pratt, *Imperial Eyes: Travel Writing and Transculturation* (London: Routledge, 1992), 2, 4, 5, 201, 205–6. See also Inderpal Grewal, *Home and Harem: Nation, Gender, Empire, and the Cultures of Travel* (Durham, NC: Duke University Press, 1996); and Ali Behdad, *Belated Travelers: Orientalism in the Age of Colonial Dissolution* (Durham, NC: Duke University Press, 1994).

48. For more information on the ways of viewing the "traveled upon," see Leah Dilworth, "Tourists and Indians in Fred Harvey's Southwest"; Sylvia Rodriguez, "Tourism, Whiteness, and the Vanishing Anglo"; and David M. Wrobel, "Introduction: Tourists, Tourism, and the Toured Upon," in *Seeing and Being Seen: Tourism in the American West*, ed. David M. Wrobel and Patrick T. Long (Lawrence: University Press of Kansas, 2001), 142–64, 194–210, and 1–34, respectively.

49. There does seem to be a new generation of scholarship emerging, a kind of post-postcolonialism that moves us beyond the easy assumptions concerning the imperialist gaze. An excellent example is Maya Jasanoff's *Edge of Empire: Lives, Culture, and Conquest in the East, 1750–1850* (New York: Alfred A. Knopf, 2005).

50. Stephens is the subject of an excellent chapter in Larzer Ziff's *Return Passages: Great American Travel Writing, 1790–1910* (New Haven, CT: Yale University Press, 2000), 58–117, from which my coverage is drawn. Stephens's works of travel include *Incidents of Travel in Egypt, Arabia Petraea, and the Holy Land* (1837); *Incidents of Travel in Greece, Turkey, Russia, and Poland* (1838); *Incidents of Travel in Central America, Chiapas, and Yucatan* (1841); and *Incidents of Travel in Yucatan* (1843).

51. Ziff recounts the meeting in *Return Passages*, 113–14. I am indebted to Andrew Cayton, who drew my attention to the Stephens-Humboldt encounter in his paper "The Imperial Republic: War and Expansion of an Empire of Liberty," in the roundtable session "United States Empire and Its Implications for History" at the annual meeting of the American Historical Association, Philadelphia, January 8, 2006. It is worth noting that German traveler Karl Heller was in Mexico at the time of the war and Humboldt's meeting with Stephens; see Karl Bartholomaeus Heller's *Reisen in Mexiko in den Jahren 1845–1848* (Leipzig: W. Engelmann, 1853; published in English as *Alone in Mexico: The Astonishing Travels of Karl Heller, 1845–1848*, ed. and trans. Terry Rugeley, Tuscaloosa: University of Alabama Press, 2007).

52. George Catlin, *Catalogue of Catlin's Indian Gallery of Portraits, Landscapes, Manners and Customs, Costumes, &c. . . . Collected During Seven Years' Travel Amongst Thirty-Eight Different Tribes, Speaking Different Languages* (New York: Piercy and Reed, 1837); and *Catlin's North American Indian Portfolio: Hunting Scenes and Amusements of the Rocky Mountains and Prairies of America from Drawings and Notes of the Author, Made During Eight Years' Travel Amongst Forty-Eight of the Wildest and Most Remote Tribes of Savages in North America* (London: George Catlin, 1844; reprinted, New York: James Ackerman, 1845).

53. See, e.g., the review of Catlin's exhibit from the *East India Chronicle*, reprinted in George Catlin, *Adventures of the Ojibbeway and Ioway Indians in England, France, and Belgium: Being Notes of Eight Years Residence in Europe with the North American Indian Collection*, 2 vols., 3rd ed. (London: George Catlin, 1852), 216. The book was originally published under the title *Catlin's Notes of Eight Years' Travels and Residence in Europe, with His North American Indian Collection: With Anecdotes and Incidents of the Travels and Adventures of Three Different Parties of American Indians Whom He Introduced to the Courts of England, France, and Belgium* (London: George Catlin, 1848). The 1852 edition of *Adventures of the Ojibbeway and Ioway Indians* has been republished in two volumes (Scituate, MA: Digital Scanning, 2001); page references are from the 1848 edition.

54. The coverage here draws on Paul Reddin's excellent account, "Trembling Excitements and Fears: Catlin and the Show Abroad," in his *Wild West Shows* (Urbana: University of Illinois Press, 1999), 27–52, quotations from 29–30.

55. A number of these broadsides are included in the George Catlin Collection, Frederick W. Beinecke Rare Book and Manuscript Library, Yale University.

56. Catlin was presenting an interesting, albeit not particularly new, reversal of the standard travel narrative form in which white travelers comment on their experience among other cultures. Voltaire and other French enlightenment thinkers had, nearly a century earlier, used the Indian travel narrative as a vehicle for illuminating the irrationality of Europeans. Moreover, it is important to note that the Iowas and Ojibways who accompanied Catlin were hardly among the first American Indians to visit Europe and have their impressions recorded. Elliott West recounts the trip of six Indians, including chiefs of the Otoes, Osages, Missourias, Illinois, and Mitchigameas, accompanied by Étienne Véniard de Bourgmont, to France in 1725. See West's essay "The West Before Lewis and Clark: Three Lives," in *The Essential West* (Norman: University of Oklahoma Press, 2012), 129–53. See also Kate Flint's excellent study *The Transatlantic Indian, 1776–1930* (Princeton, NJ: Princeton University Press, 2008).

57. Catlin, *Adventures of the Ojibbeway and Ioway Indians*, 1: 129–30.

58. King Louis Philippe abdicated the throne in 1848 and died in England in 1850. The French conquest of Algeria took place during his rule and that of his predecessor, Charles X.

59. Catlin's wife, Clara, died in 1845, and his only son, Georgie, died in 1847. Reddin's *Wild West Shows* covers these Catlin family deaths and the Indian deaths in excellent detail (45–51). John Hausdorffer also devotes a chapter, "Catlin's Tragedy: Catlin in Europe," to this topic in his careful examination of the tensions in Catlin's thinking, *Catlin's Lament: Indians, Manifest Destiny, and the Ethics of Nature* (Lawrence: University Press of Kansas, 2009), 130–49. For another useful analysis of Catlin's views on "vanishing" Indians, see Steven Conn, *History's Shadow: Native Americans and Historical Consciousness in the Nineteenth Century* (Chicago: University of Chicago Press, 2004), 54–64. For a useful treatment of Alexis de Tocqueville's views on the future of Indian peoples in the United States, see Harry Liebersohn, "Tocqueville and the Sociology of Native Aristocrats," in his *European Travelers and North American Indians* (Cambridge: Cambridge University Press, 1998), 92–112.

60. Catlin, *Adventures of the Ojibbeway and Ioway Indians*, 1: 61–62. Reddin provides coverage of the "Museum of Mankind" in *Wild West Shows*, 48.

61. Friedrich Gerstäcker may be best known to historians of the California Gold Rush as the author of a very handsome volume, *California Gold Mines* (Oakland: Biobooks, 1946), a radical abridgement of *Narrative of a Journey Round the World*, or, better, a reprinting of just the California segment of the larger work.

The book serves as a good example of how the West has literally been taken out of the world in the public memory of the Gold Rush.

Gerstäcker's *Narrative of a Journey Round the World* also was reprinted the year after its publication, in 1854, in an abridged British edition, *Gerstäcker's Travels: Rio de Janeiro, Buenos Ayres, Ride Through the Pampas, Winter Journey Across the Cordilleras, Chile, Valparaiso, California and the Gold Fields*, trans. Friedrich Gerstäcker (London: T. Nelson and Sons, 1854). Another noteworthy German travel account and memoir was published the same year, Karl Heller's *Reisen in Mexiko*. Heller's travels covered 47,500 miles in three years.

62. *The Pioneers* (1823), *The Last of the Mohicans* (1826), and *The Prairie* (1827) were all published during Gerstäcker's boyhood years; the last works in the Leatherstocking Tales series, *The Pathfinder* (1840) and *The Deerslayer* (1841), appeared during his first trip to the United States.

63. Jeffrey Sammons, "Friedrich Gerstäcker," in *DLB*, vol. 129, *Nineteenth-Century German Writers, 1841–1900*, ed. Siegfried Mews and James Hardin (Detroit: Gale Research, 1993), 110–19, notes that this trip was financed in part by a small grant from Germany's provisional government; Gerstäcker later claimed to be the only person to have ever benefited from that government. See also Irene S. Di Maio, introduction to *Gerstäcker's Louisiana: Fiction and Travel Sketches from Antebellum Times Through Reconstruction*, ed. and trans. Irene S. Di Maio (Baton Rouge: Louisiana State University Press, 2006), 1–16, esp. 1–4. Di Maio points out that in addition to being financed by the Frankfurt Parliament, the trip was also financed by the prestigious German publisher Cotta (4).

64. Howard Lamar, in his foreword to J. S. Holliday, *The World Rushed In: The California Gold Rush Experience* (Norman: University of Oklahoma Press, 2002; first published, New York: Simon and Schuster, 1981), xii, points to this global context. Holliday is certainly well aware of the world context surrounding the California Gold Rush but chooses to focus on the overlanders. For maritime journeys to the goldfields, see Charles R. Schultz, *Forty-Niners "Round the Horn"* (Columbia: University of South Carolina Press, 1999).

65. Gerstäcker's life, marked by its alternating periods of writing and wanderlust, is strangely reminiscent of Theodore Roosevelt's, which is marked by its segmented periods of public service and adventuring. For excellent overviews of Gerstäcker's travels, see Sammons, "Friedrich Gerstäcker," *DLB*; his fuller coverage in *Ideology, Mimesis, Fantasy: Charles Sealsfield, Friedrich Gerstäcker, Karl May, and Other German Novelists of America* (Chapel Hill: University of North Carolina Press, 1998), 113–200; Jeffrey Sammons, "Friedrich Gerstäcker: American Realities Through German Eyes," in his *Imagination and History: Selected Papers on Nineteenth-Century German Literature* (New York: Peter Lang, 1988), 249–63; and Di Maio, introduction to *Gerstäcker's Louisiana*, 1–16.

66. August Carl, *Friedrich Gerstäcker der Weitgereiste Ein Lebensbild* (Gera, Germany: Issleiss and Rietzchel, 1873), cited in Di Maio, *Gerstäcker's Louisiana*, 4, 278n10.

67. Erwin G. Gudde writes that Gerstäcker was "known throughout the Western world," in "Friedrich Gerstaecker: World Traveller and Author, 1816–1872," *Journal of the West* 7 (July 1968): 345–50. Renowned American travel writer Bayard Taylor recounted his meeting with Gerstäcker in his *At Home and Abroad: A Sketch-book of Life, Scenery, and Men* (New York: G. P. Putnam 1862; reprinted, New York: G. P. Putnam's Sons, 1873), 342. Taylor recounted his 1856 and 1867 meetings with the legendary Alexander von Humboldt in the same work (352–65).

68. These popular stories were fictions based on real familiarity with the settings— which places them well above the work of the average dime novelist. Friedrich Gerstäcker, *The Death Track; or, the Outlaws of the Mountain* (New York: Beadle and Adams, 1879); *The Border Bandits; or, the Horse-Thief's Trail*; *The Bush Ranger; or, the Half-Breed Brigade*; and *The Outlaw Hunter; or, Red John, the Bush Ranger* (all New York: Beadle and Adams, 1881).

69. By way of contrast, and in a departure from much of the scholarship on the California Gold Rush in recent decades, James Belich, in *Replenishing the Earth*, downplays the multicultural dimension of gold rushes in white settler societies (including California and Victoria, Australia), emphasizing instead the Anglo dimension of these phenomena. But Gerstäcker's observations certainly support the idea of significant racial and ethnic diversity in the California goldfields.

70. Gerstäcker, *Gerstäcker's Travels*, 231–33. The story of the Bombay Indian is also told at somewhat greater length in the American edition of the book, *Narrative of a Journey Round the World*, 214–17. The American edition, as the title suggests, includes coverage of the whole of Gerstäcker's trip.

71. Gerstäcker, *Narrative of a Journey Round the World*, 214.

72. See, e.g., Patrick Brantlinger, *Dark Vanishings: The Discourse on the Extinction of Primitive Peoples, 1800–1930* (Ithaca, NY: Cornell University Press, 2003).

73. Gerstäcker, *Narrative of a Journey Round the World*, 216.

74. Ibid.

75. Ibid., 214.

76. Ibid., 216.

77. Faragher and Hine, *The American West*, 249–50. Englishman William Shaw's travel account, *Golden Dreams and Waking Realities: Being the Adventures of a Gold-Seeker in California and the Pacific Islands* (London: Smith, Elder, 1851), like Gerstäcker's contemporaneous narrative, provides a disturbing picture of white violence against Indians and other peoples of color in the California gold-fields. Shaw wrote in his preface that "what he witnessed and encountered in his wanderings. . . . afford fresh evidences of the demoralizing effects of the California gold mania" and added that it would be "a source of gratification for

him to think that it has been in his power to dissipate the 'golden dreams' of others, without their having, like himself, to experience the disagreeable 'waking realities'" (v). Fellow German traveler Karl Heller also discussed indigenous population decline and decried the desultory impact of Spanish imperialism in *Alone in Mexico*, 5–51.

78. Faragher and Hine, *The American West*, 249, refer to the campaign against the California Indians as the clearest case of genocide in the history of the American frontier. See also Sherburne F. Cook, *The Population of the California Indians, 1769–1970* (Berkeley: University of California Press, 1976) and *The Conflict Between the California Indian and White Civilization* (Berkeley: University of California Press, 1976); Albert L. Hurtado, "'Extermination or Domestication': The Dilemma of California Indian Policy," in his *Indian Survival on the California Frontier* (New Haven, CT: Yale University Press, 1988), 125–48; Brendan C. Lindsay, *Murder State: California's Native American Genocide, 1846–1873* (Lincoln: University of Nebraska Press, 2012); George Harwood Phillips, *Indians and Indian Agents: The Origins of the Reservation System in California, 1849–1852* (Norman: University of Oklahoma Press, 1997), 167; William J. Bauer Jr., "They, White People, Made Slaves of Indians: Forced Labor in the Nome Cult Valley, 1850–1865," in his *We Were All Like Migrant Workers Here: Work, Community, and Memory on California's Round Valley Reservation, 1850–1941* (Chapel Hill: University of North Carolina Press, 2009), 30–57; Benjamin Madley, "California's Yuki Indians: Defining Genocide in America," *Western Historical Quarterly* 39 (Autumn 2008): 303–32; and Gary Anderson, "The Stealing of a Golden Land: Ethnic Cleansing in California," in his *Ethnic Cleansing and the Indian: The Crime that Haunts America* (Norman: University of Oklahoma Press, forthcoming). For a broader comparative approach to the topic, see Ben Kiernan's chapter "Genocide in the United States" in his *Blood and Soil: A World History of Genocide and Extermination from Sparta to Darfur* (New Haven, CT: Yale University Press, 2007), 310–63; Benjamin Madley, "Patterns of Frontier Genocide, 1803–1910: The Aboriginal Tasmanians, the Yuki of California, and the Herero of Namibia," *Journal of Genocide Research* 6 (June 2004): 167–92; and Patrick Wolfe, "Settler Colonialism and the Elimination of the Native," *Journal of Genocide Research* 8 (December 2006): 387–409.

79. Ida Pfeiffer, *A Lady's Second Journey Round the World: From London to the Cape of Good Hope, Borneo, Java, Sumatra, Celebes, Ceram, the Moluccas, etc.; California, Panama, Peru, Ecuador, and the United States* (New York: Harper and Brothers, 1856), 308–9, 319, and 321–22. Pfeiffer's first global journey, from 1846 to 1848, was recounted in *A Lady's Journey Round the World: From Vienna to Brazil, Chili, Tahiti, China, Hindostan, Persia, and Asia Minor*, a selected translation by Mrs. Percy Sinnett (London: Longman, 1856; first published as *Eine Frau fährt um die Welt*, Vienna, 1850). For more on Pfeiffer's travels, see Marion Tinling, "Ida Reyer Pfeiffer: Twice Round the World," in her *Women into the Unknown: A Sourcebook*

on Women Explorers and Travelers (Westport, CT: Greenwood Press, 1989), 225–32.

80. Gerstäcker, *Narrative of a Journey Round the World*, 395, 409, 473.

81. In addition to the indigenous population decline that accompanied the gold rushes in both California and Australia, both places saw anti-Chinese rioting by white prospectors. Furthermore, in both the United States (with California leading the way) and Australia, restrictive immigration legislation in the late nineteenth century barred Asian immigrants. The White Australia policy of 1888 remained intact until the 1970s, and in the United States, the Chinese Immigration Act of 1882 (renewed in 1892 and made permanent in 1924) remained in place until the Magnuson Act of 1943. Large-scale Asian immigration only began after the Hart-Celler Immigration Act of 1965.

82. Patrick Brantlinger, in *Dark Vanishings*, examines the discourse on extinction and argues compellingly that the language of inevitable extinction, the "ghosting of the primitive," amounted to a kind of "self-fulfilling prophesy," thereby contributing to the broader acceptance of these "dark vanishings" in western culture. However, within the broad discourse on extinction there existed a very wide range of positions—from the forceful advocacy of extermination of indigenous people to the stinging critiques of governments that allowed genocidal acts to take place. Brantlinger lumps these highly divergent, indeed antithetical, positions together into a single category—"extinction discourse"—which fails to distinguish advocates from critics. For a fuller treatment of the topic as it relates to American Indians, see Brian Dippie, *The Vanishing American: White Attitudes and U.S. Indian Policy* (Lawrence: University Press of Kansas, 1991; first published, Middletown, CT: Wesleyan University Press, 1982); and Billington, *Land of Savagery*, 129–49.

83. Gerstäcker, *Narrative of a Journey Round the World*, 569–70. Pfeiffer also commented more kindly on Dutch colonialism than she did on the English, French, and Spanish variants; see *A Lady's Second Journey*, 247–49. Pfeiffer dedicated the book to "The Dutch and the Dutch Governmental Authorities of India" (n.p.).

84. The five parts of the book cover South America, California, the Hawaiian Islands, Australia, and Java.

85. Further examples of this global positioning of the West in the mid-nineteenth century include Shaw, *Golden Dreams and Waking Realities*; L. M. Schaeffer, *Sketches of Travels in South America, Mexico, and California* (New York: James Egbert, 1860), which recounts an earlier journey in 1849; and T. Robinson Warren, *Dust and Foam; or, Three Oceans and Two Continents: Being Ten Years' Wanderings in Mexico, South America, Sandwich Islands, the East and West Indies, China, Philippines, Australia, and Polynesia* (New York: Charles Scribner; London: Sampson Low, Son, and Company, 1859).

86. Eric Sterling, "George Catlin," in *DLB*, vol. 189, *American Travel Writers, 1850–1915*, ed. Donald Ross and James J. Schramer (Detroit: Gale Research, 1998), 55–64.

87. Dippie, *The Vanishing American*, 27.

88. Renato Rosaldo, "Imperialist Nostalgia," *Representations* 26 (1989): 107–22. Cynics might argue that Catlin, by displaying Indians and offering evidence of their vanishing, was complicit in their destruction (although such arguments deemphasize the factor of Indian agency as expressed through participation). Nonetheless, Catlin's vociferous critique of his nation's Indian removal policy was clearly motivated more by anger over what was being done to Indians than by nostalgia for what was past.

Chapter Two

1. Francis Galton, *The Art of Travel; or, Shifts and Contrivances Available in Wild Countries* (London: John Murray, 1855). The previous year the Royal Geographical Society published a similar kind of guide in article form, "Hints to Travellers," in its *Journal of the Royal Geographical Society of London* 24 (1854): 329–58. For good coverage of Galton's African travels, see Nicholas Wright Gillham, *A Life of Sir Francis Galton: From African Exploration to the Birth of Eugenics* (New York: Oxford University Press, 2001), 61–92. The awarding of the Founder's Medal came after Galton had published his first account of African exploration, *The Narrative of an Explorer in Tropical South Africa* (1853). For more on the visual depiction of Africans in Galton's work and those of other British writers and explorers in the late nineteenth century, see Leila Koivunen, *Visualizing Africa in Nineteenth-Century British Travel Accounts* (New York: Routledge, 2009).

2. Dorothy Middleton, introduction to *Francis Galton's Art of Travel* (1872), a reprint of Francis Galton, *The Art of Travel; or, Shifts and Contrivances Available in Wild Countries*, 5th ed. (Harrisburg, PA: Stackpole Books, 1971), 5–17, 5, 6–7, 12.

3. The charges of plagiarism are also discussed in Nicholas T. Parson's coverage of Galton and Marcy in his *Worth the Detour: A History of the Guidebook* (Gloucester, England: Sutton Publishing, 2007), 249–52.

4. Galton, *The Art of Travel*, 1st ed. (1855), 308, 312.

5. Ibid., 58.

6. Ibid., 58–59.

7. Galton, *The Art of Travel*, 8th ed. (London: John Murray, 1893), 313. Gillham provides some good discussion of the book in *A Life of Sir Francis Galton*, 98–101. For more on Galton's African travels, see his *The Narrative of an Explorer in Tropical South Africa* (London: John Murray, 1853) and *Memories of My Life* (New

York: Dutton, 1909); see also Michael Bulmer, *Francis Galton: Pioneer of Heredity and Biometry* (Baltimore: Johns Hopkins University Press, 2003), 11–18.

8. Galton's closing comments in *The Art of Travel*, 5th ed. (London: John Murray, 1872), "On Concluding the Journey," are interesting in this regard. He reminded travelers to be sure to record their impressions very carefully at the end of the trip, even if those experiences seem absolutely unforgettable at the time. Warning those potential chroniclers, he noted that "the crowds of new impressions, during a few months or years of civilized life, will efface the sharpness of the old ones. I have conversed with men of low mental power, servants and others, the greater part of whose experience in savagedom has passed out of their memories like the events of a dream" (351).

9. Richard Francis Burton, *Personal Narrative of a Pilgrimage to El-Medinah and Meccah*, 3 vols. (London: Longman, Brown, Green, and Longmans, 1855–1856); Richard Francis Burton, *First Footsteps in East Africa; or, An Exploration of Harar* (London: Longman, Brown, Green, and Longmans, 1856); and Richard Francis Burton, *The Lake Regions of Central Africa: A Picture of Exploration*, 2 vols. (London: Longman, Green, Longman, and Roberts, 1860). The descriptions of the books and the adventures that inspired them draw on John R. Pfeiffer's excellent overview of Burton's life and work, "Sir Richard Francis Burton," in *DLB*, vol. 166, *British Travel Writers, 1837–1875*, ed. Barbara Brothers and Julia M. Gergits (Detroit: Gale Research, 1996), 98–119, esp. 105–6. See also Tim Jeal's extensive coverage of Burton's African explorations in *Explorers of the Nile: The Triumph and Tragedy of a Great Victorian Adventure* (New Haven, CT: Yale University Press, 2011). Iliya Troyanov's *The Collector of Worlds: A Novel of Sir Richard Francis Burton*, trans. William Hobson (New York: HarperCollins, 2009; first published in German, Munich: Carl Hanser Verlag, 2006) is also useful for considering Burton's travels. Isabel Burton's description of her husband's health is quoted in Fawn Brodie, introduction to Richard Francis Burton, *The City of the Saints, and Across the Rocky Mountains to California*, ed. Fawn Brodie (New York: Alfred A. Knopf, 1963), xvi–xvii; all page references are from this edition.

10. Galton, *The Art of Travel*, 2nd ed., revised and enlarged (London: John Murray, 1856), in the Sir Richard Francis Burton Library, Rare Books Collection, Henry E. Huntington Library (hereafter referred to as HEH), BL 634262. Also included among the thirty books that Burton took with him on the trip were his heavily annotated copies of James Cowles Prichard's massive tome, *The Natural History of Man: Inquiries into the Modifying Influence of Physical and Moral Agencies on the Different Tribes of the Human Family*, 3rd ed. (London: Hippolyte Bailliere, 1848), HEH RB, BL 634214; and Baron George Cuvier's equally weighty volume, *The Animal Kingdom, Arranged According to Its Organization, Forming a Natural History of Animals, and an Introduction to*

Comparative Anatomy (London: William S. Orr, 1849; first published in French as *Le Règne Animal*, 4 vols.), HEH, BL 634207.

11. Pfeiffer, "Sir Richard Francis Burton," *DLB*, 98–119, 100.

12. Richard Francis Burton, *The City of the Saints, and Across the Rocky Mountains to California* (London: Longman, Green, Longman, and Roberts, 1861; New York: Harper and Brothers, 1862).

13. Richard Francis Burton, *Wanderings in Three Continents* (London: Hutchinson, 1901), 153, 155. For the Scottsbluff-Brass comparison, see *The City of the Saints*, 87; for the Independence Rock–Jiwe la Mkoa comparison, 164; for the Utah Territory-central equatorial Africa comparison, 302; for the global comparisons of climate and elevation, 304–5. Brodie highlights these comparisons in her introduction to *The City of the Saints*, xix–xx. Elliott West also comments on the global experiences that informed Burton's descriptions of the plains in *The Way to the West: Essays on the Central Plains* (Albuquerque: University of New Mexico Press, 1995), 13.

Another early example of comparisons between the landscapes and cultures of the American West and those across the globe, in addition to Prichard's *The Natural History of Man* and Cuvier's *The Animal Kingdom*, is Harriet Martineau's comparison of Nubia and the Nubians with the Mississippi and the "Indian grounds of Wisconsin," in *Eastern Life, Present and Past*, 3 vols. (London: Edward Moxon, 1848), 1: 101–4; also cited in Lynne Withey, *Grand Tours and Cook's Tours: A History of Leisure Travel, 1750–1915* (New York: William Morrow, 1997), 244. The portion of *The City of the Saints* charting Burton's overland journey has since been published separately as *The Look of the West, 1860: Across the Plains to California* (Lincoln: University of Nebraska Press, Bison Books, 1963).

14. For more on Burton's comparative descriptions of the western American landscape and its indigenous peoples, see Richard V. Francaviglia, *Go East, Young Man: Imagining the American West as the Orient* (Logan: Utah State University Press, 2011), 47–49, 75–77, 105–6.

15. Burton compares Native American animal worship to that of the Kafir Backwana, as described in David Livingstone's *Missionary Travels and Researches in South Africa* (London: John Murray, 1857); see *The City of the Saints*, 119.

16. Burton, *The City of the Saints*, 37.

17. Ibid., 38.

18. Ibid., 41.

19. See chapter 1, notes 8, 22.

20. Burton, *The City of the Saints*, 49–50.

21. Randolph B. Marcy, *The Prairie Traveler: A Hand-book for Overland Expeditions with Maps, Illustrations, and Itineraries of the Principal Routes Between the Mississippi and the Pacific* (New York: Harper and Brothers, 1859; reprinted as *The Prairie Traveler: The 1859 Handbook for Westbound Pioneers*, Mineola, NY: Dover Books, 2006); page references from the 2006 edition.

22. Richard Francis Burton, preface to Randolph B. Marcy, *The Prairie Traveler: A Handbook for Overland Expeditions* (London: Trübner and Company, 1863), xv. Incidentally, this was not the edition of Marcy's book that Francis Galton insisted drew directly on his *The Art of Travel*. Burton also wrote in his preface that "The English reader will be disposed to criticise a book which tells so much of what has already been told, and well told too, in 'The Art of Travel,' by Mr. Francis Galton," but then went on to add: "My belief is that the more publications of the kind the better" (xv). Burton references Marcy's book in *The City of the Saints*, 6, 13–14.

    Interestingly, in his preface to *The Prairie Traveler*, Burton noted that he was working on a "system of hand-language, with which, assisted by some 100 words, any man of average abilities shall make himself understood in any country after a week's study." This system, Burton explained, was based upon the "organized pantomimic practice, by which the North American Aborigines express themselves." This hybrid language of words and signs, he wrote, "would be most useful in Africa, where within fifty miles, one meets with four or five different dialects" (xvi, 34).

23. Brodie points out (in her introduction to *The City of the Saints*, xxxii) that "Burton disliked African natives generally, openly preferring Arabs or those of mixed blood in northern Africa." Edward Said, in a probing analysis of Burton in *Orientalism*, insists that for all his cultural knowledge and empathy, Burton was in the last analysis "an imperialist." Said points to Burton's "sense of assertion and domination over all complexities of Oriental life," and further notes that "the voice of the highly idiosyncratic master of Oriental knowledge informs, feeds into the voice of European ambition for rule over the Orient" (195–198, quotations on 195, 196). Dane Kennedy, in *The Highly Civilized Man: Richard Burton and the Victorian World* (Cambridge: Harvard University Press, 2005), provides a rather more nuanced portrait of Burton than does Said, emphasizing the transition in Burton's views on race and indeed devoting separate chapters to "The Racist" and "The Relativist" (131–63 and 164–205, respectively). See also Ben Grant, *Postcolonialism, Psychoanalysis and Burton: Power Play of Empire* (London: Routledge, 2009).

24. Burton, *The City of the Saints*, 3.

25. Brodie, introduction to *The City of the Saints*, ix. See also Kennedy's excellent discussion of the "white nigger" label in *The Highly Civilized Man*, 51–57.

26. Fawn M. Brodie, "Sir Richard F. Burton: Exceptional Observer of the Mormon Scene," *Utah Historical Quarterly* 38, no. 4 (1970), 295–311. In her introduction to *The City of the Saints*, Brodie notes that Burton "was trapped in the century least capable of appraising his talents, confined and penalized by the pruderies of Victorian England" (vii). Burton probably first encountered Mormons while voyaging to the Crimean Peninsula a few years earlier; a number of recent Mormon converts fought in the British campaign there.

27. Brodie, introduction to Burton, *The City of the Saints*, xviii.

28. Burton provided, in the form of footnotes, a quite lengthy annotated bibliography of the available works on Mormonism in *The City of the Saints*, 225–38.

29. Ibid., 322.

30. Ibid., 334. Burton even went so far as to argue that "[t]he Mormon polity is, in my humble opinion,—based upon the fact that liberty is to mankind in mass, a burden far heavier than slavery—the perfection of government" (34).

31. Jules Rémy and Julius Brenchley, *A Journey to Great-Salt-Lake City, with a Sketch of the History, Religion, and Customs of the Mormons*, 2 vols. (London: W. Jeffs, 1861), 199–200. Some of Rémy's letters about Mormonism appeared in American newspapers in 1855 and 1856 and were later incorporated into the book. Selections of those letters are included in Michael W. Homer's excellent collection *On the Way to Somewhere Else: European Sojourners in the Mormon West, 1834–1930* (Salt Lake City: University of Utah Press, 2010), 67–84. Homer's collection was originally published as volume 8 in the series *Kingdom in the West: The Mormons and the American Frontier*, by the Arthur H. Clark Company, an imprint of the University of Oklahoma Press, Norman, 2006. Rémy's deeply negative assessment of polygamy appears in letter no. 7 (February 11, 1856) in *On the Way to Somewhere Else*, 80.

32. Howard Stansbury, *An Expedition to the Valley of the Great Salt Lake of Utah: Including a Description of Its Geography, Natural History, and Minerals, and an Analysis of Its Waters, with an Authentic Account of the Mormon Settlement* (Philadelphia: Lippincott, Grambo, and Company, 1852), 134, 135, 137, 144–45.

33. S. N. [Solomon Nunes] Carvalho, *Incidents of Travel and Adventure in the Far West: With Col. Fremont's Last Expedition Across the Rocky Mountains; Including Three Months' Residence in Utah, and a Perilous Trip Across the Great American Desert to the Pacific* (New York: Derby and Jackson, 1857; reprinted, Lincoln: University of Nebraska Press, Bison Books, 2004), 152, 154; page references from the 1857 edition.

34. Mrs. B. G. [Benjamin G.] Ferris, *The Mormons at Home; With Some Incidents of Travel from Mississippi to California, 1852-3, in a Series of Letters* (New York: Dix and Edwards; London: Sampson Low, Son, and Company, 1856). Mrs. Ferris spent the winter of 1852–1853 in Salt Lake City accompanying her husband, who was serving in the territorial government. For fuller coverage of women's accounts of Mormonism in this period, see Sandra L. Myres, "The Savage Within: Women, Race, Religion, and Class on the Frontier," in her *Westering Women and the Frontier Experience: 1800–1915* (Albuquerque: University of New Mexico Press, 1982), 72–98, esp. 87–98. For an earlier example of the same condemnatory tone toward Mormonism, see George Frederick Augustus Ruxton, *Life in the Far West* (Edinburgh: William Blackwood and Sons; London: John Murray, 1849); page references from the Blackwood edition. Ruxton, a British army officer, wrote that the Mormon "sect flourishes wherever Anglo-Saxon gulls are found in sufficient numbers to swallow the egregious nonsense of fanatic humbugs who

fatten upon their credulity" (270). Ruxton's tone had been a little gentler two years earlier in his observations of the Mormons in his *Adventures in the Rocky Mountains and in Mexico* (London: John Murray, 1847; New York: Harper and Brothers, 1848).

35. Mark Twain, *Roughing It* (1872), vol. 6 of *The Complete Works of Mark Twain* (New York: Harper and Brothers, 1922), 98–109, 310–14.

36. Julia M. Gergits, "Isabella Lucy Bird," in *DLB*, vol. 166, *British Travel Writers, 1837–1875*, ed. Barbara Brothers and Julia M. Gergits (Detroit: Gale Research, 1996), 29–49, 32, 30; Isabella Bird, *A Lady's Life in the Rocky Mountains* (London: John Murray; New York: G. P. Putnam's Sons, 1879; reprinted, Sausalito, CA: Comstock Editions, 1977).

37. Gergits, "Isabella Lucy Bird," *DLB*, 32, 30.

38. Bird, *A Lady's Life in the Rocky Mountains*, 86.

39. Ibid., 135–36; Gergits, "Isabella Lucy Bird," *DLB*, 29–30. For more on Bird's Hawaiian travels, see *The Hawaiian Archipelago: Six Months Among the Palm Groves, Coral Reefs, and Volcanoes of the Sandwich Islands* (London: John Murray, 1875; reprinted, New York: G. P. Putnam's Sons, 1882).

40. For more on this tendency among travelers to Japan of this era to stay on the beaten path, see Hugh Cortazzi, *Victorians in Japan: In and Around the Treaty Ports* (London: Athlone Press, 1987).

41. Bird, *A Lady's Life in the Rocky Mountains*, 4; Isabella Bird, *Unbeaten Tracks in Japan: An Account of Travels in the Interior, Including Visits to the Aborigines of Yezo and the Shrines of Nikko and Ise*, 2 vols. (London: John Murray; New York: G. P. Putnam's Sons, 1880; reprinted, Boston: Beacon Press, 1987), 259; page references from the 1987 edition.

42. Isabella Bird, *The Golden Chersonese and the Way Thither* (London: John Murray; New York: G. P. Putnam's Sons, 1883), 338–39. Monica Rico provides a transatlantic context for examining Bird in the chapter "Gender and Empire: The Earl of Dunraven and Isabella Bird in Estes Park," in her *Nature's Noblemen: Transatlantic Masculinities and the Nineteenth-Century American West* (New Haven, CT: Yale University Press, 2013); and Karen M. Morin provides some global contextualization for understanding Bird's *A Lady's Life* in her essay "Narrating Imperial Adventure: Isabella Bird's Travels in the Nineteenth-Century American West," in *Western Places, American Myths: How We Think About the West,* ed. Gary J. Hausladen (Reno: University of Nevada Press, 2003), 204–22. See also Barbara Korte's coverage of Bird in her chapter, "Women's Travel Writing," in her *English Travel Writing: From Pilgrimages to Postcolonial Explorations*, trans. Catherine Matthias (London: Macmillan; New York: St. Martin's Press, 2000), 106–26, esp. 115–18. Useful coverage of Bird is also provided by Dorothy Middleton in her *Victorian Lady Travellers* (London: Routledge, 1965), and by Marion Tinling in "Isabella Lucy Bishop Bird: A Victorian Around the World," in her *Women into the Unknown: A Sourcebook on Women Explorers and Travelers* (Westport, CT: Greenwood Press, 1989), 47–55. For women's travel writing and empire, see Sara

Mills, *Discourses of Difference: An Analysis of Women's Travel Writing and Colonialism* (London: Routledge, 1991). For gender in women's travel writing, see Kristi Siegel, ed., *Gender, Genre, and Identity in Women's Travel Writing* (New York: Peter Lang, 2004), particularly Siegel's useful introductory essay, "Intersections: Women's Travel and Theory," 3–11.

43. Ian Tyrrell, *Transnational Nation: United States History in Global Perspective Since 1789* (New York: Palgrave Macmillan, 2007), 4.

44. George Kennan, *Tent Life in Siberia and Adventures Among the Koraks and Other Tribes in Kamchatka and Northern Asia* (New York: G. P. Putnam's Sons; London: Sampson Low, Son, and Marston, 1870), 66. A second work based on subsequent travels, *Siberia and the Exile System* (New York: Century Company, 1891), established Kennan as a significant critic of Russian authoritarianism. Ian Frazier provides excellent coverage of George Kennan and George F. Kennan in *Travels in Siberia* (New York: Farrar, Straus and Giroux, 2010), 47–64; see also Helen Hundley, "George Kennan and the Russian Empire: How America's Conscience Became an Enemy of Tsarism," Kennan Institute Occasional Papers, no. 277 (Washington, D.C.: Woodrow Wilson Center, 2000).

Elliott West notes that "[b]y the early 1870s nearly fifteen million messages a year were traveling over more than 150,000 miles of wires inside the United States," and describes the advance as "easily the most dramatic in the history of communication"; see *The Last Indian War: The Nez Perce Story* (New York: Oxford University Press, 2009), 179.

45. While the bison's territory had once extended into the Humboldt Range, it had shrunk significantly by 1870, rendering this element of Verne's narrative fanciful at best.

46. The material on Cook, Verne, and Bly is drawn from Withey, *Grand Tours and Cook's Tours*, 264–72. Included among the many late-nineteenth-century works of world travel by British writers are John Boddam-Whetham, *Western Wanderings: A Record of Travel in the Evening Land* (1874); Mrs. F. D. Bridges, *Journal of a Lady's Travels Round the World* (1883); John Francis Campbell, *My Circular Notes* (1876); Sir Charles Wentworth Dilke, *Greater Britain: A Record of Travel in English-Speaking Countries During 1866–7*, 2 vols. (1868); Sir Richard Tangye, *Reminiscences of Travel in Australia, America, and Egypt* (1883); Mrs. Howard Vincent [Ethel Gwendoline Moffatt], *Forty Thousand Miles over Land and Water: The Journal of a Tour Through the British Empire and America*, 2 vols. (1885); Sir Henry Morton Stanley, *My Early Travels and Adventures in America and Asia*, 2 vols. (1895); and George Henry Peters, *Impressions of a Journey Round the World Including India, Burmah and Japan* (1897). Another fascinating travelogue from the period by a British (expatriate) writer is Thomas Stevens, *Around the World on a Bicycle*, vol. 1, *From San Francisco to Teheran* (New York: Charles Scribner's Sons, 1887). Stevens made less use of Thomas Cook's travel infrastructure than most of his contemporaries as he rode his large-wheel ("Penny Farthing") bicycle 13,500 miles in three years.

47. Nicholas Rankin retraces Stevenson's transcontinental journey, along with his other travels, in *Dead Man's Chest: Travels After Robert Louis Stevenson* (London: Faber and Faber, 1987), 118–48.

48. Robert Louis Stevenson, *Across the Plains: With Other Memories and Essays* (London: Chatto and Windus, 1890; reprinted, New York: Charles Scribner's Sons, 1892), 62, 63–64. The work was later published as part of the full account of Stevenson's trip from Scotland to California, *The Amateur Emigrant: From the Clyde to Sandy Hook* (Chicago: Stone and Kimball, 1895; reprinted, New York: Charles Scribner's Sons, 1899). For an excellent discussion of this work, see Gordon Hirsch, "Robert Louis Stevenson," in *DLB*, vol. 174, *British Travel Writers, 1876–1909*, ed. Barbara Brothers and Julia M. Gergits (Detroit: Gale Research, 1997), 268–88, 276–79.

49. Stevenson, *Across the Plains*, 66–67.

50. Ibid., 67–68.

51. The coverage of Stevenson's South Seas travels and observations is drawn from Hirsch, "Robert Louis Stevenson," *DLB*, esp. 281–87; and Barry Menikoff's insightful and nuanced essay "'These Problematic Shores': Robert Louis Stevenson in the South Seas," in *The Ends of the Earth, 1876–1918*, ed. Simon Gatrell (London: Ashfield Press, 1992), 141–56.

52. Herman Melville, *Typee: A Peep at Polynesian Life During a Four Months' Residence in a Valley of the Marquesas, with Notices of the French Occupation of Tahiti and the Provisional Cession of the Sandwich Islands to Lord Paulet* (New York: New American Library, 1979; first published, New York: Wiley and Putnam; London: John Murray, 1846). See also Melville's wonderful portrait of Queequeg in *Moby-Dick* (1851).

53. Robert Louis Stevenson, *In the South Seas: Being an Account of Experiences and Observations in the Marquesas, Paumotus, and Gilbert Islands in the Course of Two Cruises, on the Yacht "Casco" (1888) and the Schooner "Equator" (1889)* (New York: Charles Scribner's Sons, 1923; first published, 1896), 37.

54. The quotation and the coverage of cannibalism are from Hirsch, "Robert Louis Stevenson," *DLB*, 284.

55. Stevenson, *In the South Seas*, 109.

56. See Robert Louis Stevenson, *A Footnote to History: Eight Years of Trouble in Samoa* (London: Cassell; New York: Charles Scribner's Sons, 1892).

57. Robert Louis Stevenson, *In the South Seas* (London: Chatto and Windus; New York: Charles Scribner's Sons, 1896).

58. See Jeffrey Alan Melton, "Samuel Langhorne Clemens (Mark Twain), 1835–1910," in *DLB*, vol. 189, *American Travel Writers, 1850–1915*, ed. Donald Ross and James J. Schramer (Detroit: Gale Research, 1998), 65–78, quotation on 67.

59. Melton, "Samuel Langhorne Clemens (Mark Twain)," *DLB*, 68. The material that made up *The Innocents Abroad* was first published as a series of fifty letters in the *Alta Californian* newspaper. Hilton Obenzinger examines *The Innocents Abroad*

within the larger context of American travel writing about the Holy Land in his essay "Americans in the Holy Land, Israel, and Palestine," in *The Cambridge Companion to American Travel Writing*, ed. Alfred Bendixen and Judith Hamera (Cambridge: Cambridge University Press, 2009), 145–64, esp. 146–47, 150–55.

60. Melton also discusses Twain's parodying of the traveler-tourist dichotomy in "Samuel Langhorne Clemens (Mark Twain)," *DLB*, 73–74. Twain quotations are from *A Tramp Abroad*, 2 vols. (Hartford, CT: American Publishing Company), 1: 1. The character of Mr. Harris is based on Clemens's real-life travel companion at the time, Joseph Twitchell. The work has recently been republished, along with some of Twain's other travel writings: *A Tramp Abroad, Following the Equator, Other Travels*, ed. Roy Blount Jr. (New York: Library of America, 2010). A portion of *A Tramp Abroad*, along with selections from Twain's other travel writings, has recently appeared in *Mark Twain on the Move: A Travel Reader*, ed. Alan Gribben and Jeffrey Alan Melton (Tuscaloosa: University of Alabama Press, 2009).

61. Twain, *A Tramp Abroad*, 2: 1.

62. Twain's *A Tramp Abroad*, along with his other travel writing, is also clearly an inspiration for the present generation's funniest and most irreverent travel writer, Bill Bryson, whose works include *Neither Here Nor There: Travels in Europe* (New York: William Morrow, 1992); *In a Sunburned Country* (New York: Broadway Books, 2000); *A Walk in the Woods: Rediscovering America on the Appalachian Trail* (New York: Broadway Books, 1998); *I'm a Stranger Here Myself: Notes on Returning to America After Twenty Years Away* (New York: Broadway Books, 1999); *Notes from a Small Island* (New York: William Morrow, 1996); and *Bill Bryson's African Diary* (New York: Broadway Books, 2002).

63. Twain's most recent biographers, Ron Powers and David W. Levy, have little positive to say about *Following the Equator*, but Larzer Ziff, in an excellent treatment of Twain's travel writing in his book *Return Passages*, sees the enormous, even transformative significance of the work. See Powers, *Mark Twain: A Life* (New York: Free Press, 2005), 582–84; Levy, *Mark Twain: The Divided Mind of America's Best-Loved Writer* (New York: Prentice Hall, 2010), 190–91; and Ziff, "Mark Twain," in *Return Passages: Great American Travel Writing, 1780–1910* (New Haven, CT: Yale University Press, 2000), 170–221. It is worth noting that in a letter to his London publisher, Chatto and Windus, dated March 26, 1897, Twain wrote of *More Tramps Abroad* (the British title), which he had been busily revising: "I am more than satisfied with it these latter days. I wouldn't trade it for any book I have ever written—& I am not an easy person to please"; see Samuel Langhorne Clemens, Manuscripts, 1–4, "Following the Equator," folder 1, Beinecke Library, Yale University.

64. Karen Lystra explores these tragic events in *Dangerous Intimacy: The Untold Story of Mark Twain's Final Years* (Berkeley: University of California Press, 2004); see esp. chapter 2, "Heartbreak," 20–44.

65. Mark Twain, *More Tramps Abroad* (London: Chatto and Windus, 1897), 54.

66. Ibid., 134–35. In the American version, *Following the Equator: A Journey Around the World* (Hartford, CT: American Publishing Company, 1897), this coverage of aboriginal population decline in Australia is on 208–9.

67. Twain, *Following the Equator*, 155; quoted in Ziff, *Return Passages*, 215. Twain writes: "In the great museums [of Australia], you will find all the other curiosities, but in the curio of chiefest interest to the stranger all of them are lacking. We have at home an abundance of museums, and not an American Indian in them. It is clearly an absurdity, but it never struck me before."

68. Twain, *Following the Equator*, chapter 27, 256–67.

69. Twain, *More Tramps Abroad*, 138.

70. Ibid., 471–72.

71. Twain, *Following the Equator*, 352; quoted in Ziff, *Return Passages*, 218.

72. See David M. Wrobel, chapter 5, "External Solutions: New Frontiers," in his *The End of American Exceptionalism: Frontier Anxiety from the Old West to the New Deal* (Lawrence: University Press of Kansas, 1993), 53–68.

73. Mark Twain, *Roughing It*, in *The Complete Works of Mark Twain*, vol. 6 (New York: Harper and Brothers, 1925; first published, Hartford, CT: American Publishing Company, 1872), 202, 246. Ziff also argues that "Twain's siding with the islanders against Cook foreshadows the anti-imperialism of his mature career"; see *Return Passages*, 181.

74. For more on Twain's ambivalence concerning colonialism in *Roughing It*, see Ziff, *Return Passages*, 181.

75. Christopher McBride, in "Americans in the Larger World: Beyond the Pacific Coast," in *The Cambridge Companion to American Travel Writing*, ed. Alfred Bendixen and Judith Hamera (Cambridge: Cambridge University Press, 2009), 165–79, suggests that Twain's message in the letters was that "these dark-skinned people are inferior—no better than slaves recently emancipated—so America may comfortably exploit them and their land for profit" (171). McBride also suggests that these "early considerations of race in his Hawaiian writings were eventually transformed into the more probing confrontation of the issues in his later masterpieces" (171). However, McBride seems to miss Twain's critique of colonialism in the Hawaiian letters, one that developed during the course of his time on the islands. Philip Fisher places *Roughing It* and Twain's other travel writings into global context in "Mark Twain," in the *Columbia Literary History of the United States*, ed. Emory Elliott (New York: Columbia University Press, 1998), 627–44.

76. Mary H. Kingsley, *Travels in West Africa: Congo Francais, Corisco and Cameroons* (London: Macmillan, 1897), 3; coverage of polygamy, 154–56.

77. Kingsley's letter to Taylor is quoted by Deborah Birkett in "West Africa's Mary Kingsley," *History Today* 37 (May 1, 1987): 11–16, quotation on 12.

78. Mary H. Kingsley, *West African Studies* (London: Macmillan, 1899), 364, 367–68.

79. Birkett, "West Africa's Mary Kingsley," 12–13.

80. Mary H. Kingsley, quoted in Katherine Frank, *A Voyager Out: The Life of Mary Kingsley* (Boston: Houghton Mifflin, 1986), 292; cited in Rosalind I. J. Hackett's review of that work and of Kingsley's *Travels in West Africa* (reprint, Boston: Beacon Press, 1988), in *Journal of Religion in Africa* 21 (February 1991): 81.

81. Eric Hobsbawm, *The Age of Empire, 1875–1914* (London: Cardinal, 1987), 59; cited in Helen Carr, "Modernism and Travel (1880–1940)" in *The Cambridge Companion to Travel Writing*, ed. Peter Hulme and Tim Youngs (Cambridge: Cambridge University Press, 2002), 70–86, quotation on 72. It is important to note that Kingsley and Twain differed on the matter of missionary culpability for the excesses of empire; Twain viewed American missionary efforts in a much more positive light than Kingsley did British missionary activities. See Albert H. Tricomi's chapter, "The Missionary Novel in Decline: Mark Twain and America's Second Manifest Destiny," in his *Missionary Positions: Evangelicalism and Empire in American Fiction* (Gainesville: University Press of Florida, 2011), 89–106.

82. For more on Kingsley, see Frank, *A Voyager Out*; Deborah Birkett, *Mary Kingsley: Imperial Adventuress* (Hampshire, England: Palgrave Macmillan, 1992); Alison Blunt, *Travel, Gender, and Imperialism: Mary Kingsley and West Africa* (New York: Guilford Press, 1994); Laura E. Ciolkowski, "Travelers' Tales: Empire, Victorian Travel, and the Spectacle of English Womanhood in Mary Kingsley's 'Travels in West Africa,'" *Victorian Literature and Culture* 26 (1998): 337–66; and Casey Blanton, "Victorian Women Travelers: Mary Kingsley," in her *Travel Writing: The Self and the World* (New York: Twayne Publishers, 1997), 44–58.

83. For more on the theme of the "Other" in travel writing, see Mary Baine Campbell, "Travel Writing and Its Theory," in *The Cambridge Companion to Travel Writing*, ed. Peter Hulme and Tim Youngs (Cambridge: Cambridge University Press, 2002), 261–78; and Carol E. Leon, *Movement and Belonging: Lines, Places, and Spaces of Travel* (New York: Peter Lang, 2009).

84. Richard Harding Davis, *Three Gringos in Venezuela and Central America* (New York: Harper and Brothers, 1896; reprinted, 1903), 146; page references from the 1903 edition. This passage is also quoted in Terry Caeser's essay "South of the Border: American Travel Writing in Latin America," in *The Cambridge Companion to American Travel Writing*, 180–94, quotation on 185.

85. Among the works by travelers effectively acting as imperial scribes, Henry Morton Stanley's best-selling and influential account *In Darkest Africa; or, the Quest, Rescue, and Retreat of Emin, Governor of Equatoria*, 2 vols. (New York: Charles Scribner's Sons; London: Sampson Low, Marston, Searle, and Rivington, 1890).

86. Interesting in this regard are John Mackenzie's *Propaganda and Empire: The Manipulation of British Public Opinion, 1880–1960* (Manchester: Manchester University Press, 1984), and his edited collection, *Imperialism and Popular Culture* (Manchester: Manchester University Press, 1986).

Chapter Three

1. See David M. Wrobel, *The End of American Exceptionalism: Frontier Anxiety from the Old West to the New Deal* (Lawrence: University Press of Kansas, 1993).

2. Jack London, "Adventure," in *The Cruise of the* Snark (Suffolk, England: Seafarer Books, 2000; first published, New York: Macmillan, 1911), 36–46, quotations on 36, 46.

3. Jack London, "The Class Struggle," *Independent* 5 (November 1903): 2603–10; reprinted in Jack London, *The War of the Classes* (London: W. M. Heinemann, 1905), 3–49, quotations on 7–9. "How I Became a Socialist" is included in *The War of the Classes*, 267–78.

4. Jack London labeled the East End of London "the City of Degradation"; see chapter 19, "The Ghetto," in *The People of the Abyss* (New York: Macmillan, 1903), 210–31. For an examination of *The People of the Abyss* within the larger context of American travel writings about Europe, see William Merrill Decker, "Americans in Europe: Henry James to the Present," in *The Cambridge Companion to American Travel Writing*, ed. Alfred Bendixen and Judith Hamera (Cambridge: Cambridge University Press, 2009), 127–44; coverage of London, 130.

5. London, "The Ghetto," 227–29, 221. For more on the theme of racial degeneracy and attendant imperial decline in the work, see Brigitte Koenig's introduction to the Centenary Edition of *The People of the Abyss* (London: Pluto Press, 2001), v–xi. See also John Marriott, *The Other Empire: Metropolis, India and Progress in the Colonial Imagination* (Manchester: Manchester University Press, 2003), 228.

6. For more on London's time in Korea reporting on the Russo-Japanese War, see Jeanne Campbell Reesman, Sara S. Hodson, and Philip Adam, *Jack London: Photographer* (Athens: University of Georgia Press, 2010), 56–113; for the quotation from British correspondent F. A. McKenzie, see 58.

7. Jack London, *The Road* (New York: Macmillan, 1907; reprinted, New Brunswick, NJ: Rutgers University Press, 2006). Kelly's Army, named for its California leader, "General" Charles T. Kelly, was a western counterpart of Coxey's Army (named for Jacob Coxey), which moved from Ohio to Washington, D.C.; Kelly's Army traveled from California to the Ohio River in the spring of 1894, although London and several others abandoned the group in May in Missouri. From there, London headed to the World's Fair in Chicago; see Richard Etulain, introduction to *Jack London on the Road: The Tramp Diary and Other Hobo Writings*, ed. Richard Etulain (Logan: Utah State University Press, 1979), 2–3.

8. Jim Rasenberger, *America, 1908: The Dawn of Flight, the Race to the Pole, the Invention of the Model T, and the Making of a Modern Nation* (New York: Scribner, 2007), 63. The name of the Londons' vessel was drawn from Lewis Carroll's 1874 poem "The Hunting of the Snark, an Agony in 8 Fits."

9. George Byron Gordon, *In the Alaskan Wilderness* (Philadelphia: John Winston, 1917), 63–82.

10. Robert Dunn, *The Shameless Diary of an Explorer: A Story of Failure on Mount McKinley* (New York: Outing Publishing Company, 1907; reprinted with an introduction by Robert Hoagland, New York: Modern Library, 2001). For another interesting account of Alaskan exploration, see Gordon, *In the Alaskan Wilderness*, which recounts the University of Pennsylvania anthropologist's 1907 travels with his brother MacLaren Gordon. In the preface, the author explains why he thought that the publication, in 1917, of a retrospective travelogue of a frontier journey was so important in the midst of the largest military conflict the world had yet seen: "there has never been a time when the waste places of the earth possessed so great an interest for civilized man as today. To a world grown tired and sick and full of fear, there is rest and refreshment and healing power in the breath of the brooding wilderness" (11).

11. In another fascinating twist to this grand tale of adventure and questionable claims, scholars have pointed to some similarities between Cook's account and the by then long since forgotten 1864 novel by Jules Verne, *Voyages et Adventures du Capitaine Hatteras* (*The Adventures of Captain Hatteras*), which in turn drew on the experiences of the real-life British explorer John Franklin.

12. Rasenberger, *America, 1908*, 63.

13. Frederick Albert Cook, *My Attainment of the Pole: Being the Record of the Expedition that First Reached the Boreal Center, 1907–1909; With the Final Summary of the Polar Controversy* (New York: Mitchell Kennerley, 1912; first published, New York: Polar Publishing, 1911), xii. Both Peary's *The North Pole* and Cook's *My Attainment of the Pole* were recently republished (New York: Cooper Square Press, 2001).

14. Hoagland provides a good discussion of the controversy surrounding Cook in his introduction to Dunn's *The Shameless Diary of an Explorer*, xviii–xix. See also Rasenberger, *America, 1908*, 109–11, 267–70.

15. Apsley Cherry-Garrard, *The Worst Journey in the World: Antarctic, 1910–1913*, 2 vols. (London: Constable; New York: George H. Doran, 1922).

16. Reesman, Hodson, and Adam provide an excellent account of the voyage in their *Jack London: Photographer*, 148–218. For further coverage of the Londons' illnesses, see James T. Haley, *Wolf: The Lives of Jack London* (New York: Basic Books, 2010), 254, 256; and Andrew Sinclair, *Jack: A Biography of Jack London* (New York: Harper and Row, 1977), 150–54.

17. Robert Louis Stevenson made three trips to the South Seas between 1888 and 1890 and recounted his experiences and observations in three works: *In the South Seas: Being an Account of Experiences and Observations in the Marquesas, Paumotus, and Gilbert Islands* (New York: Charles Scribner's Sons, 1896); *A Footnote to History: Eight Years of Trouble in Samoa* (New York: Charles Scribner's Sons, 1892); and *Father Damien: An Open Letter to the Reverend*

Doctor Hyde of Honolulu (London: Chatto and Windus, 1890), his defense of the Belgian priest who devoted his life to the care of the lepers on Molokai. See also Jonathan Lamb's chapter "The Polynesian Person and the Spread of Leprosy, in his *Preserving the Self in the South Seas, 1680–1840* (Chicago: University of Chicago Press, 2001), 132–61, esp. 157–61. For more on Stevenson in the South Seas, see Neil Rennie, *Far-Fetched Facts: The Literature of Travel and the Idea of the South Seas* (New York: Oxford University Press, 1995); and David Farrier, *Unsettled Narratives: The Pacific Writings of Stevenson, Ellis, Melville, and London* (New York: Routledge, 2007).

18. J. M. Wood also commented positively on the efforts of Father Damien to aid the lepers of Molokai in his *A Trip Around the World on Board of a Man-of-War: Cruise of the United States Steamer "Juniata" from New York City to Yokohama* (Shanghai: Kelly and Walsh, 1888), 57.

19. London, *The Cruise of the* Snark, 105. See also London's story "Koolau the Leper," first published in *The House of Pride and Other Tales of Hawaii* (New York: Macmillan, 1912; reprinted in Jack London, *South Sea Tales*, New York: Modern Library, 2002), 18–33.

20. See Reesman, Hodson, and Adam, *Jack London: Photographer*, 167.

21. Charmian Kittredge London, *The Log of the* Snark (New York: Macmillan, 1915); published in England as *Voyaging in Wild Seas; or, A Woman Among the Head Hunters (A Narrative of the Voyage of the* Snark *in the Years 1907–1909* (London: Mills and Boon, 1915). Among the Londons' favorite readings on the trip, not surprisingly, were Melville's *Typee* and Stevenson's various works on the South Seas, as well as Isabella Bird's account of her time in Hawaii; Charmian London, *The Log of the* Snark, 23, 44. See also Charmian London's *Our Hawaii (Islands and Islanders)* (New York: Macmillan, 1917); and Clarice Stasz, *American Dreamers: Charmian and Jack London* (New York: St. Martin's Press, 1988), esp. 151–70.

22. Playbill (flyer) for the New York Criterion Theater (manager Charles Frohman) performance of "Jack London's Adventures in the South Sea Islands," by Martin Johnson, HEH RB 435918. Martin Johnson's letters to Jack and Charmian dealing with his travelogue, and seven letters of reply from the Londons, are housed in the Huntington Library's Jack London Collection. Ironically, Johnson hoped, for many years, that his travelogues about his experience with the Londons in the South Seas would help generate sufficient profit for him to pay back the financial debt to them that he had accumulated, mostly during the course of the two-year voyage.

23. Martin Johnson, *Through the South Seas with Jack London* (New York: Dodd, Mead and Company, 1913), 1.

24. For more on the Johnsons, see Osa Johnson, *I Married Adventure: The Lives of Martin and Osa Johnson* (Garden City, NY: Halcyon House, 1943; reprinted, New York: Kodansha America, 1997); and Pascal James Imperato, *They Married*

Adventure: The Wandering Lives of Martin and Osa Johnson (New Brunswick, NJ: Rutgers University Press, 1992).

25. Charmian London, *The Log of the* Snark, 95.

26. Quotations are from Michael P. Branch's excellent introduction to his edited volume, John Muir, *John Muir's Last Journey: South to the Amazon and East to Africa; Unpublished Journals and Selected Correspondence* (Washington, D.C.: Island Press; Covelo, CA: Shearwater Books, 2001), xxiii–lii, li; summary of travel itinerary, xxiii.

27. Ibid., xlv for quotation, and xlvi–xlviii for discussion of the "America-centric" nature of American nature writing and the general fascination with the youthful Muir.

28. Donald Worster, *A Passion for Nature: The Life of John Muir* (New York: Oxford University Press, 2008), 443–46, quotation on 446. Branch also notes the absence of commentary by Muir on Africa's colonial violence and puts it down to his "preference for the natural over the cultural landscape" and his effort to escape the political controversy that surrounded the Hetch Hetchy struggle; see his commentary in Muir, *John Muir's Last Journey*, 133.

29. Michael Branch's introduction to Muir, *John Muir's Last Journey*, xxvii–xxxiii.

30. Ibid., xxx; Mungo Park, *Travels in the Interior Districts of Africa: Performed Under the Direction and Patronage of the African Association in the Years 1795, 1796, and 1797* (Edinburgh: Adam and Charles Black, 1860; first published, London: G. and W. Nicol, 1799).

31. Branch devotes the closing chapter of *John Muir's Last Journey* to the matter of the writing and potential publication of these pieces; see 184–221.

32. John Muir to Douglas Aimers, June 20, 1912, in Muir, *John Muir's Last Journey*, 210–11.

33. Edmund Morris provides a detailed account of the trip in his "Prologue: The Roosevelt Africa Expedition, 1909–1910," in *Colonel Roosevelt* (New York: Random House, 2010), the concluding volume of his biographical trilogy, 3–26.

34. Theodore Roosevelt, *African Game Trails: An Account of the African Wanderings of an American Hunter-Naturalist*, 2 vols. (New York: Charles Scribner's Sons, 1922; first published, New York: Charles Scribner's Sons, 1910), 1: ix.

35. See Morris, *Colonel Roosevelt*, 112.

36. Everett Marshall, *Roosevelt's Thrilling Experiences in the Wilds of Africa Hunting Big Game* (Chicago: A. Hamming, 1910).

37. The authentic footage appeared in *Roosevelt in Africa*, directed by Cherry Kearton, released in 1910. The fake documentary, produced by the Selig Company, was released the same year.

38. For more on the Roosevelt-Hemingway connection, see Edward Whitley, "Race and Modernity in Theodore Roosevelt's and Ernest Hemingway's African Travel Writing," in *Issues in Travel Writing: Empire, Spectacle, and Displacement*, ed. Kristi Siegel (New York: Peter Lang, 2002), 13–27.

39. Roosevelt, *African Game Trails*, 1: 1.

40. Whitley provides further discussion of the themes of primitivism, modernism, savagery and civilization, and imperialism in *African Game Trails* in "Race and Modernity." Monica Rico provides excellent coverage of Roosevelt's African trip in "A White Man's Country: Elite Masculinity, Racial Decline, and the Frontier Stories of Theodore Roosevelt," in her *Nature's Noblemen: Transatlantic Masculinities and the Nineteenth-Century American West* (New Haven, CT: Yale University Press, 2013).

41. See Adam Hochschild, *King Leopold's Ghost: A Story of Greed, Terror, and Heroism in Colonial Africa* (Boston: Houghton Mifflin, 1998). Hochschild puts the death toll at ten million and discusses the horrific colonial state policy of severing the right hand of each person killed as proof of that fatality.

42. Joseph Conrad, *Heart of Darkness* (London: William Blackwood, 1902).

43. Sir Arthur Conan Doyle, *The Crime of the Congo* (New York: Doubleday, Page; London: Hutchinson, 1909); the London edition features the graphic photographs at the front of the volume.

44. Hochschild, *King Leopold's Ghost*, 241–45.

45. Richard Harding Davis, *The Congo and the Coasts of Africa* (New York: Charles Scribner's Sons, 1907; London: Unwin, 1908). The passage is quoted in James J. Schramer's insightful overview of Davis's travel writings, "Richard Harding Davis," in *DLB*, vol. 189, *American Travel Writers, 1850–1915*, ed. Donald Ross and James J. Schramer (Detroit: Gale Research, 1998), 79–98. As Schramer makes clear, while Davis abhorred Leopold's "administration" in the Congo, he was generally supportive in his account of the colonial efforts of other European powers in Africa. Vachel Lindsay's first public reading of his poem "The Congo" ("Listen to the yell of Leopold's ghost, Burning in hell for his hand-maimed host. Hear how the demons chuckle and yell. Cutting his hands off, down in Hell") was first read at the beginning of 1914, while Roosevelt was on his last wilderness adventure in the Amazon rainforest.

46. Morris, *Colonel Roosevelt*, 25–26.

47. Roosevelt, *African Game Trails*, 1: 3.

48. Theodore Roosevelt, *The Winning of the West*, vol. 1: *From the Alleghanies to the Mississippi, 1769–1776* (New York: G. P. Putnam's Sons, 1900), 127, 157.

49. Roosevelt, *African Game Trails*, 1: 23.

50. For more on the dangers of the Mungo Park expedition and the comparative good fortune of Lewis and Clark, see Elliott West, "Lewis and Park; or, Why It Matters that the West's Most Famous Explorers Didn't Get Sick (or at Least Really Sick)," in *The Essential West: Collected Essays* (Norman: University of Oklahoma Press, 2012), 15–43.

51. Burton's adventures in Africa are discussed in chapter 2 of this study.

52. Paul Belloni du Chaillu, *Explorations and Adventures in Equatorial Africa* (London: John Murray; New York: Harper and Brothers, 1861); cited in Paul

Theroux, *The Tao of Travel: Enlightenments from Lives on the Road* (New York: Mariner Books, 2012), 60.

53. For more on the famous meeting between Stanley and Livingstone, and on Livingstone's death, see chapter 9, "Canonizing Dr. Livingstone," in Tim Jeal's *Stanley: The Impossible Life of Africa's Greatest Explorer* (New Haven, CT: Yale University Press, 2007), 117–32.

54. As Leila Koivunen notes in *Visualizing Africa in Nineteenth-Century British Travel Accounts* (New York: Routledge, 2009), organized exploration of Africa by Europeans began to meet with more success by the middle of the nineteenth century as a result of new weapons technology and medical advances, most notably "the discovery of quinine as a malarial prophylactic" (2).

55. Roosevelt, *African Game Trails*, 1: 39–40.

56. Ibid., 2: 568–70 for the list of species and numbers killed; 571 for Roosevelt's justification for those numbers.

57. Theodore Roosevelt recounted the expedition in *Through the Brazilian Wilderness* (New York: Charles Scribner's Sons, 1914). The book is still in print (New York: Cooper Square Press, 2000), and available as a Project Gutenberg e-book: www.gutenberg.org/ebooks/11746. Candice Millard provides an excellent account in *The River of Doubt: Theodore Roosevelt's Darkest Journey* (New York: Doubleday, 2005), as does Morris in *Colonel Roosevelt*, 305–47. See also Joseph R. Ornig, *My Last Chance to Be a Boy: Theodore Roosevelt's South American Expedition of 1913–1914* (Mechanicsburg, PA: Stackpole Books, 1994). A short (fifteen-minute) film of the journey, composed of captions drawn from the text of Roosevelt's account and actual film footage from the expedition, was compiled by the Library of Congress and is available at: www.youtube.com/watch?v=ToqblXco5us&feature=related.

58. For the piranha description, see Roosevelt, *Through the Brazilian Wilderness*, 42.

59. Ibid., 171–72.

60. Ibid., 172–73.

61. Ibid., 217.

62. Ibid., 225. Claude Lévi-Strauss, *Tristes Tropiques* (Paris: Librairie Plon, 1955; published in English as *A World on the Wane*, trans. John Russell, London: Hutchinson, 1961).

63. Roosevelt, *Through the Brazilian Wilderness*, 254–55.

64. Ibid., 261.

65. Ibid., 269.

66. Morris provides fuller details on Roosevelt's medical condition in *Colonel Roosevelt*, 336–41.

67. Kermit would tragically take his own life in 1943.

68. These events are recounted in chapter 9, "Down an Unknown River into the Equatorial Forest," of Roosevelt, *Through the Brazilian Wilderness*, 282–320.

69. Millard describes the operation in *The River of Doubt*, 331.

70. Morris describes the official moment of deliverance for the expedition in *Colonel Roosevelt*, 344. Roosevelt describes the moment in *Through the Brazilian Wilderness*, 330.

71. For more on this transitional moment in the development of the global rubber industry, see Millard, *The River of Doubt*, 317–18.

72. Roosevelt, *Through the Brazilian Wilderness*, 323–24.

73. Nathan Miller, in *Theodore Roosevelt: A Life* (New York: William Morrow, 1992), quotes Roosevelt's friend William Roscoe Thayer's observation that "[t]he Brazilian wilderness stole ten years away of his life," along with his wife Edith's observation that the weight loss made him look younger, "younger for every pound he has lost—a year a pound, I should say" (538).

74. G. M. (George Miller) Dyott, *Man Hunting in the Jungle: Being the Story of a Search for Three Explorers Lost in the Brazilian Wilds* (Indianapolis: Bobbs-Merrill, ca. 1930).

75. Kermit Roosevelt, *The Happy Hunting-Grounds* (New York: Charles Scribner's Sons, 1920), 3. These words also served as the opening lines of a short book by Kermit Roosevelt published the following year, titled *The Long Trail* (New York: Review of Reviews/Metropolitan Magazine, 1921), 9. The volume was an expansion of Roosevelt's piece "The Happy Hunting-Grounds," the first chapter of the book that bore the same title.

76. After the South American trip with his father, Kermit Roosevelt was at this time in the business field. He founded the Roosevelt Steamship Lines and the United States Lines.

77. Theodore Roosevelt Jr. and Kermit Roosevelt, *East of the Sun and West of the Moon* (New York: Charles Scribner's Sons, 1927), 3. The scientist George K. Cherrie, who had accompanied Kermit and his father on their South American adventure, also joined the Roosevelt brothers on this expedition.

78. Ibid., 10–11.

79. Ibid., 56, 65–66, 274.

Chapter Four

1. Filmmaker Ken Burns and writer Dayton Duncan provide a fascinating account of Nelson and Crocker's trip in their film *Horatio's Drive: America's First Road Trip* (aired in 2004; available in DVD format from PBS DVD Gold, 2005).

2. The figures for miles of roads and numbers of cars are from Peter J. Blodgett, *Motoring West: Automobile Travelers in the Trans-Mississippi West, 1900–1950*, vol. 1, *Pioneering, 1900–1909* (Norman: Arthur H. Clark Company, University of Oklahoma Press, forthcoming, 2013), 4–5. Phoebe S. Kropp's chapter "The Road: El Camino Real and Mission Nostalgia," in her *California Vieja: Culture and Memory in a Modern American Place* (Berkeley: University of California Press,

2006), 47–102, provides an excellent discussion of the intersections of automotive tourism, the good roads movement, and the mission heritage in this period. See also Jim Rasenberger's *America, 1908: The Dawn of Flight, the Race to the Pole, the Invention of the Model T, and the Making of a Modern Nation* (New York: Scribner, 2007), 20. In 2009, there were more than 254 million registered vehicles in the United States, approximately five vehicles for every six Americans. For an insightful discussion of the seemingly incontrovertible tide of public passion for the automobile despite the growing awareness of the consequences of that dedication, see Brian Ladd, *Autophobia: Love and Hate in the Automotive Age* (Chicago: University of Chicago Press, 2008). See also John A. Jakle and Keith A. Sculle, *Motoring: The Highway Experience in America* (Athens: University of Georgia Press, 2008).

3. The Carey S. Bliss Collection of transcontinental automotive narratives is housed at the Huntington Library, San Marino, California, and is annotated in Bliss's useful volume *Autos Across America: A Bibliography of Transcontinental Automobile Travel, 1903–1940* (Los Angeles: Dawson's Book Shop, 1972; 2nd ed. enlarged, Austin, TX: Jenkins and Reese, 1982). Also useful are Archibald Hanna, *From Train to Plane: Travelers in the American West, 1866–1936; An Exhibition at the Beinecke Rare Book and Manuscript Library, Yale University* (New Haven, CT: Yale University Library, 1979); Michael Berger, *The Automobile in American History and Culture: A Reference Guide* (Westport, CT: Greenwood Press, 2001); and Michael Vinsen, *Motoring Tourists and the Scenic West, 1903–1948* (Dallas: DeGolyer Library, Southern Methodist University, 1989). The number of published transcontinental automotive travel books from 1903 to 1930 is approximately one hundred, depending upon definitions of what qualifies as a truly transcontinental trip (i.e., does the journey literally have to run from coast to coast, or can it begin or end inland?).

4. For more on automotive touring in this period and the development of the road infrastructure that made it possible, see Marguerite S. Shaffer, *See America First: Tourism and National Identity, 1880–1940* (Washington: Smithsonian Institution Press, 2001), esp. chapter 4, "A Nation on Wheels," and chapter 6, "Tourist Encounters," 130–68 and 221–60, respectively; and Shaffer's essay, "Seeing America First: The Search for Identity in the Tourist Landscape," in *Seeing and Being Seen: Tourism in the American West*, ed. David M. Wrobel and Patrick T. Long (Lawrence: University Press of Kansas, 2001), 165–93.

5. Anne Farrar Hyde, *An American Vision: Far Western Landscape and National Culture, 1820–1920* (New York: New York University Press, 1990), 298–99. Paul S. Sutter, in *Driven Wild: How the Fight Against Automobiles Launched the Modern Wilderness Movement* (Seattle: University of Washington Press, 2002), examines how the opposition to automotive touring catalyzed preservationist impulses.

6. For further coverage of the development of automobile technology and production and the development of road infrastructure in this period, see James J. Flink,

The Automobile Age (Cambridge: MIT Press, 1990), and *America Adopts the Automobile, 1895–1910* (Cambridge: MIT Press, 1970); Phil Patton, *Open Road: A Celebration of the American Highway* (New York: Simon and Schuster, 1986); and Michael Berger, *Devil Wagon in God's Country: The Automobile and Social Change in Rural America, 1893–1929* (Hamden, CT: Archon Books, 1979).

7. For more on the matter of the perspective of viewing landscapes through windshields, see David Louter, *Windshield Wilderness: Cars, Roads, and Nature in Washington's National Parks* (Seattle: University of Washington Press, 2006). For more on how various modes of conveyance influenced perceptions of landscape, see Anne F. Hyde, "Cultural Filters: The Significance of Perception," in *A New Significance: Re-Envisioning the History of the American West*, ed. Clyde Milner (New York: Oxford University Press, 1996), 175–201, esp. 184–88.

8. Philip Delany, "Frontiering in an Automobile," *Outing: An Illustrated Magazine of Recreation* 43 (November 1903): 2; reprinted in Blodgett, *Motoring West*, vol. 1. For another good example of this early phase of automobile travel writing about the West, see M. C. Krarup, "From Coast to Coast in an Automobile," *World's Work* (May 1904), 4740–54; reprinted in Blodgett, *Motoring West*, vol. 1.

9. Ezra Meeker, *The Busy Life of Eighty-Five Years of Ezra Meeker: Ventures and Adventures* (Seattle: published by author, 1916), and *The Ox-Team; or, The Old Oregon Trail, 1852–1906* (Lincoln, NE: Jacob North, 1906); Viola MacFadyen, *Crossing the Plains on a Prairie Schooner* (New York: David MacFadyen, 1912). For more on Meeker, see David M. Wrobel, *Promised Lands: Promotion, Memory, and the Creation of the American West* (Lawrence: University Press of Kansas, 2002, 2011), 107–14.

10. One of the best discussions of where the West begins in travel books of this period (although not a transcontinental automobile travel narrative) is Katharine Fullerton Gerould's *The Aristocratic West* (New York: Harper and Brothers, 1925), 5–6. See also Caroline Rittenberg, *Motor West* (New York: Harold Vinal, 1926), 19.

11. Blodgett, *Motoring West*, vol. 1, provides an excellent introduction to (and selection of) automotive travelogues from the period. The book is the first in Blodgett's projected five-volume series, *Motoring West: Automobile Travelers in the Trans-Mississippi West, 1900–1950*.

12. The coverage here draws heavily on Jim Rasenberger's excellent account of the Great Race, which he treats within a larger framework of other remarkable events and developments in 1908, including the race to the North Pole, in his *America, 1908*, 57–69, 80–87, 105–7, 149–51. Other published accounts of the race include George Shuster's *The Longest Auto Race* (New York: John Day, 1966)—Shuster was the co-driver of the American entry, which won the race—and German participant Hans Koeppen's *Im Auto um die Welt* (Berlin: Ullstein, 1908). The Great Race was also immortalized in celluloid, although not to great critical or popular acclaim, through the 1965 slapstick comedy movie of the same title (directed by Blake

Edwards), starring Jack Lemmon, Tony Curtis, and Natalie Wood. The film and the race itself were an inspiration for the Hanna-Barbera cartoon series "Wacky Races."

13. Jim Rasenberger, *America, 1908*, 149–51, 163–67.

14. Ibid., 60, 62–63; quotation from the *Baltimore American*, 62.

15. For more on the Züst, see the website Historic 1907 Züst, accessed December 15, 2011, http://www.greatracezust.com/.

16. Antonio Scarfoglio, *Round the World in a Motor Car*, trans. J. Parker Heyes (London: Grant Richards, 1909), 68–69. Scarfoglio's sentiments echoed those of the British woman traveler Frances Trollope, who had famously pronounced her dislike for Americans and their culture four generations earlier in *Domestic Manners of the Americans* (London: Whittaker, Treacher, and Company, 1832).

17. Scarfoglio, *Round the World in a Motor Car*, 82–83.

18. Scarfoglio's critique was echoed in George W. Pierson's cultural history *The Moving American* (New York: Alfred A. Knopf, 1973). Pierson asked, "Can 'home' be altogether divorced from place, from neighbors, from memories and ancestral associations? In the grasshopper existence to which we seem addicted, have we not converted 'home' into boardinghouse or temporary pad? And who is to measure the moral deprivations to children, the adolescent insecurities?" (119).

19. Scarfoglio, *Round the World in a Motor Car*, 145–46.

20. Van Wyck Brooks, *America's Coming of Age* (New York: B. W. Huebsch, 1915), and "The Literary Life," in *Civilization in the United States: An Inquiry by Thirty Americans*, ed. Harold Stearns (New York: Harcourt, Brace, 1922), 180–97; Waldo Frank, "The Land of the Pioneer," in his *Our America* (New York: Boni and Liverwright, 1919), 13–58, and *The Re-discovery of America: An Introduction to a Philosophy of American Life* (New York: Charles Scribner's Sons, 1929); John Dewey, "The American Intellectual Frontier," *New Republic* (May 10, 1922): 303–5.

21. Henry Miller, *The Air-Conditioned Nightmare* (New York: New Directions, 1945). For an insightful analysis of the work in the larger context of the American road narrative, see Ronald Primeau, *Romance of the Road: The Literature of the American Highway* (Bowling Green, OH: Bowling Green State University Popular Press, 1996), 33–36.

22. Walter Lippmann, *A Preface to Morals* (New York: Macmillan, 1929), 19–20, quoted in Robert Dorman's excellent study *Revolt of the Provinces: The Regionalist Movement in America, 1920–1945* (Chapel Hill: University of North Carolina Press, 1993), 24. See also T. J. Jackson Lears's seminal study *No Place of Grace: Antimodernism and the Transformation of American Culture, 1880–1920* (Chicago: University of Chicago Press, 1981).

23. Alice Huyler Ramsey was the first woman to drive an automobile across the continent. The trip was made in 1909 from New York to San Francisco, took two

months—June 9–August 9, 1909—and is recounted, retrospectively, in Ramsey's *Veil, Duster, and Tire Iron* (Pasadena, CA: Castle Press, 1961).

24. Another of the memorable women's automotive travel narratives of the period is Harriet White Fisher's *A Woman's World Tour in a Motor* (Philadelphia: J. B. Lippincott, 1911).

25. Emily Post, *By Motor to the Golden Gate* (New York: Appleton, 1916), 99, 116–18.

26. Ibid., 136, 138, 146.

27. Ibid., 160, 162. For more on the topic, see Leah Dilworth, "Tourists and Indians in Fred Harvey's Southwest," in Wrobel and Long, *Seeing and Being Seen*, 142–64; and Dilworth's larger study, *Imagining Indians in the Southwest: Persistent Visions of a Primitive Past* (Washington, D.C.: Smithsonian Institution Scholarly Press, 1996).

28. Post, *By Motor to the Golden Gate*, 230.

29. Some of those subsequent auto travelogues were inspired by Post's account; see, for example, Beatrice Larned Massey, *It Might Have Been Worse: A Motor Trip from Coast to Coast* (San Francisco: Harr Wagner, 1920).

30. Hugo Alois Taussig, *Retracing the Pioneers: From East to West in an Automobile* (San Francisco: Philopolis Press, 1910), n.p. (acknowledgments page). Emily Post, by way of contrast, did find some distinctiveness in the indigenous cultures of the Southwest, although she viewed Arizona and New Mexico as being "far more like Asia than anything in the United States or Europe" (*By Motor to the Golden Gate*, 239). Interestingly, though, Ramsey, in her recollections of Cheyenne in 1909 during her own cross-continental trip, remembered a decidedly frontier context. "Cheyenne, Wyoming, in 1909," she wrote, "was a true frontier town, of larger population and dimension than the average. It was, nevertheless, a typical one with a conglomeration of Indians, cowboys and cattlemen on its streets; its stores, naturally, carrying supplies for this mixture of people and occupations. The buildings of frame construction and the dirt streets strongly resembled the sets we see nowadays for 'Westerns' on TV"; see *Veil, Duster, and Tire Iron*, 68.

31. Winifred Hawkridge Dixon, *Westward Hoboes: Ups and Downs of Frontier Motoring* (New York: Charles Scribner's Sons, 1921), 263, 204; page references from 1925 reprinting.

32. For more on this theme, including coverage of the western journeys of Dixon and Post, see Shaffer, *See America First*, 256–58; and Virginia Scharff, *Taking the Wheel: Women and the Coming of the Motor Age* (Albuquerque: University of New Mexico Press, 1991).

33. C. K. Shepherd, *Across America by Motor-Cycle* (London: Edward Arnold, 1922), vi. The book was reprinted in 2008 by Juniper Grove, Fayetteville, Arkansas.

34. Ibid., 96.

35. Ibid., 96, 101. Post also commented on the ready availability of gasoline, even in

the desert, albeit at three to four times the regular price; see Post, *By Motor to the Golden Gate*, 246.

36. Shepherd, *Across America by Motor-Cycle*, 156, 158.

37. Although it is worth noting that Shepherd did meet a fellow motorcyclist headed in the opposite direction, from California to the east coast.

38. In addition to Dilworth's coverage of this theme in *Imagining Indians in the Southwest*, see Erika Marie Bsumek's *Indian-Made: Navajo Culture in the Marketplace, 1868–1940* (Lawrence: University Press of Kansas, 2008); and Hal K. Rothman, ed., *The Culture of Tourism, the Tourism of Culture: Selling the Past to the Present in the American Southwest* (Albuquerque: University of New Mexico Press, 2003).

39. Frank H. Trego, *Boulevarded Old Trails in the Great Southwest* (New York: Greenberg Publisher, 1929), 20, 85. Interestingly, in the late 1920s, Trego also wrote accounts of travels in Asia and South and Central America, but global contextualization is not a feature of his account of southwestern U.S. travels.

40. Ibid., 241–42. Interestingly, Post, in *By Motor to the Golden Gate*, described Isleta as "a quite large settlement where there are many Indians and also many tourists" (176). She went on to assume greater knowledge and perceptual abilities than "the average, ignorant tourist" (239).

41. Trego, *Boulevarded Old Trails*, 247.

42. For excellent coverage of the Indian Detour, see Martin Padget's chapter "Indian Detours Off the Beaten Track: Cultural Tourism and the Southwest," in his *Indian Country: Travels in the American Southwest, 1840–1935* (Albuquerque: University of New Mexico Press, 2004), 169–210, quotation on 194, from Fred Harvey, *The Indian-Detour* (New York: Rand McNally, 1926), 5–6; and Dilworth, *Imagining Indians in the Southwest*. While the Indian Detour might be dismissed as the quintessential example of the touristic commodification of experience, it is worth considering that some of the sites visited had only been known to mainstream America for a short time in 1926; for example, Rainbow Bridge was "discovered" by Anglo-Americans in 1909. For more, see Thomas Harvey, *Rainbow Bridge to Monument Valley: Making the Modern Old West* (Norman: University of Oklahoma Press, 2011).

43. Martin Padget provides a good discussion of these efforts to construct a Southwest region for popular consumption in his essay "The Southwest and Travel Writing," in *The Cambridge Companion to American Travel Writing*, ed. Alfred Bendixen and Judith Hamera (Cambridge: Cambridge University Press, 2009), 78–99, esp. 88–91.

44. Aldous Huxley, "Why Not Stay at Home?," in *Along the Road: Notes and Essays of a Tourist* (London: Chatto and Windus, 1948; first published, 1925), 3, 4–5, 9. Drawing a clear parallel with Thorstein Veblen's critique of conspicuous consumption in *The Theory of the Leisure Class* (New York: Macmillan, 1899), Huxley wrote: "People travel for the same reason as they collect art: because the best

people do it" (3–4). The notion of tourism as conspicuous consumption is evident in much of the more recent scholarship on tourism in the American West, most notably in Hal Rothman, *Devil's Bargains: Tourism in the Twentieth-Century American West* (Lawrence: University Press of Kansas, 1998). Rothman used the dismissive phrase "psychic trophies" to illustrate the motivations of tourists.

Long before Huxley asked the question "why not stay at home?" and before Alexander von Humboldt left on his famous journey to South America (1799–1804), the Frenchman Xavier de Maistre wrote a short book that might be considered the original antitravel book, examining the wonders that could be gained from explorations closer to home. The work was written in 1790, first published five years later, and titled *Journey Around My Room*. Maistre later wrote another microcosmic travelogue, *Nocturnal Expedition Around My Bedroom* (1825). The two works are available in a single edition, translated by Andrew Brown and with a foreword by Alain de Botton (London: Hesperus Press, 2004). De Botton discusses Maistre's works in his *The Art of Travel* (London: Penguin Books, 2003), 243–54.

45. Aldous Huxley, *Brave New World* (London: Chatto and Windus; Garden City, NY: Doubleday, Doran, 1932). Huxley, in his next book (which was his final travel book), *Beyond the Mexique Bay*, took up the matter of how much of the primitive might be beneficially introduced "into our civilized and industrialized way of life." In 1937, Huxley and his wife settled in the United States. For more on Huxley's travel writings, see Scott R. Christianson, "Aldous Huxley (1894–1963)," in *DLB*, vol. 195, *British Travel Writers,1910–1939*, ed. Barbara Brothers and Julia M. Gergits (Detroit: Gale Research, 1997, 155–67.

46. See, for example, Henry Otteridge Reik's *A Tour of America's National Parks* (New York: Dutton, 1920).

47. Philip J. Deloria provides an insightful exploration of the antimodernist framing of Indians in *Indians in Unexpected Places* (Lawrence: University Press of Kansas, 2004); see esp. the chapters "I Want to Ride in Geronimo's Cadillac," 136–82, quotations on 166, 146; and "The Secret History of Indian Modernity," 225–40.

48. Gerould, *The Aristocratic West*, 131.

49. Hoffman Birney, *Roads to Roam* (Philadelphia: Penn Publishing Company, 1930), 31–32. These commercial transactions—photographs of Indians for a price—are a common feature of travelogues that include the Southwest; see, for example, Rittenberg, *Motor West*, 32.

50. Gerould, *The Aristocratic West*, 132.

51. Mary Austin, *The Land of Journey's Ending* (New York: Century Company, 1924). Austin is quoted in Flannery Burke's excellent study *From Greenwich Village to Taos: Primitivism and Place at Mabel Dodge Luhan's* (Lawrence: University Press of Kansas, 2008), 141. Susan Goodman and Carl Dawson provide good coverage of Austin's travelogue in the chapter "The Call of the West," in their *Mary Austin and the American West* (Berkeley: University of California Press, 2008), 172–97.

52. Austin, *The Land of Journey's Ending*, 445.

53. The tension between Dodge Luhan's and Lawrence's visions for the place and its Indian peoples is explored in Burke's chapter "D. H. Lawrence's Place" in *From Greenwich Village to Taos*, 153–72, and by Padget in "The Southwest and Travel Writing," 93–94.

54. In "The Hopi Snake Dance," Lawrence, in the classic travel writing tendency to poke fun at the tourist, relates the gushing enthusiasm of "a girl with bobbed hair" who proclaims: "I never did see a rattlesnake, and I'm crazy to see one." The essay is included in D. H. Lawrence, *Mornings in Mexico and Other Essays*, ed. Virginia Crosswhite Hyde (Cambridge: Cambridge University Press, 2009), 79–93. *Mornings in Mexico* was originally published in London by Martin Secker, and in New York by Alfred A. Knopf, in 1927.

55. "Indians and Entertainment" originally appeared in much abbreviated form (with the quoted passage excerpted) in the *New York Times Magazine*, October 26, 1924. The full version of the essay, which Lawrence completed in April 1924, is included in Lawrence, *Mornings in Mexico*, 59–68; quotation on 67.

56. Lawrence, *Mornings in Mexico*, 68.

57. Kerouac's *On the Road*, while not strictly a travel narrative, is a work that exhibits many central features of the genre. For another example of the nostalgic search for an authentic "frontier" America, see J. R. Humphreys, *The Lost Towns and Roads of America: A Journey Revealing Early America Still Here Today* (Garden City, NY: Doubleday, 1961). The book's dust jacket reads, much in the tradition of thousands of other twentieth-century portents of the death of regionalism: "The United States is indeed becoming a nation of "strip" cities strung along super turnpikes, of gigantic shopping centers and developments."

Chapter Five

1. J. B. Priestley, *English Journey*, Seventy-Fifth Anniversary Edition (Ilkley, West Yorkshire: Great Northern, 2009; first published as *English Journey: Being a Rambling but Truthful Account of What One Man Saw and Heard and Felt and Thought During a Journey Through England During the Autumn of the Year 1933*, London: W. M. Heinemann, in association with V. Gollancz, 1934). For more on the larger context of socially conscious British travel writing of the period, see Bernard Schweizer, *Radicals on the Road: The Politics of English Travel Writing in the 1930s* (Charlottesville: University of Virginia Press, 2001).

2. *U.S. One: Maine to Florida*, compiled and written by the Federal Writers' Project of the Works Progress Administration (New York: Modern Age Books, 1938); *The Oregon Trail*, compiled and written by the Federal Writers' Project of the Works Progress Administration (New York: Hastings House, 1939).

3. Ernie Pyle, *Home Country* (New York: William Sloane, 1947), 209.

4. Ibid., 214.

5. Ibid., 226–45; Ernie Pyle to Lee G. Miller, in Lee G. Miller, *The Story of Ernie Pyle* (New York: Viking, 1950), 83.

6. Pyle, *Home Country*, 254–66.

7. Ibid., 267–70.

8. There are few moments in *Home Country* when Pyle is not deeply interested in the people he encounters, but one of those rare exceptions is his visit to the Taos Indian Pueblo. Pyle, like so many of the earlier writers who visited the Southwest in the teens and twenties, was turned off by the commercialization; he described his and Jerry's experience as a frustrating tour through an endless parade of curio shops with a thoroughly uninspiring guide (288–90). For the western Kansas description, see 291–92.

9. J. B. Priestley, *Midnight on the Desert: Being an Excursion into Autobiography During a Winter in America, 1935–1936* (New York: Harper and Brothers, 1937), 98–99.

10. Ibid., 109.

11. Ibid., 110–11, 112–13. The American writer Edmund Wilson had visited Hoover Dam half a decade before Priestley, while the construction was just getting under way and worker deaths were occurring because of accidents, heat exhaustion, and the poor initial planning for occupational health and safety; he was considerably less enamored with the site than Priestley. See Edmund Wilson, "Hoover Dam," in his *The American Jitters* (New York: Charles Scribner's Sons, 1932), 213–25.

12. Priestley, *Midnight on the Desert*, 284–85, 288. Stephen J. Pyne, in his excellent study *How the Grand Canyon Became Grand: A Short History* (New York: Viking, 1998), refers to Priestley's account as "the best Canyon essay of the era" (136). Henry Miller also provided a memorable description of the Grand Canyon in his travelogue *The Air-Conditioned Nightmare* (New York: New Directions, 1945): "It's mad, completely mad, and at the same time so grandiose, so sublime, so illusory, that when you come upon it for the first time you break down and weep with joy" (240). However, unlike Priestley, who was mesmerized by the Boulder Dam and the possibilities it provided for social engineering and uplift, Miller asked, "Why is it that in America the great works of art are all Nature's doing? . . . Nowhere in America was there anything comparable to the cathedrals of Europe, the temples of Asia and Europe—enduring monuments created out of faith and love and passion" (228).

13. Priestley, *Midnight on the Desert*, 290, 295. One might see a certain irony in the timing of Priestley's comment concerning which country might learn from the other with regard to social services. In the year that Priestley's book was published, the United States was sinking into what would be dubbed the Roosevelt Recession, and the president would in 1938 finally accept the advice of the British economist John Maynard Keynes regarding the necessity of deficit spending

during economic downturns, one that he had first discussed with FDR during their meeting in January 1934 and reiterated in a private letter to him dated February 1, 1938. Moreover, in a sense, the deficit spending that marked the early years of the New Deal and funded FDR's relief initiatives prior to his attempt to balance the budget in 1937 might also be viewed as an example of Keynesian economic policy.

14. Franklin D. Roosevelt, "Commonwealth Club Address" (September 23, 1932), in *The Public Papers and Addresses of Franklin D. Roosevelt*, ed. Samuel I. Rosenman and William D. Hassett (New York: Random House, 1938), 742–56; quotation on 754. For more on Tugwell and Wallace and the closed frontier theme during this period, see David M. Wrobel, "The New Deal Frontier," in *The End of American Exceptionalism: Frontier Anxiety from the Old West to the New Deal* (Lawrence: University Press of Kansas, 1993), 122–42, quotation on 133.

15. For more on the Federal Music Project, see Peter L. Gough, *The Music of the New Deal in the West* (Urbana: University of Illinois Press, forthcoming 2014). For the Federal Art Project, see Victoria Grieve, *The Federal Art Project and the Creation of Middlebrow Culture* (Urbana: University of Illinois Press, 2009). For full coverage of the FWP's productivity, see Jerre Mangione's concluding chapter "The Legacy" in his *The Dream and the Deal: The Federal Writers' Project, 1935–1943* (Boston: Little, Brown, 1972), 351–74.

16. Harry L. Hopkins, foreword to *A South Dakota Guide*, compiled and written by the Federal Writers' Project of the Works Progress Administration (Pierre, SD: State Publishing Company, 1938), n.p. Hopkins's quotation serves as the title of Jerrold Hirsch's *Portrait of America: A Cultural History of the Federal Writers' Project* (Chapel Hill: University of North Carolina Press, 2003).

17. A particularly noteworthy exception to the trend concerning authorship of the state guides is the Idaho guide (1937), the first of the guides to appear, and one authored largely by a single individual, Vardis Fisher (discussed later in this chapter).

18. Quotation on the travel book form is from Alan Gribben and Jeffrey Alan Melton's introduction to their anthology *Mark Twain on the Move: A Travel Reader* (Tuscaloosa: University of Alabama Press, 2009), xi–xx, see p. xi.

19. Gwendolyn Wright, introduction to *The WPA Guide to California*, compiled and written by the Federal Writers' Project of the Works Progress Administration (New York: Pantheon Books, 1984), xv–xxiv, xvii. The work was originally published as *California: A Guide to the Golden State* (New York: Hastings House, 1939).

20. These regional designations do not coincide with the U.S. Census Bureau's groupings of western states, which places Texas and Oklahoma in the South and the central and northern plains states from Kansas to North Dakota in the Midwest, dividing the West into the Pacific (Washington, Oregon, California, and Alaska and Hawaii) and mountain regions. The four regional tours

provided here would vary in distance, and dividing the West in the way I have places more than half of its population back then (and today, too, it is worth noting) in the greater southwestern borderlands region. The second tier of trans-Mississippi western states is included because it is clear from the guides that they self-identified more as western states than midwestern ones and played on their frontier heritage with as much frequency and enthusiasm as did the guides to the far western states. Similarly, Texas (and Oklahoma, too) identified far more in the WPA guides with their western heritage than their southern roots.

Bernard A. Weisberger, ed., *The WPA Guide to America: The Best of 1930s America as Seen by the Federal Writers' Project* (New York: Pantheon Books, 1985), includes sections on the northern plains states (Minnesota, North Dakota, South Dakota, Nebraska, and Kansas); the southern plains states (Arkansas, Oklahoma, and Texas); the mountain states (Montana, Wyoming, Colorado, Idaho, Utah, Washington, and Oregon), and the southwestern states (New Mexico, Arizona, Nevada, and California).

21. The guides all appeared between 1937 and 1942; population figures provided are from the 1940 census.

22. John Steinbeck's *The Red Pony*, composed of three stories, "The Promise," "The Gift," and "The Great Mountains," was published in New York by Covici-Friede in 1937. The full four-story cycle, with "The Leader of the People" included, appeared in *The Long Valley* (New York: Viking, 1938). *The Long Valley* is reprinted in John Steinbeck, *The Grapes of Wrath and Other Writings, 1936–1941*, ed. Robert DeMott and Elaine Steinbeck (New York: Library of America, 1996); for "The Leader of the People" in the reprint edition, see 190–205, quotation on 204.

23. *The WPA Guide to California*, 7.

24. California's Central Valley has itself been the subject of an enormous body of travel writing, one that stretches back long before Bidwell and that has been insightfully summarized and memorably augmented by Janet Fireman in her presidential address to the Pacific Coast Branch of the American Historical Association, in Seattle, August 2011, later published as "Between Horizons: Traveling the Great Central Valley," *Pacific Historical Review* 81 (February 2012): 1–20.

25. *The WPA Guide to California*, 38–40; quotations on 40.

26. Ibid., 64.

27. John Steinbeck, *The Harvest Gypsies*, in *The Grapes of Wrath and Other Writings, 1936–1941*, ed. Robert DeMott and Elaine A. Steinbeck (New York: Library of America, 1996). An expanded collection of *The Harvest Gypsies* articles was published in 1938 in pamphlet form as *Their Blood Is Strong* by the Simon J. Lubin Society of California to raise money for migrant workers. The original articles appeared in the *San Francisco News* between October 5 and 12, 1936. Carey McWilliams, *Factories in the Field* (Boston: Little, Brown, 1939).

28. Incidentally, Steinbeck's novels through *Of Mice and Men* (1937) are discussed in the California guide's section on literature; *The WPA Guide to California*, 149–50.

29. *The WPA Guide to California*, 65; see also 69.

30. *The WPA Guide to 1930s Arizona*, compiled and written by the Federal Writers' Project of the Works Progress Administration (Tucson: University of Arizona Press, 1989; first published as *Arizona: A State Guide*, New York: Hastings House, 1940), 5–6, 7–8.

31. Ibid., 73.

32. Ibid., 154, 193–94, 217–19, 241, 243, 469. Interestingly, by the late 1930s Barry Goldwater had joined the chorus of criticism against what was deemed the collectivist threat of the New Deal, which he contrasted with the invariably positive legacy of pioneer fortitude and self-sufficiency. By the end of the 1940s he had won a seat on the Phoenix city council, beginning a political career that would tap into the frontier heritage for its energy and that would help forge a foundation of modern American conservatism that Ronald Reagan and George W. Bush would later draw on heavily. For more on this topic, see Robert A. Goldberg, "The Western Hero in Politics: Barry Goldwater, Ronald Reagan, and the Rise of the American Conservative Movement," in *The Political Culture of the New West*, ed. Jeff Roche (Lawrence: University Press of Kansas, 2008), 13–50.

33. *The WPA Guide to 1930s New Mexico*, compiled and written by the Federal Writers' Project of the Works Progress Administration, with a foreword by Marc Simmons (Tucson: University of Arizona Press, 1989; first published as *New Mexico: A Guide to the Colorful State*, New York: Hastings House, 1940); Calendar of Annual Events on xvii–xxxvii, quotation on 4–5, coverage of festivals and events on 102–6. The guide's treatment of the arts, particularly literature and architecture, also illuminated the cultural diversity of the state; 138–39, 154–55.

34. *The WPA Guide to Texas*, compiled and written by the Federal Writers' Project of the Works Progress Administration, with an introduction by Don Graham (Austin: Texas Monthly Press, 1986; first published as *Texas: A Guide to the Lone Star State*, New York: Hastings House, 1940), 5.

35. Ibid., 95, 97, 549, 644, 113, 115, 378, 397–98, 540–41, 657.

36. Figures for emigration from the plains states are provided in Walter Nugent, *Into the West: The Story of Its People* (New York: Alfred A. Knopf., 1999), 243–44.

37. It is worth noting that North Dakota is currently experiencing strong population growth as a result of the shale oil boom; yet because single men account for the bulk of this increase, one suspects that the demographic growth may well be temporary.

38. There is no shortage of debate over whether the second tier of states west of the Mississippi ought to be considered part of the West. For an argument in favor of their inclusion, see David M. Wrobel and Michael C. Steiner, eds., *Many Wests: Place, Culture, and Regional Identity* (Lawrence: University Press of Kansas,

1997); for one that excludes those states from the West, see William E. Riebsame, ed., *Atlas of the New West: Portrait of a Changing Region* (New York: W. W. Norton, 1997); and for further discussion of the matter, see Walter Nugent, "Where Is the American West? Report on a Survey," *Montana: The Magazine of Western History* 42 (Summer 1992): 2–23; reprinted in Walter Nugent and Martin Ridge, eds., *The American West: The Reader* (Bloomington: Indiana University Press, 1999), 11–24.

39. *The WPA Guide to 1930s Oklahoma*, compiled and written by the Federal Writers' Project of the Works Progress Administration, with a restored essay by Angie Debo and a new introduction by Anne Hodges Morgan (Lawrence: University Press of Kansas, 1986; first published as *Oklahoma: A Guide to the Sooner State*, Norman: University of Oklahoma Press, 1941). For reasons that have never been fully explained, Debo's introductory essay on the history of the state was left out of the original publication, but is restored to its rightful place in the reprint.

    The Oklahoma guide, which appeared in the last weeks of 1941, was the very last of the WPA state guides to appear; the Washington state guide appeared a few weeks earlier. See Mangione, *The Dream and the Deal*, 340–41.

40. Edward Everett Dale, "The Spirit of Soonerland," *Chronicles of Oklahoma* 1 (June 1923): 167–78, quotation on 168.

41. Edward Everett Dale, "The Spirit of Oklahoma," in *The WPA Guide to 1930s Oklahoma*, 3–6, quotation on 3.

42. W. B. Bizzell also makes this point concerning temporal proximity to the state's white pioneer heritage in his foreword to *The WPA Guide to 1930s Oklahoma*, vii–viii.

43. See, for example, the coverage of the annual Pioneer Day celebration in Guymon (population 2,290) celebrating the Organic Act of May 2, 1890 (which created the boundaries of the Oklahoma Territory), *The WPA Guide to 1930s Oklahoma*, 250; coverage of Pawhuska, 290; U.S. Route 70, 314–22; U.S. Route 69, 330–44; Okay, OK, 336–37; U.S. Route 81, 368–74; and U.S. Route 283, 383–87, quotation on 383.

44. Ibid., 6, 49.

45. *Kansas: A Guide to the Sunflower State*, compiled and written by the Federal Writers' Project of the Works Progress Administration (New York: Viking, 1939; reprinted as *The WPA Guide to 1930s Kansas*, with a new introduction by James R. Shortridge, Lawrence: University Press of Kansas, 1984), essay on "Indians," 25–38; quotation on 36; page references from the 1939 edition.

46. Ibid., 16–17, photographs on 17, 19. The section entitled "Folklore," 100–104, provides coverage of the state's cowboy heritage and old settler gatherings, as do the tours along U.S. Route 24–40, and U.S. Route 40, from Kansas City to Denver, 337–69, esp. the description of the town of Wallace (population 100), 366–67; the tour along U.S. Route 160 from Springfield, Missouri, to Trinidad, Colorado, particularly the description of Ashland (population 1,232); and the tour along

U.S. Route 81 from Columbus, Nebraska, to Enid, Oklahoma, 453–64, most notably the descriptions of Wichita, 458–61, and Wellington, 461–62.

47. Craig Miner notes in his excellent study *Kansas: The History of the Sunflower
State, 1854–2000* (Lawrence: University Press of Kansas, 2002) that one of the
WPA writers in the state, Charles Edson, was critical of the Kansas volume for
bowing to the censorship of "chamber of commerce types" with the end result
being a guide that was "illiterate, inaccurate, and uninteresting" (10). However,
this criticism simply does not seem warranted given the guide's often brutally
honest portrayal of depressed economic conditions and the impact of drought
on the Kansas landscape. See also 299–300.

48. William Allen White, "Contemporary Scene," in *The WPA Guide to 1930s Kansas*,
1–3, quotations on 2.

49. *The WPA Guide to 1930s Kansas*, 126–28, quotation on 127–28. White's famous
essay, "What's the Matter with Kansas?," appeared in the *Emporia Gazette*,
August 15, 1896.

50. *Nebraska: A Guide to the Cornhusker State*, compiled and written by the Federal
Writers' Project of the Works Progress Administration, with an introduction by
Alan Boye (Lincoln: University of Nebraska Press, 2005; first Nebraska printing,
1979; first published, New York: Hastings House, 1939), page references from the
2005 edition. The FWP state guides, with their lengthy tour sections, were designed
with automotive travelers in mind, as well as vicarious travelers, of course.

51. Ibid., 3, 10, 66, 78, quotation on 3–4.

52. Ibid., 3–4, 107–8, 133.

53. Alan Boye's introduction to *Nebraska: A Guide to the Cornhusker State* illumi-
nates Sandoz's informal contributions to the guide; see v–ix, esp. vii. The guide
does include a decent chapter on the state's Indian heritage (26–42) but very little
coverage of Indian cultures in the present. Sandoz, at the time the Nebraska
guide was being compiled, was best known for her recent prize-winning work
Old Jules (Boston: Little, Brown, 1935), but would go on to write numerous important and sympathetic popular histories of Plains Indians, including *Crazy
Horse: The Strange Man of the Oglalas* (Lincoln: University of Nebraska Press,
1942); *Cheyenne Autumn* (New York: McGraw Hill, 1953); *The Buffalo Hunters*
(New York: Hastings House, 1954); and *These Were the Sioux* (New York: Hastings
House, 1961).

54. *The WPA Guide to South Dakota*, compiled and written by the Federal Writers'
Project of the Works Progress Administration, with an introduction by John E.
Miller (Minneapolis: Minnesota Historical Society Press, 2006; first published
as *A South Dakota Guide*, Pierre, SD: State Publishing Company, 1938), n.p. (preface by Lisle Reese), 1–3, 8; page references from the 2006 edition.

55. Ibid.; Deadwood, 103–5; Dupree, 237–38; Faith, 240; Buffalo Gap, 317; Gregory,
334; Winner, 335–36; and Martin, 340. It is notable that the frontispiece for the

South Dakota guide was a photograph of an elderly Indian in headdress, labeled simply, "Sioux Chieftain."

56. Ibid., 340–41.

57. *North Dakota: A Guide to the Northern Prairie State*, compiled and written by the Federal Writers' Project of the Works Progress Administration (Fargo, ND: Knight Printing Company, 1938; reprinted as *The WPA Guide to 1930s North Dakota*, Bismarck: State Historical Society of North Dakota, 1990), 3–4; page references from the 1938 edition. Frederick Jackson Turner, "The Significance of the Frontier in American History" (1893), in *Rereading Frederick Jackson Turner: "The Significance of the Frontier in American History" and Other Essays*, ed. John Mack Faragher (New Haven, CT: Yale University Press, 1998; first published, New York: Henry Holt, 1994), 31–60, quotation on 47.

58. *North Dakota: A Guide to the Northern Prairie State*, 3.

59. Ibid., 106, 123, 165, 173–81, 297–300, 327–28, 332.

60. The coverage of Indian cultures in the North Dakota guide, which occupies a chapter, "Indians and Their Predecessors" (16–34), and portions of the "History" chapter (35–58), particularly the section titled "On the Frontier" (39–46), merits an average ranking among the western state guides; it is less effective than the coverage in the Oklahoma or New Mexico guides, to name two of the better ones in this regard, but stronger than the respective sections in, for example, the Arizona, Texas, and South Dakota guides.

61. For more on this migration, see Rolland Dewing, *Regions in Transition: The Northern Great Plains and the Pacific Northwest in the Great Depression* (Lanham, MD: University Press of America, 2006), 2.

62. *Montana: A State Guide Book*, compiled and written by the Federal Writers' Project of the Works Progress Administration (New York: Viking, 1939; reprinted as *The WPA Guide to 1930s Montana*, Tucson: University of Arizona Press, 1994), 54–55, page references from the 1939 edition. Harold G. Merriam, University of Montana professor and editor of the regional journal *Frontier and Midland*, served as director of the Montana FWP.

63. Ibid., 38–39. The chapter on labor (68–78) makes up approximately twice as much of the text as the chapter on Indian peoples (31–37).

64. Ibid., 78.

65. Ibid., 36, 298, and 261, respectively.

66. Ibid., Tour 1, Section a, North Dakota Line to Billings, U.S. Route 10, 185–94, quotations on 185, 188 (Terry); and Tour 10, Section c, Miles City to Wyoming Line, 322–24, quotation on 322.

67. *Wyoming: A Guide to Its History, Highways, and People*, compiled and written by the Federal Writers' Project of the Works Progress Administration (New York: Oxford University Press, 1941), 3, 4, 5–6, 9.

68. Ibid., 9.

69. Ibid., 147–54, 335–37.

70. Mangione, *The Dream and the Deal*, 117.

71. *Wyoming: A Guide to Its History, Highways, and People*, 52–57, n.p. (photo essay).

72. Yellowstone National Park coverage encompasses pages 399–437 of the Wyoming guide and receives twenty-five additional references throughout the volume.

73. *Colorado: A Guide to the Highest State*, compiled and written by the Federal Writers' Project of the Works Progress Administration (New York: Hastings House, 1941; reprinted as *The WPA Guide to 1930s Colorado*, Lawrence: University Press of Kansas, 1987), 352, 420; page references from the 1941 edition.

74. Ralph L. Carr, governor of Colorado, in his foreword to the volume (n.p.), described the state as the "old West" and claimed that "there are to be found so many things to recall the covered wagon days," but his words do not seem to have been informed by an actual reading of the text of the guide.

75. With more than a hundred images, *Colorado* was one of the most generously illustrated of all the western guides.

76. *Colorado*, Sand Creek Massacre, 44, 293–94; vanishing Indians, 53; Consolidated Ute Agency, 358–61.

77. Ibid., 65–67, 198–99, images following 462. Mangione comments on this controversy in *The Dream and the Deal*, 338.

78. *Utah: A Guide to the State*, compiled and written by the Federal Writers' Project of the Works Progress Administration (New York: Hastings House, 1941), 3, 4, 6; Mountain Meadows massacre, 43, 303–4; Burton, 156.

79. Ibid., 3–4, 8–9; discussion of the annual Pioneer Days celebration in Ogden (population 43,719), 201.

80. Ibid., 38–44, quotation on 43, image on 44. The volume does include a photo essay on Indians (n.p., following 499), but the cumulative effect of the images is to confine the state's indigenous peoples to the past. The volume's coverage of "The Mormon Pioneers," 52–70, is three times the length of its Indian section.

81. *The WPA Guide to 1930s Nevada*, compiled and written by the Federal Writers' Project of the Works Progress Administration, with a foreword by Russell R. Elliott (Reno: University of Nevada Press, 1991; first published as *Nevada: A Guide to the Silver State*, Portland, OR: Binfords and Mort, 1940), 183; page references from the 1940 edition.

82. Lévy's coverage of Las Vegas in his *American Vertigo: Traveling America in the Footsteps of Tocqueville* (New York: Random House, 2006) is discussed in the introduction. Jean Baudrillard, *Amérique* (Paris: Bernard Grasset, 1986; published in English as *America*, trans. Chris Turner, London: Verso, 1988), 127–28; quotation and page references from the English-language edition.

83. Timothy Egan, "Chaos or Cancer: Las Vegas, Nevada," in his *Lasso the Wind: Away to the New West* (New York: Vintage, 1999; first published, New York: Alfred A. Knopf, 1998), 103, 105; page references from the 1999 edition. Egan quotes Mulroy directly; the Abbey quotation is from "The Second Rape of the

West" in Edward Abbey, *The Journey Home: Some Words in Defense of the American West* (New York: Plume, 1991). Egan's essay on Las Vegas, for all its rhetorical flourishes, does seem to exemplify the notion of the travel writer who need never have left home to render his preordained judgment on a place, as opposed to the traveler open to the possibility of learning or discovering something interesting or even unexpected. Egan did visit Las Vegas, yet one wonders whether the trip was necessary to his rendering of judgment about the place. Egan's *The Good Rain: Across Time and Terrain in the Pacific Northwest* (New York: Alfred A. Knopf, 1990), on the other hand, is more reflective of the best works of the travel narrative genre, marked by its author's deep familiarity with and connection to the places visited.

84. *The WPA Guide to 1930s Nevada*, branding quotation, 66; Twain, 81, 118, 151, 205; "Mining and Mining Jargon," 55–58; Las Vegas, 183–84; Reno, 150. The Nevada guide's coverage of the state's Indian residents is undistinguished and not terribly extensive. The phrase is used by James Shortridge in the title of his essay "The Expectations of Others: Struggles Toward a Sense of Place in the Northern Plains," in *Many Wests: Place, Culture, and Regional Identity*, ed. David M. Wrobel and Michael C. Steiner (Lawrence: University Press of Kansas, 1997), 114–35.

85. *Idaho: A Guide in Word and Picture*, compiled and written by the Federal Writers' Project of the Works Progress Administration (Caldwell, ID: Caxton Printers, 1937; rev. ed., New York: Oxford University Press, 1950). For more on Fisher and the Idaho guide, see Christine Bold's chapter "Idaho: Vardis Fisher, Local Hero," in her *The WPA Guides: Mapping America* (Jackson: University Press of Mississippi, 1999), 37–63; Tim Woodward, *Tiger on the Road: The Story of Vardis Fisher* (Caldwell, ID: Caxton Printers, 1989), 135–42; David A. Taylor's chapter "Rising Up in the West: Idaho," in his *Soul of a People: The WPA Writers' Project Uncovers Depression America* (New York: John Wiley and Sons, 2009), 97–109; and Mangione, *The Dream and the Deal*, esp. 201–8. Mangione notes that Fisher wrote "single-handedly, 374 pages of the 405-page Idaho guidebook within ten months" (203) and discusses the controversy over the order of appearance of the guides (201), as does Nick Taylor in *American Made: The Enduring Legacy of the WPA; When FDR Put the Nation to Work* (New York: Bantam Books, 2008), 311–14. Useful examinations of aspects of Fisher's involvement with the FWP are also provided in Joseph M. Flora, ed., *Rediscovering Vardis Fisher: Centennial Essays* (Moscow: University of Idaho Press, 2000); and John R Milton, *Three Wests: Conversations with Vardis Fisher, Max Evans, and Michael Straight* (Vermillion, SD: Dakota Press, 1970).

86. *Idaho: A Guide in Word and Picture*, 27.

87. Ibid., 27, 28, 29, 30; "History of Idaho Indians," 41–52; "Anthropology of Idaho Indians," 55–70.

88. Ibid., 31–32, 34–35, 36; "Emerging from the Frontier," 183–92; quotation about social development, n.p., before 183.

89. *Oregon: End of the Trail*, compiled and written by the Federal Writers' Project of the Works Progress Administration (Portland, OR: Binfords and Mort, 1940), preface, ix; National Forests, 511–18, quotation on 512.

90. Ibid., "Calendar of Events," xxvii–xxxii, 6, 8. The quoted passage concerning the pioneer legacy among "latter-day pioneers" also appears in Dewing, *Regions in Transition*, 107.

91. *Oregon: End of the Trail*, 46, 47.

92. For images of Indians, see ibid., unnumbered photo essays following 94 and 412.

93. Ibid., "Huckleberry Cakes and Venison," 86–90.

94. *Washington: A Guide to the Evergreen State*, compiled and written by the Federal Writers' Project of the Works Progress Administration (Portland, OR: Binfords and Mort, 1941).

95. For more on the controversy, see Mangione, *The Dream and the Deal*, 340–41.

96. *Washington: A Guide to the Evergreen State*, 3–4.

97. Ibid., 23, 27–28; "Lumbering" photo essay, following 372. The volume did include extensive and empathetic coverage of organized labor in the state (86–94).

98. Ibid., "Indians," 29–36, quotations on 29, 36; Indian wars and gold rush, 44–46.

99. Ibid., Colfax, 425; Ellensburg, 464; remnants of the state's pioneer past, 354–55, 449, 464, 535.

100. "Alaska Highway," *Wikipedia*, accessed January 11, 2012, http://en.wikipedia.org/wiki/Alaska_Highway.

101. *A Guide to Alaska: Last American Frontier*, compiled and written by the Federal Writers' Project of the Works Progress Administration and Merle Colby (New York: Macmillan, 1939), foreword by John W. Troy, n.p.

102. Ibid., "The Six Alaskas," xlvii–liv; quotations on 3, 8. The prefatory section, "Popular Errors About Alaska," xliii–xlv, is also fascinating.

103. Ibid., 15–16; Nome gold rush and attendant native population decline, 38–29.

104. Ibid., 44–48; native labor, 52.

105. For more on the press coverage of the colony, see Orlando Miller, *The Frontier in Alaska and the Matanuska Colony* (New Haven, CT: Yale University Press, 1975), esp. 145–60, 161–79.

106. *A Guide to Alaska: Last American Frontier*, Matanuska photo essay following 304; the photo essay includes twenty-four photographs.

107. Alfred Kazin, *On Native Grounds: An Interpretation of Modern American Prose Literature* (New York: Reynal and Hitchcock, 1942), 500–501. These passages are also quoted in Mangione, *The Dream and the Deal*, 365.

108. Notable among the midwestern guides that emphasized the frontier/pioneer heritage are *Minnesota: A State Guide*, compiled and written by the Federal Writers' Project of the Works Progress Administration (New York: Viking, 1938); and *Iowa: A Guide to the Hawkeye State*, compiled and written by the Federal Writers'

Project of the Works Progress Administration (New York: Viking, 1938). However, and not surprisingly given the more distant chronology of their settlement, all of the guides to states situated in the second tier west of the Mississippi to the Pacific coast placed greater emphasis on the theme of the western frontier heritage than any of the states to the east of that tier.

109. Malcolm Cowley, *Exile's Return: A Literary Odyssey of the 1920s* (New York: Viking, 1934; reprinted, 1956, 1986), 291; page references from the 1956 edition.

110. Frederick Jackson Turner, "Sections and Nation," *Yale Review* 12 (October 1922): 21; reprinted in *Rereading Frederick Jackson Turner*, 181–200.

111. See Daniel H. Borus, ed., *These United States: Portraits of America from the 1920s* (Ithaca, NY: Cornell University Press, 1992), 28.

112. Hirsch, *in Portrait of America*, the most insightful of the available works on the FWP, writes that the tour sections of the American Guide Series books "offered a way of rediscovering and celebrating a diverse landscape, a way of creating a consciousness of the United States that could help Americans feel at home in a diverse land" (39). Hirsch's work serves as an effective counter to Bold's *The WPA Guides*, which views the guides' celebrations of American cultural diversity in more sinister fashion by suggesting a process by which the New Deal government and FWP groups at the state level sought to control the politics of cultural representation.

113. Some travel books in these decades did position the United States within a larger global context, or at least included it in global itineraries, but these works were a less prominent part of the genre than in the nineteenth century. Particularly memorable examples include British writer Aldous Huxley's *Jesting Pilate: Travels Through India, Burma, Malaya, Japan, China, and America* (New York: George H. Doran, 1926); British writer Edward Verrall Lucas's *Roving East and Roving West* (New York: George H. Doran, 1921); and American writer and adventurer Richard Halliburton's *The Royal Road to Romance* (Indianapolis: Bobbs-Merrill, 1925).

114. There were, of course, exceptions to the tendency of travel writers in this period to turn inward and view the West outside of global contexts; a good case in point is Simone de Beauvoir's engaging account of her travels across the country in 1947 by train and Greyhound bus, *America Day by Day*, trans. Carol Cosman (Berkeley: University of California Press, 1999; first published as *L'Amérique au jour le jour*, Paris: Gallimard, 1948; first published in English translation, New York: Grove Press, 1953), with its globally comparative descriptions of western landscapes; see 151, 153.

Conclusion

1. Leacock quoted in Michael Kowalewski, "Introduction: The Modern Literature of Travel," in *Temperamental Journeys: Essays on the Modern Literature of Travel,*

ed. Michael Kowalewski (Athens: University of Georgia Press, 1992), 1–16, 3. Jacinta Matos's essay "Old Journeys Revisited: Aspects of Postwar English Travel Writing," in Kowalewski, *Temperamental Journeys*, 215–29, also begins with Evelyn Waugh's announcement of the death of travel writing.

2. Christopher Isherwood and W. H. Auden, *Journey to a War* (London: Faber and Faber, 1939).

3. Barbara Brothers and Julia M. Gergits, introduction to *DLB*, vol. 204, *British Travel Writers, 1940–1997*, ed. Barbara Brothers and Julia M. Gergits (Detroit: Gale Research, 1999), xv–xxi, xv.

4. Waugh quoted in Brothers and Gergits, introduction to *DLB*, vol. 204, and in Paul Fussell, *Abroad: British Literary Traveling Between the Wars* (New York: Oxford University Press, 1980), 215; see also Barbara Korte, *English Travel Writing: From Pilgrimages to Postcolonial Explorations*, trans. Catherine Matthias (London: Macmillan; New York: St. Martin's Press, 2000), 128. Korte provides a good discussion of "The End of Travel?," 128–33.

5. In 1955, just a few years before reliable jet service began (in 1957), British novelist and caustic cultural critic Kingsley Amis titled an essay in the *Spectator*, "Is the Travel Book Dead?" (June 17, 1955), cited in Kowalewski, *Temperamental Journeys*, 2. Recipient of the Somerset Maugham Award for his first novel, *Lucky Jim*, Amis utilized the prize money to reside in a foreign country. The aesthetic product of Amis's already caustic temperament, *I Like It Here* (1958) was both a novel and an antitravel narrative. If the travel book was dead, Amis was hardly in mourning, but his voice certainly added to a general critical acknowledgment of the end of the genre. In light of the connection drawn in this study between the end of the frontier in America and the end of the travel book, Amis's article on the death of the travel book is reminiscent of Frank Norris's 1902 essay "The Frontier, Gone at Last," *World's Work* 3 (February 1902): 1728–31.

6. Because Isherwood went on to publish a second major travel book, *The Condor and the Cows*, and made no pronouncements concerning the end of travel or the travel book, I have not included him on the list with Amis, Fussell, Waugh, and Leacock. As Korte sensibly notes, "The very fact that most 'obituaries' of travel/writing are found in travelogues themselves proves the 'death' of the genre a misnomer"; see *English Travel Writing*, 133.

7. Christopher Isherwood, *The Condor and the Cows: A South American Travel Diary* (New York: Random House, 1948; London: Methuen, 1949; reprinted, Minneapolis: University of Minnesota Press, 2003).

8. William Leach registers his disaffection with the death of regional distinctiveness, as he sees it, in post-1970 America in *Country of Exiles: The Destruction of Place in American Life* (New York: Pantheon Books, 1999; reprinted, Vintage, 2000). Wolfgang Schivelbusch's superb insights in *The Railway Journey: The Industrialization of Time and Space in the Nineteenth Century* (Berkeley: University of California Press, 1986) concerning the way in which technological

change precipitates changes in human consciousness are worth considering here. However, I would suggest that both Leach and Schivelbusch (the former in a less sophisticated manner) underestimate the significance of regionalism as a response to change.

9. For more on regions as cultural creations, see Edward Ayers, Patricia Nelson Limerick, Stephen Nissebaum, and Peter Onuff, *All Over the Map: Rethinking American Regions* (Baltimore: Johns Hopkins University Press, 1996).

10. See, for example, Leach, *Country of Exiles*.

11. For a fuller discussion of the "death of region," see Michael Steiner and David Wrobel, "Many Wests: Discovering a Dynamic Western Regionalism," in *Many Wests: Place, Culture, and Regional Identity*, ed. David Wrobel and Michael Steiner (Lawrence: University Press of Kansas, 1997), 1–30.

12. Frederick Jackson Turner, "The Significance of the Frontier in American History," in *The Frontier in American History* (New York: Henry Holt, 1921; first published, 1920), 1–38; reprinted in Frederick Jackson Turner, *Rereading Frederick Jackson Turner*, ed. John Mack Faragher (New York: Henry Holt, 1994; reprinted, New Haven, CT: Yale University Press, 1998), 31–60, quotation on 33; page references from the 1998 edition.

13. For a further discussion of this theme, see David Wrobel, *The End of American Exceptionalism: Frontier Anxiety from the Old West to the New Deal* (Lawrence: University Press of Kansas, 1993).

14. Turner, "The Significance of the Frontier in American History," 60.

15. Pico Iyer, "The Magic of Flight," *VIA Magazine* (November–December 2003): 55–60, 56.

16. See Michael Steiner, "Frontierland as Tomorrowland: Walt Disney and the Architectural Packaging of the American West," *Montana: The Magazine of Western History* 48 (Spring 1998): 2–17.

17. Lynne Withey, *Grand Tours and Cook's Tours: A History of Leisure Travel, 1750–1915* (New York: William Morrow, 1997), 176–77.

18. For more on this theme, see David Wrobel, *Promised Lands: Promotion, Memory, and the Creation of the American West* (Lawrence: University Press of Kansas, 2002), esp. chapter 3, "Remembered Journeys," 95–119.

19. Donald Ross and James J. Schramer, introduction to *DLB*, vol. 189, *American Travel Writers, 1850–1915*, ed. Donald Ross and James J. Schramer (Detroit: Gale Research, 1998), xv–xx, xvii. Ross and Schramer are summarizing James Buzard's discussion of the *Blackwood's Magazine* article in his book *The Beaten Track: European Tourism, Literature, and the Ways to Culture, 1800–1918* (New York: Oxford University Press, 2001; first published, 1993).

20. Charles Dickens, *Pictures from Italy* (1846), and John Ruskin, *Modern Painters* (1856), are quoted in Korte, *English Travel Writing*, 84. Korte provides a useful discussion of the tourist-traveler dichotomy, 96–99.

21. Francis Kilvert, quoted in Fussell, *Abroad: British Literary Traveling*, 40.

22. John Muir to Emily Pelton, April 2, 1872, in William F. Bade, *The Life and Letters of John Muir*, vol. 1 (Boston: Houghton Mifflin, 1924), 325; quoted in Earl Pomeroy, *The Pacific Slope: A History of California, Oregon, Washington, Idaho, and Nevada* (Reno: University of Nevada Press, 2003), 345.

23. Dane Kennedy, *The Highly Civilized Man: Richard Burton and the Victorian World* (Cambridge: Harvard University Press, 2005), 130.

24. William Francis Butler, *Far Out: Rovings Retold* (London: William Isbister, 1880), 149. See also Butler's *The Great Lone Land: A Narrative of Travel and Adventure in the North-West of America* (London: Sampson Low, Marston, Low, and Searle, 1872).

25. Indeed, the antitourist trope was well established by this time even in the travel accounts of those whose literary talents did not command the attentions of commercial publishing houses; see, for example, Augustus F. Tripp, "Notes of an Excursion to California in the Winter and Spring of 1893" (bound, typed ms., Henry E. Huntington Library, San Marino, CA, HM 60314). Tripp wrote, in reference to tourists' fascination with "*the* live oak" in Monterey: "Tourists do not like to miss *the* anything and there are always a good many of them to be seen" (62).

26. Rudyard Kipling, *From Sea to Sea: Letters of Travel*, vol. 2 of *The Works of Rudyard Kipling* (New York: Doubleday and McClure, 1899), 67, 68, 70, 94, 3.

27. There is a now voluminous body of scholarship on tourism and tourists in America and the West, much of it quite critical of both the phenomenon and its practitioners. An important landmark in the historiography is the late Hal Rothman's *Devil's Bargains: Tourism in the Twentieth-Century American West* (Lawrence: University Press of Kansas, 1998). Included among the scholars who play up the tourist-traveler dichotomy, much to the detriment of the former and the benefit of the latter, are the late Daniel Boorstin, "From Traveler to Tourist: The Lost Art of Travel," in his *The Image: A Guide to Pseudo Events in America*, Twenty-Fifth Anniversary Edition (New York: Atheneum, 1987), 77–117; and Ulf Hannerz, who draws the distinction between cosmopolitans and tourists in his essay "Cosmopolitans and Locals in World Culture," in *Global Culture: Nationalism, Globalization and Modernity*, ed. Mike Featherstone (London: Sage Publications, 1990), 237–51. Works that treat tourism and tourists more favorably include David Wrobel, "Introduction: Tourists, Tourism, and the Toured Upon," in *Seeing and Being Seen: Tourism in the American West*, ed. David Wrobel and Patrick Long (Lawrence: University Press of Kansas, 2001), 1–34; and John A. Jakle, *The Tourist: Travel in Twentieth-Century North America* (Lincoln: University of Nebraska Press, 1985). Jakle writes in his introduction: "I emphasize tourism not merely as a superficial spending of leisure time, although tourism has its superficial dimensions, but, rather, as a form of social glue that binds modern society together. Tourism is a principal means by which modern people define for themselves a sense of identity" (22).

28. Pico Iyer, "How Paradise Is Lost—and Found," *Time*, June 9, 1986, 82; quoted in Kowalewski, *Temperamental Journeys*, 4.

29. The first transcontinental flight, in 1911, from the Atlantic to the Pacific, was made in approximately eighty-two hours at a speed of a little over fifty miles an hour. See Seymour Dunbar, *A History of Travel in America*, vol. 4 (Indianapolis: Bobbs-Merrill, 1915). The four volumes were later republished in a single volume (New York: Tudor, 1937), 1365; page references from the 1937 edition.

30. Ann Charters, introduction to Jack Kerouac, *On the Road* (New York: Penguin Books, 1991; first published, New York: Viking, 1957), vii–xxxiii, quotation on xvii; page references from the 1991 edition.

31. For an insightful discussion of Kerouac's search for the western frontier in the novel, see Ronald Primeau's chapter "Disharmony and Protest" in his *Romance of the Road: The Literature of the American Highway* (Bowling Green, OH: Bowling Green State University Popular Press, 1996), 33–50.

32. Ibid., 3, 5, 10, 12, 16, 17, 19, 82, 85.

33. J. B. Priestley and Jacquetta Hawkes, *Journey Down a Rainbow* (New York: Harper and Brothers, 1955), 95.

34. Ibid., 187, 190, 193.

35. James (Jan) Morris, *Coast to Coast* (London: Faber and Faber, 1956; published in the United States with the title *As I Saw the U.S.A.*, New York: Pantheon, 1956), 124, 95; chapter 17, "Dams, Bridges, and Bones," 126–33; page references from the Pantheon edition. Morris's trips to the United States in 1953–1954 were interrupted by his coverage of the British Mount Everest expedition; he was the first to report on Edmund Hillary and Tenzing Norgay's famous ascent of the summit, achieved on May 29, 1953. Jan Morris wrote under the name James Morris until the early 1970s, when she underwent gender reassignment surgery. Jan Morris is one of Britain's most renowned and prolific travel writers. Excerpts from her remarkable body of work are gathered in her anthology *The World: Life and Travel, 1950–2000* (New York: W. W. Norton, 2003). For an excellent overview of her life and writings, see William Over, "Jan Morris (James Humphrey Morris)," in *DLB*, vol. 204, *British Travel Writers, 1940–1997*, ed. Barbara Brothers and Julia M. Gergits (Detroit: Gale Research, 1999), 178–94.

36. John Steinbeck, *Travels with Charley in Search of America* (New York: Penguin Books, 1962; reprinted, New York: Bantam Books, 1963), 158, 180–81; page references from the 1963 edition.

37. Ibid., 204–5, 226.

38. Robert D. Kaplan, *An Empire Wilderness: Travels into America's Future* (New York: Random House, 1998); it is worth noting that Kaplan's travelogue, informed as it is by his global travels, is less America-centric than the majority of contemporary travel books about the West. Leach, *Country of Exiles*; Richard Grant, *American Nomads: Travels with Lost Conquistadors, Mountain Men, Cowboys, Indians, Hoboes, Truckers, and Bullriders* (New York: Grove Press,

2003). Dayton Duncan, *Out West: An American Journey* (New York: Viking, 1987), retraces Lewis and Clark's 1804–1806 "Voyage of Discovery." Ian Frazier's best seller, *Great Plains* (New York: Farrar, Straus and Giroux, 1989) draws on his twenty-five thousand miles of driving back and forth across the region, observing both its contemporary distinctiveness and rich historical legacy. Frazier's *On the Rez* (New York: Farrar, Straus and Giroux, 2000) recounts his time on and around the Pine Ridge Reservation in South Dakota, home of the Oglala Sioux. Jonathan Raban's *Bad Land: An American Romance* (New York: Vintage, 1996) examines the failed early-twentieth-century homesteading efforts in eastern and central Montana against a backdrop of the region's contemporary realities; his *Old Glory: An American Voyage* (New York: Simon and Schuster, 1981), recounts his boat travels on the Mississippi River, from Minneapolis to New Orleans, inspired by Mark Twain's *Adventures of Huckleberry Finn* (1884). Kathleen Norris, *Dakota: A Spiritual Geography* (New York: Mariner Books, 2001), is one of the most powerful paeans to any American place written in recent decades.

39. Larry McMurtry, *Roads: Driving America's Great Highways* (New York: Simon and Schuster, 2000), 15. For more on regionalism in American writing, see Robert Dorman, *Revolt of the Provinces: The Regionalist Movement in America, 1920–1945* (Chapel Hill: University of North Carolina Press, 1993) and *Hell of a Vision: Regionalism and the Modern American West* (Tucson: University of Arizona Press, 2012); Richard Etulain, *Re-Imagining the Modern American West: A Century of Fiction, History, and Art* (Tucson: University of Arizona Press, 1996); and Michael C. Steiner, ed., *Regionalists on the Left: Radical Voices from the American West* (Norman: University of Oklahoma Press, 2013).

40. *The Grapes of Wrath* (1940; dir. John Ford); *Easy Rider* (1969; dir. Dennis Hopper); *Rain Man* (1988; dir. Barry Levinson); *Powwow Highway* (1989; dir. Jonathan Wacks); *Thelma and Louise* (1991; dir. Ridley Scott); *Smoke Signals* (1998; dir. Chris Eyre); *Borat* (2006; dir. Larry Charles); *Little Miss Sunshine* (2006; dir. Valerie Faris and Jonathan Dayton); and *Cars* (2006; dir. John Lasseter and Joe Ranft).

41. Bobby Troup, "(Get Your Kicks) on Route 66" (first recorded in 1946, covered by Chuck Berry in 1961 and the Rolling Stones in 1964); Hank Snow, "I've Been Everywhere" (1962; later recorded by Johnny Cash, 1996); Bob Dylan, "Highway 61 Revisited" (1965, *Highway 61 Revisited*); Simon and Garfunkel, "America" (1968, *Bookends*); Janis Joplin, "Me and Bobby McGee" (1971, *The Pearl*; written by Kris Kristofferson and Fred Foster); the Grateful Dead, "Truckin'" (1970, *American Beauty*); Lowell George (of Little Feat), "Willin'" (1971, *Little Feat*; 1972, *Sailin' Shoes*); the Eagles, "Take It Easy" (1972, *Eagles*; written by Jackson Browne and Glenn Frey and later recorded by Jackson Browne, *For Everyman*, 1973); the Eagles, "Life in the Fast Lane" (1977, *Hotel California*); Jackson Browne, "Running on Empty" (1977, *Running on Empty*); Bruce Springsteen, "Born to Run" and "Thunder Road" (both 1975, *Born to Run*), and "The Promised Land" (1978,

Darkness on the Edge of Town); Willie Nelson, "On the Road Again" (1980, *Honeysuckle Rose* movie soundtrack); Dire Straits, "Telegraph Road" (1982, *Love Over Gold*; written by Mark Knopfler); Bob Dylan and Sam Shepard, "Brownsville Girl" (1986, Bob Dylan, *Knocked Out Loaded*); U2, *The Joshua Tree* (1987); Tom Petty, "Runnin' Down a Dream" (1989, *Full Moon Fever*); Tom Cochrane, "Life Is a Highway" (1991, *Mad Mad World*; covered by Rascal Flatts on the *Cars* soundtrack, 2006); Red Hot Chili Peppers, "Road Trippin'" (2000, *Californication*).

42. Douglas Brinkley, *The Magic Bus: An American Odyssey* (New York: Harcourt, Brace, 1993).

43. The United States' formal military involvement in Iraq came to an end on December 15, 2011.

44. John Gaddis, in the chapter "The Landscapes of History" in his *The Landscapes of History: How Historians Map the Past* (New York: Oxford University Press, 2002), rightly emphasizes the role historians play in constructing rich landscapes with the benefit of an enhanced angle of vision that develops as time passes, one that contemporary observers of a particular event could not have enjoyed. However, it is worth adding that historians do often exhibit a tendency to imagine the contours of the past and the intellectual horizons of past actors as somehow simpler than those of the present and its participants.

45. The best account of the demographic dimension of American expansion is Walter Nugent's *Into the West: The Story of Its People* (New York: Alfred A. Knopf, 1999).

46. See John Diggins, *The Rise and Fall of the American Left* (New York: W. W. Norton, 1992), 187–200. Among historians, there were of course exceptions to the trend of turning inward and creating nation-centric histories in the first half or so of the twentieth century: Herbert Eugene Bolton's *The Spanish Borderlands: A Chronicle of Old Florida and the Southwest* (New Haven, CT: Yale University Press, 1921; reprinted, Albuquerque: University of New Mexico Press, 1996); Earl Pomeroy's *The Territories and the United States, 1861–1890: Studies in Colonial Administration* (Philadelphia: University of Pennsylvania Press/American Historical Association, 1947); and Walter Prescott Webb's *The Great Frontier* (Boston: Houghton Mifflin, 1952; reprinted, Las Vegas: University of Nevada Press, 2003) are three notable examples.

SELECTED BIBLIOGRAPHY

Primary Sources

Manuscript Collections

Everett D. Graff Collection of Western Americana, Newberry Library, Chicago.

Raymond and Whitcomb First Person Travel Accounts, Henry E. Huntington Library, San Marino, CA, hereafter referred to as HEH.

Western Americana Collection, Beinecke Rare Book and Manuscript Library, Yale University.

Rare Book Collections

Carey Bliss Collection (transcontinental automotive travel narratives) (HEH).

American Travelers

Abbey, Edward. *The Journey Home: Some Words in Defense of the American West*. New York: Plume, 1991.

Austin, Mary. *The Land of Journey's Ending*. New York: Century Company, 1924.

Ballou, Maturin Murray (Lieutenant Murray). *Aztec Land: Central America, The West Indies, and South America*. Boston: Houghton Mifflin, 1890.

——. *The New Eldorado: A Summer Journey to Alaska*. Boston: Houghton Mifflin, 1889.

Birney, Hoffman. *Roads to Roam*. Philadelphia: Penn Publishing Company, 1930.

Bly, Nellie. *Around the World in Seventy-Two Days*. New York: Pictorial Weeklies Company, 1890.

Bowles, Samuel. *Across the Continent: A Summer's Journey to the Rocky Mountains, the Mormons, and the Pacific States, with Speaker Colfax*. Springfield, MA: S. Bowles, 1866.

——. *Our New West: Records of Travel Between the Mississippi River and the Pacific Ocean*. Hartford, CT: Hartford Publishing Company, 1869.

Brinkley, Douglas. *The Magic Bus: An American Odyssey*. New York: Harcourt, Brace, 1993.

Bryson, Bill. *Bill Bryson's African Diary*. New York: Broadway Books, 2002.

———. *I'm a Stranger Here Myself: Notes on Returning to America After Twenty Years Away*. New York: Broadway Books, 1999.

———. *In a Sunburned Country*. New York: Broadway Books, 2000.

———. *Neither Here Nor There: Travels in Europe*. New York: William Morrow, 1992.

———. *Notes from a Small Island*. New York: William Morrow, 1996.

———. *A Walk in the Woods: Rediscovering America on the Appalachian Trail*. New York: Broadway Books, 1998.

Carvalho, S. N. [Solomon Nunes]. *Incidents of Travel and Adventure in the Far West: With Col. Fremont's Last Expedition Across the Rocky Mountains; Including Three Months' Residence in Utah, and a Perilous Trip Across the Great American Desert to the Pacific*. New York: Derby and Jackson, 1857. Reprinted, Lincoln: University of Nebraska Press, Bison Books, 2004.

Catlin, George. *Catalogue of Catlin's Indian Gallery of Portraits, Landscapes, Manners and Customs, Costumes, & c. . . . Collected During Seven Years' Travel Amongst Thirty-Eight Different Tribes, Speaking Different Languages*. New York: Piercy and Reed, 1837.

———. *Catlin's North American Indian Portfolio: Hunting Scenes and Amusements of the Rocky Mountains and Prairies of America from Drawings and Notes of the Author, Made During Eight Years' Travel Amongst Forty-Eight of the Wildest and Most Remote Tribes of Savages in North America*. London: George Catlin, 1844. Reprinted, New York: James Ackerman, 1845.

———. *Catlin's Notes of Eight Years' Travels and Residence in Europe, with His North American Indian Collection: With Anecdotes and Incidents of the Travels and Adventures of Three Different Parties of American Indians Whom He Introduced to the Courts of England, France, and Belgium*. London: George Catlin, 1848. Reprinted as *Adventures of the Ojibbeway and Ioway Indians in England, France, and Belgium: Being Notes of Eight Years' Residence in Europe with the North American Indian Collection*, 2 vols., 3rd ed., London: George Catlin, 1852; and 2 vols., Scituate, MA: Digital Scanning, 2001.

Cook, Frederick Albert. *My Attainment of the Pole: Being the Record of the Expedition that First Reached the Boreal Center, 1907–1909; With the Final Summary of the Polar Controversy*. New York: Mitchell Kennerley, 1912. First published, New York: Polar Publishing, 1911. Reprinted, New York: Cooper Square Press, 2001.

———. *To the Top of the Continent: Discovery, Exploration and Adventure in Sub-Arctic Alaska; The First Ascent of Mt. McKinley, 1903–1906*. New York: Doubleday, Page, 1908.

Dana, Richard Henry. *Two Years Before the Mast: A Personal Narrative of Life at Sea*. New York: Harper and Brothers, 1840.

Davis, Richard Harding. *The Congo and the Coasts of Africa*. New York: Charles Scribner's Sons, 1907. Reprinted, London: Unwin, 1908.

———. *Three Gringos in Venezuela and Central America*. New York: Harper and Brothers, 1896. Reprinted, 1903.

——— *The West from a Car Window*. New York: Harper and Brothers, 1892.

Delaney, Philip. "Frontiering in an Automobile." *Outing: An Illustrated Magazine of Recreation* 43 (November 1903): 131–35.

Dixon, Winifred Hawkridge. *Westward Hoboes: Ups and Downs of Frontier Motoring*. New York: Charles Scribner's Sons, 1921.

Du Chaillu, Paul Belloni. *Explorations and Adventures in Equatorial Africa*. London: John Murray; New York: Harper and Brothers, 1861.

Dumbell, K. E. M. *Seeing the West*. Garden City, NY: Doubleday, 1920.

Duncan, Dayton. *Miles from Nowhere: Tales from American's Contemporary Frontier*. New York: Viking, 1993. Reprinted, Lincoln: University of Nebraska Press, 2000.

———. *Out West: An American Journey*. New York: Viking, 1987.

Duniway, Abigail Scott. *From the West to the West: Across the Plains to Oregon*. Chicago: A. C. McClurg, 1905.

Dunn, Edward. *Double-Crossing America by Motor: Routes and Ranches of the West*. New York: G. P. Putnam's Sons, 1933.

Dunn, Robert. *The Shameless Diary of an Explorer: A Story of Failure on Mount McKinley*. New York: Outing Publishing Company, 1907. Reprinted with an introduction by Robert Hoagland, New York: Modern Library, 2001.

Dyott, G. M. (George Miller). *Man Hunting in the Jungle: Being the Story of a Search for Three Explorers Lost in the Brazilian Wilds*. Indianapolis: Bobbs-Merrill, ca. 1930.

Eaton, Walter P. *Skyline Camps: A Note Book of a Wanderer in Our Northwestern Mountains*. Boston: W. A. Wilde, 1922.

Egan, Timothy. *The Good Rain: Across Time and Terrain in the Pacific Northwest*. New York: Alfred A. Knopf. 1990.

———. *Lasso the Wind: Away to the New West*. New York: Vintage, 1999. First published, New York: Alfred A. Knopf, 1998.

Enock, Charles Reginald. *Farthest West: Life and Travel in the United States*. New York: Appleton, 1910.

———. *The Great Pacific Coast, Twelve Thousand Miles in the Golden West: Being an Account of Life and Travel in the Western States of North and South America, from California, British Columbia, and Alaska to Mexico, Panama, Peru, and Chile; and a Study of Their Physical and Political Conditions*. New York: Charles Scribner's Sons, 1910.

Fairbanks, Harold Wellman. *The Western Wonder-Land: Half-Hours in the Western United States*. London: D. C. Heath, 1905.

Faris, John T. *Seeing the Far West*. Philadelphia: J. B. Lippincott, 1920.

Ferguson, Melville F. *Motor Camping on Western Trails*. New York: Century Company, 1925.

Ferris, Mrs. B. G. [Benjamin G.]. *The Mormons at Home: With Some Incidents of Travel from Mississippi to California, 1852–3, in a Series of Letters*. New York: Dix and Edwards; London: Sampson Low, Son, and Company, 1856.

Field, H. M. *Our Western Archipelago*. New York: Charles Scribner's Sons, 1895.

Finger, Charles J. *Adventure Under Sapphire Skies*. New York: William Morrow, 1931.

———. *Foot-loose in the West: Being the Account of a Journey to Colorado and California and Other Western States*. New York: William Morrow, 1932.

Fireman, Janet. "Between Horizons: Traveling the Great Central Valley." *Pacific Historical Review* 81 (February 2012): 1–20.

Fisher, Harriet White. *A Woman's World Tour in a Motor*. Philadelphia: J. B. Lippincott, 1911.

Fitzpatrick, James A. *Fireside Travels in North America*. Chicago: Rand McNally; Saint Paul: Brown and Bigelow, 1948.

Frazier, Ian. *Great Plains*. New York: Farrar, Straus and Giroux, 1989.

———. *On the Rez*. New York: Farrar, Straus and Giroux, 2000.

———. *Travels in Siberia*. New York: Farrar, Straus and Giroux, 2010.

Frothingham, Robert. *Trails Through the Golden West*. New York: R. M. McBride, 1932.

Gerould, Katharine Fullerton. *The Aristocratic West*. New York: Harper and Brothers, 1925.

Gilpin, William. *The Cosmopolitan Railway Compacting and Fusing Together All the World's Continents*. San Francisco: The History Company, 1890.

Gladding, Effie P. *Across the Continent by the Lincoln Highway*. New York: Brentano's, 1915.

Gordon, George Byron. *In the Alaskan Wilderness*. Philadelphia: John Winston, 1917.

Greeley, Horace. *An Overland Journey from New York to San Francisco in the Summer of 1859*. New York: C. M. Saxton, Barker; San Francisco: H. H. Bancroft, 1860.

Gregg, Josiah. *Commerce of the Prairies*. New York: J. and H. G. Langley, 1845. Reprinted as *Scenes and Incidents in the Western Prairies*, Philadelphia: J. W. Moore, 1856.

Halliburton, Richard. *The Royal Road to Romance*. Indianapolis: Bobbs-Merrill, 1925.

Harvey, Fred. *The Indian-Detour*. New York: Rand McNally, 1926.

Hearndon, William. *Exploration of the Valley of the Amazon, 1851–1852*. Edited by Gary Kinder. New York: Grove Press, 2000. First published, Washington: Robert Armstrong, Public Printer, 1853.

Heat-Moon, William Least. *Blue Highways: A Journey into America*. Boston: Little, Brown, 1982.

———. *River Horse: The Logbook of a Boat Across America*. New York: Houghton Mifflin Harcourt, 1999.

Hulme, Kathryn. *How's the Road?* San Francisco: privately printed, 1928.

Irving, Washington. *Adventures of Captain Bonneville; or, Scenes Beyond the Rocky Mountains of the Far West*. London: R. Bentley; Paris: Baudry's European Library, 1837.

———. *Astoria; or, Anecdotes of an Enterprise Beyond the Rocky Mountains.* 2 vols. Chicago: Donohue, Henneberry; Philadelphia: Carey, Lea and Blanchard, 1836.

———. *A Tour on the Prairies.* No. 1 of the Crayon Miscellanies. London: John Murray, 1835.

Jackson, Helen Hunt. *Glimpses of Three Coasts.* Boston: Roberts Brothers, 1886.

Johnson, Martin. *Through the South Seas with Jack London.* New York: Dodd, Mead and Company, 1913.

Kaplan, Robert D. *An Empire Wilderness: Travels into America's Future.* New York: Random House, 1998.

Kennan, George. *Siberia and the Exile System.* New York: Century Company, 1891.

———. *Siberia and the Exile System.* Abridged edition, with an introduction by George Frost Kennan. Chicago: University of Chicago Press, 1958.

———. *Tent Life in Siberia and Adventures Among the Koraks and Other Tribes in Kamchatka and Northern Asia.* New York: G. P. Putnam's Sons; London: Sampson Low, Son, and Marston, 1870. Republished by CreateSpace Independent Publishing Platform, 2011.

Kent, Rockwell. *Wilderness: A Journal of Quiet Adventure in Alaska.* New York: Modern Library, 1930.

King, Clarence. *Mountaineering in the Sierra Nevada.* Boston: J. R. Osgood, 1872.

Krarup, M. C. "From Coast to Coast in an Automobile." *World's Work* (May 1904): 4740–54.

Kuralt, Charles. *Charles Kuralt's America.* New York: G. P. Putnam's Sons, 1995.

———. *A Life on the Road.* New York: Ballantine Books, 1990.

Lambourne, Alfred. *The Pioneer Trail.* Salt Lake City: Deseret News, 1913.

Laut, Agnes C. *The Overland Trail: The Epic Path of the Pioneers to Oregon.* New York: Fredrick A. Stokes, 1929.

Leach, William. *Country of Exiles: The Destruction of Place in American Life.* New York: Pantheon Books, 1999. Reprinted, New York: Vintage, 2000.

Leland, Lilian. *Travelling Alone: A Woman's Journey Around the World.* New York: American News, 1890.

Lewis, Meriwether, and William Clark. *The Original Journals of the Lewis and Clark Expedition, 1804–1806.* 2 vols. Philadelphia: J. Maxwell for Bradford and Inskeep and Abraham H. Inskeep of New York, 1814. Reprinted in 8 vols., edited by Reuben Gold Thwaites, New York: Dodd, Mead and Company, 1904–1905.

London, Charmian Kittredge. *The Log of the* Snark. New York: Macmillan, 1915. Published in England as *Voyaging in Wild Seas; or, A Woman Among the Head Hunters (A Narrative of the Voyage of the* Snark *in the Years 1907–1909).* London: Mills and Boon, 1915.

———. *Our Hawaii (Islands and Islanders).* New York: Macmillan, 1917, 1922.

London, Jack. "The Class Struggle." *Independent* 5 (November 1903): 2603–10.

———. *The Cruise of the* Snark. Suffolk, England: Seafarer Books, 2000. First published, New York: Macmillan, 1911.

———. "Koolau the Leper." In *The House of Pride and Other Tales of Hawaii*. New York: Macmillan, 1912.

———. "The Lepers of Molokai." *Women's Home Companion* 35 (January 1908): 7–8, 45.

———. *The People of the Abyss*. With an introduction by Brigitte Koenig. London: Pluto Press, 2001. First published, New York: Macmillan, 1903.

———. *The Road*. New York: Macmillan, 1907. Reprinted, New Brunswick, NJ: Rutgers University Press, 2006.

———. *South Sea Tales*. New York: Modern Library, 2002.

———. *The War of the Classes*. London: W. M. Heinemann, 1905.

MacFadden, Harry A. *Rambles in the Far West*. Hollidaysburg, PA: Standard Printing House, 1906.

MacFadyen, Viola. *Crossing the Plains on a Prairie Schooner*. New York: David MacFadyen, 1912.

Magoffin, Susan S. *Down the Santa Fe Trail and into Mexico: The Diary of Susan Shelby Magoffin, 1846–1847*. Edited by Stella M. Drumm. New Haven, CT: Yale University Press, 1926. Reprinted with a foreword by Howard R. Lamar, New Haven, CT: Yale University Press, 1962. Reprinted, Lincoln: University of Nebraska Press, 1982.

Marcy, Randolph B. *The Prairie Traveler: A Hand-book for Overland Expeditions with Maps, Illustrations, and Itineraries of the Principal Routes Between the Mississippi and the Pacific*. New York: Harper and Brothers, 1859. Reprinted as *The Prairie Traveler: The 1859 Handbook for Westbound Pioneers*. Mineola, NY: Dover Books, 2006.

Massey, Beatrice Larned. *It Might Have Been Worse: A Motor Trip from Coast to Coast*. San Francisco: Harr Wagner, 1920.

McGill, Vernon. *Diary of a Motor Journey from Chicago to Los Angeles*. Los Angeles: Grafton, 1922.

McMurtry, Larry. *Roads: Driving America's Great Highways*. New York: Simon and Schuster, 2000.

Meeker, Ezra. *The Busy Life of Eighty-Five Years of Ezra Meeker: Ventures and Adventures*. Seattle: published by the author, 1916.

———. *The Ox-Team; or, The Old Oregon Trail, 1852–1906*. Lincoln, NE: Jacob North, 1906.

Melville, Herman. *Typee: A Peep at Polynesian Life During a Four Months' Residence in a Valley of the Marquesas, with Notices of the French Occupation of Tahiti and the Provisional Cession of the Sandwich Islands to Lord Paulet*. New York: New American Library, 1979. First published, New York: Wiley and Putnam; London: John Murray, 1846.

Miller, Henry. *The Air-Conditioned Nightmare*. New York: New Directions, 1945.

Mills, Enos A. *The Rocky Mountain Wonderland*. Boston: Houghton Mifflin, 1915.

———. *The Spell of the Rockies*. Boston: Houghton Mifflin, 1911.

Moyers, Bill. *Listening to America: A Traveler Rediscovers His Country*. New York: Harper and Row, 1971.

Muir, John. *John Muir's Last Journey: South to the Amazon and East to Africa; Unpublished Journals and Selected Correspondence.* Edited by Michael P. Branch. Washington, D.C.: Island Press; Covelo, CA: Shearwater Books, 2001.

———. *The Mountains of California.* New York: Century Company, 1894.

———. *My First Summer in the Sierra.* Mineola, NY: Dover Books, 2004. First published, Boston: Houghton Mifflin, 1911.

———. *Travels in Alaska.* Boston: Houghton Mifflin, 1915.

Murphy, Thomas D. *Three Wonderlands of the American West: Being the Notes of a Traveler, Concerning the Yellowstone Park, the Yosemite National Park, and the Grand Canyon of the Colorado River, with a Chapter on the Other Wonders of the Great American West.* Boston: L. C. Page, 1912.

Norris, Frank. "The Frontier, Gone at Last." *World's Work* 3 (February 1902): 1728–31.

Norris, Kathleen. *Dakota: A Spiritual Geography.* New York: Mariner Books, 2001.

O'Sullivan, John L. "Annexation." *Democratic Review* 17 (July–August 1845): 5–10.

Parkman, Francis. *The Oregon Trail: Sketches of Prairie and Rocky-Mountain Life.* Boston: Little, 1872. First published as *The California and Oregon Trail,* New York: G. P. Putnam's Sons, 1849.

Peary, Robert E. *The North Pole: Its Discovery in 1909 Under the Auspices of the Peary Arctic Club.* New York: Frederick A. Stokes, 1910. Reprinted, New York: Cooper Square Press, 2001.

Peixotto, Ernest C. *Our Hispanic Southwest.* New York: Charles Scribner's Sons, 1916.

Pike, Zebulon Montgomery. *Exploratory Travels Through the Western Territories of North America.* London: Longman, Hurst, Rees, Orme and Brown, 1811.

Post, Emily. *By Motor to the Golden Gate.* New York: Appleton, 1916.

Powell, E. Alexander. *The End of the Trail: The Far West from New Mexico to British Columbia.*
New York: Charles Scribner's Sons, 1914.

Powell, John Wesley. *The Exploration of the Colorado River and Its Canyons.* New York: Penguin Books, 1997. First published as *Exploration of the Colorado River of the West and Its Tributaries,* Washington, D.C.: Government Printing Office, 1875.

Putnam, George P. *In the Oregon Country: Out-doors in Oregon, Washington, and California, Together with Some Legendary Lore, and Glimpses of the Modern West in the Making.* New York: G. P. Putnam's Sons, 1915.

Pyle, Ernie. *Home Country.* New York: William Sloane, 1947.

Ramsey, Alice Huyler. *Veil, Duster, and Tire Iron.* Pasadena, CA: Castle Press, 1961.

Reeves, Richard. *American Journey: Traveling with Tocqueville in Search of Democracy in America.* New York: Simon and Schuster, 1982.

Reik, Henry Otteridge. *A Tour of America's National Parks.* New York: Dutton, 1920.

Rinehart, Mary R. *Nomad's Land.* New York: George H. Doran, 1926.

Rittenberg, Caroline. *Motor West.* New York: Harold Vinal, 1926.

Roosevelt, Kermit. *The Happy Hunting-Grounds*. New York: Charles Scribner's Sons, 1920.

———. *The Long Trail*. New York: Review of Reviews/Metropolitan Magazine, 1921.

Roosevelt, Theodore. *African Game Trails: An Account of the African Wanderings of an American Hunter-Naturalist*. 2 vols. New York: Charles Scribner's Sons, 1922. First published, New York: Charles Scribner's Sons, 1910.

———. *Through the Brazilian Wilderness*. New York: Charles Scribner's Sons, 1914. Reprinted, New York: Cooper Square Press, 2000.

———. *The Winning of the West*. 4 vols. New York: G. P. Putnam's Sons, 1889–1896.

Roosevelt, Theodore, Jr., and Kermit Roosevelt. *East of the Sun and West of the Moon*. New York: Charles Scribner's Sons, 1927.

Sanders, Helen F. *Trails Through Western Woods*. New York: Alice Harriman, 1910.

Sanford, Francis B. *Letters of the Rambler: A Trip Across the Continent*. Garden City, NY: Country Life Press, 1921.

Schaeffer, L. M. *Sketches of Travels in South America, Mexico, and California*. New York: James Egbert, 1860.

Schuyler, Montgomery. *Westward the Course of Empire: "Out West" and "Back East" on the First Trip of the "Los Angeles Limited."* New York: G. P. Putnam's Sons, 1906.

Shuster, George. *The Longest Auto Race*. New York: John Day, 1966.

St. John de Crèvecoeur, Hector. *Letters from an American Farmer*. New York: Fox, Duffield, 1904. First published, 1782.

Stansbury, Howard. *An Expedition to the Valley of the Great Salt Lake of Utah: Including a Description of Its Geography, Natural History, and Minerals, and an Analysis of Its Waters, with an Authentic Account of the Mormon Settlement*. Philadelphia: Lippincott, Grambo, and Company, 1852.

Steele, David M. C. *Going Abroad Overland: Studies of Places and People in the Far West*. New York: G. P. Putnam's Sons, 1917.

Steinbeck, John. *Travels with Charley in Search of America*. New York: Viking, 1961. Reprinted, New York: Bantam Books, 1963.

Stephens, John L. *Incidents of Travel in Central America, Chiapas, and Yucatan*. 2 vols. New York: Harper and Brothers, 1841. Reprinted, Cambridge: Cambridge University Press, 2010.

———. *Incidents of Travel in Egypt, Arabia Petraea, and the Holy Land*. New York: Harper and Brothers, 1837.

———. *Incidents of Travel in Greece, Turkey, Russia, and Poland*. New York: Harper and Brothers, 1838.

———. *Incidents of Travel in Yucatan*. New York: Harper and Brothers, 1843.

Taussig, Hugo Alois. *Retracing the Pioneers: From East to West in an Automobile*. San Francisco: Philopolis Press, 1910.

Taylor, Bayard. *At Home and Abroad: A Sketch-book of Life, Scenery, and Men*. New York: G. P. Putnam, 1862. Reprinted, New York: G. P. Putnam's Sons, 1873.

———. *Eldorado; or, Adventures in the Path of Empire, Comprising a Voyage to California, via Panama; Life in San Francisco and Monterey; Pictures of the Gold Region; and Experiences of Mexican Travel.* New York: G. P. Putnam, 1850.

Theroux, Paul. *The Old Patagonian Express: By Train Through the Americas.* Boston: Houghton Mifflin, 1997. First published, 1979.

———. "Round the World in 80 Clichés." *Sunday Times* (London), December 11, 1977, 41.

Trego, Frank H. *Boulevarded Old Trails in the Great Southwest.* New York: Greenberg Publisher, 1929.

Tripp, Augustus F. "Notes of an Excursion to California in the Winter and Spring of 1893." Bound, typed ms. Henry E. Huntington Library, San Marino, CA, HM 60314.

Twain, Mark (Samuel Langhorne Clemens). *Autobiographical Writings.* Edited by R. Kent Rasmussen. New York: Penguin Books, 2012.

———. *The Complete Works of Mark Twain.* New York: Harper and Brothers, 1922. First published, Hartford, CT: American Publishing Company, 1903.

———. *Following the Equator: A Journey Around the World.* Hartford, CT: American Publishing Company, 1897. Reprinted as *More Tramps Abroad*, London: Chatto and Windus, 1897.

———. *The Innocents Abroad, or the New Pilgrims' Progress.* Hartford, CT: American Publishing Company, 1869. Reprinted as *The Innocents Abroad* and *The New Pilgrims' Progress*, 2 vols., London: Hotten, 1870.

———. *Life on the Mississippi.* London: Chatto and Windus; Hartford, CT: Osgood, 1883.

———. *Mark Twain on the Move: A Travel Reader.* Edited by Alan Gribben and Jeffrey Alan Melton. Tuscaloosa: University of Alabama Press, 2009.

———. *Roughing It.* London: Routledge, 1872.

———. *A Tramp Abroad.* 2 vols. London: Chatto and Windus; Hartford, CT: American Publishing Company, 1880.

———. *A Tramp Abroad, Following the Equator, Other Travels.* Edited by Roy Blount Jr. New York: Library of America, 2010.

Warren, T. Robinson. *Dust and Foam; or, Three Oceans and Two Continents: Being Ten Years' Wanderings in Mexico, South America, Sandwich Islands, the East and West Indies, China, Philippines, Australia, and Polynesia.* New York: Charles Scribner; London: Sampson Low, Son, and Company, 1859.

Whiting, Lilian. *The Land of Enchantment: From Pike's Peak to the Pacific.* Boston: Little, Brown, 1909.

Wilkes, Charles. *The Narrative of the United States Exploring Expedition: During the Years 1838, 1839, 1840, 1841, 1842.* 5 vols. Philadelphia: Lea and Blanchard, 1844; London: Whittaker, 1845.

———. *Western America, Including California and Oregon, with Maps of Those Regions, and the "Sacramento Valley."* Philadelphia: Lea and Blanchard, 1849.

Wilson, Edmund. *The American Jitters.* New York: Charles Scribner's Sons, 1932.

———. *Travels in Two Democracies.* New York: Harcourt, Brace, 1936.

Wood, J. M. *A Trip Around the World on Board of a Man-of-War: Cruise of the United States Steamer "Juniata" from New York City to Yokohama.* Shanghai: Kelly and Walsh, 1888.

British Travelers

Amis, Kingsley. "Is the Travel Book Dead?" *The Spectator* 194, no. 6625 (June 17, 1955): 774–75.

Berger, Max. *The British Traveller in America, 1836–1860.* New York: Columbia University Press, 1943.

Bird, Isabella Lucy. *Among the Tibetans.* London: Religious Tract Society; New York: Fleming H. Revell, 1894.

———. *Chinese Pictures: Notes on Photographs Made in China.* London: Cassell, 1900.

———. *The Englishwoman in America.* London: John Murray, 1856; New York: Arno, 1859.

———. *The Golden Chersonese and the Way Thither.* London: John Murray; New York: G. P. Putnam's Sons, 1883.

———. *The Hawaiian Archipelago: Six Months Among the Palm Groves, Coral Reefs, and Volcanoes of the Sandwich Islands.* London: John Murray, 1875. Reprinted, New York: G. P. Putnam's Sons, 1882.

———. *Journeys in Persia and Kurdistan: Including a Summer in the Upper Karun Region and a Visit to the Nestorian Rayahs.* London: John Murray; New York: G. P. Putnam's Sons, 1891.

———. *Korea and Her Neighbors: A Narrative of Travel, with an Account of the Recent Vicissitudes and Present Position of the Country.* New York: Fleming H. Revell; London: John Murray, 1898.

———. *A Lady's Life in the Rocky Mountains.* London: John Murray; New York: G. P. Putnam's Sons, 1879. Reprinted, Sausalito, CA: Comstock Editions, 1977.

———. *Unbeaten Tracks in Japan: An Account of Travels in the Interior, Including Visits to the Aborigines of Yezo and the Shrines of Nikko and Ise.* 2 vols. London: John Murray; New York: G. P. Putnam's Sons, 1880. Reprinted, Boston: Beacon Press, 1987.

———. *The Yangtze Valley and Beyond: An Account of Journeys in China, Chiefly in the Province of SzeChuan and Among the Man-Tze of the Somo Territory.* London: John Murray, 1899; New York: G. P. Putnam's Sons, 1900.

Bird, Isabella Lucy, and Henrietta A. Bird. *Letters to Henrietta.* Edited by Kay Chubbuck. Boston: Northeastern University Press, 2003.

Boddam-Whetham, John. *Western Wanderings: A Record of Travel in the Evening Land.* London: Richard Bentley, 1874.

Bridges, F. D. *Journal of a Lady's Travels Round the World.* London: John Murray, 1883.

Bryce, James. *The American Commonwealth.* 2 vols. New York: Macmillan, 1893–1895.

Burton, Richard Francis. *The City of the Saints, and Across the Rocky Mountains to California*. Edited by Fawn Brodie. New York: Alfred A. Knopf, 1963. Reprinted, Santa Barbara, CA: Narrative Press, 2003. First published, London: Longman, Green, Longman, and Roberts, 1861; New York: Harper and Brothers, 1862.

———. *First Footsteps in East Africa; or, An Exploration of Harar*. London: Longman, Brown, Green, and Longmans, 1856.

———. *The Lake Regions of Central Africa: A Picture of Exploration*. 2 vols. London: Longman, Green, Longman, and Roberts, 1860.

———. *The Look of the West, 1860: Across the Plains to California*. Lincoln: University of Nebraska Press, Bison Books, 1963, 1966.

———. *Personal Narrative of a Pilgrimage to El-Medinah and Meccah*. 3 vols. London: Longman, Brown, Green, and Longmans, 1855–1856.

———. *Selected Papers on Anthropology, Travel and Exploration*. Introduction by Norman M. Penzer. London: A. M. Philpot, 1924.

———. *Wanderings in Three Continents*. London: Hutchinson, 1901.

Butler, William Francis. *Far Out: Rovings Retold*. London: William Isbister, 1880.

———. *The Great Lone Land: A Narrative of Travel and Adventure in the North-West of America*. London: Sampson Low, Marston, Low, and Searle, 1872.

Campbell, John Francis. *My Circular Notes: Extracts from Journals, Letters Sent Home, Geological and Other Notes, Written While Travelling Westwards Round the World, from July 6, 1874, to July 6, 1875*. London: Macmillan, 1876.

Carver, Jonathan. *Travels Through the Interior Parts of North America in the Years 1766, 1767, and 1768*. London: printed for the author and sold by J. Walter, 1778. Reprinted as *Three Years' Travels Through the Interior Parts of North-America, for More Than Five Thousand Miles*, Philadelphia: Key and Simpson, 1796. Reprinted, Minneapolis: Ross and Haines, 1956.

Cherry-Garrard, Apsley. *The Worst Journey in the World: Antarctic, 1910–1913*. 2 vols. London: Constable; New York: George H. Doran, 1922.

Chesterton, G. K. *What I Saw in America*. London: Hodder and Stoughton, 1922.

Cohen, David. *Chasing the Red, White, and Blue: A Journey in Tocqueville's Footsteps Through Contemporary America*. New York: Picador, 2001.

Dickens, Charles. *American Notes for General Circulation*. 2 vols. London: Chapman and Hall, 1842. Published in a single volume, New York: Harper and Brothers, 1842.

Dilke, Charles Wentworth. *Greater Britain: A Record of Travel in English-Speaking Countries During 1866–7*. 2 vols. London: Macmillan, 1868.

Galton, Francis. *The Art of Travel; or, Shifts and Contrivances Available in Wild Countries*. London: John Murray, 1855.

———. *Memories of My Life*. New York: Dutton, 1909.

———. *The Narrative of an Explorer in Tropical South Africa*. London: John Murray, 1853.

Graham, Stephen. *The Gentle Art of Tramping*. New York: Appleton, 1926; London: Holden, 1927.

———. *In Quest of El Dorado*. New York: Appleton, 1923; London: Macmillan, 1924.

———. *Tramping with a Poet in the Rockies*. London: Macmillan; New York: Appleton, 1922.

———. *A Tramp's Sketches*. London: Macmillan, 1912.

Grant, Richard. *American Nomads: Travels with Lost Conquistadors, Mountain Men, Cowboys, Indians, Hoboes, Truckers, and Bullriders*. New York: Grove Press, 2003.

Haldane, J. W. C. *3,800 Miles Across Canada*. London: Simpkin, Marshall, Hamilton, Kent, 1900.

Humphreys, J. R. *The Lost Towns and Roads of America: A Journey Revealing Early America Still Here Today*. Garden City, NY: Doubleday, 1961.

Huxley, Aldous. *Along the Road: Notes and Essays of a Tourist*. London: Chatto and Windus; New York: George H. Doran, 1925.

———. *Beyond the Mexique Bay*. London: Chatto and Windus; New York: Harper and Brothers, 1934.

———. *Brave New World*. London: Chatto and Windus; Garden City, NY: Doubleday, Doran, 1932.

———. *Jesting Pilate: Travels Through India, Burma, Malaya, Japan, China, and America*. New York: George H. Doran, 1926.

Isherwood, Christopher. *The Condor and the Cows: A South American Travel Diary*. New York: Random House, 1948; London: Methuen, 1949. Reprinted, Minneapolis: University of Minnesota Press, 2003.

———. *Goodbye to Berlin*. London: Minerva, 1939.

Isherwood, Christopher, and W. H. Auden. *Journey to a War*. London: Faber and Faber, 1939.

Kemble, Francis Anne (Butler). *Journal of a Residence on a Georgia Plantation in 1838–1839*.

London: Longman, Green, Longman, Roberts, and Green, 1863.

Kingsley, Mary Henrietta. *Travels in West Africa: Congo Francais, Corisco and Cameroons*. London: Macmillan, 1897. Reprinted, Boston: Beacon Press, 1988.

———. *West African Studies*. London: Macmillan, 1899.

Kipling, Rudyard. *American Notes*. New York: M. J. Ivers, 1891. Reprinted as *American Notes: Rudyard Kipling's West*, edited by Arrell Morgan Gibson, Norman: University of Oklahoma Press, 1981.

———. *From Sea to Sea: Letters of Travel*. Vol. 2 of *The Works of Rudyard Kipling*. New York: Doubleday and McClure, 1899.

Lawrence, D. H. "Indians and Entertainment." *New York Times Magazine*, October 26, 1924.

———. *Mornings in Mexico and Other Essays*. Edited by Virginia Crosswhite Hyde. London: Martin Secker; New York: Alfred A. Knopf, 1927. Reprinted, Cambridge: Cambridge University Press, 2009.

Livingstone, David. *Missionary Travels and Researches in South Africa*. London: John Murray, 1857.

Lucas, Edward Verrall. *Roving East and Roving West*. New York: George H. Doran, 1921.

Martineau, Harriet. *Eastern Life, Present and Past*. 3 vols. London: Edward Moxon, 1848.

McGrath, Melanie. *Motel Nirvana: Dreaming of the New Age in the American Desert*. New York: Picador, 1996.

Morris, Elizabeth Keith. *An Englishwoman in the Canadian West*. London: Simpkin Marshall, 1913.

Morris, Jan (James Humphrey Morris). *Coast to Coast*. London: Faber and Faber, 1956. Published in the United States with the title *As I Saw the U.S.A.*, New York: Pantheon, 1956.

———. *The World: Life and Travel, 1950–2000*. New York: W. W. Norton, 2003.

Park, Mungo. *Travels in the Interior Districts of Africa: Performed Under the Direction and Patronage of the African Association in the Years 1795, 1796, and 1797*. Edinburgh: Adam and Charles Black, 1860. First published, London: G. and W. Nicol, 1799.

Peters, George Henry. *Impressions of a Journey Round the World Including India, Burmah and Japan*. London: Waterlow and Sons, 1897.

Priestley, J. B. *English Journey*. Seventy-Fifth Anniversary Edition. Ilkley, West Yorkshire: Great Northern, 2009. First published as *English Journey: Being a Rambling but Truthful Account of What One Man Saw and Heard and Felt and Thought During a Journey Through England During the Autumn of the Year 1933*. London: W. M. Heinemann, in association with V. Gollancz, 1934.

———. *Midnight on the Desert: Being an Excursion into Autobiography During a Winter in America, 1935–1936*. New York: Harper and Brothers, 1937.

Priestley, J. B., and Jacquetta Hawkes. *Journey Down a Rainbow*. New York: Harper and Brothers, 1955.

Raban, Jonathan. *Bad Land: An American Romance*. New York: Vintage, 1996.

———. *Hunting Mister Heartbreak: A Discovery of America*. New York: Edward Burlingame, 1991; first published, London: Collins Harvill, 1990.

———. *Old Glory: An American Voyage*. New York: Simon and Schuster, 1981.

Rankin, Nicholas. *Dead Man's Chest: Travels After Robert Louis Stevenson*. London: Faber and Faber, 1987.

Roberts, Cecil. *And So to America*. New York: Doubleday, 1947.

Ruxton, George Frederick Augustus. *Adventures in the Rocky Mountains and in Mexico*. London: John Murray, 1847; New York: Harper and Brothers, 1848.

———. *Life in the Far West*. Edinburgh: William Blackwood and Sons; London: John Murray, 1849.

Shaw, William. *Golden Dreams and Waking Realities: Being the Adventures of a Gold-Seeker in California and the Pacific Islands.* London: Smith, Elder, 1851.

Shepherd, C. K. *Across America by Motor-Cycle.* London: Edward Arnold, 1922. Reprinted, Fayetteville, AR: Juniper Grove, 2008.

Stanley, Henry Morton. *How I Found Livingstone.* London: Sampson Low, Marston, Low, and Searle; New York: Scribner, Armstrong, 1872.

————. *In Darkest Africa; or, the Quest, Rescue, and Retreat of Emin, Governor of Equatoria.* 2 vols. New York: Charles Scribner's Sons; London: Sampson Low, Marston, Searle, and Rivington, 1890.

————. *My Early Travels and Adventures in America and Asia.* 2 vols. London: Sampson Low, Marston, 1895.

Stevens, Thomas. *Around the World on a Bicycle.* Vol. 1, *From San Francisco to Teheran.* New York: Charles Scribner's Sons, 1887.

Stevenson, Robert Louis. *Across the Plains: With Other Memories and Essays.* London: Chatto and Windus, 1890. Reprinted, New York: Charles Scribner's Sons, 1892.

————. *The Amateur Emigrant: From the Clyde to Sandy Hook.* Chicago: Stone and Kimball, 1895. Reprinted, New York: Charles Scribner's Sons, 1899.

————. *Essays of Travel.* London: Chatto and Windus, 1905.

————. *Father Damien: An Open Letter to the Reverend Doctor Hyde of Honolulu.* London: Chatto and Windus, 1890.

————. *A Footnote to History: Eight Years of Trouble in Samoa.* London: Cassell; New York: Charles Scribner's Sons, 1892.

————. *From Scotland to Eldorado.* Edited by James D. Hart. Cambridge: Belknap Press of Harvard University Press, 1966.

————. *In the South Seas: Being an Account of Experiences and Observations in the Marquesas, Paumotus, and Gilbert Islands in the Course of Two Cruises, on the Yacht "Casco" (1888) and the Schooner "Equator" (1889).* New York: Charles Scribner's Sons, 1923. First published, London: Chatto and Windus; New York: Charles Scribner's Sons, 1896.

————. *The Letters of Robert Louis Stevenson.* Vol. 1. Edited by Sidney Colvin. London: Methuen, 1901.

————. *The Silverado Squatters.* London: Chatto and Windus, 1883; New York: Munro, 1884.

———— *The Works of Robert Louis Stevenson.* Edinburgh: Longmans, Green, 1894.

Tangye, Richard. *Reminiscences of Travel in Australia, America, and Egypt.* London: Sampson Low, Marston, Searle, and Rivington, 1883.

Theroux, Louis. *The Call of the Weird: Travels in American Subcultures.* London: Macmillan, 2005. Reprinted, Boston: Da Capo Press, 2007.

Trollope, Anthony. *North America.* Edited by Donald Smalley and Bradford Allen Booth. New York: Da Capo Press, 1986. This edition first published, New York: Alfred A. Knopf, 1951. First published, New York: Harper and Brothers; London: Chapman and Hall, 1862.

———. *Travelling Sketches*. London: Chapman and Hall, 1866.

Trollope, Frances. *Domestic Manners of the Americans*. 2 vols. London: Whittaker, Treacher, and Company, 1832.

Vincent, Howard, Mrs. (Ethel Gwendoline Moffatt). *Forty Thousand Miles over Land and Water: The Journal of a Tour Through the British Empire and America*. 2 vols. London: Sampson Low, Marston, Searle, and Rivington, 1885.

White, John. *Sketches from America: Part I.—Canada; Part II.—A Pic-nic to the Rocky Mountains; Part III.—the Irish in America*. London: Sampson Low, Son, and Marston, 1870.

Wortley, Lady Emmeline Stuart. *Sketches of Travel in America: North America, Caribbean and Peru*. London: Bosworth, 1853.

———. *Travels in the United States, etc., During 1849 and 1850*. London: Richard Bentley, 1851.

Wortley, Victoria Stuart. *A Young Traveler's Journal of a Tour in North and South America*. London: Bosworth, 1852.

Canadian Travelers

McEvoy, Bernard. *From the Great Lakes to the Wide West: Impressions of a Tour Between Toronto and the Pacific*. Toronto: W. Briggs, 1902.

Continental European Travelers

Baudrillard, Jean. *Amérique*. Paris: Bernard Grasset, 1986. Translated by Chris Turner as *America*, London: Verso, 1988.

De Beauvoir, Simone. *America Day by Day*. Translated by Carol Cosman. Berkeley: University of California Press, 1999. First published as *L'Amérique au jour le jour*, Paris: Gallimard, 1948. First published in English translation, New York: Grove Press, 1953.

Gerstäcker, Friedrich. *California Gold Mines*. Oakland: Biobooks, 1946.

———. *Gerstäcker's Travels: Rio de Janeiro, Buenos Ayres, Ride Through the Pampas, Winter Journey Across the Cordilleras, Chile, Valparaiso, California and the Gold Fields*. Translated by Friedrich Gerstäcker. London: T. Nelson and Sons, 1854.

———. *Narrative of a Journey Round the World, Comprising a Winter Passage Across the Andes to Chili, with a Visit to the Gold Regions of California and Australia, the South Sea Islands, Java, &c*. New York: Harper and Brothers, 1853.

Heller, Karl Bartholomaeus. *Reisen in Mexiko in den Jahren 1845–1848*. Leipzig: W. Engelmann, 1853. Translated by Terry Rugeley as *Alone in Mexico: The Astonishing Travels of Karl Heller, 1845–1848*, Tuscaloosa: University of Alabama Press, 2007.

Humboldt, Alexander von, and Aimé Bonpland. *Personal Narrative of Travels to the Equinoctial Regions of America, During the Years 1799–1804*. Edited and translated by Thomasina Ross. 3 vols. London: H.G. Bohn, 1852.

Koeppen, Hans. *Im Auto um die Welt*. Berlin: Ullstein, 1908.

Lévi-Strauss, Claude. *Tristes Tropiques*. Paris: Librairie Plon, 1955. Translated by John Russell as *A World on the Wane*, London: Hutchinson, 1961.

Lévy, Bernard-Henri. *American Vertigo: Traveling America in the Footsteps of Tocqueville*. New York: Random House, 2006.

Maistre, Xavier de. *A Journey Around My Room; and A Nocturnal Expedition Around My Room*. Translated by Andrew Brown. With a foreword by Alain de Botton. London: Hesperus Press, 2004.

Pfeiffer, Ida. *A Lady's Journey Round the World: From Vienna to Brazil, Chili, Tahiti, China, Hindostan, Persia, and Asia Minor*. A selected translation by Mrs. Percy Sinnett. London: Longman, 1856. First published as *Eine Frau fährt um die Welt*, Vienna, 1850.

———. *A Lady's Second Journey Round the World: From London to the Cape of Good Hope, Borneo, Java, Sumatra, Celebes, Ceram, the Moluccas, etc.; California, Panama, Peru, Ecuador, and the United States*. New York: Harper and Brothers, 1856.

Rémy, Jules, and Julius Brenchley. *A Journey to Great-Salt-Lake City, with a Sketch of the History, Religion, and Customs of the Mormons*. 2 vols. London: W. Jeffs, 1861.

Scarfoglio, Antonio. *Round the World in a Motor Car*. Translated by J. Parker Heyes. London: Grant Richards, 1909.

Tocqueville, Alexis de. *Democracy in America*. Translated, edited, and introduced by Harvey C. Mansfield and Delba Winthrop. Chicago: University of Chicago Press, 2000.

———. *Democracy in America*. Henry Reeve text as revised by Francis Bower. Edited by Phillips Bradley. 2 vols. New York: Alfred A. Knopf, 1945. Reprinted, 1945, 1946, 1948, 1951, 1953, 1957.

——— *Writings on Empire and Slavery*. Edited and translated by Jennifer Pitts. Baltimore: Johns Hopkins University Press, 2001.

Wied, Prince Maximilian. *The North American Journals of Prince Maximilian of Wied*. Vol. 1, *May 1832–April 1833*; vol. 2, *April–September 1833*; vol. 3, *September 1833–August 1834*. Edited by Stephen S. Witte and Marsha V. Gallagher. Translated by William J. Orr, Paul Schach, and Dieter Karch. Norman: University of Oklahoma Press, 2008, 2010, 2012.

American Guide Series

Arizona: A State Guide. Prepared by the Federal Writers' Project of the Works Progress Administration. New York: Hastings House, 1940. Reprinted as *The WPA Guide to 1930s Arizona*, Tucson: University of Arizona Press, 1989.

California: A Guide to the Golden State. Prepared by the Federal Writers' Project of the Works Progress Administration. New York: Hastings House, 1939. Reprinted as *The WPA Guide to California: The Federal Writers' Project Guide to 1930s California*, New York: Pantheon Books, 1984.

Colorado: A Guide to the Highest State. Prepared by the Federal Writers' Project of the Works Progress Administration. New York: Hastings House, 1941. Reprinted as *The WPA Guide to 1930s Colorado*, Lawrence: University Press of Kansas, 1987.

A Guide to Alaska: Last American Frontier. Prepared by the Federal Writers' Project of the Works Progress Administration and Merle Colby. New York: Macmillan, 1939.

Idaho, a Guide in Word and Picture. Prepared by the Federal Writers' Project of the Works Progress Administration. Caldwell, ID: Caxton Printers, 1937. Rev. ed., New York: Oxford University Press, 1950.

Iowa: A Guide to the Hawkeye State. Prepared by the Federal Writers' Project of the Works Progress Administration. New York: Viking, 1938.

Kansas: A Guide to the Sunflower State. Prepared by the Federal Writers' Project of the Works Progress Administration. New York: Viking, 1939. Reprinted as *The WPA Guide to 1930s Kansas*, with a new introduction by James R. Shortridge, Lawrence: University Press of Kansas, 1984.

Minnesota: A State Guide. Prepared by the Federal Writers' Project of the Works Progress Administration. New York: Viking, 1938.

Montana: A State Guide Book. Prepared by the Federal Writers' Project of the Works Progress Administration. New York: Viking, 1939. Reprinted as *The WPA Guide to 1930s Montana*, Tucson: University of Arizona Press, 1994.

Nebraska: A Guide to the Cornhusker State. Prepared by the Federal Writers' Project of the Works Progress Administration. New York: Hastings House, 1939. Reprinted, with an introduction by Alan Boye, Lincoln: University of Nebraska Press, 1979, 2005.

Nevada: A Guide to the Silver State. Prepared by the Federal Writers' Project of the Works Progress Administration. Portland, OR: Binfords and Mort, 1940. Reprinted as *The WPA Guide to 1930s Nevada*, with a foreword by Russell R. Elliot, Reno: University of Nevada Press, 1991.

New Mexico: A Guide to the Colorful State. Prepared by the Federal Writers' Project of the Works Progress Administration. New York: Hastings House, 1940. Reprinted as *The WPA Guide to 1930s New Mexico*, with a foreword by Marc Simmons, Tucson: University of Arizona Press, 1989.

North Dakota: A Guide to the Northern Prairie State. Prepared by the Federal Writers' Project of the Works Progress Administration. Fargo, ND: Knight Printing Company, 1938. Reprinted as *The WPA Guide to 1930s North Dakota*, Bismarck: State Historical Society of North Dakota, 1990.

Oklahoma: A Guide to the Sooner State. Prepared by the Federal Writers' Project of the Works Progress Administration. Norman: University of Oklahoma Press, 1941. Reprinted as *The WPA Guide to 1930s Oklahoma*, with a restored essay by Angie Debo and a new introduction by Anne Hodges Morgan, Lawrence: University Press of Kansas, 1986.

Oregon: End of the Trail. Prepared by the Federal Writers' Project of the Works Progress Administration. Portland, OR: Binfords and Mort, 1940.

The Oregon Trail. Prepared by the Federal Writers' Project of the Works Progress Administration. New York: Hastings House, 1939.

Remembering America: A Sampler of the WPA American Guide Series. Edited by Archie Hobson. New York: Columbia University Press, 1995.

A South Dakota Guide. Prepared by the Federal Writers' Project of the Works Progress Administration. Pierre, SD: State Publishing Company, 1938. Reprinted as *The WPA Guide to South Dakota*, with an introduction by John E. Miller, Minneapolis: Minnesota Historical Society Press, 2006.

Texas: A Guide to the Lone Star State. Prepared by the Federal Writers' Project of the Works Progress Administration. New York: Hastings House, 1940. Reprinted as *The WPA Guide to Texas*, with an introduction by Don Graham, Austin: Texas Monthly Press, 1986.

U.S. One: Maine to Florida. Prepared by the Federal Writers' Project of the Works Progress Administration. New York: Modern Age Books, 1938.

Utah: A Guide to the State. Prepared by the Federal Writers' Project of the Works Progress Administration. New York: Hastings House, 1941.

Washington: A Guide to the Evergreen State. Prepared by the Federal Writers' Project of the Works Progress Administration. Portland, OR: Binfords and Mort, 1941.

Wyoming: A Guide to Its History, Highways, and People. Prepared by the Federal Writers' Project of the Works Progress Administration. New York: Oxford University Press, 1941.

The WPA Guide to America: The Best of 1930s America as Seen by the Federal Writers' Project. Edited by Bernard A. Weisberger. New York: Pantheon Books, 1985.

Primary Sources General

Amis, Kingsley. *I Like It Here.* London: Victor Gollancz, 1958.

Bolton, Herbert Eugene. *The Spanish Borderlands: A Chronicle of Old Florida and the Southwest.* New Haven, CT: Yale University Press, 1921. Reprinted, Albuquerque: University of New Mexico Press, 1996.

Boorstin, Daniel. *The Genius of American Politics.* Chicago: University of Chicago Press, 1953.

Brooks, John Graham. *As Others See Us: A Study of Progress in the United States.* New York: Macmillan, 1908.

Brooks, Van Wyck. *America's Coming of Age.* New York: B. W. Huebsch, 1915.

Commager, Henry Steele. *The American Mind: An Interpretation of American Thought and Culture Since the 1880s.* New Haven, CT: Yale University Press, 1950.

Conrad, Joseph. *Heart of Darkness.* London: William Blackwood, 1902. Originally published in three parts in *Blackwood's Magazine* 165 (February 1899): 164–460; (March 1899): 460–621; (April 1899): 620–781.

Cowley, Malcolm. *Exile's Return: A Literary Odyssey of the 1920s.* New York: Viking, 1934. Reprinted, 1956, 1986.

Cuvier, Baron George. *The Animal Kingdom, Arranged According to Its Organization, Forming a Natural History of Animals, and an Introduction to Comparative Anatomy*. London: William S. Orr, 1849. First published in French as *Le Règne Animal*, 4 vols.

Dale, Edward Everett. "The Spirit of Soonerland." *Chronicles of Oklahoma* 1 (June 1923): 167–78.

Dewey, John. "The American Intellectual Frontier." *New Republic* (May 10, 1922): 303–5.

Doyle, Arthur Conan. *The Crime of the Congo*. New York: Doubleday, Page; London: Hutchinson, 1909.

Frank, Waldo D. *Our America*. New York: Boni and Liverwright, 1919.

———. *The Re-discovery of America: An Introduction to a Philosophy of American Life*. New York: Charles Scribner's Sons, 1929.

Franklin, Benjamin. *The Writings of Benjamin Franklin*. Vol. 10. Edited by Albert K. Smythe. New York: Macmillan, 1907.

Hartz, Louis. *The Liberal Tradition in America: An Interpretation of American Political Thought Since the Revolution*. New York: Harcourt, Brace, 1955.

Hofstadter, Richard. *The American Political Tradition and the Men Who Made It*. New York: Alfred A. Knopf, 1948.

Jackson, Helen Hunt. *A Century of Dishonor: A Sketch of the United States Government's Dealings with Some of the Indian Tribes*. New York: Harper and Brothers, 1881.

Jefferson, Thomas. *The Writings of Thomas Jefferson*. Edited by H. A. Washington. Vol. 2. Washington, D.C.: Taylor and Maury, 1854.

Kazin, Alfred. *On Native Grounds: An Interpretation of Modern American Prose Literature*. New York: Reynal and Hitchcock, 1942.

Linscott, Robert N., ed. *The Best American Humorous Short Stories*. New York: Random House, 1945.

Lippmann, Walter. *A Preface to Morals*. New York: Macmillan, 1929.

Marshall, Everett. *Roosevelt's Thrilling Experiences in the Wilds of Africa Hunting Big Game*. Chicago: A. Hamming, 1910.

McWilliams, Carey. *Factories in the Field*. Boston: Little, Brown, 1939.

O'Sullivan, John L. "Annexation." *Democratic Review* 17 (July–August 1845): 5–10.

———. "Manfest Destiny." *New York Morning News*, editorial, December 27, 1845.

Pomeroy, Earl S. *In Search of the Golden West: The Tourist in Western America*. Lincoln: University of Nebraska Press, 1990. First published, New York: Alfred A. Knopf, 1957.

———. *The Territories and the United States, 1861–1890: Studies in Colonial Administration*. Philadelphia: University of Pennsylvania Press/American Historical Association, 1947.

Potter, David M. *People of Plenty: Economic Abundance and the American Character*. Chicago: University of Chicago Press, 1954.

Prichard, James Cowles. *The Natural History of Man: Inquiries into the Modifying Influence of Physical and Moral Agencies on the Different Tribes of the Human Family.* 3rd ed. London: Hippolyte Bailliere, 1848.

Roosevelt, Franklin D. *The Public Papers and Addresses of Franklin D. Roosevelt.* Edited by Samuel I. Rosenman and William D. Hassett. New York: Random House, 1938.

Royal Geographical Society. "Hints to Travellers." *Journal of the Royal Geographical Society of London* 24 (1854): 329–58.

Royce, Josiah. *California, from the Conquest in 1846 to the Second Vigilance Committee in San Francisco: A Study of American Character.* Boston: Houghton Mifflin, 1886.

Sandoz, Mari. *The Buffalo Hunters.* New York: Hastings House, 1954.

———. *Cheyenne Autumn.* New York: McGraw Hill, 1953.

———. *Old Jules.* Boston: Little, Brown, 1935.

———. *These Were the Sioux.* New York: Hastings House, 1961.

Smith, Henry Nash. *Virgin Land: The American West as Symbol and Myth.* Cambridge: Harvard University Press, 1950.

Stearns, Harold. *Civilization in the United States: An Inquiry by Thirty Americans.* New York: Harcourt, Brace, 1922.

Turner, Frederick Jackson. *The Frontier in American History.* New York: Henry Holt, 1920.

———. *Rereading Frederick Jackson Turner: "The Significance of the Frontier in American History" and Other Essays.* Edited by John Mack Faragher. New York: Henry Holt, 1994. Reprinted, New Haven, CT: Yale University Press, 1998.

———. "Sections and Nation," *Yale Review* 12 (October 1922).

Veblen, Thorstein. *The Theory of the Leisure Class.* New York: Macmillan, 1899.

Ward, John William. *Andrew Jackson: Symbol for an Age.* New York: Oxford University Press, 1955.

Webb, Walter Prescott. *The Great Frontier.* Boston: Houghton Mifflin, 1952. Reprinted, Las Vegas: University of Nevada Press, 2003.

White, William Allen. "What's the Matter with Kansas?" *Emporia Gazette*, August 15, 1896.

Whitman, Walt. *Leaves of Grass.* 2nd ed. Brooklyn, NY: Fowler and Wells, 1856.

Works on Travel and Travelers

Reference Works

Berger, Michael. *The Automobile in American History and Culture: A Reference Guide.* Westport, CT: Greenwood Press, 2001.

Bliss, Carey S. *Autos Across America: A Bibliography of Transcontinental Automobile Travel, 1903–1940.* Los Angeles: Dawson's Book Shop, 1972. 2nd ed. enlarged, Austin, TX: Jenkins and Reese, 1982.

Dictionary of Literary Biography. Vol. 129, *Nineteenth-Century German Writers, 1841–1900*. Edited by Siegfried Mews and James Hardin. Detroit: Gale Research, 1993.

———. Vol. 166, *British Travel Writers, 1837–1875*. Edited by Barbara Brothers and Julia M. Gergits. Detroit: Gale Research, 1996.

———. Vol. 174, *British Travel Writers, 1876–1909*. Edited by Barbara Brothers and Julia M. Gergits. Detroit: Gale Research, 1997.

———. Vol. 183, *American Travel Writers, 1776–1864*. Edited by James J. Schramer and Donald Ross. Detroit: Gale Research, 1997.

———. Vol. 189, *American Travel Writers, 1850–1915*. Edited by Donald Ross and James J. Schramer. Detroit: Gale Research, 1998.

———. Vol. 195, *British Travel Writers, 1910–1939*. Edited by Barbara Brothers and Julia M. Gergits. Detroit: Gale Research, 1997.

———. Vol. 204, *British Travel Writers, 1940–1997*. Edited by Barbara Brothers and Julia M. Gergits. Detroit: Gale Research, 1999.

Elliott, Emory, ed. *Columbia Literary History of the United States*. New York: Columbia University Press, 1998.

Hanna, Archibald. *From Train to Plane: Travelers in the American West, 1866–1936; An Exhibition at the Beinecke Rare Book and Manuscript Library, Yale University*. New Haven, CT: Yale University Library, 1979.

Literary History of the United States. Edited by Robert E. Spillier, Willard Thorp, Thomas H. Johnson, and Henry Seidel Canby. New York: Macmillan, 1948.

Smith, Harold F. *American Travelers Abroad: A Bibliography of Accounts Published Before 1900*. 2nd ed. Lanham, MD: Scarecrow Press, 1999.

Strupp, Christoph, and Birgit Zischke, eds. *German Americana, 1800–1955*. Washington, D.C.: German Historical Institute, 2005.

Thwaites, Reuben G., ed. *Early Western Travels, 1748–1846: A Series of Annotated Reprints of Some of the Best and Rarest Contemporary Volumes of Travel*. 32 vols. Cleveland: A. H. Clark, 1904–1907.

Tinling, Marion. *Women into the Unknown: A Sourcebook on Women Explorers and Travelers*. Westport, CT: Greenwood Press, 1989.

Anthologies

Adams, Percy G., ed. *Travel Literature Through the Ages: An Anthology*. New York: Garland, 1988.

Agosín, Marjorie, and Julie H. Levison. *Magical Sites: Women Travelers in 19th Century Latin America*. Buffalo: White Pine Press, 1999.

Bear, Mary R., ed. *America Through Women's Eyes*. New York: Macmillan, 1933.

Borus, Daniel H., ed. *These United States: Portraits of America from the 1920s*. Ithaca, NY: Cornell University Press, 1992.

Di Maio, Irene S., ed. *Gerstäcker's Louisiana: Fiction and Travel Sketches from Antebellum Times Through Reconstruction*. Baton Rouge: Louisiana State University Press, 2006.

Farrier, David. *Unsettled Narratives: The Pacific Writings of Stevenson, Ellis, Melville, and London*. New York: Routledge, 2007.

Fraser, Keath, ed. *Bad Trips*. New York: Vintage Departures, 1991.

———. ed. *Worst Journeys: The Picador Book of Travel*. New York: Picador, 1993.

Fussell, Paul, ed. *The Norton Book of Travel*. New York: W. W. Norton, 1987.

Handlin, Oscar. *This Was America: True Accounts of People and Places, Manners and Customs, as Recorded by European Travelers to the Western Shore in the Eighteenth, Nineteenth, and Twentieth Centuries*. Cambridge: Harvard University Press, 1949.

Homer, Michael W. *On the Way to Somewhere Else: European Sojourners in the Mormon West, 1834–1930*. Salt Lake City: University of Utah Press, 2010.

Hooper, Glen, and Tim Youngs, eds. *Perspectives on Travel Writing*. Aldershot, England: Ashgate, 2004.

Hulme, Peter, and Tim Youngs, eds. *The Cambridge Companion to Travel Writing*. Cambridge: Cambridge University Press, 2002.

Jutzi, Alan H., ed. *In Search of Sir Richard Burton: Papers from a Huntington Library Symposium*. San Marino, CA: Henry E. Huntington Library, 1993.

Kowalewski, Michael, ed. *Temperamental Journeys: Essays on the Modern Literature of Travel*. Athens: University of Georgia Press, 1992.

Mochring, Eugene P. *Urban America and the Foreign Traveler, 1815–1855*. New York: Arno Press, 1974.

Morris, Mary, ed. *Maiden Voyages: Writings of Women Travelers*. New York: Vintage, 1993.

Nevins, Allan. *American Social History as Recorded by British Travellers*. New York: Henry Holt, 1923. Reprinted as *America Through British Eyes*, New York: Oxford University Press, 1948.

Robinson, Jane, ed. *Unsuitable for Ladies: An Anthology of Women Travelers*. Oxford: Oxford University Press, 1994.

Schriber, Mary Suzanne, ed. *Telling Travels: Selected Writings by Nineteenth-Century American Women Abroad*. DeKalb: Northern Illinois University Press, 1994.

Slung, Michelle, ed. *Living with Cannibals and Other Women's Adventures*. Washington, D.C.: National Geographic Society, 2000.

Theroux, Paul. *The Tao of Travel: Enlightenments from Lives on the Road*. New York: Mariner Books, 2012.

Tomlinson, H. M., ed. *An Anthology of Modern Travel Writing*. New York: T. Nelson, 1936.

Tuckerman, Henry T. *America and Her Commentators: With a Critical Sketch of Travel in the United States*. New York: Charles Scribner, 1864.

Watts, Edward, and David Rachels. *The First West: Writings from the American Frontier, 1776–1860*. New York: Oxford University Press, 2002.

Wrobel, David M., and Patrick T. Long, eds. *Seeing and Being Seen: Tourism in the American West*. Lawrence: University Press of Kansas, 2001.

Monographs and Articles

Adams, Percy G. *Travel Literature and the Evolution of the Novel*. Lexington: University Press of Kentucky, 1983.

Appleby, Joyce, Lynn Hunt, and Margaret Jacob. *Telling the Truth About History*. New York: W. W. Norton, 1994.

Athearn, Robert G. *Westward the Briton: The Far West, 1865–1900, as Seen by British Sportsmen and Capitalists, Ranchers and Homesteaders, Lords and Ladies*. New York: Charles Scribner's Sons, 1953. Reprinted, Lincoln: University of Nebraska Press, Bison Books, 1962.

Behdad, Ali. *Belated Travelers: Orientalism in the Age of Colonial Dissolution*. Durham, NC: Duke University Press, 1994.

Bendixen, Alfred, and Judith Hamera, eds. *The Cambridge Companion to American Travel Writing*. Cambridge: Cambridge University Press, 2009.

Berger, Max. *The British Traveller in America, 1836–1860*. New York: Columbia University Press, 1943.

Billington, Ray Allen. *Land of Savagery, Land of Promise: The European Image of the American Frontier in the Nineteenth Century*. New York: W. W. Norton, 1981.

———. *Westward Expansion: A History of the American Frontier*. New York: Macmillan, 1949.

Birkett, Deborah. "West Africa's Mary Kingsley." *History Today* 37 (May 1, 1987): 11–16.

Blanton, Casey. *Travel Writing: The Self and the World*. New York: Twayne Publishers, 1997.

Blodgett, Peter J. *Motoring West: Automobile Travelers in the Trans-Mississippi West, 1900–1950*. Vol. 1, *Pioneering, 1900–1909*. Norman: Arthur H. Clark Company, University of Oklahoma Press, forthcoming 2013.

Blunt, Alison. *Travel, Gender, and Imperialism: Mary Kingsley and West Africa*. New York: Guilford Press, 1994.

Bold, Christine. *The WPA Guides: Mapping America*. Jackson: University Press of Mississippi, 1999.

Boorstin, Daniel. *The Image: A Guide to Pseudo Events in America*. Twenty-Fifth Anniversary Edition. New York: Atheneum, 1987.

Bowen, Frank C. *A Century of Atlantic Travel: 1830–1930*. Boston: Little, Brown, 1930.

Brodie, Fawn M. "Sir Richard F. Burton: Exceptional Observer of the Mormon Scene." *Utah Historical Quarterly* 38, no. 4 (1970): 295–311.

Buzard, James. *The Beaten Track: European Tourism, Literature, and the Ways to Culture, 1800–1918*. New York: Oxford University Press, 2001. First published, 1993.

Caesar, Terry. *Forgiving the Boundaries: Home as Abroad in American Travel Writing*. Athens: University of Georgia Press, 1995.

Caldwell, Genoa, ed. *The Man Who Photographed the World: Burton Holmes Travelogues, 1886–1938*. New York: Harry N. Abrams, 1977.

Campbell, Robert. *In Darkest Alaska: Travel and Empire Along the Inside Passage*. Philadelphia: University of Pennsylvania Press, 2007.

Carr, E. H. "The Historian and His Facts." In *What Is History?* 2nd ed. London: Penguin Books, 1987. First published, 1961.

Cavitch, David. *D. H. Lawrence and the New World*. New York: Oxford University Press, 1969.

Ciolkowski, Laura E. "Travelers' Tales: Empire, Victorian Travel, and the Spectacle of English Womanhood in Mary Kingsley's 'Travels in West Africa.'" *Victorian Literature and Culture* 26 (1998): 337–66.

Clark, Steve, ed. *Travel Writing and Empire: Postcolonial Theory in Transit*. London: Zed Books, 1999.

Clark, Thomas D. "The Great Visitation to American Democracy." *Mississippi Valley Historical Review* 44 (June 1957): 3–28.

Cocker, Mark. *Loneliness and Time: The Story of British Travel Writing*. New York: Pantheon Books, 1992.

Cocks, Catherine. *Doing the Town: The Rise of Urban Tourism in the United States, 1850–1915*. Berkeley: University of California Press, 2001.

Cortazzi, Hugh. *Victorians in Japan: In and Around the Treaty Ports*. London: Athlone Press, 1987.

De Botton, Alain. *The Art of Travel*. London: Penguin Books, 2003. First published, London: Hamish Hamilton, 2002.

Diggins, John. *The Rise and Fall of the American Left*. New York: W. W. Norton, 1992.

Dodd, Philip, ed. *The Art of Travel: Essays on Travel Writing*. London: Frank Cass, 1982.

Dulles, Foster Rhea. *Americans Abroad: Two Centuries of European Travel*. Ann Arbor: University of Michigan Press, 1954.

Dunbar, Seymour. *A History of Travel in America*. Vol. 4. Indianapolis: Bobbs-Merrill, 1915. Four volumes reprinted in a single volume, New York: Tudor, 1937.

Etulain, Richard, ed. *Jack London on the Road: The Tramp Diary and Other Hobo Writings*. Logan: Utah State University Press, 1979.

Flink, James J. *America Adopts the Automobile, 1895–1910*. Cambridge: MIT Press, 1970.

———. *The Automobile Age*. Cambridge: MIT Press, 1990.

Flint, Kate. *The Transatlantic Indian, 1776–1930*. Princeton, NJ: Princeton University Press, 2008.

Flora, Joseph M., ed., *Rediscovering Vardis Fisher: Centennial Essays*. Moscow: University of Idaho Press, 2000.

Foreman, Carolyn T. *Indians Abroad, 1493–1938*. Norman: University of Oklahoma Press, 1943.

Francaviglia, Richard V. *Go East, Young Man: Imagining the American West as the Orient*. Logan: Utah State University Press, 2011.

Fussell, Paul. *Abroad: British Literary Traveling Between the Wars.* New York: Oxford University Press, 1980.

Gaddis, John Lewis. *The Landscape of History: How Historians Map the Past.* New York: Oxford University Press, 2002.

Gatrell, Simon, ed. *The Ends of the Earth, 1876–1918.* London: Ashfield Press, 1992.

Gilman, Carolyn. *Lewis and Clark: Across the Divide.* Washington, D.C.: Smithsonian Books, 2003.

Goetzmann, William H. *Exploration and Empire: The Explorer and the Scientist in the Winning of the American West.* New York: W. W. Norton, 1966.

Goodman, Susan, and Carl Dawson. *Mary Austin and the American West.* Berkeley: University of California Press, 2008.

Grant, Ben. *Postcolonialism, Psychoanalysis and Burton: Power Play of Empire.* London: Routledge, 2009.

Grewal, Inderpal. *Home and Harem: Nation, Gender, Empire, and the Cultures of Travel.* Durham, NC: Duke University Press, 1996.

Gudde, Erwin G. "Friedrich Gerstaecker: World Traveller and Author, 1816–1872." *Journal of the West* 7 (July 1968): 345–50.

Hackett, Rosalind I. J. "*Travels in West Africa* by Mary H. Kingsley and *A Voyager Out: The Life of Mary Kingsley* by Katherine Frank." *Journal of Religion in Africa* 21 (February 1991): 78–82.

Hausdorffer, John. *Catlin's Lament: Indians, Manifest Destiny, and the Ethics of Nature.* Lawrence: University Press of Kansas, 2009.

Hayes, Kevin J. *An American Cycling Odyssey, 1887.* Lincoln: University of Nebraska Press, 2002.

Hundley, Helen. "George Kennan and the Russian Empire: How America's Conscience Became an Enemy of Tsarism." Kennan Institute Occasional Papers, no. 277. Washington, D.C.: Woodrow Wilson Institute, 2000.

Iyer, Pico. "How Paradise Is Lost—and Found." *Time*, June 9, 1986, 82.

———. "The Magic of Flight." *VIA Magazine* (November–December 2003): 55–60.

Jakle, John A. *The Tourist: Travel in Twentieth-Century North America.* Lincoln: University of Nebraska Press, 1985.

Jakle, John A., and Keith A. Sculle. *Motoring: The Highway Experience in America.* Athens: University of Georgia Press, 2008.

Jeal, Tim. *Explorers of the Nile: The Triumph and Tragedy of a Great Victorian Adventure.* New Haven, CT: Yale University Press, 2011.

Kagle, Steven E., ed. *America: Exploration and Travel.* Bowling Green, OH: Bowling Green State University Popular Press, 1979.

Koivunen, Leila. *Visualizing Africa in Nineteenth-Century British Travel Accounts.* New York: Routledge, 2009.

Korte, Barbara. *English Travel Writing: From Pilgrimages to Postcolonial Explorations.* Translated by Catherine Matthias. London: Macmillan; New York: St. Martin's Press, 2000.

Lackey, Kris. *Roadframes: The American Highway Narrative*. Lincoln: University of Nebraska Press, 1997.

Ladd, Brian. *Autophobia: Love and Hate in the Automotive Age*. Chicago: University of Chicago Press, 2008.

Lamb, Jonathan. *Preserving the Self in the South Seas, 1680–1840*. Chicago: University of Chicago Press, 2001.

Leask, Nigel. *Curiosity and the Aesthetics of Travel Writing, 1770–1840: "From an Antique Land."* Oxford: Oxford University Press, 2002.

Leed, Eric J. *The Mind of the Traveler: From Gilgamesh to Global Tourism*. New York: Basic Books, 1991.

Leon, Carol E. *Movement and Belonging: Lines, Places, and Spaces of Travel*. New York: Peter Lang, 2009.

Liebersohn, Harry. *European Travelers and North American Indians*. Cambridge: Cambridge University Press, 1998.

Limerick, Patricia Nelson. *Desert Passages: Encounters with American Deserts*. Albuquerque: University of New Mexico Press, 1985.

Louter, David. *Windshield Wilderness: Cars, Roads, and Nature in Washington's National Parks*.
Seattle: University of Washington Press, 2006.

Lystra, Karen. *Dangerous Intimacy: The Untold Story of Mark Twain's Final Years*. Berkeley: University of California Press, 2004.

MacCannell, Dean. *Empty Meeting Grounds: The Tourist Papers*. New York: Routledge, 1992.

———. *The Ethics of Sightseeing*. Berkeley: University of California Press, 2011.

———. *The Tourist: A New Theory of the Leisure Class*. Berkeley: University of California Press, 1999. First published, New York: Schocken Books, 1976.

McDermott, John Francis, ed. *Travelers on the Western Frontier*. Urbana: University of Illinois Press, 1970.

Mesick, Louise. *The English Traveler in America, 1785–1835*. New York: Columbia University Press, 1922.

Middleton, Dorothy. *Victorian Lady Travellers*. London: Routledge, 1965.

Millard, Candice. *The River of Doubt: Theodore Roosevelt's Darkest Journey*. New York: Doubleday, 2005.

Mills, Sara. *Discourses of Difference: An Analysis of Women's Travel Writing and Colonialism*. London: Routledge, 1991.

Mulvey, Christopher. *Anglo-American Landscape: A Study of Nineteenth-Century Anglo-American Travel Literature*. London: Cambridge University Press, 1983.

———. *Transatlantic Manners: Social Patterns in Nineteenth-Century Anglo-American Travel Literature*. Cambridge: Cambridge University Press, 1990.

Myres, Sandra L. *Westering Women and the Frontier Experience: 1800–1915*. Albuquerque: University of New Mexico Press, 1982.

Nichols, Roger L. "Western Attractions: Europeans and America." *Pacific Historical Review* 74 (2005): 1–17.

Ornig, Joseph R. *My Last Chance to Be a Boy: Theodore Roosevelt's South American Expedition of 1913–1914*. Mechanicsburg, PA: Stackpole Books, 1994.

Padget, Martin. *Indian Country: Travels in the American Southwest, 1840–1935*. Albuquerque: University of New Mexico Press, 2004.

Parsons, Nicholas T. *Worth the Detour: A History of the Guidebook*. Gloucester, England: Sutton Publishing, 2007.

Patton, Phil. *Open Road: A Celebration of the American Highway*. New York: Simon and Schuster, 1986.

Phillips, Kate. *Helen Hunt Jackson: A Literary Life*. Berkeley: University of California Press, 2003.

Pierson, George W. *The Moving American*. New York: Alfred A. Knopf, 1973.

Poole, Robert M. *Explorer's House: National Geographic and the World It Made*. New York: Penguin Press, 2004.

Porter, Dennis. *Haunted Journeys: Desire and Transgression in European Travel Writing*. Princeton, NJ: Princeton University Press, 1991.

Pratt, Mary Louise. *Imperial Eyes: Travel Writing and Transculturation*. London: Routledge, 1992.

Primeau, Ronald. *Romance of the Road: The Literature of the American Highway*. Bowling Green, OH: Bowling Green State University Popular Press, 1996.

Rapson, Richard L. *Britons View America: Travel Commentary, 1860–1935*. Seattle: University of Washington Press, 1971.

Rasenberger, Jim. *America, 1908: The Dawn of Flight, the Race to the Pole, the Invention of the Model T, and the Making of a Modern Nation*. New York: Scribner, 2007.

Reddin, Paul. *Wild West Shows*. Urbana: University of Illinois Press, 1999.

Rennie, Neil. *Far-Fetched Facts: The Literature of Travel and the Idea of the South Seas*. New York: Oxford University Press, 1995.

Rico, Monica. *Nature's Noblemen: Transatlantic Masculinities and the Nineteenth-Century American West*. New Haven, CT: Yale University Press, 2013.

Roberts, Jason. *A Sense of the World: How a Blind Man Became History's Greatest Traveler*. New York: HarperCollins, 2006.

Ronda, James P. *Lewis and Clark Among the Indians*. Lincoln: University of Nebraska Press, 1984; Bison Books First Printing, 1998; Bison Books Centennial Edition, 2002.

Rose, Kenneth. *Unspeakable Awfulness: America Through the Eyes of European Travelers, 1865–1900*. New York: Routledge, forthcoming 2013.

Rothman, Hal K., ed. *The Culture of Tourism, the Tourism of Culture: Selling the Past to the Present in the American Southwest*. Albuquerque: University of New Mexico Press, 2003.

———. *Devil's Bargains: Tourism in the Twentieth-Century American West*. Lawrence: University Press of Kansas, 1998.

Sachs, Aaron. *The Humboldt Current: Nineteenth-Century American Exploration and the Roots of American Environmentalism.* New York: Viking, 2006.

Sammons, Jeffrey L. *Ideology, Mimesis, Fantasy: Charles Sealsfield, Friedrich Gerstäcker, Karl May, and Other German Novelists of America.* Chapel Hill: University of North Carolina Press, 1998.

———. *Imagination and History: Selected Papers on Nineteenth-Century German Literature.* New York: Peter Lang, 1988.

Scharff, Virginia. *Taking the Wheel: Women and the Coming of the Motor Age.* Albuquerque: University of New Mexico Press, 1991.

Schivelbusch, Wolfgang. *The Railway Journey: The Industrialization of Time and Space in the Nineteenth Century.* Berkeley: University of California Press, 1986.

Schriber, Mary Suzanne. *Writing Home: American Women Abroad, 1830–1920.* Charlottesville: University of Virginia Press, 1997.

Schultz, Charles R. *Forty-Niners "Round the Horn."* Columbia: University of South Carolina Press, 1999.

Schwantes, Carlos A. *Going Places: Transportation Redefines the Twentieth-Century West.* Bloomington: Indiana University Press, 2003.

———. *Long Day's Journey: The Steamboat and Stagecoach Era in the Northern West.* Seattle: University of Washington Press, 1999.

———. *Railroad Signatures Across the Pacific Northwest.* Seattle: University of Washington Press, 1996.

Schwantes, Carlos A., and James P. Ronda. *The West the Railroads Made.* Seattle: University of Washington Press, 2008.

Schweizer, Bernard. *Radicals on the Road: The Politics of English Travel Writing in the 1930s.* Charlottesville: University of Virginia Press, 2001.

Shaffer, Marguerite S. *See America First: Tourism and National Identity, 1880–1940.* Washington, D.C.: Smithsonian Institution Press, 2001.

Siegel, Kristi, ed. *Gender, Genre, and Identity in Women's Travel Writing.* New York: Peter Lang, 2004.

———. ed. *Issues in Travel Writing: Empire, Spectacle, and Displacement.* New York: Peter Lang, 2002.

Spurr, David. *The Rhetoric of Empire: Colonial Discourse in Journalism, Travel Writing, and Imperial Administration.* Durham, NC: Duke University Press, 1993.

Stetler, Julia. "Buffalo Bill's Wild West in Germany: A Transnational History." PhD dissertation, University of Nevada, Las Vegas, 2012.

Tompkins, Jane. "At the Buffalo Bill Museum, June 1988." In *West of Everything: The Inner Life of Westerns,* 178–203. New York: Oxford University Press, 1992.

Vinsen, Michael. *Motoring Tourists and the Scenic West, 1903–1948.* Dallas: DeGolyer Library, Southern Methodist University, 1989.

Withey, Lynne. *Grand Tours and Cook's Tours: A History of Leisure Travel, 1750–1915.* New York: William Morrow, 1997.

Youngs, Tim. *Travellers in Africa: British Travelogues, 1850–1900*. Manchester: Manchester University Press, 1994.

Ziff, Larzer. *Return Passages: Great American Travel Writing, 1780–1910*. New Haven, CT: Yale University Press, 2000.

Biographies

Bade, William F. *The Life and Letters of John Muir*. Vol. 1. Boston: Houghton Mifflin, 1924.

Barr, Pat. *A Curious Life for a Lady: The Life of Isabella Bird*. London: Macmillan, 1970.

Bedford, Sybille. *Alduous Huxley: A Biography*. 2 vols. London: Chatto and Windus, 1973, 1974. Published in a single volume, New York: Harper and Row, 1974.

Benson, Jackson. *John Steinbeck: Writer*. New York: Penguin Books, 1990. First published as *The True Adventures of John Steinbeck, Writer*, New York: Viking, 1984.

Birkett, Deborah. *Mary Kingsley: Imperial Adventuress*. Hampshire, England: Palgrave Macmillan, 1992.

Brodie, Fawn M. *The Devil Drives: A Life of Sir Richard Burton*. London: Eye and Spottiswoode; New York: W. W. Norton, 1967.

Bulmer, Michael. *Francis Galton: Pioneer of Heredity and Biometry*. Baltimore: Johns Hopkins University Press, 2003.

Bume, Glenn S. *Richard F. Burton*. Boston: Twayne Publishers, 1985.

Carl, August. *Friedrich Gerstäcker der Weitgereiste Ein Lebensbild*. Gera, Germany: Issleiss and Rietzchel, 1873.

Chinard, Gilbert. *Thomas Jefferson: The Apostle of Americanism*. Boston: Little, Brown, 1929.

Frank, Katherine. *A Voyager Out: The Life of Mary Kingsley*. Boston: Houghton Mifflin, 1986.

Gatti, Anne. *Isabella Bird Bishop*. London: Hamish Hamilton, 1988.

Gillham, Nicholas Wright. *A Life of Sir Francis Galton: From African Exploration to the Birth of Eugenics*. New York: Oxford University Press, 2001.

Gilmour, David. *The Long Recessional: The Imperial Life of Rudyard Kipling*. London: John Murray, 2002.

Haley, James T. *Wolf: The Lives of Jack London*. New York: Basic Books, 2010.

Imperato, Pascal James. *They Married Adventure: The Wandering Lives of Martin and Osa Johnson*. New Brunswick, NJ: Rutgers University Press, 1992.

Jeal, Tim. *Stanley: The Impossible Life of Africa's Greatest Explorer*. New Haven, CT: Yale University Press, 2007.

Kennedy, Dane. *The Highly Civilized Man: Richard Burton and the Victorian World*. Cambridge: Harvard University Press, 2005.

Levy, David W. *Mark Twain: The Divided Mind of America's Best-Loved Writer*. New York: Prentice Hall, 2010.

Lovell, Mary S. *A Rage to Live: A Biography of Richard and Isabel Burton*. New York: W. W. Norton, 1998.

Miller, Lee G. *The Story of Ernie Pyle*. New York: Viking, 1950.

Miller, Nathan. *Theodore Roosevelt: A Life*. New York: William Morrow, 1992.

Morris, Edmund. *The Rise of Theodore Roosevelt*. New York: Coward, McCann, and Geoghegan, 1979.

———. *Theodore Rex*. New York: Random House, 2001.

———. *Colonel Roosevelt*. New York: Random House, 2010.

Powers, Ron. *Mark Twain: A Life*. New York: Free Press, 2005.

Rice, Edward. *Captain Sir Richard Francis Burton: A Biography*. Cambridge, MA: Da Capo Press, 2001.

Sandoz, Mari. *Crazy Horse: The Strange Man of the Oglalas*. Lincoln: University of Nebraska Press, 1942.

Sinclair, Andrew. *Jack: A Biography of Jack London*. New York: Harper and Row, 1977.

Stasz, Clarice. *American Dreamers: Charmian and Jack London*. New York: St. Martin's Press, 1988.

Stoddart, Anna. *The Life of Isabella Bird (Mrs. Bishop)*. London: John Murray, 1906; New York: Dutton, 1907.

Woodward, Tim. *Tiger on the Road: The Story of Vardis Fisher*. Caldwell, ID: Caxton Printers, 1989.

Worster, Donald. *A Passion for Nature: The Life of John Muir*. New York: Oxford University Press, 2008.

Autobiographies

Clemens, Samuel Langhorne. *The Autobiography of Mark Twain*. Edited by Charles Neider. New York: Harper Perennial, 2000.

———. *The Autobiography of Mark Twain*. Vol. 1. Edited by Harriet Elinor Smith. Berkeley: Mark Twain Project, Bancroft Library/University of California Press, 2010.

Johnson, Osa. *I Married Adventure: The Lives of Martin and Osa Johnson*. Garden City, NY: Halcyon House, 1943. Reprinted, New York: Kodansha America, 1997.

Novels and Short Story Collections

Babb, Sanora. *Whose Names Are Unknown*. Norman: University of Oklahoma Press, 2004.

Conrad, Joseph. *Heart of Darkness*. London: William Blackwood, 1902.

Kerouac, Jack. *On the Road*. New York: Viking, 1957. Reprinted with an introduction by Ann Charters, New York: Penguin Books, 1991.

Lewis, Sinclair. *The Man Who Knew Coolidge: Being the Soul of Lowell Schmaltz, Constructive and Nordic Citizen*. New York: Harcourt, Brace, 1928.

McCarthy, Cormac. *The Road*. New York: Vintage, 2006.

Melville, Herman. *Moby-Dick*. London: Richard Bentley; New York: Harper and Brothers, 1851.

Steinbeck, John. *The Grapes of Wrath and Other Writings, 1936–1941*. Edited by Robert DeMott and Elaine A. Steinbeck. New York: Library of America, 1996.

———. *The Long Valley*. New York: Viking, 1938.

———. *The Red Pony*. New York: Viking, 1937.

Troyanov, Iliya. *The Collector of Worlds: A Novel of Sir Richard Francis Burton*. Translated by William Hobson. New York: HarperCollins, 2009. First published in German, Munich: Carl Hanser Verlag, 2006.

Verne, Jules. *Around the World In Eighty Days*. New York: Penguin Books, 2004. First published as *Le tour du monde en quatre-vingts jours*, Paris: Pierre-Jules Hetzel, 1873.

Nonfiction Novels

Tom Wolfe. *The Electric Kool-Aid Acid Test*. New York: Farrar, Straus and Giroux, 1968.

Personal Journals

Steinbeck, John. *Working Days: The Journals of* The Grapes of Wrath. Edited by Robert DeMott. New York: Viking Penguin, 1989.<bibtxt>

Secondary Works General

Anderson, Fred, and Andrew Cayton. *The Dominion of War: Empire and Liberty in North America, 1500–2000*. New York: Viking, 2005.

Anderson, Gary. *Ethnic Cleansing and the Indian: The Crime that Haunts America*. Norman: University of Oklahoma Press, forthcoming.

Athearn, Robert G. *The Mythic West in Twentieth-Century America*. Lawrence: University Press of Kansas, 1989.

Ayers, Edward, Patricia Nelson Limerick, Stephen Nissebaum, and Peter Onuff. *All Over the Map: Rethinking American Regions*. Baltimore: Johns Hopkins University Press, 1996.

Bauer, William J., Jr. *We Were All Like Migrant Workers Here: Work, Community, and Memory on California's Round Valley Reservation, 1850–1941*. Chapel Hill: University of North Carolina Press, 2009.

Belich, James. *Replenishing the Earth: The Settler Revolution and the Rise of the Anglo-World, 1783–1939*. Oxford: Oxford University Press, 2009.

Bender, Thomas. *Nation Among Nations: America's Place in World History*. New York: Hill and Wang, 2006.

Berger, Michael. *Devil Wagon in God's Country: The Automobile and Social Change in Rural America, 1893–1929*. Hamden, CT: Archon Books, 1979.

Bhabha, Homi K. *The Location of Culture*. New York: Routledge, 1994.

Billington, Ray Allen, and Martin Ridge, eds. *Westward Expansion: A History of the American Frontier*. 6th ed. Albuquerque: University of New Mexico Press, 2001.

Brantlinger, Patrick. *Dark Vanishings: The Discourse on the Extinction of Primitive Peoples, 1800–1930*. Ithaca, NY: Cornell University Press, 2003.

———. *Rules of Darkness: British Literature and Imperialism, 1830–1914*. Ithaca, NY: Cornell University Press, 1988.

Bsumek, Erika Marie. *Indian-Made: Navajo Culture in the Marketplace, 1868–1940*. Lawrence: University Press of Kansas, 2008.

Burke, Flannery. *From Greenwich Village to Taos: Primitivism and Place at Mabel Dodge Luhan's*. Lawrence: University Press of Kansas, 2008.

Campbell, Neil. *The Rhizomatic West: Representing the American West in a Transnational, Global, Media Age*. Lincoln: University of Nebraska Press, 2008.

Cannadine, David. *Ornamentalism: How the British Saw Their Empire*. New York: Oxford University Press, 2001.

Cayton, Andrew. "The Imperial Republic: War and Expansion of an Empire of Liberty." Paper presented at the roundtable session, United States Empire and Its Implications for History, at the annual meeting of the American Historical Association, Philadelphia, January 8, 2006.

Conn, Steven. *History's Shadow: Native Americans and Historical Consciousness in the Nineteenth Century*. Chicago: University of Chicago Press, 2004.

Cook, Sherburne F. *The Conflict Between the California Indian and White Civilization*. Berkeley: University of California Press, 1976.

———. *The Population of the California Indians, 1769–1970*. Berkeley: University of California Press, 1976.

Cox Richardson, Heather. *West from Appomattox: The Reconstruction of America After the Civil War*. New Haven, CT: Yale University Press, 2007.

Craven, Avery, ed. *Essays in Honor of William E. Dodd: By His Former Students at the University of Chicago*. Chicago: University of Chicago Press, 1935.

Cummings, Bruce. *Dominion from Sea to Sea: Pacific Ascendancy and American Power*. New Haven, CT: Yale University Press, 2009.

Deloria, Philip J. *Indians in Unexpected Places*. Lawrence: University Press of Kansas, 2004.

Deverell, William, ed. *The Blackwell Companion to the American West*. Malden, MA: Blackwell, 2004.

Dewing, Rolland. *Regions in Transition: The Northern Great Plains and the Pacific Northwest in the Great Depression*. Lanham, MD: University Press of America, 2006.

Diggins, John. *The Rise and Fall of the American Left*. New York: W. W. Norton, 1992.

Dilworth, Leah. *Imagining Indians in the Southwest: Persistent Visions of a Primitive Past*. Washington, D.C.: Smithsonian Institution Scholarly Press, 1996.

Dippie, Brian. *The Vanishing American: White Attitudes and U.S. Indian Policy*. Lawrence: University Press of Kansas, 1991. First published, Middletown, CT: Wesleyan University Press, 1982.

Dorman, Robert. *Hell of a Vision: Regionalism and the Modern American West.* Tucson: University of Arizona Press, 2012.

———. *Revolt of the Provinces: The Regionalist Movement in America, 1920–1945.* Chapel Hill: University of North Carolina Press, 1993.

Etulain, Richard. *Re-Imagining the Modern American West: A Century of Fiction, History, and Art.* Tucson: University of Arizona Press, 1996.

———. *Telling Western Stories: From Buffalo Bill to Larry McMurtry.* Albuquerque: University of New Mexico Press, 1999.

Faragher, John Mack, and Robert Hine. *The American West: A New Interpretive History.* New Haven, CT: Yale University Press, 2000.

Featherstone, Mike, ed. *Global Culture: Nationalism, Globalization and Modernity.* London: Sage Publications, 1990.

Foster, Jonathan. "Stigma Cities: Dystopian Urban Identities in the United States West and South in the Twentieth Century." PhD dissertation, University of Nevada, Las Vegas, 2009.

Fry, Joseph A. "Place Matters: Regionalism and the Formation of American Foreign Policy," with Commentaries and Author Response. *Diplomatic History* 36 (June 2012): 451–514.

Gaddis, John. *The Landscapes of History: How Historians Map the Past.* New York: Oxford University Press, 2002.

Gough, Peter L. *The Music of the New Deal in the West.* Urbana: University of Illinois Press, forthcoming 2014.

Grieve, Victoria. *The Federal Art Project and the Creation of Middlebrow Culture.* Urbana: University of Illinois Press, 2009.

Harvey, Thomas. *Rainbow Bridge to Monument Valley: Making the Modern Old West.* Norman: University of Oklahoma Press, 2011.

Hausladen, Gary J., ed. *Western Places, American Myths: How We Think About the West.* Reno: University of Nevada Press, 2003.

Haynes, Sam W., and Christopher Morris, eds. *Manifest Destiny and Empire: Antebellum American Expansionism.* College Station: Texas A&M University Press, 1997.

Hietala, Thomas R. *Manifest Design: Anxious Aggrandizement in Late Jacksonian America.* Ithaca, NY: Cornell University Press, 1985.

Hirsch, Jerrold. *Portrait of America: A Cultural History of the Federal Writers' Project.* Chapel Hill: University of North Carolina Press, 2003.

Hobsbawm, Eric. *The Age of Empire, 1875–1914.* New York: Pantheon Books, 1987. Reprinted, New York: Vintage Books, 1989.

Hochschild, Adam. *King Leopold's Ghost: A Story of Greed, Terror, and Heroism in Colonial Africa.* Boston: Houghton Mifflin, 1998.

Holliday, J. S. *The World Rushed In: The California Gold Rush Experience.* Norman: University of Oklahoma Press, 2002. First published, New York: Simon and Schuster, 1981.

Hurtado, Albert L. *Indian Survival on the California Frontier*. New Haven, CT: Yale University Press, 1988.

Hutson, James Paul. "Benjamin Franklin and the West." *Western Historical Quarterly* 4 (October 1973): 425–34.

Hyde, Anne Farrar. *An American Vision: Far Western Landscape and National Culture, 1820–1920*. New York: New York University Press, 1990.

Igler, David. "Diseased Goods: Global Exchanges in the Eastern Pacific Basin, 1770–1850." *American Historical Review* 109 (June 2004): 693–719.

———. *The Great Ocean: Pacific Worlds from Captain Cook to the Gold Rush*. New York: Oxford University Press, 2013.

Jasanoff, Maya. *Edge of Empire: Lives, Culture, and Conquest in the East, 1750–1850*. New York: Alfred A. Knopf, 2005.

Kammen, Michael, "The Problem of American Exceptionalism: A Reconsideration." *American Quarterly* 45 (March 1993): 1–43.

Kastor, Peter J. *The Louisiana Purchase and the Creation of America*. New Haven: Yale University Press, 2004.

Kennedy, Paul. *The Rise and Fall of the Great Powers: Economic Change and Military Conflict from 1500 to 2000*. New York: Random House, 1987.

Kiernan, Ben. *Blood and Soil: A World History of Genocide and Extermination from Sparta to Darfur*. New Haven, CT: Yale University Press, 2007.

Kropp, Phoebe S. *California Vieja: Culture and Memory in a Modern American Place*. Berkeley: University of California Press, 2006.

Lamar, Howard, and Leonard Thompson. *The Frontier in History: North America and South Africa Compared*. New Haven, CT: Yale University Press, 1981.

Lears, T. J. Jackson. *No Place of Grace: Antimodernism and the Transformation of American Culture, 1880–1920*. Chicago: University of Chicago Press, 1981.

Limerick, Patricia Nelson. *The Legacy of Conquest: The Unbroken Past of the American West*. New York: W. W. Norton, 2006. First published, 1987.

Limerick, Patricia Nelson, Clyde Milner II, and Charles Rankin, eds. *Trails: Toward a New Western History*. Lawrence: University Press of Kansas, 1991.

Lindsay, Brendan C. *Murder State: California's Native American Genocide, 1846–1873*. Lincoln: University of Nebraska Press, 2012.

Mackenzie, John, ed. *Imperialism and Popular Culture*. Manchester: Manchester University Press, 1986.

———. *Propaganda and Empire: The Manipulation of British Public Opinion, 1880–1960*. Manchester: Manchester University Press, 1984.

Madley, Benjamin. "California's Yuki Indians: Defining Genocide in America." *Western Historical Quarterly* 39 (Autumn 2008): 303–32.

———. "Patterns of Frontier Genocide, 1803–1910: The Aboriginal Tasmanians, the Yuki of California, and the Herero of Namibia." *Journal of Genocide Research* 6 (June 2004): 167–92.

Madsen, Deborah L. *American Exceptionalism*. Jackson: University Press of Mississippi, 1998.

Malin, James C. *The Contriving Brain and the Skillful Hand in the United States*. Ann Arbor, MI: Edwards Brothers, 1955.

Mangione, Jerre. *The Dream and the Deal: The Federal Writers' Project, 1935–1943*. Boston: Little, Brown, 1972.

Marriott, John. *The Other Empire: Metropolis, India and Progress in the Colonial Imagination*. Manchester: Manchester University Press, 2003.

Miller, Orlando. *The Frontier in Alaska and the Matanuska Colony*. New Haven, CT: Yale University Press, 1975.

Milner, Clyde, ed. *A New Significance: Re-Envisioning the History of the American West*. New York: Oxford University Press, 1996.

Milton, John R. *Three Wests: Conversations with Vardis Fisher, Max Evans, and Michael Straight*. Vermillion, SD: Dakota Press, 1970.

Miner, Craig. *Kansas: The History of the Sunflower State, 1854–2000*. Lawrence: University Press of Kansas, 2002.

Mitchell, Lee Clark. *Witnesses to a Vanishing America: The Nineteenth-Century Response*. Princeton, NJ: Princeton University Press, 1981.

Noble, David. *Death of a Nation: American Culture and the End of Exceptionalism*. Minneapolis: University of Minnesota Press, 2002.

Nugent, Walter. "Comparing Wests and Frontiers." In *The Oxford History of the American West*, 803–33. Edited by Clyde A. Milner II, Carol A. O'Connor, and Martha Sandweiss. New York: Oxford University Press, 1994.

———. *Crossings: The Great Transatlantic Migrations, 1870–1914*. Bloomington: Indiana University Press, 2002.

———. *Habits of Empire: A History of American Expansion*. New York: Alfred A. Knopf, 2008.

———. *Into the West: The Story of Its People*. New York: Alfred A. Knopf, 1999.

———. "Where Is the American West? Report on a Survey." *Montana: The Magazine of Western History* 42 (Summer 1992): 2–23.

Nugent, Walter, and Martin Ridge, eds. *The American West: The Reader*. Bloomington: Indiana University Press, 1999.

Peck, Gunther. *Reinventing Free Labor: Padrones and Immigrant Workers in the North American West, 1880–1930*. Cambridge: Cambridge University Press, 2000.

Phillips, George Harwood. *Indians and Indian Agents: The Origins of the Reservation System in California, 1849–1852*. Norman: University of Oklahoma Press, 1997.

Pletcher, David M. *The Diplomacy of Annexation: Texas, Oregon, and the Mexican War*. Columbia: University of Missouri Press, 1973.

Pomeroy, Earl. *The Pacific Slope: A History of California, Oregon, Washington, Idaho, and Nevada*. Reno: University of Nevada Press, 2003.

Pratt, Julius. "John L. O'Sullivan and Manifest Destiny." *New York History* 14 (July 1933): 213–34.

———. "The Origin of Manifest Destiny." *American Historical Review* 32 (July 1927): 795–98.

Pyne, Stephen J. *How the Grand Canyon Became Grand: A Short History.* New York: Viking, 1998.

Reesman, Jeanne Campbell, Sara S. Hodson, and Philip Adams. *Jack London: Photographer.* Athens: University of Georgia Press, 2010.

Reichard, Gary W., and Ted Dickson, eds. *America on the World Stage: A Global Approach to U.S. History.* Urbana: University of Illinois Press; Chicago: Organization of American Historians, 2008.

Riebsame, William E., ed. *Atlas of the New West: Portrait of a Changing Region.* New York: W. W. Norton, 1997.

Roberts, J. M. *The New Penguin History of the World.* New York: Penguin Books, 2004. First published, 1976.

Roche, Jeff, ed. *The Political Culture of the New West.* Lawrence: University Press of Kansas, 2008.

Rosaldo, Renato. "Imperialist Nostalgia." *Representations* 26 (1989): 107–22.

Ross, Dorothy. "Historical Consciousness in Nineteenth-Century America." *American Historical Review* 89 (October 1984): 909–28.

Said, Edward. *Culture and Imperialism.* New York: Vintage Books, 1994. First published, New York: Alfred A. Knopf, 1993.

———. *Orientalism.* New York: Pantheon Books, 1978.

Slotkin, Richard. *The Fatal Environment: The Myth of the Frontier in the Age of Industrialization, 1800–1890.* New York: Atheneum, 1985.

———. *Gunfighter Nation: The Myth of the Frontier in Twentieth-Century America.* New York: Atheneum, 1992.

———. *Regeneration Through Violence: The Mythology of the American Frontier, 1600–1800.* Middletown, CT: Wesleyan University Press, 1973.

Steiner, Michael C. "Frontierland as Tomorrowland: Walt Disney and the Architectural Packaging of the American West." *Montana: The Magazine of Western History* 48 (Spring 1998): 2–17.

———. ed. *Regionalists on the Left: Radical Voices from the American West.* Norman: University of Oklahoma Press, 2013.

Streeby, Shelley. *American Sensations: Class, Empire, and the Production of Popular Culture.* Berkeley: University of California Press, 2002.

Sutter, Paul S. *Driven Wild: How the Fight Against Automobiles Launched the Modern Wilderness Movement.* Seattle: University of Washington Press, 2002.

Taylor, David A. *Soul of a People: The WPA Writers' Project Uncovers Depression America.* New York: John Wiley and Sons, 2009.

Taylor, Nick. *American Made: The Enduring Legacy of the WPA; When FDR Put the Nation to Work.* New York: Bantam Books, 2008.

Tricomi, Albert H. *Missionary Positions: Evangelicalism and Empire in American Fiction.* Gainesville: University Press of Florida, 2011.

Tyrrell, Ian. "American Exceptionalism in an Age of International History." *American Historical Review* 96 (October 1991): 1031–55.

———. *Transnational Nation: United States History in Global Perspective Since 1789.* New York: Palgrave Macmillan, 2007.

West, Elliott. *The Essential West: Collected Essays.* Norman: University of Oklahoma Press, 2012.

———. *The Last Indian War: The Nez Perce Story.* New York: Oxford University Press, 2009.

———. *The Way to the West: Essays on the Central Plains.* Albuquerque: University of New Mexico Press, 1995.

White, Richard. *"It's Your Misfortune and None of My Own": A New History of the American West.* Norman: University of Oklahoma Press, 1991.

———. *Railroaded: The Transcontinentals and the Making of Modern America.* New York: W. W. Norton, 2011.

Wolfe, Patrick. "Settler Colonialism and the Elimination of the Native." *Journal of Genocide Research* 8 (December 2006): 387–409.

Worster, Donald. *Rivers of Empire: Water, Aridity, and the Growth of American West.* New York: Oxford University Press, 1985.

Wrobel, David M. *The End of American Exceptionalism: Frontier Anxiety from the Old West to the New Deal.* Lawrence: University Press of Kansas, 1993.

———. "Exceptionalism and Globalism: Travel Writers and the Nineteenth-Century American West." *The Historian* 68 (Fall 2006): 430–60.

———. "Global West, American Frontier." *Pacific Historical Review* 78 (February 2009): 1–26.

———. *Promised Lands: Promotion, Memory, and the Creation of the American West.* Lawrence: University Press of Kansas, 2002, 2011.

———. "The West in the World, the World in the West: Gerstäcker, Burton, and Bird on the Nineteenth-Century Frontier." *Montana: The Magazine of Western History* 58 (Spring 2008): 24–34.

Wrobel, David M., and Michael C. Steiner, eds. *Many Wests: Place, Culture, and Regional Identity.* Lawrence: University Press of Kansas, 1997.

Documentary Films

Burns, Ken, and Dayton Duncan, producers. *Horatio's Drive: America's First Road Trip.* DVD. Directed by Ken Burns. PBS DVD Gold, 2005.

INDEX